Voluntary but not Amateur

A guide to the law
for voluntary
organisations
and community groups

Seventh edition

Ruth Hayes and Jacki Reason

updated from previous editions
by Duncan Forbes, Ruth Hayes and Jacki Reason

London Voluntary Service Council
356 Holloway Road, London N7 6PA

March 2004

London Voluntary Service Council
356 Holloway Road
London N7 6PA

tel	020 7700 8107
fax	020 7700 8108
email	publications@lvsc.org.uk
website	www.actionlink.org.uk/lvsc

Registered charity 276886

Typeset by Jacki Reason
Cover design by Bananadesign
Printed by Hendy Banks Colour Print, London

British Library Cataloguing in Publication Data
A catalogue record for this book is available from the British Library
ISBN 1 872582 32 X

Foreword

Now in its seventh edition and with many thousands of copies sold, *Voluntary but not Amateur* has become the bible for those charged with setting up or managing voluntary sector organisations

This edition has been completely revised and updated to help readers keep track of all the changes in law and practice that affect voluntary sector managers. Over the next two years a mass of new and enhanced legislation affecting employment, equal opportunities and disability discrimination will come into force. *Voluntary but not Amateur* brings it all together in one easy to use up to date reference and good practice guide.

Voluntary but not Amateur gives practical information in an easy style. It is ideal for newcomers – staff or management committee members – and also for people with experience who need to keep up to date with the latest developments. It is also designed to be accessible to people from the many diverse communities in London. Others who will find this book useful are managers in the public and private sectors as well as university and college students and anyone wanting to understand management and good practice in voluntary organisations.

It is an important part of the London Voluntary Service Council's services to strengthen London's voluntary organisations. *Voluntary but not Amateur* is one of the tools used to achieve that goal, together with other LVSC services such as Personnel Employment Advice and Conciliation Service (PEACe), support and advice, information and training. Used in conjunction with *Just about Managing?*, a complementary publication, it is an invaluable and powerful aid to voluntary sector managers.

Mark Clarke
Acting Chief Executive, London Voluntary Service Council

Acknowledgements

LVSC would like to thank Ruth Hayes and Jacki Reason for writing this book, Sandy Adirondack for her invaluable input and Rob Good for checking the law.

The authors would like to thank a number of people for their comments, including the following: Jimi Adeleye (Local Government Capacity and Modernisation Division, ODPM) – local authority companies, David Birley (Environment Director, Safe Neighbourhoods Unit) – green office, John Bryan (ODPM) – Landlord and Tenant Act, Chris Chiton (Pensions Trust) – pensions, Jonathan Dawson (honorary legal advisor, Community Matters) – deed of trust and conditions of hire, Jane Grenfell (Head of Charity Status, Charity Commission) – charity matters, Mick Holder (London Hazards Centre) – health and safety, Julie Howell (Digital Policy Development Officer, RNIB) – creating accessible websites, Information Rights Division of the Department for Constitutional Affairs – Freedom of Information Act, Veronica Karrington (Community Matters) – premises, Jon Lord (West Midlands Planning Aid) – planning and building regulations, Ken Pennykid (Keegan & Pennykid) – insurance, Mark Restell (Information Officer, National Centre for Volunteering) – volunteers, Will Roden (FSA) – industrial and provident societies, Lucy Ryan (HM Treasury) – Cooperatives and Benefits Society Act, Jon Thorne (Head of Financial Regulation, Charity Commission) – charity finance, Paul Ticher – data protection and monitoring.

Introduction

In November 2003 the government announced its intention to publish a draft Charities Bill. We have made reference where appropriate to the likely content of the Bill, based on the content of *Charities and Not-for-Profits: a Modern Legal Framework*, the government's response to the Strategy Unit review *Private Action, Public Benefit*. For further details see the 'Community and Race' section of the Home Office website: www.homeoffice.gov.uk/

Sources of further information appear throughout the publication: contact details are listed on pages 213-215.

Reference is made throughout to *Voluntary but not Amateur*'s companion volume *Just about Managing?*, also published by the London Voluntary Service Council, and *The Voluntary Sector Legal Handbook*, published by the Directory of Social Change.

All Acts of Parliament are available from the Stationery Office: see page 215 for contact information.

This book is intended for guidance only, and is not a substitute for professional advice. No responsibility for loss occasioned as a result of any person acting or refraining from acting can be accepted by the publisher or authors. The law as stated is correct as at 15 December 2003.

The law in this book is the law applying in England and Wales. Readers from Scotland and Northern Ireland should obtain legal advice as to whether the same law applies.

Contents

Chapter 4:
Responsibilities during employment

Chapter 5:
Health and safety

Chapter 1:
Before you start – legal structures and charitable status

Related chapters
Chapter 2 – Running an organisation
Chapter 6 – Premises
Chapter 7 – Insurance
Chapter 9 – Public activities
Chapter 10 – Winding up

This chapter examines the advantages and disadvantages of each of the legal structures open to a voluntary organisation. It then describes which organisations are eligible for charity status, and the advantages and disadvantages of becoming a charitable organisation. Reference is made to a number of Charity Commission publications (usually indicated by a CC reference), which, unless otherwise indicated, are available from its website *www.charitycommission.gov.uk* or publications line 01823 345 427.

Legal structures

The legal structures for a voluntary organisation are currently:

- unincorporated association
- a charitable trust
- company limited by guarantee
- an industrial and provident society (IPS).

Two new structures are proposed under forthcoming legislation: the charitable incorporated organisation (CIO), under the draft Charities Bill (see page 4), and the community interest company (CIC), included in the Companies (Audit, Investigations and Community Enterprise) Bill (see page 5).

Any organisation – whatever its size – needs a set of **governing rules** defining what it is set up to achieve, and a set of internal rules and procedures (outlined in chapter 2). The governing rules are set out in the **governing document**. The precise form depends on the legal structure adopted.

Legal structure	Governing document
unincorporated association	constitution or rules
charitable trust	trust deed, deed of trust or declaration of trust
company limited by guarantee	memorandum and articles of association*
industrial and provident society	rules

*Under company and charity law proposals, private companies (which include most voluntary sector companies and charitable incorporated organisations – see page 4) will be able to use a shorter, simplified single-document constitution.

Throughout the book, we will be using the term constitution to cover all forms of governing document. Constitutions are described in detail on pages 16 and 17.

Most voluntary organisations will be run by a committee. A management committee can be known by a number of different titles, including the following:

- committee
- executive committee
- management committee
- council of management
- board of trustees (most commonly used by charities)
- board of directors (most commonly used by companies and IPSs).

Unincorporated associations

An unincorporated association is not required by law to seek approval of any kind before setting up, nor does it have to register with any regulatory body unless it is legally charitable (see *Charitable status,* page 9). However, it may still have to register with some bodies before starting to operate – for example, the Inland Revenue, the local environmental health department, the National Care Standards Commission (Commission for Social Care Inspection from April 2004) or Ofsted. An unincorporated association with very low income, which does not intend to employ staff or acquire property may need only a set of basic rules under which all members will operate. These should state the organisation's aims, the powers it has to achieve them and its management procedures.

Advantages

An unincorporated association is quick and cheap to set up. Unless it is applying for charitable status no other agency need be involved in the setting up process. There are no fees to pay, unless it takes legal advice about drawing up a constitution. It does not have to answer to an external authority, for example by submitting accounts (unless the organisation is a charity, or accounts are required by a funding body). Unlike trusts, unincorporated associations have the flexibility to design a democratic constitution. Finally, they can generally be wound up more easily than companies or IPSs, provided the constitution allows for this (see chapter 10).

Unincorporated associations can register as charities and gain all the advantages of charity status listed later in this chapter. They *must* register if their objects are charitable and their annual income is over £1000 (under the draft Charities Bill the limit will be increased to £5000).

Disadvantages

An unincorporated association has no separate legal existence, and remains for most purposes a collection of individuals. As a result, in most cases:

- it cannot acquire property in its own name; property must be held by individuals or an incorporated body acting on behalf of the organisation
- legal proceedings cannot be taken by the organisation in its own name, but must be taken by individuals representing the organisation
- individual members of the management committee can be held personally responsible for the organisation's obligations and debts; this is an important factor to consider when choosing a legal structure, and is further discussed below (see *Liability of committee members*, page 15).

As an organisation develops, the trustees of a charitable unincorporated association may apply to the Charity Commission to become an **incorporated body of trustees**. If the Commission accepts the application, this overcomes the first two disadvantages listed above, as the charity property is then held in the name of the organisation and the trustees can enter into contracts or take proceedings in the name of the incorporated body. See *Incorporation of charity trustees* (CC43) for further details. Applications must be made on the form in the application pack *How to apply to the Charity Commission for a Certificate of Incorporation* (CHY 1093), available from Charity Commission offices.

Only incorporation, as a company or an industrial and provident society,* will protect committee members against being personally responsible, in most situations, for the organisation's liabilities and debts. Registering an unincorporated association as a charity does not provide this kind of protection, nor does incorporating the charity trustees. If liability of management committee members is a concern you should seriously consider forming a company limited by guarantee or an industrial and provident society. See *Minimising the risk of personal liability*, page 15.

*Two other forms of incorporation are proposed in forthcoming legislation – the charitable incorporated organisation (see page 4) and the community interest company (see page 5)

An unincorporated association may find it difficult to borrow money. Loans can be made only to individual committee members, who become personally responsible for ensuring repayments.

The constitution

The Charity Commission and other organisations have devised model constitutions. Alternatively, the organisation could adapt one being used by a similar organisation; see *Models*, page 25.

Charitable trusts

An organisation with no need for members, that wants a simple structure which allows a small number of people to manage money or property for a charitable purpose, could consider setting up as a trust. However, only organisations with charitable aims may use this structure, and if they meet the requirements for charity registration detailed on page 9 must register with the Charity Commission.

There are three parties involved in a trust:

- the donors of money or property (the people who started the trust by making the first donation) and all future donors
- the trustees (the Charity Commission usually requires three), who become the nominal owners of the trust property
- the beneficiaries (the people who will benefit from the trust).

As with all voluntary organisations, the trustees must ensure that the property or money is used for the purposes set out in the trust deed (a trust's constitution); as with all charities it is generally illegal for them to benefit personally from trust property.

Advantages

Trusts can be set up quickly and cheaply although you may need legal advice. Apart from asking the Charity Commission to approve the trust's constitution (the trust deed) and paying stamp duty (£5 in 2003) at the local Inland Revenue Stamp Office, no other regulatory body need be involved (although it may be necessary to register with some bodies once operating). Small trusts are also cheap to administer. If there is provision for changes in the trust deed, amendments can be made fairly easily. However, as with any charity, the Charity Commission must approve any alterations to the section on aims and objectives.

Trustees can acquire and manage property on behalf of the trust, and the trust deed can give trustees powers to raise and borrow money to fulfil its aims.

Disadvantages

Organisations set up as charitable trusts must register as charities and therefore have all the restrictions facing registered charities set out later in this chapter.

Trusts are essentially non-democratic organisations. Unlike other legal structures, there is generally no membership structure – although the trust deed can be written in a way that allows for members and elected trustees. Trustees are generally the only people with legal powers to make decisions relating to the trust.

Trustees can apply to the Charity Commission to be incorporated (see page 2). This enables them to hold property, enter into contracts and take court action in the name of the trust. But even when incorporated in this way trustees can be personally liable. They are not protected from personal liability by registering the organisation as a charity.

The constitution

The constitution of a charitable trust is called a **trust deed, deed of trust** or **declaration of trust**. There are several models available, including *A model declaration of trust for a charitable trust* (GD2), available from *www.charitycommision.gov.uk* and the Charity Law Association's *Trust deed for a charitable trust* – approved by the Charity Commission – available (for a charge) from *Charitylaw@aol.com*

Limited companies

There are two types of limited company. In a **company limited by share**s members (shareholders) invest money in the hope of gaining a profit; this type of company is generally found in the commercial sector.

The second kind is a **company limited by guarantee**. This is appropriate for organisations which aim to pursue some social or political cause. There are no shareholders and any profits are reinvested in the company. All members must guarantee to pay a nominal sum (usually £1, and almost always no more than £10) if the company becomes insolvent.

A limited company with charitable aims must register with the Charity Commission if it meets the requirements listed on page 9.

Advantages

A company limited by guarantee is an **incorporated organisation**. This means that it has a separate legal identity as distinct from that of its members, and therefore:
- can buy, own and sell property in its own name
- may take or defend legal proceedings in its own name
- can protect individual members of the organisation and, in most circumstances, members of the management committee from personal liability.

The liability of individual members (people with a right to vote at an annual general meeting) and board members (also known as **committee members** or **directors**) is different. The extent of members' personal liability is limited to the amount they agree to guarantee. Individual members are therefore almost totally protected against personal liability in an incorporated organisation.

Under company law the board of directors is responsible for running the company; the directors generally have no personal liability unless they:
- act fraudulently
- are fined for breach of a statutory duty or a criminal offence
- act in breach of trust, or
- continue running the company when they know or ought to know it has no reasonable chance of avoiding insolvent liquidation.

Committee members' liability is discussed further under *Minimising the risk of personal liability*, on page 15. Insolvent liquidation is dealt with in chapter 10.

Companies must have a membership, which usually has the power to elect, and always has the power to remove, officers and committee members. The structure works equally well for any size of organisation.

Because a company limited by guarantee is incorporated and therefore has a separate legal identity, owning and transferring property is relatively simple. Even when the committee or membership changes, ownership of the property remains in the name of the company, so there is no need for any formal process to transfer ownership. Although most companies have to use the word 'Limited' as part of their name, the majority of voluntary organisations are exempt from this requirement (see *Decide on the name*, in chapter 2).

It may be easier for a company to borrow money because the lender knows that the organisation, rather than a changing group of individuals, is responsible for repayment. However, banks may still ask for personal guarantees from individual committee members who will then be liable to repay the loan if the company defaults.

Once the memorandum and articles of association (the company's constitution) is agreed, company registration (with the Registrar of Companies) takes two to three weeks provided there are no complications. The registration fee is low (£20 in 2003/04).

Disadvantages

Companies' activities are regulated by the Companies Acts and are usually subject to more controls and bureaucracy than other legal structures.

Annual returns and accounts must be submitted to the Registrar of Companies (for which there is a charge, £15 in 2003/04) and these are open to the public. The company must keep registers of members and directors, which must be available for public inspection (see *Setting up registers*, in chapter 2).

Companies limited by guarantee have to notify the Registrar of Companies whenever a committee member leaves or a new one is appointed, or a committee member's personal details change. They must also notify the Registrar if they enter into any legal charge (for example if they borrow money from a bank and the bank has a mortgage over the company's property).

Companies limited by guarantee are one of the categories of organisation that may come under the definition of a company under local authority influence. See *Local authority companies*, page 8.

The constitution

The constitution of a limited company consists of two parts:*

- the **memorandum of association**, which contains the company's aims, the powers it has to pursue them, and the extent of members' liability
- the **articles of association**, which describe the company's rules, including its procedures for electing the board (management committee) and keeping accounts.

Under new company law proposals, private companies (which include most voluntary sector companies) will be able to use a shorter, simplified single-document constitution.

Charitable incorporated organisations

The draft Charities Bill will introduce a new form of incorporated charity – the charitable incorporated organisation (CIO). CIOs will only have to register with the Charity Commission, not with Companies House, and so many of the disadvantages listed above will not apply.

CIOs will have the following characteristics:
- Limited liability for members
- Membership and foundation formats (ie they will be appropriate for charities with or without a membership structure)
- Flexible administrative powers
- Model constitutions prepared by coordinating bodies, tailor-made for particular parts of the sector
- Straightforward plain English constitutions
- An explicit statement of trustees' duty of care, consistent with the **Trustee Act 2000**

Charitable associations and trusts are likely to be able to convert to a CIO by a special or unanimous written resolution and it will be straightforward to convert from other incorporated forms.

New and existing charities will be able to choose whether to incorporate as a CIO or a company limited by guarantee.

Community interest companies

The **Companies (Audit, Investigations and Community Enterprise) Bill**, published in December 2003, provides for the establishment of community interest companies (CICs). The form will be available to non-charitable, not-for-profit organisations pursuing community benefit (also known as 'social enterprises').

A CIC will be registered as a company in the usual way, but will also need to satisfy a 'community interest test', ie show that its purposes are in the interests of the community or wider public and that access to its benefits will not be confined to an unduly restricted group. CICs will not be able to distribute profits and assets to their members – an 'asset lock'.

CICs limited by shares will have the option of issuing shares that pay a dividend to investors. The dividend payable will be capped in order to protect the asset lock.

CICs will not have the benefits or obligations of charitable status, and organisations that are legally charitable (see page 9) will not be able to register as CICs.

A new independent regulator will have the job of maintaining public confidence in CICs, by ensuring they comply with the law.

All organisations, including charities, but excluding political parties, will be able to establish CICs as subsidiaries.

For further details see *www.dti.gov.uk/cics*

Industrial and provident societies

To qualify for registration under the **Industrial and Provident Societies Act 1965** a society must generally have at least three members, carry on an industry, business or trade and be either a **bona fide cooperative society** or acting for the **benefit of the community**.

A **bona fide cooperative society** must meet the following criteria:
- members should have a common economic, social or cultural need or interest
- its constitution must have no artificial restrictions on membership, designed to increase other members' interests and rights
- business must be conducted for the members' mutual benefit
- if a workers' coop, membership must be open to everyone who works in the coop
- all members must have an equal say in running the society
- the interest paid to members who have invested money in the society must be restricted
- if profits are distributed to members, this must be according to the extent to which they have participated in the business of the society.

An organisation for the **benefit of the community** (a community benefit society*) must usually:
- not be set up with the purpose of making a profit
- have rules forbidding the distribution of its assets among members
- allow all members an equal say in controlling its affairs
- restrict the interest rate paid on its share or loan capital
- be able to show it will benefit non-members
- have 'special reasons' for registering as an industrial and provident society, rather than as a company (ie some concrete advantage or benefit that would be lost or unobtainable as a company).

Examples of acceptable special reasons include:
- wanting to operate on the basis of 'one member, one vote'
- practical business reasons (which should be explained)
- being part of a group structure of societies sharing common accounting and/or IT systems.

Such organisations may, under forthcoming legislation, be able to register as community interest companies – see above.

Advantages

Like companies limited by guarantee, industrial and provident societies (IPSs) are incorporated organisations, which means that they can hold property and take legal action in their own name. Most importantly, committee members are protected from personal liability under contracts and can generally be personally liable only if they act fraudulently or in breach of trust, or continue to run the organisation when they ought to know that it has no reasonable chance of avoiding insolvent liquidation (see chapter 10).

IPSs use a set of rules to register with the Financial Services Authority (FSA). Most societies applying for registration do so through one of the organisations (**sponsoring bodies**) that has agreed model rules with the FSA. Using model rules limits the chance of mistakes, may reduce the fee payable and can shorten the time taken to register. For details contact the FSA.

Disadvantages
If the organisation doesn't use model rules, registration can be a lengthy, expensive process (£950 in 2003/04). If model rules are used, the fee is reduced (to between £100 and £950, depending on the number of changes made to the model) although the umbrella organisation which produced the model rules and that will help with registration may charge an additional fee. Even registration using model rules can take several months.

Annual returns and accounts must be submitted to the FSA, and these are open to the public. Registers of members and officers must be kept and be available for public inspection (see *Setting up registers*, in chapter 2). An IPS has to pay the FSA an annual fee, in 2003/04 between £60 and £370, depending on its total assets.

Probably the greatest disadvantage is that an IPS cannot register with the Charity Commission, even if it is a charitable organisation, and therefore will not receive a registered charity number. Some funders, for example charitable trusts, can award grants only to registered charities.

A charitable IPS should submit its constitution to the Inland Revenue for recognition as charitable, otherwise it will not be able to claim the tax advantages of charitable status (see page 10) and may have to pay corporation tax. A charitable IPS is eligible for rate relief in the same way as other charities (see page 11).

Provided their rules don't specify an earlier date, IPSs have seven months to submit their annual return after the end of a financial year. This period is shorter than that required for companies.

Proposed company law changes include reducing the time limit for filing the accounts of private companies (which include most voluntary sector companies) to seven months.

IPSs may fall within the definition of a company under local authority influence (see page 8) and they are more likely to do so than companies limited by guarantee.

Further information about IPSs is available from Mutual Societies Registration at the Financial Services Authority (*www.fsa.gov.uk/mutual_societies_registration/*).

Cooperatives and Community Benefit Societies Act 2003
This Act makes some changes to the law relating to IPSs. From 1 April 2004 it:
- enables the Treasury to make regulations to allow community benefit IPSs to set in place an 'asset lock', so that, if they wish, they can ensure that some or all of their assets can only ever be used or dealt with for the benefit of the community
- helps IPSs enter into contracts and conduct business by bringing some aspects of IPS law into line with corresponding company legislation.

For further information contact the FSA.

Changing the structure
It is possible to move from one form of legal structure to another as an organisation develops and its needs change. For example, it may start with a steering group with no constitution, merely a set of agreed objectives, and move on to develop a more formal constitution.

Changing from unincorporated to incorporated
In time an organisation may want to own property, take on staff or enter into long-term contracts. It may then want to consider becoming a company limited by guarantee. This is perfectly possible. A new organisation (the company) will need to be established, the assets and liabilities of the original organisation will be transferred to the company, and the original organisation is likely to be wound up.

The following points need to be considered when making such a change.

Date of transfer: It is most convenient to choose a date that fits in with the original organisation's financial year – either the last day or half-way through. In this way both the old and the new organisation will have either a full or a six-month period of accounts.

Bank accounts: The company must open new bank accounts and the new committee of the company will therefore have to pass resolutions appointing new cheque signatories.

Officers: Company officers will need to be elected, following procedures laid down in the company's articles of association.

Contracts of employment: Employees will need to have their employment transferred. The company must inform them, on or shortly after the transfer, of the name and address of their new employer, stating that they have continuity of employment from the original organisation.

Premises: If the original organisation leases premises, the landlord will need to agree to transfer the lease to the company. If the trustees hold property for the unincorporated organisation, ownership will need to be transferred to the company. In both circumstances it is essential to take legal advice. The rules on disposal of premises are discussed in more detail in chapter 6.

Equipment: On the date of transfer, all equipment belonging to the original organisation must be transferred to the company. The best way is for an officer representing the original organisation and a committee member or officer from the company to sign a single sheet of paper confirming the transfer of all equipment. Check whether any guarantees on the equipment are invalidated by a transfer of ownership. If so, it may be advisable to leave them in the name of the committee members of the original organisation until the guarantee has expired.

Insurance: The company will need new insurance policies (although if ownership of equipment is kept in the original name (see above) the insurance must also be in the original name). Additional types of insurance may be needed (for further details see chapter 7).

Funding: Funding agreements will have to be transferred to the company, with the funders' permission. Many funders require unincorporated organisations to get their consent before even starting the conversion process, and may need to confirm that a grant payable to an unincorporated organisation will continue to be payable to the new company.

Membership: When the company is set up, the only members will be those people who signed the memorandum and articles of association (the constitution). One of the first tasks of the new committee is to ensure all members from the original organisation are admitted into membership, following the procedures laid down in the articles of association.

Cooptions: The first committee members (company directors) are the people who signed Form 10 (see *Adopt the constitution*, in chapter 2) as part of the process of setting up the company. Any additional committee members should be elected, appointed or coopted under the provisions in the articles of association.

Letterheads: The new company will need a new letterhead (see *Letterheads*, in chapter 2). It is illegal to continue to use the original organisation's letterhead without the company registration number.

Charity number: If registered as a charity the company will have to apply for a new charity registration number, using the form in the Charity Commission's incorporation pack *Charity incorporation – how to 'incorporate' an unincorporated charity and apply for registration* (RTN 1302).

Action on the transfer date

The following transfers will take place:
* money in bank or building society accounts
* responsibility for outstanding cheques and liabilities
* employees' contracts
* equipment and premises (unless they are to be left in the names of the original trustees).

The original organisation will continue to exist until the final accounts have been prepared and audited (if required – see chapter 8), and submitted to a general meeting, and the winding up procedures in the constitution or trust deed have been followed.

The final meeting

After the transfer date a general meeting of the original organisation should be held to discuss:
* agreement of the audited accounts for the final period up to the date of transfer
* a resolution to wind up the organisation.

Charities

The Charity Commission's pack *Charity incorporation: How to 'incorporate' an unincorporated charity and apply for registration* (RTN 1302) is designed to help charities through the process of winding up the original charity, transferring its assets and registering the new company. It can be downloaded from *www.charity-commission.gov.uk* or ordered from 0870 3330123.

Converting to a charitable incorporated organisation (see page 4) will involve a simplified process.

Converting an industrial and provident society to a company

An industrial and provident society (IPS) that wishes to covert into a company must pass a special resolution. Under the **Industrial and Provident Societies Act 1965**, the resolution can serve as the memorandum and articles (constitution) of the new company.

The **Industrial and Provident Societies Act 2002** sets out the following voting requirements for a special resolution:
- not less than 50% of the qualifying members must vote on the resolution, and
- not less than 75% of those who vote must vote in favour.

The IPS must hold a second meeting to confirm the special resolution not less than 14 days and not more than one month after the first meeting. The resolution to confirm must be passed by the majority of those qualifying members who vote.

For further details see *www.fsa.gov.uk/ mutual_societies_registration/company_conversion.html*

Local authority companies

The **Local Government and Housing Act 1989** established a statutory framework to regulate local authorities' interest in companies.* The Act defines two categories – those subject to local authority control and those subject to **local authority influence**. The framework came into effect in 1995, under **the Local Authorities (Companies) Order 1995**.

In the context of this Act 'companies' includes industrial and provident societies (IPSs) as well as companies limited by guarantee, and so could apply to voluntary organisations. Some details are given below. However, this is a particularly complicated area of law, which is subject to change, and it is particularly important to seek legal advice about this subject.

Local authority control

A company is controlled by the local authority where one or more local authorities control the majority of the voting rights at a general meeting, or control the appointment of the majority of committee members. As this is unlikely to apply to small, local voluntary organisations, it is not discussed further here.

Local authority influence

A company is considered to be influenced by the local authority if there is a business relationship between the company and local authority (see below) and:
- at least 20% of the voting rights of members entitled to vote at a general meeting are held by people associated with the local authority (see below), *or*
- at least 20% of its committee or board of directors are people associated with the local authority, *or*
- at least 20% of the voting rights at a committee or board meeting are held by people who are associated with the local authority.

Business relationship

A company has a business relationship with the local authority if:
- within a period of 12 months, more than half its turnover is associated with the local authority, or
- more than half its assets originated with the local authority, or
- it occupies local authority land leased or sold for less than the commercial rate.

Associated with the local authority

A person is 'associated with the local authority' if he or she:
- is or has been a local authority councillor within the past four years
- is currently an employee of the local authority, or
- is currently an employee or director of a company that is under the control of the local authority (see above).

Controls

A voluntary organisation defined as a company subject to local authority influence:
- must state this fact and the name(s) of the relevant authority/authorities on headed paper, other formal documents and cheques
- has restrictions on travel and other expenses it can pay to local authority representatives on the committee
- is subject to the same restrictions as local authorities in publishing material which appears 'wholly or in part to be designed to effect public support for a political party' (**Section 2, Local Government Act 1986**)
- must provide financial information to the local authority's auditors
- must reply to requests for information about its work from individual local authority councillors (subject to normal rules of confidentiality)
- may have certain financial transactions treated as if they were financial transactions of the local authority.

Exemptions

The Secretary of State has powers to exempt an individual organisation, or particular types of organisations from the rules on local authority controlled and influenced companies. At the time of writing (December 2003) these included some citizens advice bureaux and registered housing associations. A full list of exempt organisations is available from the Office of the Deputy Prime Minister on 020 7944 8766.

For further information on local authority companies contact the Local Authority Companies, Trading and Partnership Branch of the Office of the Deputy Prime Minister.

Charitable status

This section describes which organisations are eligible for charitable status and which have to register with the Charity Commission; it then examines the advantages and disadvantages of being a charity.

In the strict legal sense, a charity is an organisation established exclusively for charitable purposes (ie set up for the benefit of the public) and will generally have to register under the **Charities Act 1993**.

A charitable unincorporated association, trust or company limited by guarantee which owns or occupies land, has permanent endowment (ie where expenditure of capital is restricted and (normally) only income can be spent on the organisation's purposes) or has an annual income of £1000 or more must register with the Charity Commission.

The draft Charities Bill will increase the registration threshold to £5000 and remove the criteria relating to land and permanent endowment. Charities under the threshold will be able to register voluntarily.

Excepted charities

Some charities are excepted from registering. These include some very small charities (see above), some churches and other registered places of worship, and voluntary schools. They can register voluntarily.

Under the draft Charities Bill, currently excepted charities will eventually have to register with the Charity Commission.

Exempt charities

Some charities are exempt from registering (and cannot register voluntarily) because they are considered to be adequately supervised by, or accountable to, some other authority. These include charitable industrial and provident societies (see page 5), many state schools, registered social landlords, and some universities, medical schools and museums. They are, however, subject to the legal rules generally applicable to charities and the provisions of the 1993 Charities Act (unless specifically excluded).

The draft Charities Bill will propose requiring exempt charities (or groups of exempt charities) whose income is above £100,000 to register if no acceptable alternative regulator can be identified.

Charitable purposes

To be a charity an organisation must have exclusively charitable purposes (its objects or aims, which are usually stated in its constitution).

Charitable purposes can be grouped under four broad headings:
*   the relief of financial hardship
*   the advancement of education
*   the advancement of religion
*   certain other purposes beneficial to the community.

All purposes must also be for the public benefit (ie for the benefit of the community or a significant section of it).

The meaning of 'charitable purposes' is largely based on decisions of the Charity Commission and the Court. For further information see *Recognising new charitable purposes* (RR1A), available from *www.charity-commission.gov.uk*

Relief of financial hardship

The Charity Commission uses a broad definition of financial hardship, and states that 'generally speaking, anyone who does not have access to the normal things of life which most people take for granted would probably qualify for help'. A person does not have to be destitute to qualify, and the hardship need not be long-term, for example temporary hardship caused by an accident or a death in the family may qualify.

Relief of financial hardship can be provided directly, for example through financial help, food, clothing, equipment or housing, or indirectly by helping people become more self-sufficient, for example through providing welfare advice or supporting another organisation which helps people suffering hardship. Unlike the other charitable purposes described below, financial hardship charities can work with a narrowly defined group of people. For further information see *Charities for the relief of the poor* (CC4) and *Charities for the relief of sickness* (CC6).

Advancement of education

There is no precise definition of education. It is not limited to formal education, and can include:

- promoting aesthetic education, for example through concerts and drama
- providing work-related training
- research activities for public benefit
- playgroups
- education in the academic sense (the Charity Commission would not accept an organisation promoting a particular point of view).

The advancement of education must be for general public benefit.

Advancement of religion

The definition includes the provision and upkeep of places of worship, paying ministers and other faith leaders, and holding services. In order to qualify under this heading the religion being promoted has to:

- be founded on a belief in a supreme being or beings, and
- involve expression of that belief through worship.

The organisation must also be able to demonstrate that its activities will benefit the general public.

Other purposes beneficial to the community

As long as an organisation can demonstrate that its activities are beneficial to the community (or a substantial part of it) there is scope for extending the traditional charitable frontiers, for example:

- promoting racial harmony
- the relief of old age, sickness or disability, where there is no financial need
- conserving and protecting the natural environment and endangered species
- providing help for victims of natural or civil disasters
- resettlement and rehabilitation of ex-offenders and drug misusers
- promoting industry, commerce or art for the public benefit.

Review of the Register

As a result of the Charity Commission's review of the Register of Charities, the following are now recognised as charitable purposes:

- promoting religious harmony
- promoting equality and diversity for the benefit of the public
- urban and rural regeneration
- the relief of unemployment
- community capacity building
- preservation and/or conservation
- museum and art gallery collections
- promoting community participation in healthy recreation by providing facilities for playing particular sports
- promoting human rights.

For further information see *www.charity-commission.gov.uk*

A self-help organisation that has a closed membership would not be eligible for charitable status, as it does not operate for the general public benefit. However, a self-help group might be able to obtain charitable status if it is open to anyone (or anyone living in a defined area) with a certain condition or in a specific situation.

Draft Charities Bill

The proposed legislation will expand the four headings above to twelve more specific ones:

- The prevention and relief of poverty
- The advancement of education
- The advancement of religion
- The advancement of health
- Social and community advancement
- The advancement of science, culture, arts and heritage
- The advancement of amateur sport
- The promotion of human rights, conflict resolution and reconciliation
- The provision of social housing
- The promotion of animal welfare
- The advancement of environmental protection and improvement
- Other purposes beneficial to the community

To qualify as charitable, an organisation will have to show first, that its purposes (as set out in its constitution) fall within one or more of the above list and, second, that it is established for the public benefit.

Advantages

Tax relief

The main advantages of charitable status lie in the field of taxation. Charities have the following tax advantages:

income and corporation tax: charities do not pay income

tax on their income or corporation tax on their profits. Profits earned from trading activities can be exempt from tax, but only if:

- they are used solely for the purposes of the charity, and
- the trade is part of its main function or the work is mainly carried out by the beneficiaries, or
- the profits fall within the annual turnover limit described on page 12

stamp duty: charities are exempt from stamp duty when buying or leasing property or buying shares in England, Wales, Scotland or Northern Ireland, but they need to obtain an exemption stamp from the local Inland Revenue Stamp Office

capital gains tax: charities do not pay capital gains tax as long as any gain is used for charitable purposes

inheritance tax: many gifts to charities are exempt from inheritance tax

Value Added Tax (VAT): sales or the hire of donated goods to the general public, to disabled people or to people receiving means tested benefits, and some charity fundraising events are exempt from VAT. Most other trading by charities is, however, taxed in the normal way – even if the profits from the trading are exempt from other forms of tax. Organisations that charge for goods or services, or that are considering contracting with public authorities should check with their accountants and with Customs and Excise to see whether they must charge VAT

donations: under *Gift Aid* charities can recover tax on donations from individuals, and companies can reclaim the tax on charity donations, making charity giving more attractive. There is no limit on the amount or number of donations individuals or companies can make. For further details see *Gift Aid*, in chapter 9.

Rate relief

A charity is entitled to an 80% reduction on the non-domestic rate on any building it uses wholly or mainly for charitable purposes (**mandatory relief**). The local authority has the discretion to waive the remaining 20% so that the charity pays no rates at all (**discretionary relief**). There is no statutory requirement to submit applications for mandatory rate relief but it is advisable to inform the rating authority (see *Paying rates*, in chapter 6, for further details).

Fundraising

Some funders, particularly trusts, have a policy of grant-aiding only registered charities. Having charitable status and, in particular, having a registered charity number (which registered charities are automatically given) also provides credibility when raising money from the public.

Advice

The Charity Commission can offer free advice on all aspects of charity law (telephone 0870 333 0123, minicom 0870 333 0125). It also produces a number of free publications, available via *www.charity-commission.gov.uk* or from the publications line 01823 345 427.

Small charities

The Charity Commission takes a 'light touch' approach to charities whose annual income is under £10,000. There are two Small Charities Units, in Liverpool (charities in England) and Taunton (Welsh charities), which publish a number of information sheets specifically for small charities. For further details see *www.charity-commission.gov.uk/supportingcharities*

Disadvantages

Political activity

Charities must not have directly political aims, and are therefore restricted in the nature of their campaigning work. The law does, however, allow some political activity by charities as long as it is directly relevant to their work and does not involve party politics.

The general principles are that a charity can engage in political activity if:

- there is a reasonable expectation that the activity would further the charity's objectives and so help its beneficiaries to an extent justified by the resources devoted to the activity
- it is within the charity's powers under the terms of its constitution.

In addition, the views expressed must be based on a well-founded and reasoned case and be expressed in a responsible way.

The Charity Commission publishes two sets of guidelines on political activities and campaigning by charities: *Political activities and campaigning by charities* (CC9) and *Political activities and campaigning by local community charities* (CC9a).

The guidelines list acceptable and unacceptable political activities under the following headings:

- Influencing government or public opinion
- Responding to proposed legislation
- Advocating and opposing changes in the law and public policy
- Supporting, opposing and promoting legislation
- Commenting on public issues
- Supporting political parties

- Acting with other bodies
- Providing information
- Responding to forthcoming elections
- Conducting and publishing research
- Seeking support for government grants
- Demonstrations and direct action

At the time of writing (December 2003) the Charity Commission intended to revise its guidelines on campaigning to make the tone less cautionary and place greater emphasis on the campaigning and other non-party political activities that charities can undertake. The legal position will remain the same.

To avoid problems with the Charity Commission charities should avoid using words such as 'campaign', 'pressure' or 'action' in their published material unless the activities clearly fall within the Charity Commission's guidelines.

Charities that overstep the mark on political activity may receive a demand for income tax or corporation tax on at least part of their income. Committee members may, in rare cases, be liable for breach of trust. If non-charitable activities continue, the Charity Commission is likely to remove the organisation from the Register of Charities.

To clarify whether a proposed political activity (including the content of publications or advertisements) would be acceptable to the Charity Commission, telephone its advice line on 0870 333 0123.

Some charities have a parallel non-charitable organisation to carry out their political activity. For example Liberty is not a charity, and so is free to campaign. The linked but separate Civil Liberties Trust is registered as a charity. An organisation that adopts this strategy must ensure that the charitable and non-charitable bodies have completely separate accounts, committees and decision-making procedures. If the charity's premises, equipment and staff time are used by the non-charity, the charity must charge an appropriate amount. Get advice from an accountant or solicitor if considering this approach.

Trading

There are some restrictions on the trading activities a charity can carry out. Permitted activities are:
- selling its services as part of its charitable work, for example by providing educational or community care services, or a charity which is a theatre charging people to see productions
- trading if the trading is ancillary to the charity's primary purpose, for example selling food and drink in a theatre restaurant or bar to members of the audience

- selling goods produced by its beneficiaries, for example items made in a sheltered workshop
- selling donated goods, land, building and investments
- running a lottery, provided it complies with all requirements for small lotteries (see *Lotteries and raffles*, in chapter 9)
- organising fundraising events (see *Fundraising*, in chapter 9)

For further information about all aspects of charity trading see *Charities and trading* (CC35) and the Inland Revenue booklet *Trading by charities* (IR2001).

Sometimes charities will want to run a trading activity connected to their main activities. For example a shop run by a charitable art gallery or museum may sell a range of goods. Some may be directly related to the gallery or museum, for example works of art or educational books, but other goods such as mugs or sweatshirts may be sold solely to raise funds. Or a charity may want to run trading activities that are not directly linked to its main activities. Such non-primary purpose trading by a charity is exempt from tax if:
- the total turnover from all trading and other incidental fundraising activities does not exceed the annual turnover limit (see below), or
- if the total turnover exceeds the annual turnover limit, there was a reasonable expectation that it would not do so, and
- the profits are used for the purposes of the charity.

The Charity Commission can still refuse, or retract, charitable status if it believes any trading falls outside the exemptions for charities, so if in doubt check with the Commission before starting to trade.

Annual turnover limit
The annual turnover limit is:
- £5000, or
- if greater than £5000, but not more than £50,000, less than 25% of the charity's gross income (for example, if the charity's total gross income is £160,000, all the turnover from its non-charitable trading will be taxable if it exceeds £40,000 (ie 25% of £160,000)).

If the proposed trading does not comply with the above requirements it is advisable to set up a trading company (see below).

Charities and contracts (CC37) describes the issues to be considered when contracting with public bodies to provide services (see *Contracting to provides services*, in chapter 9).

There are special difficulties with conducting private research, for example research for a commercial organisation or where a charity is seeking commercial sponsorship. Refer to the Inland Revenue's *Trading by charities* if your charity is considering undertaking these kinds of activities.

Using a separate trading company

Where a charity is not permitted to carry out certain trading itself, it can set up a separate trading company, in a way that ensures it is controlled by the charity or its trustees.

The charity which sets up the trading company must meet the following requirements:
- the charity's constitution must not include any restrictions on purchasing shares in a private company
- the trading venture must not be too speculative
- there must be some clear benefits to the charity in having the trading company – a reasonable expectation of profits and income based on proper assessments of risk and income
- the two organisations must have totally separate accounts and, if the same staff are employed by both, it must be possible to distinguish the work staff do for each organisation. It must also be possible to distinguish the separate costs of any shared premises, equipment and stationery
- the charity must not subsidise the trading company; costs for shared staff, premises, equipment etc must be properly apportioned and the charity must charge the trading company for all resources used by the company (note that there may be VAT implications in these recharges)
- the charity can lend money to the trading company only if it has power under its constitution to make such loans, the loan is considered to be a reasonable investment, it charges market interest rates and takes steps to obtain security for the loan.

There may be some disadvantages in setting up a trading company, including:
- the possibility of losing rate relief if premises are partly used for non-charitable purposes
- the additional costs and staff time of operating a trading company
- the additional time involved in running two separate organisations with two separate committees
- the potential conflict of interest between trustees or directors of the two bodies (the Charity Commission recommends that at least one director of each body is not a director of the other)
- restrictions on investment in the trading company (this must be subject to the rule of charity law)

- any profit made by the trading company is subject to corporation tax. Generally, most of the profits will be covenanted or donated to the charity and attract tax relief through Gift Aid (see *Tax relief*, page 10) but any profits retained, including money the trading company uses to invest in its development, are taxable
- arrangements may be needed between the two bodies for the use of land. The **Charities Act 1993** may require that these arrangements operate on a commercial basis (see chapter 6)
- the difficulty of apportioning costs between the charity and non-charity
- the potential VAT implications for the charity when it recharges the non-charity for staff time, use of premises, use of equipment, etc.

Users on the committee

Many voluntary organisations see user participation as a vital way of ensuring services are relevant and accessible. However, a charity that is considering having its service users on the management committee must take care to ensure there is no conflict of interest.

The Charity Commission advises that user committee members should be excluded from taking any part in decisions directly affecting their interests or those of anyone closely connected to them. For example, in a charity helping people in financial need, a user committee member may need to be excluded from decisions where grants are allocated.

There is no legal bar to all committee members being users, but as a guide the Charity Commission suggests that users make up no more than a third of the committee.

For further information see *Users on board* (CC24).

Payments to committee members

A charity can only remunerate its committee members (either by financial payments or benefits in kind) if it has the legal right to do so. This applies both to payment for a specific service such as legal advice or designing a poster, and paying a trustee to act as a trustee.

A committee member can only receive financial benefit from the charity if:
- the constitution allows such a payment, *or*
- the Charity Commission has given written consent, *and*
- the member withdraws from any meeting when payment is discussed.

In addition, one of the two following conditions must be met:

- the constitution limits payment to a 'reasonable sum' for services provided by a committee member, or
- the payment is a fair price for the work, the charity can afford it and the payment is related to actual services provided and is not simply a gift.

Any such payments are subject to tax, either through PAYE or self-assessment, may be subject to the national minimum wage (see chapter 3), and may affect any state benefits the trustee is receiving.

Amending the constitution

If there is no clause in the constitution allowing remuneration, a charity will need to get authority from the Charity Commission before it can amend its constitution to allow this.

Payment for acting as trustee

The Commission will take the following into account when considering such a request:

- the charity's size and administrative complexity
- the charity's ability to pay
- the nature and complexity of the charity's activities
- whether committee members need to be involved in the charity's day-to-day management
- the specialist nature of the skills required, and whether these could be supplied by employees or external advisers
- the comparative cost of buying in the necessary skills rather than paying committee members.

In general, the Charity Commission believes committee members should not receive any payment if staff are employed. However, it recognises that in some cases at least one of the committee members, for example the chair, may be so heavily involved that remuneration may be justified.

Remuneration for professional services

The Commission will only agree to such an amendment for professional services where:

- safeguards are in place
- the service is necessary
- the service is best provided by a trustee rather than an independent person (this could be because of a combination of in-house knowledge and price).

Under the draft Charities Bill a committee will be able to pay an individual trustee to provide a service to a charity (outside his or her duties as a trustee) if it reasonably believes this would be in the charity's interests. The
government will introduce safeguards to prevent deliberate or unintentional misuse.

One-off payments

Charities can apply to the Commission for permission to make a one-off payment to a committee member, under **Section 26** of the **Charities Act 1993**, if they can show that:

- the work is exceptional and not part of the committee member's normal duties
- the work is necessary
- the payment is genuine, for example the member is not being employed at a greater cost than would be charged elsewhere, and
- payment is appropriate for the work done.

For further details see *Payment of charity trustees* (CC11).

Small charities

Charities whose annual income is under £10,000 can pay up to a total of £1000 each year to trustees for providing an extra service to the charity without reference to the Charity Commission, provided that:

- the service is necessary
- the payment is reasonable
- a majority of trustees are not being paid
- the trustee concerned withdraws from discussions about remuneration, and is not counted as being part of the quorum (the minimum number of voting members needed to take decisions, see page 21)
- the payment is declared in the charity's accounts.

For further details see *Small payments for providing a service to the charity* (SCU8), available from *www.charity-commission.gov.uk/supportingcharities*

Employees on the committee

A new charity can include a provision within its constitution allowing an employee to be appointed as a committee member if:

- it is in the interests of the good administration of the charity, and
- the employee is excluded from meetings where terms of employment are discussed.

However, the number of employee places will generally be restricted, and they must be in the minority.

The Charity Commission will not permit existing charities to amend their constitutions to allow employee membership unless they can make a very strong case.

Even though restrictions mean that most employees cannot play any formal role in making the most important management decisions, they can still be involved through consultation. Unless prohibited by the organisation's constitution, it is always possible to invite employees to attend and speak (but not vote) at trustee meetings.

For further details see *Payment of charity trustees* (CC11).

Liability for breach of trust

A charity's committee members can be personally liable if any losses result where they have acted in breach of trust. This is discussed further under Minimising the risk of personal liability, below.

Publicity and administrative requirements

All charities must make their annual accounts available to any member of the public on request. Charities whose annual income or expenditure exceeds £10,000 must submit an annual return (containing information specified in the **Charities (Annual Return) Regulations 1997)**, their annual accounts and a trustees' annual report to the Charity Commission (see *Annual reports on the accounts*, in chapter 8). Charities whose income and expenditure is below this threshold are advised to submit their annual return to the Charity Commission, and must inform the Commission of any changes to the details held on the Charity Register (an annual Register Check Form is issued for this purpose).

Standard Information Return

The government has agreed to the introduction of a Standard Information Return (SIR) for charities whose income exceeds £1 million, the format and content of which will be developed by the Charity Commission, in consultation with charities and others. It is possible the SIR information will be collected as part of the current annual return.

Minimising the risk of personal liability

All voluntary organisations will want to ensure that members and committee members do not end up being personally liable for losses in any way. In many voluntary organisations there is minimal risk. In others there *are* risks, and these organisations need to choose a legal structure designed to prevent personal liability as far as possible.

Liability of committee members

It is important to understand the following ways in which committee members can become personally liable:

- for breach of trust if the organisation is a charity
- for negligence to service users, staff, or anyone else
- for breach of statutory duties in carrying out the organisation's activities
- under contracts entered into by the organisation.

Where there is no management committee the liability rules below will apply to the organisation's members.

Breach of trust

Committee members of a charity who have acted in breach of trust may be personally required to repay the charity for any losses incurred, whatever the legal structure. This can include where:

- a committee member has acted fraudulently (for example stealing money from the charity)
- someone has gained personal benefit from being a committee member (for example receiving payment or other benefits not allowed under the terms of the constitution and not authorised by the Charity Commission)
- committee members have allowed the charity to carry out an activity not permitted under the terms of the constitution or under charity law (for example engaging in a political campaign or trading which was not within its powers or within charity law). However, even if the committee has acted in breach of trust in allowing this activity, members would be required to repay the charity only if financial costs were incurred. For example, if the charity engaged in political campaigning which was not allowed, committee members might have to repay to the charity the cost of any publicity material produced
- the committee has acted outside the charity's objects, beneficiary group or area of benefit
- the committee has been seriously negligent and this has resulted in losses to the charity (for example by allowing it to engage in some risky venture without taking proper steps to protect its position).

Provided trustees act sensibly and seek advice when necessary from, for example, valuers, solicitors, accountants or the Charity Commission, there should be no reason for them to act in breach of trust. It is particularly important for organisations that operate on the fringe of acceptable charity activity (for example campaigning), to get advice if they have any doubt whether the activities are permitted under charity law.

Even if a committee member has acted in breach of trust, the court has power to relieve him or her of personal liability if it is satisfied that the individual acted reasonably and honestly.*

It may also be possible for the charity to obtain trustee indemnity insurance against personal liability for an act taken in breach of trust by an honest mistake (see chapter 7).

Under the draft Charities Bill, trustees will be able to apply to the Charity Commission as well as the court for relief from personal liability for breach of trust where they have acted honestly and reasonably.

Negligence

In a company limited by guarantee or an industrial and provident society the organisation itself would usually be liable for negligence if it is sued for a loss, damage or injury arising as a result of an organisation's action or inaction (for example giving incorrect legal advice, or failing to repair a dangerous building). The committee members would generally be protected from individual liability to the person who has been injured or suffered damage or loss. But in unincorporated associations and charitable trusts, individual committee members would be liable for negligence.

In practice, organisational and personal liability can be avoided by taking out adequate insurance (public liability and/or professional indemnity insurance), and the committee should take responsibility for arranging this (see chapter 7). If the organisation has employees, it must take out employer's liability insurance.

Breach of statutory duties

Committee members have a number of statutory duties, for example in relation to employees, health and safety and company law. There are many statutory duties, such as those under the Health and Safety at Work Act or related regulations (see chapter 5), and the duty to send in company accounts and reports on time, where failure to act is an offence that may be punishable by fines or, in some cases, imprisonment (see chapter 8).

The organisation can reduce the risk of such offences occurring by ensuring there are people connected to the organisation – whether committee members, staff, volunteers or professional advisors – who are aware of the full range of obligations, and by having proper procedures and monitoring in place.

Contracts

Voluntary organisations can enter into a number of contracts including:
- employment contracts
- contracts with consultants or freelance workers
- leases on premises

- other leases, for example for photocopiers or cars
- contracts to provide services
- opening an account, for example with a stationery supplier.

Many contracts, especially those relating to leasing premises, vehicles or equipment, contain clauses requiring payment over a number of years. Unless there is provision to terminate the contract or assign (transfer) it, an organisation will continue to be liable to make the payments until the lease has ended.

In an incorporated organisation (industrial and provident society or company limited by guarantee) the organisation itself will be liable to make the payments even if its funding has ceased. If the organisation cannot afford to meet the obligations, it is wound up and such assets as it has are distributed among the people to whom it owes money (see chapter 10).

For unincorporated organisations there is no such escape, so taking on contracts and leases increases the risk of personal liability for the committee members of unincorporated associations and trusts.

An unincorporated organisation cannot itself enter into a lease or contract of any kind. It must do so through:
- named individuals or the whole committee, who will be responsible for making payments under the terms of any contract or lease
- appointing holding trustees (see page 22) or a custodian trustee (for leases or investments); if there are holding trustees this is best done using a trust deed which states that they are entitled to indemnification from the main body or its committee members
- applying to the Charity Commission, if a charity, to become an incorporated body of trustees (see page 2).

Personal liability can be limited to some extent by:
- ensuring the contract can be terminated at least on reasonable notice if funding runs out
- stating in the contract that it is being entered into by a person in the capacity of a trustee on behalf of the organisation and that the trustee is not to be personally liable for any breach of contract.

The constitution

A constitution is the legal document that sets out the rules for governing an organisation. Some rules are determined by an organisation's legal structure and whether it wishes to be legally charitable; others will

depend on how it wants to manage its own affairs. It is necessary for the following reasons:
- to ensure an organisation's aims are clear and agreed by its members
- to provide mechanisms for making decisions and resolving disputes
- to ensure accountability
- to gain credibility with banks and funders
- to clarify liability and lines of responsibility
- to enable an organisation to take advantage of the benefits of charitable status
- to enable holding or custodian trustees to be formally appointed and, if necessary, hold property on trust for an organisation (see chapter 6)
- to enable an organisation which is legally charitable to register as a charity
- to enable an organisation which wishes to do so, to register as a company or an industrial and provident society
- to enable an organisation to affiliate to the local council for voluntary service or other second tier (umbrella) organisation.

Broadly, a constitution has the following sections:
- name of the organisation
- objects and beneficiaries (and area of benefit, if defined)
- powers
- procedures and rules for running the organisation – these will include details relating to membership, annual general meetings and other membership meetings, the management committee, officers and committee meetings, keeping financial accounts
- alterations to the constitution
- dissolution.

Name

A constitution should start with the name of the organisation (for further details, including restrictions on names, see *Setting up the organisation*, in chapter 2).

Objects, beneficiaries and area of benefit

Aims and objectives: This clause defines the organisation's main purposes (why it exists or what it hopes to achieve), its beneficiaries (the people it is set up to work with or for, and if applicable its area of benefit (the geographic area it serves). It is preferable, where relevant, to write the aims in order of priority.

To register as a charity, all objects written in the constitution must be recognised by the Charity Commission as being charitable (see *Charitable purposes*, page 9). Once registered, charities cannot change any of their objects without the consent of the Charity Commission.

The Charity Commission publishes example charitable objects for a range of charitable purposes, available from *www.charity-commission.gov.uk/registration*

The **Sex Discrimination Act 1975**, the **Race Relations Act 1976** and the **Disability Discrimination Act 1995** forbid discrimination in the provision of services on grounds of sex, marital status, racial group and disability. The exceptions are where objects specifically state that an organisation is providing services to women or men only and/or to one racial group (which cannot be defined by reference to colour) and/or where an organisation is set up to provide services to people with a specific disability. If the organisation intends to use these provisions, check with the Equal Opportunities Commission, the Commission for Racial Equality and/or the Disability Rights Commission, as appropriate.

Area of benefit: This clause describes the catchment area of an organisation, for example ward, town or local authority area.

Powers

This clause allows the organisation to undertake the activities necessary in order to achieve its objectives. It would include, for example, the power to employ and pay staff, own land or property, borrow or raise money, and take out most insurances.

If an organisation wants to be able to insure members of its management committee against personal liability for acting in breach of trust (or in the case of a company or industrial and provident society for any liability for wrongful trading) then the power to do so must be explicitly included in the constitution. The Charity Commission will allow a charity to include powers to take out this kind of insurance (trustee indemnity) provided that it does not extend to a deliberate breach of trust, criminal activity, or recklessness. For further details see chapter 7.

If a charity wants to remunerate its committee members (whether in cash or kind) it must include this power in its constitution. For further information see *Payments to committee members*, page 13.

Procedures and rules for running the organisation

Membership

All voluntary organisations, apart from some charitable trusts, will have a membership structure. In legal terms a member is a person or an organisation who agrees to abide by the terms of the constitution in return for rights given under that constitution, for example the right to vote at general meetings.

The constitution should define who is eligible for membership, categories of membership (see below), how membership is approved, membership subscriptions and members' meetings. There should also be clauses on conditions of membership, members' rights and the circumstances in which membership ends.

Eligibility: Who is eligible for membership will depend on the organisation's aims and objectives, key activities and catchment area. Remember that most charities must operate for the benefit of the general public, and organisations operating purely for specific people may not be eligible for charitable status.

If the organisation has a defined area of benefit, its constitution must be clear about whether membership is open only to people who live (or live or work) in that area.

Membership categories: In general there are two categories of membership – voting and non-voting. The categories of voting members must be defined in the constitution.

Non-voting categories of membership can be set up even if they are not included in the constitution. It is important to remember that, although non-voting members are recognised as supporting the organisation and having a close connection with it, they are not technically 'members' and they will not have rights such as being able to attend and vote at the annual general meeting (AGM).

Group membership

It is possible to allow organisations as well as individuals to become members. An incorporated organisation (company or industrial and provident society) can become a member of any other body, as long as its constitution allows this. The organisation will appoint a representative (or representatives) who will act on its behalf. Unless the constitution states otherwise, such representatives will have the same rights and obligations as individual members.

Technically, an unincorporated association cannot be a member of another organisation (because it has no separate legal existence – see page 2) and must appoint a nominee to join on its behalf. The nominee then becomes a member, whose name must appear in the membership register (see *Setting up registers*, in chapter 2). However, many organisations ignore this and will allow an unincorporated association to join in the same way as an incorporated organisation and to appoint a representative to act on the organisation's behalf.

New members

The constitution may describe procedures for applying for membership and approving new members.

Resignation

The procedures for resigning from membership should also be described and include a requirement for resignations to be made in writing.

Terminating membership

This clause describes the circumstances in which membership will end. The rule could state that individuals would cease to be members upon death, if they resigned, stopped working or living in the area or did not pay their subscriptions (see *Subscriptions*, below).

There could also be a rule setting out grounds for expulsion, for example by bringing the organisation into general disrepute. The decision making procedures also need to be spelt out. One method is for the management committee to propose an expulsion, an appeals committee to review the case, and the final decision to be taken by ordinary members in a general meeting. Whatever method is chosen, there must be a balance between members' rights and the ability of an organisation to protect its reputation. The member concerned must be given an opportunity to know why the expulsion is being proposed, and to state their case. The reasons for expulsion should be recorded.

When a person or organisation ceases to be a member for any reason the list of members must be updated (within 14 days for a company). Members of industrial and provident societies should have the value of their share (usually £1) refunded in exchange for their share certificate (see *Conditions of membership*, below).

Subscriptions

Many organisations have subscriptions, or membership fees. Sometimes a nominal amount is charged, to cover the administrative costs involved in running a membership organisation; other organisations see subscriptions as a useful way of generating income. It is common to charge different members different rates, for example unwaged people may have free or subsidised membership.

There should be a rule stating who is responsible for setting the amount of the subscription (usually the management committee, or the members of the organisation in a general meeting), how often the sum is reviewed, when fees are to be paid (usually either annually or quarterly), and any arrangements for reduced payments for people joining throughout the year. Generally these matters are decided either at the AGM or by the management committee.

Procedures for dealing with lapsed subscriptions and termination of membership should be included.

Rather than including the details of membership procedures, the constitution may say that the management committee, or a general meeting of the members, has power to decide the rules relating to membership and subscriptions. This allows more flexibility, because the rules can subsequently be changed by the management committee or a general meeting without having formally to amend the constitution.

Conditions of membership
Members of a company limited by guarantee agree to pay a fixed amount (usually £1 or £5) if the company becomes insolvent. Industrial and provident society members agree to buy a share from the society (usually for £1).

There are no specific requirements for members of unincorporated associations. Some have 'open membership', where the constitution states that anyone fulfilling certain criteria (for example living on a specific estate or in a particular ward) is automatically a member. Arrangements of this kind do not impose any obligations on members.

Members' rights
In some cases, the rights of members are automatically implied by law – see the table overleaf. Any non automatic rights must be included in the constitution. Non-automatic rights could include rights to:
- put resolutions to the AGM
- have copies of non-confidential committee meeting minutes
- attend committee meetings as observers
- stand for election to the committee
- nominate candidates to stand in committee elections.

Members' rights implied by law

Members' rights	Unincorporated association– (non-charity)	Unincorporated association (registered charity)	Company (non-charity or registered charity)	IPS (non-charitable or charitable)
To attend and vote at the AGM	Depends on the constitution	✗	✓	✓
To receive a copy of the constitution on request	✗	No, but copies can be obtained from the Charity Commission	✓	✓
To receive a copy of the accounts and auditors' report	✗	Yes, on request	✓	✓
To inspect the register of members, officers and committee members	✗	✗	✓	✓
To call a special or extraordinary meeting (if requested by a specified number of members)	✗	✗	✓	✓

Members' meetings

Members' meetings are usually called 'general meetings', but may also be described as 'open meetings' or 'council meetings'. In most cases incorporated organisations (industrial and provident societies and companies) must hold an annual general meeting which all members with voting rights are entitled to attend and at which these members can vote.

Annual general meetings (AGMs)

It is good practice for an organisation to have one formal meeting of all members each year. This is a legal requirement for companies (although it is possible for a company to elect not to hold an AGM) and industrial and provident societies, who must hold their first AGM within 18 months of setting up and then once in each calendar year, with no more than 15 months between AGMs.

Under proposed company law changes AGMs will not be necessary unless companies positively opt for them or company members want them; if held, they will have to be held within ten months of the end of the financial year.

An organisation's constitution will determine some of the content of the AGM. In many cases this will include approving the minutes of the previous AGM, receiving the accounts (and is a legal requirement of an industrial and provident society), receiving a report from the committee on the organisation's activities, appointing auditors if necessary, electing committee members and officers, approving any changes to the constitution and considering any resolutions put forward.

The constitution should state how much notice must be given to members and by what means, the quorum needed for the meeting to be valid, and voting procedures.

Motions or resolutions

If members are to be able to put forward motions at a general meeting the constitution should explain where and by when they have to be sent, and how other members will be notified.

Other members' meetings

The constitution could include a clause stating that a certain number of general meetings should be held, say three a year, or at regular intervals. The organisation may also want to allow a specified number of members to write to the secretary requesting a general meeting. A general meeting arranged in this way may be called a 'special general meeting' or an 'extraordinary general meeting'.

As with the AGM, the constitution should specify how much notice must be given to members, the means of giving notice, the quorum needed for the meeting to be valid and voting procedures.

The minimum notice required for company meetings is laid down by law. This is usually 14 days, but 21 days' notice is needed for the AGM and if certain proposals, for example changes to the constitution, are to be considered.

Under the **Companies Act 1985 (Electronic Communications) Order 2000**, companies can give notice electronically, including via a website, see *Communicating electronically*, in chapter 2.

All meetings

It is important to add a clause stating that accidentally failing to give a member notice of a meeting does not invalidate that meeting.

Dispensing with meetings

Many constitutions contain provision for a resolution to be passed in writing, provided a copy of the resolution is signed by all voting members (ie by 100% of those who are entitled to attend and vote at general meetings). Company members have this right even if it is not explicit in the constitution. For relatively small organisations this can be a useful way of making decisions quickly while avoiding the administrative costs of calling a meeting.

Under proposed company law changes, if members unanimously agree a decision, they will be able to do so informally, without having to observe the provisions of the Companies Act or their company's constitution, and it will be easier for members to make decisions by written resolution, without having to hold a formal meeting.

Voting procedures

The constitution should explain voting procedures. The clause should specify:
- who may vote at each meeting
- whether the same voting procedure is used for motions and for elections
- whether a motion has to be agreed by a majority of those eligible to vote, or of those actually present
- whether the chair has a normal vote, a casting vote, or both.

The constitution could include a provision allowing members to appoint a proxy – a person who is entitled to vote on behalf of someone who is unable to attend a meeting. If so, there should be a rule requiring written proof of the appointment of a proxy to be sent to the organisation before the meeting so its validity can be checked (under the **Companies Act 1985 (Electronic Communications) Order 2000**, in companies proxies can be sent by e-mail (see *Communicating electronically*, in chapter 2).

Members of a company have a right to require a poll to be taken. This involves checking the votes against a membership list rather than voting simply on a show of hands. Many constitutions allow the members to ask for a secret ballot if they wish.

Quorum

A clause should specify the minimum number of voting members needed to take decisions. The constitution should state the procedures for an inquorate meeting (ie with too few voting members present). One option is to adjourn the meeting until the same time the following week, which would be deemed to be quorate regardless of how many people attended.

A committee that does not have enough members to form a quorum obviously cannot hold a quorate meeting. However it does legally have the power to meet to co-opt new committee members (if allowed by its constitution) or it can call a general meeting at which new committee members can be elected.

For further information on running effective meetings see chapter 4 of *Just about managing?* and for more about legal aspects of meetings see chapter 17 of *The voluntary sector legal handbook*.

The committee, officers and committee meetings

Management committee membership

Committees' powers vary, but their key role is to manage an organisation's affairs on behalf of the members of the organisation. The constitution should include clauses stating how many people should serve on the committee and how long someone remains in office once elected – in some organisations the whole committee retires at each AGM but can stand for re-election; other organisations prefer to elect committee members for a two or three-year term, or to have a proportion (say, a third) retiring each year on rolling programme.

Included should be a clause stating who is eligible for committee membership. In particular, it should clarify:
- whether members of the management committee must also be members of the organisation
- whether certain people are ineligible for committee membership.

NB: Committee members of unincorporated charities must be aged 18 or over. Members of IPS must be aged 16 or over. There is no minimum age limit for committee members (directors) of companies (including charitable companies), but a person must be old enough to understand the duties of a director.

The following people cannot be committee members of charities:
- those who have been convicted of any offence involving deception or dishonesty, unless the conviction is spent under the **Rehabilitation of Offenders Act 1974** (see *Ex-offenders*, in chapter 3)
- undischarged bankrupts and people who have made formal agreements with creditors under the **Insolvency Act 1986***
- anyone who has previously been removed from trusteeship of a charity by the court or the Charity Commission
- anyone disqualified from being a company director*
- anyone who is not legally capable of managing their own affairs.*

It is an offence to act as a charity trustee or a company director whilst disqualified unless the Charity Commission has given a waiver under **Section 72(4)** of the **Charities Act 1993**.

**These rules also apply to non-charitable companies.*

A committee member found to be in one of the above categories cannot vote at committee meetings. The constitution should state whether the person concerned will be excluded from attending further committee meetings automatically and/or ceases to be a committee member. If so, there will be an immediate vacancy.

If there is no such provision, anyone disqualified will remain as a committee member unless they resign, but cannot act on behalf of the organisation. They remain in effect suspended, until removed under the terms of the constitution (see *Terminating the period of office*, page 23) or if a waiver is obtained from the Charity Commission (see above). If a waiver is obtained, they can then resume work on the committee as before.

Selecting the committee

The constitution should explain how the first management committee will be chosen and how members are to be appointed in successive years.

Election

The most usual way of becoming a committee member is

through election by the membership at the AGM or by postal or electronic ballot. Branch organisations may have a two-stage process whereby people are elected locally and their names are put to the AGM at which the management committee is chosen.

Organisations wishing to elect their committee at the AGM should state in their constitutions how many votes members have and explain the procedures for:

nominations — nominations could be required in advance, for example at least 14 days before the AGM, alternatively nominations could be made at the AGM itself

informing members about candidates, where relevant – for example through written notification at least one week before the AGM

voting – whether by post, electronically or at the meeting, and if at the meeting, whether by secret ballot or by a show of hands.

If elections are held using a postal or electronic ballot, the constitution should explain how the ballot is organised, the procedures and timescales for nominations, how members are informed about candidates and the number of votes each category of member has. The whole process could take up to two months.

Some constitutions do not set out the details of election procedures. Instead, they allow the committee to make rules (which may be called 'standing orders' or 'bylaws') on how elections must be held.

Appointment

The organisation may also wish to allow committee members to be appointed by other organisations, or by organisations using its services. Such members would not have to stand for election unless the constitution says they have to be approved by a general meeting or by the committee.

Cooption

Some constitutions include rules to allow the committee to coopt additional committee members in order to:
- fill a vacancy on the committee (sometimes called a 'casual vacancy'), see *Filling vacancies*, below.
- introduce specific skills on to the committee, for example financial expertise
- introduce additional perspectives on to the committee, for example those of service users or people from socially excluded groups.

In most cases the management committee chooses coopted members. Their status may differ from that of full members, and sometimes they do not have the power to vote.

Filling vacancies

The constitution should also describe the procedures for filling committee vacancies if, for example, a member resigns between elections. How a member is replaced may be determined by their category of membership. The options for replacing a person elected by the membership could be:
- a cooption made by the committee
- holding another election.

Subcommittees

It is often useful to have a clause in the constitution allowing the management committee to appoint subcommittees to deal with specific topics, for example staff, finance or service activities. It is possible to word the constitution so it allows subcommittees to include people who are not members of the main management committee, but in charities the Charity Commission may require that committee members form the majority in decision making subcommittees.

Holding trustees

An unincorporated association's constitution should allow the appointment of 'holding trustees' or a custodian trustee to make it easier to own or lease property. Since an unincorporated association has no separate legal existence, a lease will usually be granted to named individuals or an incorporated body. As it would be impracticable to have the whole committee named as trustees, the organisation is given the power to appoint a few people or an incorporated body to represent it. Holding trustees can, but do not have to be members of the committee.

Holding trustees entering into any form of contract (including a photocopier or premises lease) will continue their responsibilities until that lease expires, even if they cease to be committee members or no longer have any involvement with the organisation. If any of these arrangements are likely to be long term, or involve financial risk, the organisation should consider becoming incorporated as a company limited by guarantee or an industrial and provident society (see *Minimising the risk of personal liability,* page 15). This will then enable the organisation to enter into the lease or own the property, without having to appoint holding trustees or a custodian trustee. For further details see chapter 6.

Officers

The constitution should state the officers needed and who is eligible, and describe how they are to be appointed.

Companies must appoint a **company secretary** and industrial and provident societies must have a **secretary** to meet statutory responsibilities. In charities, a paid employee can be the secretary but cannot generally be a member of the committee (see *Employees on the committee*, page 14).

Proposed company law changes dispense with the need for private companies (which includes most voluntary sector companies) to appoint a company secretary.

Most organisations also appoint a chair, committee secretary and treasurer. Some have other officers such as a vice chair and membership secretary. For details about officers' duties see *The responsibilities of officers*, in chapter 2 and *Duties of the treasurer*, in chapter 8.

The constitution should set out the procedures for electing officers. The main options are elections by the membership at the AGM or election by the management committee from amongst themselves at their first meeting after the AGM. There should also be clauses specifying how long officers can stay in post and the procedure for filling vacancies.

Sometimes, the constitution allows the committee to decide how much power is delegated to individual officers. In this case the committee could make its own rules (standing orders) which set out the powers that have been delegated to subcommittees and officers.

The constitution should also state:
- who is responsible for keeping minutes and preparing and distributing agendas
- that the treasurer is responsible for keeping accounts
- that subcommittees must report on their activities to the full management committee (the Charity Commission will usually require this, and it is good practice for all voluntary organisations to include this requirement).

In companies and industrial and provident societies (IPSs) the company secretary/secretary has responsibilities laid down by law (see chapter 2). It may be necessary to distinguish in the constitution between the company secretary/secretary and an 'honorary' secretary who does not have duties under company or IPS law.

Terminating the period of office

The constitution should describe ways in which people can cease to be committee members and officers, for example when their term of office expires, through non-attendance without good reason (in this case the minimum number of meetings should be defined), or on grounds of misconduct

(again the grounds should be defined). It should be clear whether their membership is automatically terminated, or if the committee takes that decision. There should be a provision stating that if an appointing organisation withdraws its appointee (see *Appointment*, page 22), that person automatically ceases to be a committee member.

Members of a company can remove a committee member by passing a resolution by a simple majority at a general meeting. Special rules govern the notice that must to be given of any such resolution.

If a committee member can be dismissed through non-attendance ensure:
- regular checks are kept on attendance
- any member nearing the limit is warned
- the committee is informed if someone's limit is reached.

If a committee member can be dismissed on grounds of misconduct ensure:
- any proposed resolution conforms with the constitution and that proper notice has been given
- the committee member is informed of the meeting at which the removal is to be considered and is given written details of any allegations
- enough time is allocated at the meeting for the matter to be properly considered and for the committee member to have an opportunity to speak
- the vote on any resolution is counted and recorded in the minutes
- any provisions of the equal opportunities policy are complied with
- reasons for removal are recorded.

To ensure fairness it may be worth setting up an external appeal system using independent people to consider the case.

Powers to suspend

The constitution could include powers to suspend officers or committee members, or at the very least, require them to leave the committee meeting. To avoid such a power being misused, consider including a provision enabling the officer or committee member to appeal to a general meeting.

Management committee meetings

The constitution or attached standing orders should state:
- how often the committee should meet
- who is responsible for calling meetings. This is usually the secretary, but it may be worth giving the power to two or three other members of the committee to arrange a meeting if the secretary fails to do so

- the length of notice that must be given. Often this is seven days, but a clause could state that a meeting can be called at shorter notice if a specified number of committee members agree
- that the notice of a meeting must include the venue, date and time, together with the agenda
- voting procedures (see page 20)
- the quorum, and the procedures for an inquorate meeting (see page 21).

There could also be a clause saying that certain items cannot be discussed unless members have been given advance notice. If this is the case, include provision for overriding this clause in an emergency.

Written resolutions

There could be a clause saying the committee can make decisions without actually meeting, by all the members signing a written resolution.

Vested interests

There should be a clause stating that committee members must declare any personal financial interest in a decision and cannot take part in discussions or vote on that subject. This is a requirement of charity law. There should also be a rule saying committee members must declare any other conflict of interest (for example, being an employee or committee member of another organisation that is trying for the same grant or contract as this organisation) and that the committee will decide whether they can take part in discussions or vote on that subject.

Minutes

There should be a clause stating that committee meeting minutes must be kept in a proper minute book. The task is generally the responsibility of the secretary. This is a requirement of charity, company and industrial and provident society law.

Observers at committee meetings

Some constitutions specify who can attend meetings as observers; alternatively the decision could be left to the discretion of the management committee.

Keeping accounts

All voluntary organisations are advised to keep accounts, and most are legally required to do so. Limited companies must keep accounts in a specified form laid down by the **Companies Act 1985** and submit copies to Companies House. If the company is charitable, its accounts must comply with certain aspects of charity accounting rules, and must be submitted to the Charity Commission as well

as Companies House. Industrial and provident societies are governed by the **Friendly and Industrial and Provident Societies Act 1968** and must send their accounts to the Financial Services Authority. Unincorporated charities are governed by the **Charities Act 1993** and must submit copies of their accounts to the Charity Commission if their annual income is more than £10,000. For further details of the legal requirements see chapter 8.

The constitution should lay down the basic procedures for handling accounts and state that any funds raised will be used only for the organisation. There should also be clauses:
- giving the management committee or general meeting the right to determine the financial year
- specifying that the management committee can decide rules relating to signatories
- stating that the accounts must be audited or examined in accordance with legal requirements (see chapter 8).

The auditors are generally formally elected at the AGM. They have the right to see financial records, the minutes of meetings and bank statements, and must also be given the right to be notified of any general meeting.

Under company law the members of a company are able to dismiss auditors, and all organisations should consider including this power in their constitutions. Anyone auditing the accounts of a charity, company or industrial and provident society is required by law to be independent of the organisation. Other organisations should specify certain people who may not act as auditors. These would include committee members, trustees, employees and their relatives.

Altering the constitution

This clause explains the procedure for making changes to the constitution. Generally amendments to the rules of an unincorporated organisation are made at the AGM or a special meeting called for this purpose. The clause should state:
- the amount of notice required to hold the meeting
- how members will be notified of proposed changes
- the majority required (usually two-thirds or three-quarters of those voting or those eligible to vote) for alterations to be carried
- where relevant, that the Charity Commission must give prior approval for changes in the objects clause and certain other clauses relating to use of the charity's money or property. The Commission is likely to insist that the constitution contains a clause requiring its written consent before such changes are made.

Guidance on the wording of these clauses can be found in *Choosing and preparing a governing document* (CC22).

The Charity Commission has introduced a fast track approach to amending the constitutions of small unincorporated charities (ie those with gross annual income under £10,000). For further details see *Public guidance for small charities who wish to amend their governing documents* (SCU11), available from *www.charity-commission.gov.uk/supportingcharities/sculist.asp*

The **Companies Act 1985** describes the process for altering companies' constitutions, and where the company is also a registered charity some alterations need the Charity Commission's consent.

Dissolution

The dissolution or termination clause describes the procedures for winding up an organisation. In unincorporated organisations the power to decide such a move usually rests with members of the organisation at a general meeting. The clause must also describe how any remaining assets are to be dealt with. They should first be used to pay off any debts.

The procedures for winding up a company or industrial or provident society depend on whether the organisation is solvent or insolvent, and are governed by the **Insolvency Act 1986** (even if the organisation is solvent).

The dissolution clause will specify what happens to any assets remaining after the debts have been paid. In general any remaining assets will have to be transferred to an organisation with similar objectives. In legal terms this is called the *cy-pres* rule. There is usually a rule forbidding the distribution of assets or property, directly or indirectly,

among members. Charities usually have to consult the Charity Commission over the transfer of remaining assets. For further details on winding up see chapter 10.

Models

Model constitutions are available. The Charity Commission has models for organisations wishing to register as charities, either as an unincorporated association (GD3) or as a company limited by guarantee (GD1). It has also produced a *Model declaration of trust* (GD2) for organisations wishing to become charitable trusts. All are available from *www.charity-commission.gov.uk* The Commission will advise any charitable organisation on developing a constitution. The Charity Law Association has also produced models for charitable companies, charitable trusts and charitable associations, approved by the Charity Commission, available (for a charge) from Charitylaw@aol.com in both printed and disk form. Some large national charities have agreed standard constitutions with the Charity Commission for their branches or affiliates or for specific types of organisation. They are listed on the Charity Commission's website at *www.charity-commission.gov.uk/registration/govdoclist.asp*

Industrial and provident societies (IPSs) planning to use a set of model rules can get advice from the sponsoring organisation (see *Industrial and provident societies – advantages*, page 5). The Financial Services Authority can provide forms and guidance notes on how to register a new IPS as well as general advice on registration.

Inevitably model constitutions are general and will probably need adapting to meet an organisation's specific needs. It is advisable to seek legal advice or advice from a voluntary sector support organisation such as a council for voluntary service when drawing up a constitution.

Chapter 2:
Setting up and running the organisation

Related chapters
Chapter 1 – Legal status
Chapter 3 – Employment
Chapter 6 – Premises
Chapter 8 – Trasurer's role; accounts
Chapter 9 – Services
Chapter 10 – Winding up

Chapter 1 describes the legal structures possible for a voluntary organisation and explains how a constitution works. This chapter covers the process for getting an organisation up and running once you have decided whether to be charitable and which structure to use.

Throughout the chapter we use 'constitution' to refer to all forms of governing document (see *Legal structures*, in chapter 1 for further details).

Unless otherwise indicated, Charity Commission publications mentioned in the text (usually indicated by a CC reference) are available from its website *www.charitycommisison.gov.uk* or publications line 01823 345 427.

Setting up the organisation
Decide on the name
Companies limited by guarantee and industrial and provident societies (IPSs) cannot use a name that is the same as or very similar to the name of another company or IPS, and charities cannot use a name that is the same as or very similar to that of another charity. You can check whether a proposed name is already is use by telephoning Companies House, the Financial Services Authority (for IPSs) or the Charity Commission. All authorities have the power to restrict use of certain names.

A non-charitable unincorporated association can use virtually any name, but be careful about choosing a name already in use, because the organisation runs the risk of having a claim of 'passing off' brought against it and besides, this could be confusing to potential users.

A company limited by guarantee does not have to use the word 'limited' or the Welsh equivalent 'cyfngedig' at the end of its name if:
- its objects are the promotion of commerce, art, science, education, religion, charity or any profession or anything incidental or conducive to those objects, and

- its memorandum and articles (constitution):
  - require its profits or other income to be used to promote its objects
  - prohibit the payment of dividends to members, and
  - on winding up, require the assets to be transferred to another body with similar objects, or to one whose objects are the promotion of charity.

If a company wants to use this exemption, its solicitor, a director or the company secretary (see page 46) must complete **Form 30(5)(a)** – a statutory declaration that the company complies with the above requirements.

An IPS must end its name with 'limited' or 'cyfngedig'. It is possible to apply to the Financial Services Authority for exemption.

Draft and agree the constitution
Charities
To register as a charity an organisation must have exclusively charitable objects. The Charity Commission can provide examples of objects, or it is possible to use or adopt objects used by similar organisations. Remember that the **Sex Discrimination Act 1975**, the **Race Relations Act 1976** and the **Disability Discrimination Act 1995** forbid discrimination in the provision of services on grounds of sex, racial group and disability. The exception is where the objects of a charity specifically state that the charity is set up to provide services to women or men only, to one racial group (which cannot be defined by reference to colour) or to people with specific disabilities. If the organisation intends to use these provisions, check with the Equal Opportunities Commission, the Commission for Racial Equality or the Disability Rights Commission, as appropriate.

Anyone considering setting up as a charity should get a copy of *Registering as a charity* (CC21) and *Choosing and preparing a governing document* (CC22) and the registration application pack *Application to register a charity*.

The Charity Commission publishes model constitutions for organisations wishing to register as charities, as either an unincorporated association (GD3), a charitable trust (GD2) or a company limited by guarantee (GD1), available from *www.charity-commission.gov.uk*. A number of organisations have standard constitutions approved by the Charity Commission which can be used by organisations associated with that charity: these are listed on the Commission's website at *www.charity-commission.gov.uk/registration/govdoclist.asp*. The Charity Law Association also has models approved by the Charity Commission (for which a charge is made), available by e-mailing *Charitylaw@aol.com*

Industrial and provident societies

Industrial and provident societies (IPSs) planning to use a set of model rules can get advice from the sponsoring organisation (see chapter 1) or the Financial Services Authority. Legal advice will be needed to draw up a tailor-made constitution.

Non-charitable companies

The constitution (memorandum and articles) of a non-charitable company will depend on the nature of the company. If it is a voluntary organisation, the constitution is likely to be quite similar to a charity's, but with non-charitable objects. If the company is going to be a trading company, the constitution will be more like a business's. Your local council for voluntary service or similar organisation should be able to advise on an appropriate constitution for a non-charitable company.

Non-charitable associations

There are no rules regarding the constitution for a non-charitable association. It may be quite similar to a charitable association's but with non-charitable objects, or it may be much shorter.

Adopt the constitution

Unincorporated associations

Once the constitution has been agreed between yourselves (and, if applicable, your solicitor and/or funders) the next step is for those involved formally to adopt the constitution, either by holding a meeting or by the first members signing the document.

Companies limited by guarantee

Under **Section 1** of the **Companies Act 1985** it is possible for a limited company to have only one director. However, it is nearly always advisable for voluntary sector companies to have more than one. The company must also appoint a company secretary.

Under company law proposals the requirement for private companies (which includes most voluntary sector companies) to appoint a company secretary, will be abolished, although they will still be able to do so voluntarily. However, the company secretary's duties will still need to be carried out.

Follow the procedures below to adopt a constitution (the memorandum and articles of association):

* at least one person must sign both the memorandum and the articles of association as the 'subscriber(s)' (ie the founder member(s)) of the company
* the first director(s) must complete and sign **Form 10** saying they have agreed to be the company's director(s). The form (which also gives details of the company's registered office and the company secretary) must also be signed by the subscribers (ie the people who signed the memorandum and articles) or their agent. If there are more than two directors photocopy page 2 of the form or use **Form 10 continuation sheets**
* at least one director, the company secretary or the solicitor handling the registration must sign a Declaration (**Form 12**)* confirming compliance with company law – this must be done after the other documents have been signed and dated
* a voluntary sector company using a name which does not include the word 'limited' must complete **Form 30(5)(a)**.*

All the above must be submitted to the New Companies Department at Companies House, together with two bound and signed copies of the memorandum and articles of association and payment of £20 (in 2003/04), payable to 'The Registrar of Companies'.

*Forms 12 and 30(5)(a) must be witnessed by a commissioner for oaths, notary public, justice of the peace or solicitor, once the memorandum and articles have been completed.

All forms mentioned above are available free of charge from Companies House, either from *www.companieshouse.gov.uk* or by telephoning 0870 3333636. They are also available from legal stationers, accountants, solicitors and company formation agents – see the phone book for addresses.

Provided the correct documentation is submitted and the name is acceptable, the Registrar of Companies will register the company, give it a registered number and send a Certificate of Incorporation to its registered office. This process will take between five and seven working days.

Charitable trusts

Charitable trusts must follow the following procedures:

- the first trustees must 'execute' the trust deed, ie sign it in front of an independent witness (who must also sign against each signature, and give his or her address)
- send the trust deed to the local Inland Revenue stamp office within 30 days, with the stamping fee (£5 in 2003/04)
- send two certified* copies of the stamped deed to the Charity Commission, together with completed forms **APP1** (charity registration application form) and **DEC1** (trustees' declaration) – see *Register as a charity*, below.

*A declaration on the document by a person authorised by the trustees, saying 'I certify that this is a true copy of [name of the document]'.

Industrial and provident societies (IPSs)

If the organisation is not using model rules, it is advisable to check with the Financial Services Authority (FSA) about the proposed rules. Once the rules are agreed in principle and, for a charitable IPS, accepted by the Inland Revenue, submit the application using **Form A**, available from the FSA, with the registration fee (which will depend on whether the organisation is using model, adapted or new rules) and two bound copies of the rules.

Register as a charity

Once the constitution has been formally adopted or the company has been formally incorporated, send the Charity Commission the following:

- the charity registration application form **APP1** and trustees' declaration **DEC1** (both forms are included in the registration application pack), and
- two certified copies (see above) of the organisation's constitution, and
- a certified copy (see above) of the minutes of the general meeting at which it was adopted (unincorporated association), or
- a certified copy of the certificate of incorporation and certified copies of any special resolution showing subsequent amendments (company).

The Charity Commission will either approve the application, ask for additional information or reject the application, giving reasons. Any changes needed to the constitution will have to be adopted according to the appropriate amendment procedures. (It is not always necessary to make all the changes suggested by the Commission, but if you are not going to you will need to explain why, and you may need legal advice for this.)

Because of the complex nature of charity law, it takes on average 88 working days (in 2003) to reach a decision on an application. Organisations using a standard or model governing document are normally dealt with more quickly.

Once the Commission is satisfied with the constitution the charity is entered on the Register of Charities and will be notified of:

- its registration number
- the details of the charity recorded in the Register's index
- the requirements after registration.

Appointing the committee

Unincorporated associations

The only initial members of an unincorporated association will be those people who attended the meeting to agree the constitution or who signed the constitution. The procedure for admitting new members will have to be used before anyone else can join and is given the right to vote (see *Changes in organisational membership*, page 34).

If a meeting is used to set up the group and agree its constitution, those attending generally elect the first committee members and officers. If the group is set up by signing a constitution it will need to follow the procedures for electing a committee and officers, probably by holding a general meeting.

Companies and industrial and provident societies (IPSs)

The initial members are those who signed the memorandum and articles of association (companies) or rules (IPSs). A company must name its first committee members and company secretary* in its application for incorporation (**Form 10**). It may need to follow the procedures in the articles of association to increase the committee membership by cooptions or elections and to appoint other officers. An IPS will have a secretary named in its application for registration and will have to hold a general meeting to elect a committee.

Proposed company law changes dispense with the need for private companies (which includes most voluntary sector companies) to appoint a company secretary.

Trusts

A trust does not generally have members. The first trustees (committee members) are generally named in the trust deed, or will be named in the trustees' declaration DEC 1 (see *Register as a charity*, page 28).

Committee members' and officers' roles

Potential committee members and officers should be clear about their roles and responsibilities, which should be agreed at the first committee meeting. It is useful to draw up 'role descriptions' for all committee members: the checklist on page 45 should help (for details of the treasurer's role see *Duties of the treasurer*, in chapter 8).

For the rest of this chapter the body which runs the organisation will be called 'the committee', the members of the committee 'committee members', and the company secretary of a company limited by guarantee, the secretary of an industrial and provident society and the secretary of any other organisation 'the secretary'.

The first committee meeting

The procedures to be followed before, during and after the first committee meeting are outlined in the checklist *The first committee meeting* (page 42).

The agenda should include the following items.

Cooptions to the committee

Check whether the constitution gives powers to coopt others onto the committee and, if so, decide whether to exercise these powers. If an election at a general meeting is the only method of expanding committee membership, it may be necessary to hold such a meeting fairly quickly.

Election of officers

The usual options for electing officers (if they have not already been appointed as part of the setting-up process) are:
- by members at an annual general meeting (AGM)
- by the committee at its first meeting, or
- by the committee pending an AGM.

If the constitution does not allow the committee to appoint officers the organisation will have to wait until the first AGM.

Membership

Organisations may want to expand their membership as soon as possible. The constitution should describe the necessary procedures. In some cases only the committee can agree new members, but other constitutions allow the responsibility to be delegated to a subcommittee, individual officers or staff.

Address for administrative purposes

All charities must notify the Charity Commission of their contact address and of any changes to that address. Companies must notify the Registrar of Companies, and industrial and provident societies (IPSs) the Financial Services Authority of their first registered office, and of any changes to that address.

The registered address must be printed on all correspondence and many other documents.

Companies and IPSs must have their full registered name clearly displayed outside the premises (or visible from the outside during normal working hours).

Bank accounts

The constitution may describe the requirements for cheque signatories. Before the first meeting, obtain the necessary bank forms (**bank mandates**) – most banks have different forms for different legal structures. The bank will require the committee to pass and minute a standard resolution which includes the decision to appoint cheque signatories. The signatories will need to sign the necessary paperwork; the person chairing the meeting, and possibly the secretary, will need to sign to confirm the appointment of the signatories.

Registered charities should inform the bank of their charitable status because charities with an annual income above £10,000 must state on their cheques that they are a registered charity.

Under the **Co-operatives and Community Benefit Societies Act 2003** from 1 April 2004 charitable industrial and provident societies which don't include 'charity', 'charitable' or the Welsh equivalents in their name will have to include a statement that they are charitable on cheques.

In order to avoid fraud banks have stringent requirements to set up a bank account and may require personal information about cheque signatories.

Insurance

Chapter 7 describes the insurances that organisations

must or should consider. It is advisable to have insurance proposals completed and ready to send off as soon as the organisation is set up. If this is not possible, insurance must certainly be sorted out before the organisation takes on any legal responsibilities, including premises, or allows employees to start working.

Premises
Organisations planning to take on premises should consider the requirements set out in chapter 6 relating to leasing or owning premises.

Developing organisational policies
There are a number of policies that an organisation should develop – either as a legal requirement or as good practice. These include the following.

Health and safety: Organisations with employees are legally required to have a health and safety policy and carry out a risk assessment, and these must be in writing if there are five or more employees. It is good practice to have these in writing even if there are no employees, or less than five. See chapter 5 for further details.

Disciplinary and grievance: All organisations employing 20 or more people must have disciplinary and grievance procedures. This will be extended to all employers in October 2004. See chapter 4 for further details.

Equal opportunities: It is good practice to develop an equal opportunities policy as soon as possible. This should form the basis of any decisions made about services, membership, staff and volunteer recruitment, and committee membership. Equal opportunities policy and practice are discussed at the end of this chapter and in chapters 3 and 9.

Data protection: A data protection policy is essential, to ensure the organisation complies with the law (see chapter 9).

Confidentiality: It is good practice to have a policy on confidentiality (see chapter 4).

E-mail and internet use: Although there is no obligation for organisations to develop an e-mail/internet policy for their staff, it is advisable to do so, to avoid risk from inappropriate use (see chapter 4).

Environmental: It is also good practice to develop a policy that ensures the organisation has environmentally friendly policies and procedures. This is discussed further in chapter 6.

The financial year
The constitution may stipulate a financial year; if not, then the committee has discretion. Many organisations link their financial year to that of their major funder(s). Companies House must be informed of any change of a company's accounting reference date on **Form 225** before the end of the period allowed for sending in the accounts.

Auditors
Many voluntary groups have a statutory requirement to have their accounts audited (see chapter 8). Some funders may also require audited accounts. Before the first committee meeting clarify the requirements and in particular check whether the auditor needs to be a qualified accountant.

If an auditor is to be appointed, this should be done as soon as possible and certainly before the end of the first financial year.

Letterheads
The headed paper of companies limited by guarantee and industrial and provident societies must contain reference to their legal status ('Company limited by guarantee no ... registered in ...' or 'Registered as an industrial and provident society no ...') and must give the address of the registered office.

Organisations that count as local authority influenced or controlled (see chapter 1) must state this fact on their letterhead and identify the relevant local authority or authorities.

Registered charities whose income exceeded £10,000 in the previous financial year must give their status on their letterhead ('Registered charity'). It is useful to include the registration number ('Registered charity number ...').

From 1 April 2004 charitable industrial and provident societies which don't include 'charity', 'charitable' or the Welsh equivalents in their name must declare their charitable status on all correspondence.

Companies are not legally obliged to have directors' names on their stationery. However, if they do so they must include the names of all directors and must amend the stationery whenever there is a change of director.

Other printed material
Registered charities whose income exceeded £10,000 in the previous financial year must have their status printed on fundraising material and financial stationery such as order forms and invoices.

From 1 April 2004 charitable industrial and provident societies which don't include 'charity', 'charitable' or the Welsh equivalents in their name must declare their charitable status on official doeuments.

A company must ensure that its full registered name is included on these documents and that the registration number and address of its registered office is included on all orders for goods or services.

Electronic communications

External e-mails and other electronic communications sent outside the organisation and websites should include the same information as printed materials. E-mails sent within an organisation do not need to contain the information.

Delegating powers

Check the constitution to see whether decision making can be delegated. Larger organisations may wish to establish standing orders to delegate powers to a number of subcommittees. Smaller organisations could delegate responsibility to officers or individual committee members. Under the Charities Act 1993 all charity trustees have the right to delegate to one or more trustees.

Annual general meetings (AGMs)

The constitution may allow for an AGM to be held before the end of the first financial year and if so, the first committee meeting may want to consider when to hold it. It could be combined with a launch and, if required, election of committee members. Thereafter AGMs will be held after each financial year, to receive the accounts of that year. Companies must hold their first AGM within 18 months of incorporation. Note that because trusts do not have a membership, there is generally no constitutional requirement to have an AGM.

Proposed company legislation removes the requirement for private companies (which includes most voluntary sector companies) to hold AGMs unless members want them. If they are to be held, they will need to be held within ten months of the financial year end.

Taking over from a previous organisation

If one organisation has been set up to take over the activities of another, additional decisions have to be made. The new organisation will need to agree formally to take responsibility for the employees, equipment and property as well as all liabilities of the old organisation so that it can be wound up (for further details see *Changing the structure*, in chapter 1).

Appointing staff

In organisations appointing staff the committee should agree:
- an equal opportunities policy, which includes recruitment procedures
- shortlisting and interview procedures
- a health and safety policy
- job particulars
- terms and conditions of employment, and in particular any entitlements which are greater than the statutory minimum (for example sickness pay, maternity, paternity and adoption leave and pay, parental leave entitlement, annual leave entitlement, and redundancy pay)
- disciplinary and grievance procedures.

Staff recruitment is covered in chapter 3.

Setting up registers

Companies and industrial and provident societies are legally required to keep certain registers (lists), some of which must be open to public inspection. Failure to keep registers up to date can lead to imposition of a fine. There must be separate pages for the different kinds of register: company/IPS members, committee members and secretaries.

Registers can be contained in a simple bound book, purchased from any stationers, or they can be kept on computer, provided they are secure and can be printed out. Preprinted company registers are largely for share companies and contain primarily share certificates, which are irrelevant to voluntary organisations. The *Sinclair Taylor & Martin company handbook and registers for voluntary sector companies limited by guarantee* (2nd edn), available from Sandy Adirondack, includes registers appropriate for voluntary organisations, with explanations of how to complete them.

Although unincorporated associations are not obliged to keep such registers, it is good practice to do so.

Register of members

Companies limited by guarantee and industrial and provident societies (IPSs) must have a register of members. It must include:
- names and addresses of all members
- date of joining
- date of ceasing to be a member.

If an organisation is a member, the register should list the organisation's name and can also include (but does not have to) the name of its representative. Unincorporated organisations cannot generally be members of a company or IPS, so in this case the organisation's representative becomes the company or IPS member, and the name of the organisation they represent can also be included in the register.

The date a member resigns or is removed from membership must be entered, but the name must not be deleted for at least 20 years after the person ceased to be a member.

The register, or a duplicate, is usually held at the registered office. If the company's register of members is not kept at the registered office, Companies House has to be notified on **Form 353** where it is kept. (This can be done online, see *www.companieshouse.gov.uk/services* for further details.) The register of company members must be available for public inspection, and kept in a form that prevents it being falsified.

If a company limited by guarantee has more than 50 members, the register must have an alphabetical index unless the membership list itself is in alphabetical order.

An IPS' register of members must state the number of shares owned by each member.

Registers of officers and committee members

Industrial and provident societies must keep a separate register of officers' names and addresses, showing when they were appointed and when they ceased to hold office.

Companies limited by guarantee must have a register of directors (committee members) and a register of company secretaries. A company secretary who is also a member of the committee has to be entered in both registers.

The register of company directors must contain the following:
- date of appointment or election
- date of ceasing to be a director
- full name
- any previous name used in the past 20 years or since the director was aged 18 (apart from any change of name on marriage)
- home address, including post code*
- date of birth
- nationality
- business occupation
- every company of which the person concerned is, or has been a director at any time in the previous five

years, including companies limited by guarantee. If there are no such companies, the register should say so.

The register of company secretaries need include only their name, home address,* date of appointment as secretary and date of ceasing to be secretary.

*Under the **Companies (Particulars of Usual Residential Address) (Confidentiality Orders) Regulations 2002** company directors and secretaries can apply to the Secretary of State for permission to keep their private address confidential. This facility is only available to those who can demonstrate actual or serious risk of violence or intimidation. For further information telephone 0845 303 2400.*

Register of charges

This is necessary if a company or industrial and provident society enters into any charges, ie takes out a loan that requires security or collateral.

Completing the necessary forms

Registration authorities will send most of the forms that have to be completed. There is one important exception. Companies will need to get their own supply of **Forms 288a, 288b and 288c**, which must be submitted to Companies House whenever a director (committee member) or company secretary is appointed or elected or ceases to hold the position, or there is any change in the details on form 288a (which are the same as the details in the register of directors). These forms are available free from *www.companieshouse.gov.uk* or by telephoning 0870 3333636. They can also be supplied by legal stationers, accountants, solicitors and company formation agents – see the phone book for addresses. These forms can be submitted online – see *www.companieshouse.gov.uk/services* for further details.

Noting important dates

The secretary and treasurer need to ensure that dates and periods of notice stated in the constitution are met, and that deadlines for charity and/or company forms are met.

Auditing accounts

Some organisations need to have their accounts audited before their AGM (see *Auditing or examining accounts*, in chapter 8). This involves:
- getting the year's financial records to the auditor in time for them to be audited and draft accounts prepared

- submitting draft accounts to a committee meeting for approval*
- having approved accounts signed by committee members* and the auditors
- sending them to members, usually at least 21 days before the AGM.

In some unincorporated organisations, accounts are, under the constitution, approved by the organisation's members, not the committee.

This process could take up to six months.

Committee elections

In many organisations a management committee is elected at the AGM. Proxies, postal and electronic methods of election can be used only if allowed by the constitution. If elections are carried out using these methods check the timetable laid out in the constitution.

Filing accounts

Charities with annual income or expenditure over £10,000, companies limited by guarantee and industrial and provident societies must file their annual accounts, audited if required, with the relevant registrar. The secretary and treasurer need to note the date by which these accounts must be filed. For companies, late submission incurs an automatic fine.

Running the organisation

Meetings

Notice of meetings

The constitution should set out the notice required for general meetings. This is usually either 14 or 21 days. Some also specify notice for committee meetings, and the method of giving notice. If the constitution does not specify notice for meetings the committee should adopt standing orders setting out its requirements.

Communicating electronically

Under the **Companies Act 1985 (Electronic Communications) Order 2000** registered companies can communicate electronically with company members, including through e-mail and websites. There are strict rules regarding electronic communications, which must be followed. The Institute of Chartered Secretaries and Administrators has published detailed guidance, which includes 25 points of recommended good practice, 23 other points for companies to consider before offering this facility, and a specimen invitation to use electronic communications. For further details see *www.icsa.org.uk/products*

Preparing for the meeting

Some constitutions describe the content of agendas and conduct of meetings. If not set out in the constitution, issues which need to be clear before any meeting are:
- whether the chair has a casting vote in the case of a tie
- who is taking minutes
- whether a subcommittee has delegated powers to make required decisions.

Auditors of companies and IPSs must receive notice of all general meetings and are entitled to speak on matters concerning the audit, accounts and other financial matters.

Virtual or electronic meetings

Unless the constitution specifically prohibits it, organisations (including charities) may choose to conduct meetings by electronic means, as long as members can both see and hear each other, for example by using video conferencing or internet video facilities. This could be useful if the organisation needs to make an emergency decision, and it may make it easier for some disabled committee members to participate (although could exclude visually or hearing impaired members).

Some constitutions permit resolutions to be passed without holding meetings, for example, by each member or committee member signing a copy of the resolution. If the technology is available, this can be achieved very quickly using e-mail and secure electronic signatures.

Proposed company legislation includes simplifying rules on written resolutions to make it easier for private companies (which includes most voluntary sector companies) to take decisions.

For further details on running meetings see *Charities and meetings* (CC48) and chapter 5 of *Just about managing?*

Annual general meetings (AGMs)

An organisation's constitution will specify some of the content of the AGM. In many cases this will include approving the minutes of the previous AGM, receiving the accounts (and is a legal requirement of an industrial and provident society), receiving a report from the committee on the activities of the organisation, appointing auditors, electing committee members and officers, approving any changes to the constitution and considering any resolutions put forward.

Proposed company law removes the requirement for private companies (which includes most voluntary sector companies) to hold an AGM unless required to do by the members. However most funders are likely to expect organisations to hold one.

Changes in organisational membership

New members

The constitution should describe the procedures for admitting new members – both individual and, where relevant, organisational (see *Organisational membership*, in chapter 1). In some cases the committee must make the decision, if so, new membership should be an item on every agenda. If permitted by the constitution it may be possible to delegate the decision to a subcommittee, officers or staff. If this is the case, the committee should pass a resolution to this effect, which should be recorded in the minute book.

In IPSs, members usually pay £1 for their share and receive a share certificate. Other organisations may charge a membership subscription, if this is allowed in the constitution.

All organisations should have a method of recording acceptance of membership, for example an application form that includes the statement 'I wish to become a member of ... and agree to abide by its constitution', together with the member's signature. All new members should be given appropriate written material, for example a copy of the constitution, annual report, equal opportunities policy and code of practice.

An equal opportunities policy should ensure that any decision to refuse membership is justified and that reasons are recorded.

Terminating membership

Terminating membership is covered under *Procedures and rules for running the organisation*, in chapter 1.

Recording changes

Companies and IPSs must enter details of membership changes in the register of members (see page 31). Other organisations should keep a record, in order to ensure all members are invited to the AGM and other general meetings and are given the other privileges of membership.

Changes in committee membership

Procedures for electing or appointing committee members, terminating committee membership and filling vacancies are covered in *The committee, officers and committee meetings*, in chapter 1.

Information for new committee members

All new committee members should be given information required to carry out their responsibilities, for example a copy of the constitution, induction pack, role description, annual report and accounts, minutes and papers for the last two or three committee meetings (and the next meeting, if available), and the organisation's main policies (see *Developing organisational policies*, page 30).

Changes in officers

The constitutions of industrial and provident societies (IPSs) and companies limited by guarantee usually require that secretaries are appointed by the committee, who can remove them at any time. For other officers the rules are as set out in the constitution.

Always ensure that the appointment of officers is clearly stated in the minutes of the general or committee meeting at which the appointment took place.

Recording changes

Companies limited by guarantee and IPSs must update the relevant register (directors and secretaries for companies, and officers for an IPS) when there is a change.

Companies must inform Companies House within 14 days of any changes in committee membership or committee members' details using Form **288a** (new committee members and changes in secretary), **288b** (resignations), or **288c** (changes in personal details). This can be done online; for further details see *www.companieshouse.gov.uk/services*

Where officers' names appear on an organisation's stationery, ensure it is amended as necessary. Note that if the name of one director of a company appears on the stationery, then all directors must be included.

The law and good practice on organisational and committee membership are covered in greater details in The voluntary sector legal handbook.

Changing the administrative office

An organisation changing its administrative office should carry out the following procedure:

- check whether the constitution has specific rules about changes to the office
- ensure that the decision is made by a meeting and recorded in the minutes
- ensure other organisations have the new address including, in particular, the bank, insurers, funders and the Charity Commission if relevant
- include the new registered office address on stationery and some other documents, if a company limited by guarantee or an industrial and provident society (IPS) – see *Letterheads*, page 30.
- submit **Form 287** to Companies House, if a company, within 14 days (see *www.companieshouse.gov.uk/ services* for details of how to submit this online)
- inform the Financial Services Authority if an IPS
- ensure the full registered name is outside the new registered office or visible during working hours, if a company or IPS.

Annual accounts, annual reports and annual returns

Accounts and reports

Chapter 8 covers the law and good practice concerning bookkeeping and producing accounts. It also explains when an audit or independent inspection of a charity's, company's or IPS's accounts is required by law. This section looks at the role of the committee in managing the annual accounts and audit and producing annual reports.

The accounts of a company limited by guarantee or an IPS, audited if required, must be approved by the committee before being presented to the membership at a general meeting (which, in the case of an IPS, must be an AGM). Company members must receive approved accounts at least 21 days before the meeting. Most IPSs' rules allow 14 days' notice. It is possible to distribute accounts electronically, with members' agreement. See *Communicating electronically*, page 33.

A company or IPS will therefore need to carry out the following procedure:

- the organisation's finance staff and/or treasurer prepare initial accounts
- the committee, working with senior staff, prepares a report that expands on the accounts and explains the organisation's work during the year and contains information required under company, IPS and/or charity law (the **annual report**)

- the audit, if required, is completed and the auditor is satisfied that he or she can give the necessary certificate
- the auditor presents a draft set of accounts and the report on the accounts to the committee
- the committee approves the draft and authorises the necessary signatures to the accounts and report as required by company or IPS law
- those authorised sign a copy of the accounts and report
- signed copies of the accounts and report are sent to members with a copy of the auditor's certificate.

For organisations which are not companies or IPSs the process will be similar, but the constitution may require final approval to be given by the AGM. In this case the committee would approve the draft and circulate it to members before the AGM, and it would be approved at the AGM.

The timescale of organising the audit means that a committee meeting to approve the accounts and report will generally need to take place at least two months before an AGM.

The first auditor of any organisation will have been appointed by the committee or at a general meeting or AGM. After that, in companies limited by guarantee and IPSs, the membership appoints the auditor at the general meeting that approves the accounts,* and either decides how much the auditor should be paid or passes a resolution delegating this responsibility to the committee.

Under proposed company legislation there will be no need to reappoint auditors annually, unless companies opt for this, or members request this in a particular year.

In those unincorporated charities which must have an audit (see chapter 8), the committee should appoint the auditor unless the constitution specifies that this is to be done at a general meeting.

Submitting the accounts and report

Companies must send their annual accounts and report to Companies House within ten months from the end of their financial year. (*Company law changes propose reducing this to seven months.*)

Industrial and provident societies must submit their annual return to the Financial Services Agency within seven months of the end of the financial year.

Registered charities must send their annual accounts and

report to the Charity Commission within ten months of the end of each financial year. Smaller charities only need to send them to the Charity Commission if asked to do so. Charitable companies with income exceeding £10,000 must also send their accounts and report to Companies House.

The draft Charities Bill is likely to require charities whose income exceeds £1 million to include further information in the format of the Standard Information Return (SIR). The SIR will highlight key qualitative and quantitative information about the charity, focusing on how it sets objectives and measures its outcomes against these.

Annual returns

Registered charities whose annual income or expenditure exceeds £10,000, industrial and provident societies and companies limited by guarantee have to submit annual returns to the relevant regulatory bodies. Charitable companies must submit separate annual returns to both the Registrar of Companies and the Charity Commission.

Charities with an annual income of £10,000 or less must provide the Charity Commission with information to keep their entry in the Central Register of Charities up to date (including income and expenditure figures). The most convenient way to do this is using the annual Register Check Form, automatically sent out by the Charity Commission.

In each case the relevant regulatory body will send the annual return for completion. It is then simply a case of following the necessary instructions on the form and submitting it by the deadline. Companies must pay a fee (£15 in 2003/04).

Changes to the constitution

Most constitutions describe procedures for amending clauses. This will often involve a specific meeting, with a certain amount of notice to be given of any resolution, and for a particular majority voting in favour of any amendment.

A registered charity must receive the Charity Commission's written consent before considering any amendment to the constitution's objects or any provision relating to the use of its income or property. As soon as any amendment has been passed, a copy of the resolution making the change must be sent to the Charity Commission. If there are major changes the Commission will also need a copy of the revised constitution.

The Charity Commission has introduced a 'light touch' regime for smaller charities (ie those whose annual income is under £10,000), which speeds up some processes, including agreement to constitution changes for unincorporated charities. For further details see *www.charity-commission.gov.uk/supportingcharities*

Company constitutions (memorandum and articles) do not usually contain amendment procedures. This is because under company law, the constitution can be changed at the AGM or other general meeting for which 21 days' notice of the full resolution has been given, and on a resolution passed by 75% of those voting. This includes any change of name. A copy of the revised constitution must be submitted to the Registrar of Companies, with a signed copy of the special resolution which made the change showing the date on which it was passed, within 15 days. If the change required prior consent from the Charity Commission, a copy of the consent must be submitted to Companies House. Charitable companies must also send the Charity Commission a copy of the revised constitution.

An industrial and provident society (IPS) must submit a copy of its amended constitution (rules) to the Financial Services Authority. A special meeting may be needed to amend the constitution, although it could be held immediately before or after the AGM.

Most banks need to be informed of any amendment to the constitution; check the original bank mandate for details.

Funders may also need to be informed of any amendment, and some funders require that they be informed or even that they must give consent before any change can take place. Failure to comply with this requirement could put grants at risk.

If an organisation changes its name, it should ensure the new name is immediately used on all stationery, external e-mails, website, cheques and other necessary financial documents and publications. Companies limited by guarantee and IPSs must also change their name on their registered office.

Dealing with crises

Emergency decisions

Constitutions may include provisions for making decisions in between the normal committee meeting cycle. The main methods are:
- allowing a committee meeting to be held at short notice at the chair's discretion
- allowing a decision to be made by circulating a copy of

a proposed resolution to each committee member and obtaining their signatures

- delegating decision making to a subcommittee or officers
- making a decision by telephone or e-mail then ratifying it at the next meeting. This procedure should only be used if the organisation is absolutely certain that the decision will be ratified. In some situations it may be possible to make a decision by a written resolution signed by 100% of the people entitled to vote.

No quorum

Without a quorum (which should be specified in the constitution, see *Procedures and rules for running the organisation*, in chapter 1), a meeting cannot make a decision.

If there are not enough committee members to make a quorum, or the committee membership falls below the minimum specified in the constitution, the committee can usually meet only to call a general meeting or, if allowed to do so under the constitution, coopt or appoint new members to the committee.

Some constitutions give procedures for dealing with inquorate general meetings, for example adjourning the meeting to a later date and deeming the reconvened meeting as being quorate however many people turn up, thus enabling decisions to be made.

Misconduct by officers or committee members

The members of a company limited by guarantee can remove a committee member by passing a resolution with an ordinary majority at a general meeting of which 28 days' notice ('special notice') has been given. As soon as the company receives such a notice it must send a copy to the director concerned.

In other organisations the constitution must include specific provision in the constitution to remove a committee member or officer. If not, a general meeting must be called to amend the constitution so that the committee or the general meeting is given the power to remove the person concerned. However, this option is likely to cause considerable friction within the organisation and is unlikely to impress funders and supporters.

In all cases, if a committee member or officer is guilty of misusing funds, if the constitution gives the committee the right to appoint signatories, the committee has authority to remove that person's ability to sign cheques. The committee also has the power to require the person concerned to return any property belonging to the organisation immediately, and can take legal action to recover this property if required.

The person to be removed must, in all cases, be given an opportunity to present their case at the meeting at which the removal is discussed, and under company law has the right to ask the company to circulate written representations at the company's expense.

Equal opportunities

People are discriminated against both intentionally and unintentionally because of their race, skin colour, ethnic origin, religion, cultural beliefs, nationality, national origin, gender and sexuality. Young people, older people and disabled people are discriminated against due to lack of understanding about their capabilities and experiences. People who are HIV positive or who are living with AIDS face discrimination because of other people's ignorance.

The overall result is that some people are denied equal access to employment, training, financial and other services and opportunities.

Discrimination manifests itself in various ways, both directly and indirectly. It means that certain people are denied social interaction that others enjoy or take for granted, and are excluded from the decision making processes on matters that affect their lives.

The law

All employers must be aware of their legal obligations, which include those under the following:

- Equal Pay Act 1970
- Rehabilitation of Offenders Act 1974
- Race Relations Act 1976
- Sex Discrimination Act 1975
- Disability Discrimination Act 1995 and subsequent regulations
- Sex Discrimination (Gender Reassignment) Regulations 1999, amending the Sex Discrimination Act 1999
- Race Relations (Amendment) Act 2000
- Race Relations Act 1976 (Amendment) Regulations 2003
- Employment Equality (Religion or Belief) Regulations 2003
- Employment Equality (Sexual Orientation) Regulations 2003.

By December 2006 there will be employment equality regulations relating to age.

Employment issues covered by the above Acts and Regulations are discussed under *Discrimination*, in chapter 3, and in chapter 4. Chapter 9 describes the law and good practice in relation to the delivery of services.

Good practice

As well as fulfilling their legal duties, voluntary organisations generally consider it important to oppose discrimination, highlight injustice and promote good practice. They should ensure that their services, employment opportunities and decision making processes are accessible to everyone, even groups not covered by legislation. Every voluntary organisation should develop, and keep under review, an equal opportunities policy and the procedures necessary to implement the policy. The essential aims of the policy should be to help both the staff and committee eliminate direct and indirect discrimination in decision making, employment practices and opportunities and in service provision, and to provide a framework for taking positive action that is required or allowed under the legislation.

Organisations should not simply adopt someone else's equal opportunities policy. Developing your own policy will increase the organisation's awareness of different forms of discrimination and how these are manifested, at both an individual and organisational level. This awareness enables individuals and the organisation to develop appropriate ways of addressing discrimination and to bring about change. Furthermore, an essential part of developing equality of opportunity is the process of examining current practices and ensuring that access to services is not denied by discriminatory practices or behaviour or by a failure to make changes that would enable people to participate.

Finally, in developing an equal opportunities policy and procedures it is important to involve people who use or could use the organisation, especially those who have traditionally been underrepresented in the decision making processes. It is vital to involve the staff, trade union and committee in drawing up the policy and in monitoring its implementation and effectiveness, as this ensures that everyone's skills and experiences are drawn upon and the policy and procedures are owned by the organisation.

The following sections describe the points to consider when developing and implementing an equal opportunities policy.

Developing the policy

An equal opportunities policy should have four components:
- a policy statement or declaration of the organisation's commitment to combating discrimination and taking positive action to encourage participation
- the organisation's objectives concerning equal opportunities
- procedures for implementation
- monitoring and review processes.

Declaration of intent

This is a public statement that an organisation recognises that certain groups of people experience discrimination, is opposed to this situation, and will take steps to challenge it.

The committee, staff and trades unions should be involved in drafting the statement. It should be agreed by the committee members and be issued to and supported by all staff and committee members. Many organisations include the statement in their publications and other written material, and incorporate it into their job advertisements. Some also have the statement clearly visible in their public areas.

Objectives

These could include:
- to ensure that no member or potential member of staff, committee member, volunteer or service user experiences unfair or unlawful discrimination
- to ensure that staff and committee members understand the various forms and effects of discrimination
- to increase membership from socially excluded people and, where relevant, from organisations representing people who experience exclusion
- to seek to ensure that the composition of the committee reflects that of the population eligible to use the organisation
- to make adaptations to premises and equipment and ensure that they are accessible to staff and users
- to take legally permitted action to increase the number of staff from underrepresented groups, especially in senior positions and in posts that have access to the decision making process
- to establish better links with socially excluded groups
- to increase awareness within the organisation of the needs of groups who experience discrimination in order to provide more relevant services
- to review and adapt the organisation's, policies, procedures and services to meet the needs of people facing discrimination

- to introduce an equal opportunities dimension in all areas of current and proposed work, recruitment and service provision
- to consider establishing special projects to combat discrimination, where these are allowed under the relevant legislation
- to advocate equal opportunities policies (for example by stating that an organisation will only be considered for membership if it has, or is in the process of developing a policy).

Procedures for implementation

There are explicit requirements under the **Disability Discrimination Act 1995** for organisations with 15 or more employees* to make reasonable adjustments to enable a disabled person to apply for jobs and do the work if appointed, or to enable an existing employee who becomes disabled to continue working. The Act also requires all providers of goods, services or facilities to make reasonable adjustments to policies and procedures where disabled people are excluded from access to services and, from October 2004 to make reasonable adjustments to premises. For further details see chapters 3, 4 and 9.

The small employers exemption will be removed from October 2004.

As well as meeting their legal obligations, organisations should identify other ways to challenge discrimination. Some may choose to tackle all forms of inequality at once, others may decide to address one issue at a time. For example an organisation may feel that racial inequality is the major problem within its organisation and the area it serves. It would therefore develop a programme aimed at ensuring that black and minority ethnic people are treated fairly.

Once this programme is in motion, the organisation may then begin to focus on other forms of discrimination, having learned from the experiences of developing and implementing a policy to redress one form of inequality. It is important to remember that some people experience discrimination because of a combination of prejudicial views.

Points to consider when drawing up procedures to implement a policy include:
- examining the organisation to identify where discrimination exists and what form it takes
- examining the structure and composition of the committee and other decision making groups
- monitoring and reviewing services

- developing procedures and making them available publicly so that everyone involved with the organisation, including staff, members, committee members, officers, volunteers, self-employed workers, trainees and users know the standards of conduct expected and what to do if discrimination occurs
- developing procedures for dealing with breaches of the code of conduct, not just by staff in the form of a disciplinary policy, but by anyone involved with the organisation, including members, committee members, honorary officers, paid staff, volunteers, self-employed workers, trainees and users. For example, this may include a commitment to take steps to remove a committee member who is guilty of misconduct. It is important to build in safeguards to ensure that these actions are taken only in appropriate cases and are not themselves used in a discriminatory way
- staff recruitment
- staff training
- conditions of service
- staff support
- physical access and working arrangements
- allocating responsibility for implementing the equal opportunities policy; some groups set up a subcommittee, with staff representation, for this purpose.

Monitoring and review

Equal opportunities policies and procedures need to be continually monitored, to evaluate their effectiveness and highlight those areas which need to be revised.

Monitoring involves collecting statistical information, and should cover:
- job applicants (advertising, applications, shortlisting and selection)
- the workforce (including promotion, training and use of disciplinary and grievance procedures)
- members of the organisation
- the committee, subcommittees and working groups (composition and expertise)
- service users.

It is important to state the process clearly and identify who is responsible for collecting and analysing the information and implementing any necessary revision.

Equal opportunities monitoring may involve collecting information classed as 'sensitive' under the **Data Protection Act 1998** (see chapter 9) and so it may be necessary to get people's explicit consent to collect and hold the information. However, if information is made anonymous and is not linked to an individual by name or code number, it is unlikely to come under the Act.

Managing the policy

Membership

An equal opportunities policy should require a regular analysis of an organisation's membership to identify which communities are underrepresented. This may point to the need to alter the membership recruitment practice. This could include:

- consulting groups on how to make the organisation more relevant to people facing discrimination
- translating written material into other community languages and into Braille, making it available on tape and producing versions appropriate for people with learning difficulties
- preparing publicity material aimed at people from specific communities
- organising open days and conferences to describe the organisation's work and making interpreters and signers available at these events.

Management committees

Composition: A voluntary organisation's management committee (referred to here as the committee) is often made up of representatives of service users, people with a specialist knowledge of its work, and people with specialist expertise, for example in finance, personnel, fundraising or marketing.

An equal opportunities policy should require a regular analysis of the composition of the committee, subcommittees and working parties to ensure they reflect the diversity of people who experience discrimination.

As well as examining who is involved in formal decision making, informal decision making processes should be reviewed. Quite often key decisions are made in discussions that take place before and after meetings. This practice can lead to exclusion.

The policy should also describe measures to encourage representation from minority groups. This could include, for example, a commitment to producing committee papers in large print, in other languages, in Braille and in a form suitable for people with learning difficulties; ensuring meeting rooms have an induction loop; arranging signers; paying members' expenses for care of children or other dependants; and taking into account dates of all faiths' festivals when arranging meetings (see the *Shap calendar of religious festivals*, published by the Shap Working Party, available from *www.support4learning.org.uk/shap*).

Make sure that all committee members are encouraged to participate.

Check the constitution's procedures for appointing committee members. If people have to be members for some time before they can be nominated for election, some may be discouraged from standing. But at the same time, it is good practice to ensure people have an understanding of the organisation before they are elected to a committee.

Access to committee meetings: Think about where and when committee meetings take place. Some members may dislike travelling at night. As well as measures described above under *Composition*, consider whether committee members need to be offered escorts or drivers to take them to and from meetings, or need to know they can be reimbursed for using a taxi or registered minicab.

Training committee members: The equal opportunities policy should consider committee members' training needs. These would include:

- the committee's role and responsibilities
- equal opportunities legislation (see *The law*, page 37)
- involving all members. Existing members must learn how to work as a team, involve new members and challenge discriminatory actions, whether made intentionally or otherwise
- equal opportunities in recruitment and service delivery.

Implementing the policy

The committee should delegate responsibility for ensuring that the equal opportunities policy is implemented and developed to a named committee member and the most senior member of staff, although final responsibility will still lie with the committee as a whole.

This includes:

- ensuring all employees and committee members know how the policy operates and the process for its review and development. Make sure information is included in all induction programmes, for both staff and committee members, and that everyone is kept informed about any changes in the policy and procedures
- identifying staff and committee members' equal opportunities training needs – for both individuals and the staff and/or committee as a whole. This could cover, for example recruitment or changes in legislation
- involving the union at all stages
- carrying out monitoring procedures (see *Monitoring and review*, page 39)

- regularly reviewing recruitment, selection, promotion and training procedures, in discussion with the personnel officer and/or staffing subcommittee where appropriate
- handling harassment, bullying and discrimination complaints (see *Setting standards and dealing with complaints*, in chapter 3)
- reporting to the committee and membership on the progress of implementing the policy.

Make sure whoever has the responsibility is given time to perform these duties effectively and has the appropriate authority, including:

- being able to report directly to the committee
- powers to invoke an investigation into a complaint of discrimination, bullying or harassment (which should be carried out by more than one person)
- powers to examine written material in the organisation (but bear in mind confidentiality issues)
- a budget to cover the costs involved in carrying out this work.

Checklist
The first committee meeting

Before the meeting
❑ set up the necessary registers
❑ set up a system for keeping minutes of committee meetings and general meetings. Companies must keep minutes in a form which prevents tampering or forgery (for example a book or numbered loose leaf pages initialled by the chair), and it is good practice for all organisations to do so
❑ organise safe storage for:
- the original of the constitution
- copies of documents submitted to the Financial Services Authority, the Registrar of Companies and/or the Charity Commission and other registration bodies if necessary (such as Ofsted, the local environmental health department or the National Care Standards Commission (Commission for Social Care Inspection from April 2004))
- registers of members, committee members and officers
- minute books (which should generally also include minutes and papers distributed for the meeting)
- financial records
- signed copies of annual accounts and reports
- legal documents such as leases, employment contracts and insurance policies
❑ check the constitution for procedures to elect officers
❑ draft role descriptions for officers and committee members
❑ check the constitution for rules on cheque signatories
❑ obtain bank mandate forms and clarify the documentation required by the bank
❑ consider what insurances are necessary and obtain quotes and proposal forms
❑ obtain information necessary for the committee to make decisions about entering into licences or leases for premises
❑ where relevant, invite organisations entitled to appoint (nominate) committee members to put forward appointees
❑ check the constitution for:
- the committee's powers to coopt additional members
- rules on admitting new members and whether the committee can delegate this responsibility
- the date of the financial year end
- rules about delegation to subcommittees, officers or staff
❑ check funders' requirements regarding year end
❑ check constitutional, funder, charity law and/or IPS or company law rules on audit of accounts and, in particular, whether a qualified accountant is required
❑ draft stationery, ensuring that it complies with legal requirements
❑ make a note of deadlines that have to be met for the AGM.

At the meeting
Ensure that decisions are formally made and minuted about:
❑ cheque signatories
❑ insurance policies
❑ delegating authority for completing and signing insurance proposal forms
❑ staff recruitment
❑ taking on premises
❑ delegating responsibility (where relevant)
❑ developing the organisation's policies and procedures
❑ taking over from a previous group.

After the meeting
❑ update the necessary registers
❑ order stationery, ensuring it complies with legal requirements
❑ notify, as appropriate, Companies House, the Financial Services Authority and/or the Charity Commission of any change to the registered office
❑ obtain necessary signatures on the bank mandate and any additional information the bank requires from signatories if not already done at the meeting
❑ enter into the minute book the requirements for the bank resolutions and sign the bank mandate to confirm that this has been done
❑ return forms to the bank to set up account(s) and, where relevant, ensure that cheques include the words 'registered charity'
❑ obtain and file the necessary insurance policies, ensuring copies of proposal forms are made and kept
❑ ensure everyone involved with the organisation is made aware of their responsibilities, including under equal opportunities, health and safety and data protection law and policies, environmental and confidentiality policies, and charity, IPS and company law
❑ if a company limited by guarantee:
- inform Companies House of new committee members (**Form 288a**), resignations (**Form 288b**), or changes in committee members' personal details (**Form 288c**)*

- inform Companies House on **Form 225** of any change in the accounting reference date*
- notify Companies House on **Form 353** if the register of members is to be kept somewhere other than the registered office*
- ensure the organisation's name and a statement that it is a company appears on all letterheads, external e-mails, websites, cheques, bills, receipts and publications
❑ if a registered charity whose annual income is over £10,000, ensure the organisation's name and, if required, a statement that it is a charity appears on all letterheads, external e-mails, websites, cheques, bills, receipts and publications

❑ from 1 April 2004, if a charitable industrial and provident society whose name doesn't include 'charity', 'charitable' or the Welsh equivalents, a statement that it is charitable must appear on all letterheads, external e-mails, websites, cheques, bills, receipts and publications
❑ if a local authority influenced or controlled company (see chapter 1), ensure this is made clear on all documents and that the authority/authorities is/are identified
❑ keep a record of all decisions to delegate authority.

All these forms can be submitted online – see www.companieshouse.gov.uk

Checklist
Elections

Some constitutions detail the election procedures. If there are no requirements, the committee should agree the format for the election, including procedures for taking nominations, methods of making sure that only those entitled to vote do so, and whether it should take place by secret ballot or open show of hands (see *Elections*, chapter 1).

Before the meeting
Check:
❑ categories of elected committee members
❑ who can vote for which categories
❑ nomination procedures, including timescales.

Circulate (as appropriate):
❑ requests for nominations with instructions
❑ information about nominees, if this is being sent out before the meeting
❑ proxy, electronic or postal ballot papers, if allowed under the constitution.

Prepare (as appropriate):
❑ ballot papers
❑ a list of those entitled to vote for each category of member
❑ the agenda in such a way that vote counting can take place without interrupting the flow of the meeting.

At the meeting
Ensure (as appropriate):
❑ ballot papers are given to those entitled to vote, with an explanation of the voting procedure (including who can vote for particular categories of members)
❑ people not running for election are available to count votes
❑ results are announced, and recorded in the minutes
❑ the necessary information relating to new members is completed for the register of committee members, and that companies complete **Form 288a** (appointments) and **Form 288b** (resignations)

Checklist

Annual general meeting

Before the meeting

❏ check the period within which the AGM must be held (incorporated organisations – within 18 months of incorporation, and then at least once in each calendar year and no more than 15 months since the previous AGM; unincorporated – as stated in the constitution) (*proposed company legislation removes the requirement for private companies to hold AGMs unless members want them: those that choose to hold AGMs will have to hold them within ten months of the financial year-end*).

❏ where relevant, ensure the accounts are submitted to the auditor in time for the audit to be completed and for approved accounts to be sent to members

❏ if a company, ensure that audited accounts and report and the balance sheet, approved by the committee and signed as required are ready for distribution to members with the AGM agenda (although the accounts do not need to be laid before the AGM, see *The auditing or examining process*, in chapter 8)

❏ check the constitution for any agenda requirements

❏ check the rules on elections

❏ ensure correct notice is given of the AGM and that notices are sent in accordance with the constitution

❏ ensure that the auditor is informed of the meeting (this is a legal requirement for companies and industrial and provident societies)

❏ if a company, ensure there is a sufficient supply of **Form 288a** to be completed at the AGM by new committee members (the form can be downloaded from *www.companieshouse.gov.uk*)

❏ prepare the necessary material to hold elections.

At the meeting

❏ ensure resolutions are passed receiving, and, if required under the constitution, approving the accounts and the committee's report

❏ ensure elections are held

❏ ensure minutes are kept.

After the meeting

❏ ensure a company's new committee members complete and sign **Form 288a**, and **Form 288b** is completed for committee members who are no longer serving

❏ submit accounts (audited if required), balance sheet and the committee's report to Companies House or Financial Services Authority and/or the Charity Commission within the correct timescale – see *Submitting the accounts and report*, page 35

❏ ensure that a copy of the audited accounts and balance sheets and annual report are available for inspection by all members in line with the constitution and, in the case of a company limited by guarantee or an industrial and provident society, at the registered office

❏ for a company limited by guarantee, inform Companies House on **Form 288a** of any new committee members, and on **Form 288b** of any committee members who are no longer on the committee (these can be submitted online)

❏ update the appropriate registers

❏ ensure that the minutes are written up

❏ carry out induction procedures for new committee members (existing committee members may also find this useful).

Checklist
Committee members' roles and responsibilities

Duties of all committee members

Committee members have overall responsibility for meeting an organisation's legal duties and ensuring it is properly managed, and for promoting good practice in all its activities.

Legal duties

- ❏ ensuring the organisation meets its objectives as set out in the constitution (see chapter 1)
- ❏ ensuring the organisation complies with the rules set out in its constitution and acts legally in all its activities (getting advice when necessary)
- ❏ acting in the interests of the organisation and its beneficiaries (if a charity) or members (if a non-charity), and not for personal benefit
- ❏ informing meetings of any interest in a contract or other decision that could lead to conflict of interest
- ❏ providing proper accounts of the organisation's activities to its members, funders (and the Charity Commission, Companies House and other regulatory bodies as appropriate), producing annual reports and directors' reports as required by law and ensuring that accounts, annual returns and other required information is filed on time
- ❏ seeking professional advice where relevant
- ❏ ensuring the organisation's resources and assets are well managed and used to pursue its objects
- ❏ keeping up to date with the organisation's activities to ensure informed decision making at all times
- ❏ keeping abreast of legislation that may affect the organisation's work and direction
- ❏ complying with relevant legislation
- ❏ ensuring that the organisation has effective health and safety policies and procedures covering all its premises and activities and that they are effectively monitored
- ❏ ensuring that necessary insurance policies are taken out and periodically reviewed
- ❏ ensuring the organisation meets all its contractual and other obligations, including employment contracts, tenancy and/or licence agreements, funding contracts and equipment licences
- ❏ regularly attending committee meetings and working jointly with other members.

Managerial tasks

- ❏ setting overall policy and short, medium and long-term objectives
- ❏ identifying, discussing and agreeing new areas of work

- ❏ ensuring there are systems for regularly monitoring and evaluating the organisation's work
- ❏ being a good employer
- ❏ supervising and supporting senior staff and ensuring other employees and volunteers are properly supervised and supported
- ❏ ensuring the organisation's equal opportunities policy and other policies and procedures are implemented and monitored
- ❏ promoting the organisation.

Main duties of the chair

The tasks of a chair can be divided into four key areas, some of which could be delegated to a vice chair.

Planning and running the organisation's meetings

These include the AGM, any other members' meetings and committee meetings. *NB: Chairing meetings is the only legal duty of a chair.*

Planning meetings involves:

- ❏ ensuring the organisation holds the meetings required by its constitution
- ❏ helping to plan the agendas for each meeting, checking the minutes of previous meetings and ensuring that these and any background papers are distributed beforehand
- ❏ being briefed about each item on the agenda
- ❏ ensuring outstanding matters are followed up
- ❏ ensuring compliance with the procedures for giving notice of meetings (although this is more likely to be a secretary's duty).

Running meetings involves:

- ❏ ensuring the meeting is quorate (ie there are enough voting members present to take decisions)
- ❏ gaining agreement of the minutes of the previous meeting and then signing them
- ❏ making sure all relevant items on the agenda are discussed
- ❏ ensuring all participants who wish to do so have the opportunity to make a contribution, or in large meetings deciding who is chosen to speak
- ❏ fairly summarising issues and options before a decision is taken
- ❏ making sure voting procedures are complied with
- ❏ clarifying decisions made so everyone is clear what has been decided
- ❏ ensuring proper minutes are taken.

Dealing with matters relating to the membership, other officers and users

This involves:

- ❏ ensuring members' rights as stated in the constitution are met
- ❏ helping to deal with disciplinary action against members and other officers
- ❏ helping to deal with disputes between members, users and the organisation.

Supervising senior staff

The chair is often responsible for supervising and supporting the work of the senior member of staff, although this may be done by another committee member.

Helping with the management of the organisation

This involves:

- ❏ making decisions and taking action between committee meetings (taking 'chair's action') if this is allowed by the constitution or has been authorised by the committee
- ❏ acting as a sounding board for senior staff
- ❏ signing cheques and liaising with the treasurer
- ❏ helping to deal with any staff problems
- ❏ assisting with staff recruitment.

Other duties

The chair may also act as a spokesperson, which could include:

- ❏ representing the organisation at external events
- ❏ liaising with the press on behalf of the organisation (this could be delegated to a press officer)
- ❏ taking an active role in fundraising campaigns.

Main duties of a company secretary

Companies limited by guarantee must have a company secretary, whose post requires meeting certain legal obligations under company law. If the constitution allows, some of the tasks may be delegated to paid staff, volunteers, a solicitor or others. A member of staff (or anyone else with the necessary knowledge) can be the company secretary.

Under proposed company legislation, private companies (which includes most voluntary sector companies) will no longer need to appoint a company secretary, although they will be able to do so, if they wish. However, the company secretary's duties will still need to be carried out.

NB: In this section we refer to 'directors', which are a company's committee members.

Maintaining and updating the registers

This involves:

- ❏ maintaining a register of members and a register of directors and company secretaries
- ❏ notifying the Registrar of Companies within 14 days of any changes of director(s) or secretary – on **Form 288a** for appointments or **Form 288b** for resignations – and any changes in a director's or secretary's details as given on Form 288a – on **Form 288c** (these forms can be submitted online)
- ❏ where relevant, maintaining a register of charges, ie loans made to the company where the bank has a form of security, such as a mortgage.

If the company has a seal, it is good practice to keep a sealing register – the list of documents on which the company seal has been used.

Ensuring meetings are called and recorded

This involves:

- ❏ ensuring that an AGM is held within 18 months of incorporation and then at least every 15 months (*under proposed company legislation, private companies – which includes most voluntary sector companies – will only have to hold AGMs if members wish; if AGMs are held they will need to be held within ten months of the end of the company's financial year*)
- ❏ ensuring that 21 days' written notice of the AGM is given to members and auditors (notice can be given electronically to members who have agreed to this, provided company law rules on electronic notice are followed) and that business is transacted in accordance with the constitution
- ❏ calling other general meetings as required by the constitution, ensuring that 14 days' written notice is given and business is transacted according to the rules
- ❏ understanding which resolutions need to comply with the rules for special, extraordinary or elective resolutions or ordinary resolutions with special notice
- ❏ informing the Registrar of Companies of any special, extraordinary or elective resolution (and certain types of ordinary resolution) with 15 days of them being passed by the company
- ❏ ensuring minute books are kept for general meetings and directors' meetings, and for any other meetings, such as subcommittees or staff, where decisions are made.

Administration of annual returns and accounts

This involves:

- ❏ ensuring an income and expenditure account and balance sheet, and if required, either a compilation report or full audit are prepared (see chapter 8 for more about these requirements)

❏ preparing the directors' annual report on the accounts

❏ ensuring the accounts and directors' report are approved by the directors and signed by the directors and/or company secretary, as required under company law

❏ circulating audited or examined accounts to all members of the company at least 21 days before the AGM (provided company law rules are met, this can be done electronically)

❏ submitting the income and expenditure account, balance sheet and directors' report to the Registrar of Companies within ten months of the end of the organisation's financial year

❏ submitting an annual return to the Registrar of Companies by the due date

❏ for charitable companies, submitting accounts to the Charity Commission within ten months of the end of the financial year

❏ submitting an annual return to the Charity Commission by the due date

❏ keeping copies of all company annual returns, accounts and reports for at least three years and all unincorporated charity returns, accounts and reports for at least six years (it is good practice to keep them forever, as they are a formal record of the organisation's history).

Supervising legal agreements

Ensuring all legal agreements or contracts are properly discussed, agreed and recorded by the directors.

Meeting other requirements

This involves:

❏ notifying the Registrar of Companies of changes to the organisation's registered office within 14 days – using **Form 287** (which can be submitted electronically)

❏ ensuring the organisation's stationery includes its registered name and address, the fact that it is a company limited by guarantee and its company registration number (and where relevant the fact that it is a registered charity)

❏ if the organisation is registered for VAT, ensuring the VAT number is printed on its invoices and certain other documents

❏ ensuring people who are entitled to do so can inspect company records

❏ having custody of the company seal, if there is one, and ensuring it is properly used.

Main duties of a committee secretary

'Company secretary' is a legal position, required under current company law. Many organisations, both incorporated and unincorporated, have an elected committee secretary.

Companies

In a company the elected secretary might help the company secretary prepare for and administer meetings and assist with other administration.

Unincorporated associations

In unincorporated associations, the secretary often takes on responsibilities similar to those of the company secretary – specifically in relation to meetings, maintaining lists of members' and committee members' names and addresses, and ensuring annual reports and accounts are submitted to the relevant agencies.

Unless required by the constitution there is no obligation to have an elected secretary, and the relevant tasks can be undertaken by committee members or staff.

Preparing for meetings

This involves:

❏ sending notices of all meetings to members, within the time required by the constitution

❏ making arrangements for meetings, for example organising refreshments, booking rooms, ensuring appropriate facilities for participants with special needs

❏ preparing the agenda, in consultation with the chair, and distributing the agenda with any background papers

❏ checking that members have carried out tasks agreed at the previous meeting.

Helping in meetings

This involves:

❏ making sure the minutes of the previous meeting are agreed and that they are signed by the chair

❏ taking and producing minutes of the meetings, recording names of those attending and apologies, major decisions, any votes taken and agreed further action.

Other administration

This involves:

❏ dealing with incoming correspondence

❏ keeping records of outgoing correspondence

❏ keeping records of membership subscriptions

❏ ensuring members are provided with the organisation's constitution, annual report and policies

❏ sending out publicity about the organisation.

Chapter 3:
Responsibilities in recruitment

Related chapters
Chapter 4 – Employment
Chapter 5 – Health and safety
Chapter 7 – Insurance
Chapter 9 – Data protection

Employing people brings new responsibilities, and before taking these on employers must be aware of their legal obligations and employees' rights. They should also have an equal opportunities policy covering all forms of paid employment and volunteering, to ensure the best people are attracted to work in the organisation and that everyone is treated fairly.

The terminology

In this and the following chapter we use the following terminology:

- **employees**: people who work for the organisation on a regular basis and meet the legal definition of employee (see below)

- **workers**: employees and others such as casuals and freelances who are entitled to workers' rights (see below)

- **volunteers**: people who do not receive any pay or other reward in return for their work (though they may receive reimbursement for genuine out-of-pocket expenses)

- **staff**: everyone who works for the organisation, ie all of the above.

Further information about many of the employees' and workers' rights described in this chapter is available on the Department of Trade and Industry's website *www.dti.gov.uk*

Some definitions

Employees

Whether someone is an employee and therefore entitled to employment rights is a matter of law and is ultimately determined by the employment tribunals and courts. Many legal criteria (called 'tests') are used to determine whether someone is legally an employee. Generally a person is likely to be an employee if they are required to work for an organisation on a regular basis (whether this is, for example, every day or a certain number of hours per week or fortnight), are under the organisation's control and receive pay or something else of value in return for the work.

An employee no longer has to work a minimum number of hours per week. In one case, for example, a person who worked two hours on alternate Fridays was held to be an employee. So a cleaner or carer who is employed to work for an hour every week or fortnight is likely to be an employee, unless they are genuinely running their own business as a cleaner or carer and invoice the organisation.

Temporary workers, people on fixed-term contracts, job-sharers and part-timers are all likely to be employees. A volunteer who receives money (other than reimbursement for genuine out-of-pocket expenses) or something else of value and is obliged to work for an organisation on a regular basis could be held to be legally an employee.

Workers

Even if a person is not an employee they could meet the wider legal definition of a worker and be entitled to some (although not all) employment rights. A worker is anyone who is being paid or receiving something of value for providing work himself or herself and who does not run their own business as a self-employed person. Casuals and freelances might be workers but not employees. They work as and when the organisation requires them but with no obligation on the part of the organisation to offer work and no obligation on the person to accept it if it is offered.

A volunteer who receives money (other than genuine reimbursement) or something else of value in return for their work, and who works for the organisation on an occasional basis rather than being required to work regularly, could legally be a 'worker' and be entitled to workers' rights.

Rights
The main workers' rights are:
- protection under the employment provisions of equal opportunities legislation (see *Discrimination*, page 57), this applies to employees, other workers, and people who run their own business as a self-employed person
- the national minimum wage (see page 51), this applies to employees and other workers, but not to people who are genuinely self-employed
- working time rights, including four weeks' paid holiday (see *Working Time Regulations*, page 52, these apply to employees and other workers, but not people who are genuinely self-employed.

There are other workers' rights. In this book when we refer to employees we mean only people who are legally employees; when we refer to workers we mean employees and others who meet the legal definition of worker. When we refer to the self-employed we mean people who genuinely run their own business and are registered with the Inland Revenue as being self-employed.

Note that just because a person is paid via PAYE doesn't necessarily mean that they are an employee for the purposes of employment rights. Most will be, but the method of payment is just one part of the test of whether someone is an employee.

Employment rights

All employees (see page 48) have rights during employment: those given by statute (**statutory rights**) and those acquired through their contract of employment (**contractual rights**). Some rights apply to all employees as soon as they start work; others depend upon length of service and continuity of employment. Continuity of employment, or **continuous service**, means how long the person has worked for the same employer, even if the job has changed. In some cases work with a previous employer also counts towards continuity.

Below we outline employment rights for **workers** (which include employees), then additional rights for **employees** only.

Workers' rights

When someone applies for a job
Everyone has the right not to be discriminated against because of their race, sex, sexuality, religion or belief or trade union membership. Applicants also have the right not to be discriminated against on the grounds of disability in organisations with 15 or more employees unless this is objectively justified. The 15-worker limit will be removed in October 2004 (see *Disability discrimination*, page 60).

As soon as someone starts work
All workers, from their first day at work, have a number of rights.

In relation to pay
- An itemised pay statement showing how much they earn and any deductions (see *Paying people*, in chapter 4).
- The national minimum wage if aged 18 or over, and not to be dismissed because they qualify for the national minimum wage or because they have sought to enforce their right to do so (see *Minimum wage*, page 51).
- Not to have unauthorised deductions made from wages (see *Paying people*, in chapter 4).

In relation to annual leave and working hours
(see *Working Time Regulations*, page 52).
- Four weeks' paid annual leave
- To rest breaks and maximum working hours per week and, if night workers, access to health checks.

In relation to protection from discrimination
(see *Discrimination*, page 57)
- Equal pay for work of equal value.
- Not to be discriminated against on grounds of race.
- Not to be discriminated against on grounds of sex or marital status.
- Not to be discriminated against because of past, current or future actions in relation to gender reassignment.

- Not to be discriminated against on grounds of disability (except where different treatment is justified), when employed by an organisation with 15 or more workers (this exemption will disappear in October 2004).
- Not to be discriminated against on grounds of sexuality.
- Not to be discriminated against on the grounds of religion or belief.

In relation to trades union activity

(see *Unions*, in chapter 4)

- In organisations employing 20 or more people, to have an independent trade union recognised by the employer if the majority of the workforce wants one.
- Union membership (in almost all cases) and to take part in union activities.
- Not to belong to a trade union.
- Not to be victimised or unfairly dismissed on grounds of trade union membership or activities.
- Not to be discriminated at work or when applying for a job through an employer keeping a record of trade union members.
- Reasonable paid time off to carry out duties and undergo relevant training as an official of a recognised trade union or as an employee representative.
- Reasonable time off to perform duties as a union learning representative.
- Reasonable time off (which need not be paid) for activities of a recognised trade union.

In relation to protection from dismissal and victimisation

- Not to be dismissed for any reason connected with racial group, sex, sexuality, religion or belief (see *Discrimination*, page 57).
- In organisations with 15 or more employees, not to be dismissed for any reason connected with disability unless this is justified (see *Discrimination*, page 57). This small organisation exemption will no longer apply from October 2004.
- Not to be dismissed in breach of their contract.
- Not to be victimised or dismissed after 'blowing the whistle' on illegal or dangerous activities carried out by their employer (see *Public interest disclosure*, in chapter 4).

Other rights

- To be accompanied by a colleague or trade union official during disciplinary or grievance hearings (see *Disciplinary policy and procedures*, in chapter 4).
- To compensation if they become ill or injured during the course of employment as a result of the employer's negligence (see *Legislation*, in chapter 5).

Additional rights for employees
As soon as someone starts work
In relation to time off (apart from trade union activity)

- Reasonable time off with pay to perform functions as a safety representative (in organisations with five or more staff) (see *Safety representatives*, in chapter 5).
- Reasonable time off (which need not be paid) for public activities (see *Time off for public duties*, in chapter 4).
- If aged 16 or 17 and without having achieved a certain educational or training standard, to reasonable paid time off to study or train for a relevant qualification to help them achieve that standard. Certain employees aged 18 have the right to complete training already begun (*Employment Rights Act 1996* amended by the *Teaching and Higher Education Act 1996*).

In relation to protection from dismissal and victimisation

- Not to be dismissed during the first eight weeks of lawfully organised industrial action (*Employment Relations Act 1999*).
- Not to be dismissed for activities relating to being a representative for consultation about redundancy or business transfer (see *Redundancy*, in chapter 4).
- Not to be dismissed for participating in the election of an employee representative (see *Redundancy*, in chapter 4).
- Not to be victimised or dismissed on grounds of activities as a safety representative, for making a complaint about a health and safety matter or for taking steps to protect themselves or leaving a place where they reasonably believe they are in danger (see *Safety representatives*, in chapter 5).
- Not to be victimised or dismissed because they have asserted a statutory right (ie have required the employer to comply with statutory obligations) (*Employment Rights Act 1996*).

In relation to family responsibilities

- To reasonable unpaid time off to deal with unexpected or sudden emergencies relating to dependants. A 'dependant' would include a partner, parent, child and more distant relative who is dependent on the employee (see *Dependants leave*, in chapter 4).
- Female employees are also entitled to:
- paid time off for antenatal care (see *Maternity*, in chapter 4)
- 26 weeks' ordinary maternity leave – even if the woman was pregnant when she started the job (see *Maternity*, in chapter 4)
- the right to return to the same job on the same pay and conditions after ordinary maternity leave (see *Maternity*, in chapter 4)
- the right not to be unfairly dismissed for any reason

connected with their pregnancy (see *Maternity*, in chapter 4)
- the right to a written statement of the reasons for dismissal if she is dismissed at any time while she is pregnant or after childbirth where her ordinary maternity leave period ends (see *Right not to be dismissed*, in chapter 4).

Other rights
- To work in a healthy, safe environment (see *General duties under the HSW Act*, in chapter 5).
- To statutory sick pay after they have been off sick for four days in a row and are earning more than the national insurance lower earnings limit (£77 in 2003/04, £79 in 2004/05) (there are some exceptions; see *Sickness*, in chapter 4).

After one calendar month
- One week's notice of dismissal (*Employment Rights Act 1996*).
- Pay during medical suspension (*Health and Safety at Work Act 1974*).
- Wages if laid off (*Employment Rights Act 1996*).
- A statement of terms of employment particulars (see chapter 4). The employer has two months in which to issue a statement (*Employment Rights Act 1996*).

After 26 weeks
- Twenty-six weeks' statutory maternity pay during ordinary maternity leave (see *Maternity*, in chapter 4), if earning more than the national insurance lower earnings limit (£77 in 2003/04, £79 in 2004/05).
- Twenty-six weeks' additional maternity leave (unpaid).
- The option of one week's or two consecutive weeks' paternity leave and, if earning more than the lower earnings limit – LEL) statutory paternity pay (see *Paternity*, in chapter 4).
- Twenty-six weeks' ordinary adoption leave followed by 26 weeks' additional adoption leave, and (if earning more than the LEL) statutory adoption pay (see *Adoption*, in chapter 4).
- Parents of children aged under 6 (or 18 if disabled) can make a written request for more flexible working arrangements (see *Flexible ways of working*, in chapter 4).

After one year
- Not to be dismissed for an unfair reason or through an unfair procedure (note that for some unfair dismissals there is no qualifying period) (*Employment Rights Act 1996*)
- To be given written reasons for dismissal within 14 days of a request (*Employment Rights Act 1996*)

- To take up to 13 weeks' unpaid parental leave to care for each child born after 15 December 1999 during their first five years or, in the case of a disabled child, up to 18 weeks' leave until the child's eighteenth birthday. Similar rights exist for adopted children. Employees of children born or adopted between 15 December 1994 and 14 December 1999 need one year's continuous service with their current employer or a previous employer between 15 December 1998 and 9 January 2002, and must take parental leave before 31 March 2005 (or in the case of adoption, up to the child's eighteenth birthday if that is sooner) (see *Parental leave*, in chapter 4).
- Employees affected by **Transfer of Undertakings (Protection of Employment) Regulations 1981** (TUPE) who consider that their rights have been infringed may complain to an employment tribunal (see *Taking on other organisations' staff*, in chapter 4).

After two years
- To redundancy payment, if earning more than the national insurance lower earnings limit (£77 in 2003/04).
- To reasonable time off work to look for work or training if under notice of redundancy (see *Redundancy*, in chapter 4).

After employment ends
- To protection against discrimination on the grounds of race, sex, disability, religion or belief, or sexuality once the employment had ended. Such discrimination could include failure to provide a reference and not dealing with a grievance post termination (see *Post employment discrimination*, in chapter 4).

Minimum wage
The **National Minimum Wage Act 1998** sets a minimum hourly rate for almost all employees and others who are paid for their work. At the time of writing (December 2003) the minimum hourly rates were:
- £4.50 for workers aged 22 years and over
- £3.80 for those aged between 18 and 21
- £3.80 for people aged 22 or over for six months after starting a new job with a new employer if they receive accredited training on at least 26 days during that six-month period.

The government has provisionally accepted the Low Pay Commission's recommendations of £4.85 for adult workers and £4.10 for younger workers from 1 October 2004.

The minimum rates apply to most workers, including pieceworkers, homeworkers, sessional staff, agency workers, part-time staff and casual workers and freelance workers who fall within the definition of worker (see chapter 4). The main exceptions include:

- people who are 'genuinely self-employed' (see *Self-employed people*, page 54)
- anyone aged under 18 years*
- a volunteer worker in a hostel with charitable status who receives free accommodation and food as well as expenses for any work related travel, but who does not receive monetary payments
- some apprentices and some trainees on government schemes including the New Deal and Work Based Learning for Adults and on European Social Fund programmes
- residential members of charitable religious communities
- volunteers who receive no pay, or only out-of-pocket expenses, and/or whose only benefit is the training necessary for their work
- volunteers who receive no benefits in kind other than reasonable subsistence and accommodation, and training necessary for them to do their voluntary work.

Volunteers could be entitled to a minimum wage if organisations give them additional non-job related training, or provide any payment above genuine reimbursement for expenses, or provide other benefits.

At the time of writing (December 2003) the government was considering a proposal to increase the national minimum wage to 16 and 17 year olds.

Employers must keep adequate records to show that the minimum wage is being paid to all workers. If there is a dispute, the employer must prove that the national minimum wage has been paid. They must keep records for three years, but DTI advice is to keep them for at least six years, as employees can take out a claim for up to this period.

Employees must be given access to their records within 14 days of a written request, although this deadline can be extended with the employee's agreement.

For information and advice on the national minimum wage telephone 0845 6000 678. For free copies of the DTI publication *A detailed guide to the national minimum wage* ring 0845 8450 360 or visit *www.dti.gov.uk*

Working Time Regulations 1998

These regulations provide the following rights for workers:
- a 48-hour limit on the working week, in most cases averaged over 17 weeks, unless people agree in writing to work more hours, or more hours have been negotiated with the relevant union(s) or employees' representatives
- four weeks' annual paid leave, which can include public holidays
- 20-minute in-work rest breaks where the working day is longer than six hours
- rest breaks of 11 consecutive hours each 24-hour period
- a day off each week, or two days off each fortnight.

Night workers
A night worker is defined as someone who works at least three hours between 11pm and 6am. Night workers can work no more than eight hours in any 24-hour period and cannot opt out of this limit. They also have the right to free health assessments to ensure they are suitable for night work.

Young workers
Workers aged 16 and 17 years must not work more than eight hours a day or 40 hours a week and generally cannot work at night (but there are some exceptions). They also have the following rights:
- a 30-minute rest period if the work day is longer than 4.5 hours
- a 12-hour rest period in each 24 hours
- in addition to this a weekly rest period of 48 hours.

Working time hours include overtime, job-related training, time travelling during the course of work and working lunches. Not included are hours travelling to and from work, lunch breaks, evening classes or day release courses.

Part-time workers must receive the same entitlements (with paid holiday on a pro rata basis). Workers in some sectors, for example transport, currently remain outside the scope of the regulations.

Employers must keep records to show that staff are taking their daily, weekly and annual entitlements to time off, and are not working more the maximum allowed hours. It is not necessary to keep records of the working hours of anyone who has opted out of the 48-hour week, but employers must still keep a record of their names.

Employers must offer regular health assessments to night workers. They should keep a record of the name of the night worker, when an assessment was offered (or when they had the assessment if there was one) and the result of any assessment. Records must be kept for two years.

Enforcement of the regulations is split between two bodies. The entitlements (for example rest periods and breaks and paid annual leave) are enforced through employment tribunals. The working time limits are enforced by the Health and Safety Executive and by local authorities.

Fixed-term employees

The **Fixed-term Employees (Prevention of Less Favourable Treatment) Regulations 2002** prevent employees on fixed-term contracts being treated less favourably than comparable employees on permanent contracts. The regulations apply to people on contracts that last for a specific period, or until a specific task has been completed or a specified event takes place or does not take place. It would include, for example, seasonal staff employed for a specific period, as well as employees covering for maternity leave. The regulations do not apply to agency workers.

Employees on fixed-term contracts do not necessarily have to receive the same pay and benefits as comparable permanent employees, but must receive a comparable package. This includes:
- pay, holidays, sick pay, and the same or similar benefits, for example season ticket loans and car allowances
- access to occupational pension schemes, or salary equivalent to the employer pension contribution, or a contribution to a stakeholder or private pension scheme.

Fixed-term employees may write to their employers asking for written statements explaining the reasons for any discrepancy between them and permanent staff. Employers must respond within 21 days. Less favourable treatment can be justified in one of two ways. The employer must show:
- there are genuine business reasons, or
- that, in terms of pay and benefits, the fixed-term employee's package as a whole is at least equal to that of permanent colleagues.

Rights

Fixed-term employees have the right to:
- protection from unfair dismissal
- receive information on suitable internal vacancies and to apply for permanent jobs
- receive suitable training and apply for promotion
- receive statutory redundancy pay if they have at least two years' continuous service and their contract is ending because of redundancy, unless they entered into a contract with a waiver of this right before 1 October 2002 (see below).

The use of successive fixed-term contracts is limited to four years unless a longer period can be justified on objective grounds. A renewal of the fixed-term contract after four years' continuous service will be treated as a permanent contract.

Employees on fixed-term contracts can no longer be asked to waive their rights to statutory redundancy payments in their contracts, and any waiver included in a fixed-term contract after 30 September 2002 is invalid. As with their permanent colleagues, fixed-term workers with at least at least two years' continuous service are entitled to statutory redundancy payments.

Part-time workers

The **Part-time Workers (Prevention of Less Favourable Treatment) Regulations 2000** give part-time workers the same rights as comparable full-time workers. Unlike fixed-term rights, which apply only to employees, part-time rights apply to workers (see page 49), including employees and most other people working under a contract. Under the regulations 'full-time' is defined as the number of hours considered by the employer to be full-time for that type of work, and 'part-time' is anything which is not full-time.

Part-time workers have the same statutory rights as if they were full-time (annual leave, sick pay, maternity, paternity, adoption, parental and dependants leave, calculated on a pro rata basis). In addition they are entitled to the same contractual rights. This means that part-time workers should always:
- receive the same basic rate of pay (pro rata) as comparable full-time workers, unless a different rate can be justified on objective grounds (for example performance-related pay)
- receive the same hourly rate of overtime as comparable full-time workers
- not be excluded from training simply because they work part time: employers should try to schedule training sessions so that part-time workers can attend
- have the same access to any career break schemes as comparable full-timers
- have the same entitlements (pro rata) to contractual sick pay, annual leave, maternity, parental, adoption and dependants leave as full-time workers
- have the same access to occupational pension schemes as full-timers
- have the right to be treated no less favourably when being selected for redundancy.

A part-timer who believes they are being treated less favourably than a full-timer can ask their employer for a written statement of reasons. The employer must respond within 21 days.

Agency staff

Agency staff are placed to work for an organisation for a limited period. There is usually a contract between the agency and the organisation, as well as one between the agency and the individual. In these situations, the organisation is unlikely to be the employer. Towards the end of 2002, the government began consulting on an EU proposal for a directive on working conditions for agency workers. The proposed directive would require equal treatment for agency workers after their first six weeks.

Even if an organisation is not the employer, it is unlawful to discriminate against an agency worker on grounds of sex, marital status, racial group, religion or belief, sexuality or disability (see *Discrimination*, page 57). Agency workers have the right to receive the national minimum wage (see *Minimum wage*, page 51) and have the same rights as employees under the Working Time Regulations (see page 52), part-timers' rights (see page 53), and the right to be accompanied at disciplinary and grievance hearings (see *Disciplinary policy and procedures*, in chapter 4).

Seconded staff

Seconded staff are employed by one organisation, for example a local authority or company, and are placed with another organisation for a limited period. The original organisation generally remains the employer, although in some situations the host organisation could legally be considered the employer. There should be a written agreement between the seconding employer, the host organisation and the secondee, clarifying management arrangements.

As employees, seconded staff have the same rights as any employee. In addition it is unlawful for the host organisation to discriminate against a secondee on grounds of sex, marital status, racial group, religion or belief, sexuality or disability (see *Discrimination*, page 57).

Self-employed people

People are generally legally defined as self-employed if they run their own business, can choose the work they take, work for a number of clients, and are registered as self-employed with the Inland Revenue. They pay their own tax and national insurance and are responsible for their own public liability insurance (and professional indemnity insurance if they provide a professional service, see chapter 7). They are not entitled to employment rights or to workers' rights (except protection under anti-discrimination legislation), but the organisations they work for owe them a responsibility under the **Health and Safety at Work Act 1974** (see chapter 5).

For suggestions about the content of a self-employed person's contract see *Taking on freelance and self-employed workers and consultants*, page 74.

It may be tempting to contract people on a self-employed basis to avoid employment responsibilities, in particular the duty to operate PAYE and pay employer's national insurance payments. However, to qualify for self-employed status, people have to meet a number of criteria relating to their working practices. If people are treated as self-employed when they should legally be treated as employees, the Inland Revenue PAYE and National Insurance Contributions Offices can demand tax and national insurance payments from the employing organisation even though these have not been deducted from the fees paid to the individual. There may also be penalties for and interest due on late payment. It is advisable to check with your PAYE office before treating anyone as self-employed.

As well as the tax implications, an organisation may end up in an employment tribunal if the person subsequently claims that they are legally an employee and therefore entitled to employment rights (such as the right to paid holiday or to claim unfair dismissal).

Trainees

Whether trainees have employees' rights depends on the circumstances and the specific legislation. Those placed by colleges, and who are not paid by the host organisation, are not usually classified as employees or workers and therefore will have no rights associated with employment. Those placed for longer periods or who are paid may acquire employment or workers' rights. Always clarify whether trainees are to be treated as employees. In all cases the host organisation has responsibilities to trainees under the **Health and Safety at Work Act 1974** (see chapter 5).

There are special responsibilities owed to trainees aged under 18 in health and safety legislation, to compensate for their lack of experience or lower awareness of risks (see *The management of health and safety at work*, in chapter 5).

Trainees who are not employees will not be covered by employers' liability insurance if they are injured due to the employer's negligence or failure to comply with health and safety law. It is therefore essential to ensure that your public liability insurance covers any trainees working for your organisation (see chapter 7).

An organisation's equal opportunities policy should cover trainee recruitment and management and include procedures for dealing with complaints of discrimination, harassment or bullying.

Volunteers

Volunteers who are unpaid (apart from reimbursement of genuine out-of-pocket expenses) and who do not receive anything else of value in return for their work are unlikely to be legally employees or workers. Volunteers who are paid anything other than reimbursement of genuine, documented out-of-pocket expenses may legally be employees or workers, become entitled to employment or workers' rights and could, for example, qualify for the national minimum wage. They may also be entitled to employment or workers' rights where they receive:
- training or perks which are not necessary for their work, or
- training or benefits necessary for their work, but where they are required to provide a specified amount or period of work (for example 'After you complete the training, you must volunteer for at least six months').

For advice on this, contact the National Centre for Volunteering Infoline on 0800 028 3304.

Organisations have a duty of care towards their volunteers, and all volunteers are owed responsibilities under the **Health and Safety at Work Act 1974** (see chapter 5). Volunteers should be insured either under employers' or public liability cover, and their actions covered by public liability insurance and/or professional indemnity insurance (see chapter 7).

The equal opportunities policy should cover volunteer recruitment and management and include procedures for dealing with complaints of discrimination, harassment or bullying. Points to consider when recruiting volunteers are discussed under *Taking on volunteers*, page 75.

Workers from abroad

The Work Permit Scheme is run by Work Permits (UK), which is part of the Home Office's Immigration and Nationality Directorate.

The aim is to allow organisations to employ, train or provide work experience to people who are not nationals of a European Economic Area (EEA)* country or Switzerland.

The European Union (EU) member states (Austria, Belgium, Denmark, Finland, France, Germany, Greece, Holland, Ireland, Italy, Luxembourg, Portugal, Spain, Sweden, and United Kingdom) together with Iceland, Liechtenstein and Norway currently (2003) comprise the EEA. The following countries will gain full membership of the EU and therefore the EEA in 2004: Cyprus, Czech Republic, Estonia, Hungary, Latvia, Lithuania, Malta, Poland, Slovakia, and Slovenia.

All EEA citizens can work in this country in any type of job. Most people from non-EEA countries require a work permit. Exceptions include:
- commonwealth citizens with at least one grandparent born in the UK
- people born in Gibraltar
- those in permit-free employment, including journalists and ministers of religion, but entry clearance is still required
- spouses and dependent children aged under 18 of people who hold work permits
- people who do not have conditions attached to their stay in the UK.

For further details contact Work Permits (UK).

Work permits

It is the employer's responsibility to apply for a work permit and pay an application fee of £95 (2003/04). Generally, Work Permits (UK) considers an application against four basic criteria:
- whether there is a genuine vacancy for an employee in Great Britain. To this end posts must be advertised within the UK and EEA before candidates from elsewhere can be considered
- what skills, qualifications and experience are necessary to do the job – with the exception of 'keyworkers' work permits are generally issued for jobs that need high level skills
- occupations that are acknowledged to be in short supply
- whether the person is suitably qualified.

There are six main categories of work permit arrangements:

Business and commercial allows employers to recruit people from outside the EEA who are going to be filling a vacancy that may otherwise be filled by a 'resident worker'.

Training and work experience enables people from outside the EEA to undertake work-based training for a professional or specialist qualification, or a period of work experience.

Sportspeople and entertainers allows employers to recruit established sportspeople, entertainers, cultural artists and some technical/support people from outside the EEA.

Internships allows students from outside the EEA studying first or higher degree courses overseas to accept an internship with an employer in this country.

General Agreement on Trade in Services (GATS) allows employees of companies that are based outside the EU to work in the UK on a service contract awarded to their employer by a UK-based organisation.

The Highly Skilled Migrant Entry Programme (HSMP) allows highly skilled individuals to migrate to the United Kingdom.

Details are available on the Work Permits (UK) website at *www.workpermits.gov.uk*. For general advice contact the general inquiry service on 0114 259 4074.

Overseas students

Students will normally have a stamp in their passports stating that they cannot work 'without the consent of the Secretary of State'.

Students studying at UK institutions who are not nationals of an EEA country can work subject to certain conditions. Neither the organisation nor the student needs to obtain permission for this, although there are conditions covering the hours and type of work they can do. Students may not:

- work more than 20 hours per week during term time unless on a placement necessary for their studies
- engage in business or self-employment
- pursue a career by filling a permanent full-time vacancy.

Restrictions on employing people from abroad

Under the **Asylum and Immigration Act 1996** it is a criminal offence to employ someone who is not entitled to work in the United Kingdom. At the time of writing (December 2003) the government was consulting employers about extending proof of eligibility to work under provisions in the **Nationality, Immigration and Asylum Act 2002.**

Employers can protect themselves by proving that, before the employment began:

- one of a number of documents which appeared to relate to the employee was shown to the employer, and

- the employer either kept the document(s) or made a copy.

The following documents are acceptable (the full list can be found in the guides published by the Home Office and Commission for Racial Equality – see below):

- a document issued by a previous employer, Contributions Agency, Inland Revenue PAYE Office, Benefits Agency or Employment Service which contains the person's national insurance number
- a birth certificate or certificate of naturalisation from the UK or another EU/EEA country
- a passport showing that the person has a right to be in the UK without conditions
- a Home Office letter indicating the person has permission to take employment
- a work permit
- a passport or national identity card issued by an EEA state.

At the time of writing (December 2003) the employee only needed to produce one of these documents, which all had equal validity.

To avoid the risk of a claim of racial discrimination, organisations should ask all potential employees to provide one of the documents.

It is a criminal offence to recruit or continue to employ someone if you discover (for example through information received from the Immigration Service or the Police, or from documentation) that the person concerned is not entitled to work.

Under the Act it is the employer who is liable. However, if the employer is a corporate body (a company or industrial and provident society), anyone responsible for its overall management can also face prosecution if the offence was committed with their consent or knowledge, or they did not take reasonable care to ensure that procedures for checking were in place.

There are two useful sets of guidance on how to comply with the Act: *Prevention from illegal working: Guidance for employers*, free from the Home Office, and *Racial equality and the Asylum and Immigration Act 1996: A guide for employers on compliance with the Race Relations Act 1976*, published by the Commission for Racial Equality (CRE). The CRE's publication includes good practice recommendations to ensure equal and fair treatment of all job applicants and prospective employees.

For further information on employing people from abroad contact the Joint Council for the Welfare of Immigrants or the Refugee Training and Employment Section of the Refugee Council.

Discrimination

Context

The European Union has established a common framework to tackle unfair discrimination in the fields of employment, self-employment, occupation and vocational training on six grounds: sex, race, sexual orientation, religion, age and disability. The framework comprises three directives: the **Race Directive 2000**, the **Employment Directive 2000**, and the **Equal Treatment Directive 1975** (amended 2002). To comply with these directives the government has:

- amended earlier race and sex discrimination legislation through the **Race Relations Act 1976 (Amendment) Regulations 2000** and the **Sex Discrimination Act 1975 (Amendment) Regulations 2003**
- introduced new legislation to ban discrimination on the grounds of religion and sexuality **Employment Equality (Religion or Belief) Regulations 2003** and **Employment Equality (Sexual Orientation) Regulations 2003**
- introduced the **Disability Discrimination Act 1995 (Amendment) Regulations 2003** which are in force from 1 October 2004
- started a consultation process to introduce new laws to ban age discrimination which will be implemented in 2006.

The **Race Relations Act 1976** makes it illegal to discriminate against anyone because of their race, colour, ethnic origin, nationality or national origin. Ethnic origin is not defined in the legislation. However, discrimination cases have clarified the position of certain groups of people. For example, Jews, Romany gypsies and Sikhs were found to be ethnic groups, whereas travellers were not. Scottish and English people are racial groups.

The **Sex Discrimination Act 1975** makes it illegal to discriminate against anyone because of their sex or (for employment purposes) marital status, or because of gender reassignment.

The **Sex Discrimination (Gender Reassignment) Regulations 1999** cover discrimination in employment and vocational training on the grounds of gender reassignment (often known as transsexuality). The regulations make it illegal to discriminate against anyone who plans to undergo, is undergoing or who has undergone gender reassignment, unless that person's sex is a genuine occupational qualification for the job.

The **Disability Discrimination Act 1995** (DDA) governs disability discrimination. The Act has been amended by the **Disability Discrimination Act 1995 (Amendment) Regulations 2003**, which come into force on 1 October 2004.

Under the Act someone is considered to have a disability if they have:

- a physical, sensory or mental impairment which has a substantial and long-term (over 12 months) adverse effect on their ability to carry out normal day-to-day activities. 'Normal day-to-day activities' include: mobility; manual dexterity; physical coordination; continence; ability to lift, carry or move everyday objects; speech, hearing or eyesight; ability to communicate; memory or ability to concentrate or understand; and perception of risk of physical danger
- a progressive illness, such as multiple sclerosis, which has any adverse effect on their ability to carry out normal day-to-day activities
- a severe disfigurement, such as a burns injury, even if it has no adverse effect on day-to-day activities.

Included in the illnesses and disabilities so far accepted as falling within the definition of the Act are AIDS, long-term depression, diabetes, epilepsy and ME.

Under the **Disability Discrimination (Blind and Partially Sighted Persons) Regulations 2003** anyone registered with the local authority as blind or partially sighted, or certified as blind or partially sighted by an ophthalmologist is defined as disabled for the purposes of the DDA. They do not have to show that the condition has a substantial adverse effect on their day-to-day activities. From October 2004 the DDA will be amended to include people with serious cancer or diagnosed as HIV+, who may not meet the statutory definition of disabled.

People who have had a disability within the meaning of the Act are protected even if they no longer have that disability. For example it would be discrimination to refuse to interview or recruit someone if they revealed they had had a disability in the past.

The **Employment Equality (Religion or Belief) Regulations 2003** outlaw discrimination in employment and vocational training on the grounds of religion, religious belief or similar philosophical belief. Religion or belief is not explicitly defined, but would include collective worship, a clear belief system, a profound belief affecting the way of life or view of the world. The regulations cover beliefs such as Paganism and Humanism and those without religious or similar beliefs.

The **Employment Equality (Sexual Orientation) Regulations 2003** outlaw discrimination in employment and vocational training on the grounds of sexuality towards people of the same sex (lesbians and gay men), the opposite sex (heterosexuals) and the same and opposite sex (bisexuals). They cover discrimination on grounds of perceived as well as actual sexuality (ie assuming – correctly or incorrectly – that someone is lesbian, gay, heterosexual or bisexual).

All the anti-discrimination provisions apply to the self-employed, contract workers and job applicants as well as employees and workers.

Discrimination is forbidden in:
- arrangements for recruiting
- shortlisting and appointment
- terms and conditions of work
- promotion and training
- pay and fringe benefits*
- redundancy
- retirement ages.

*Under the **Employment Equality (Sexual Orientation) Regulations 2003** if organisations give benefits to opposite sex unmarried partners, refusing to give them to same sex partners would be discrimination. Benefits which specify married partners only do not have to be extended to include unmarried partners.*

Sources of advice

Three organisations promote equality, in relation to sex, race and disability: the Equal Opportunities Commission (*www.eoc.org.uk*), the Commission for Racial Equality (*www.cre.gov.uk*) and the Disability Rights Commission (*www.drc-gb.org*). As well as providing advice to individuals and to employers, the Commissions have a law-enforcing role. They offer legal advice and support to some individuals in making complaints about discrimination, usually in test cases. They also have the power to carry out formal investigations, to issue non-discrimination notices and, where necessary, to seek an injunction to prevent discrimination from continuing. Each Commission has issued a Code of Practice which contains practical guidance on eliminating discrimination and promoting equality of opportunity. Although there is no legal requirement to comply with these Codes, an employment tribunal will take an organisation's non-compliance into account when determining a case of unlawful discrimination.

Equality Direct is a telephone helpline (0845 600 3444) and website service (*www.equalitydirect.org.uk*) managed by ACAS that provides advice on equality legislation and good practice. ACAS has also produced guidance on the Employment (Equality) Regulations 2003: *Sexual orientation and the workplace* and *Religion or belief in the workplace*, visit *www.acas.org.uk* or ring 08457 47 47 47 (textphone users ring 08456 06 16 00).

Definitions

Direct discrimination
This means treating someone less favourably than another person is or would be treated in the same or comparable circumstances.

Indirect discrimination
In general terms this means applying an unjustified condition in relation to selection criteria, policies, rules or any other formal practices which puts certain people at a disadvantage. The EU equal treatment directives have or will introduce a wider statutory definition of indirect discrimination as a 'provision, criterion or practice' which put people of a particular group at a disadvantage and is not justified in relation to the job. See *Context*, page 57, for the timetable for implementing these directives.

Victimisation
This means treating people less favourably because they have made a complaint under the anti-discrimination legislation or supported someone else in making a complaint.

Harassment
The **Race Relations Act 1976 (Amendment) Regulations 2003** state that harassment on the grounds of race or ethnic or national origins is unlawful. Harassment occurs when someone's actions or words, based on race or ethnic or national origins, are unwelcome and violate another person's dignity or create an environment that is intimidating, hostile, degrading, humiliating or offensive. Similar definitions exist in the **Employment Equality (Religion or Belief) Regulations 2003** and **Employment Equality (Sexual Orientation) Regulations 2003** and the **Disability Discrimination Act 1995 (Amendment) Regulations 2003** (in force from 1 October 2004). The **Equal Treatment Amendment Directive 2002** provides the first statutory definition of sexual harassment ('unwanted conduct related to the sex of a person') and sexual harassment (when 'any form of unwanted verbal, non-verbal or physical conduct of a sexual nature occurs'). The Directive has to be implemented by new legislation in the UK by October 2005, although case law has already defined sexual harassment in this way in the UK.

Not only is the employer liable for any damages arising from harassment in the workplace, the perpetrators can also be ordered to pay compensation.

The **Disability Discrimination Act 1995** (DDA) introduces specific definitions of discrimination in relation to disabled workers – **Less favourable treatment**: treating a disabled person less favourably for a reason relating to their disability and **Failing to make reasonable adjustments in relation to a disabled person**. See *Disability discrimination*, page 60.

Advertising

It is illegal to publish advertisements which might reasonably be understood to indicate an intention to discriminate. 'Advertisements' has a wide meaning including all publications, notices, radio, television and computer based publications.

Burden of proof

The **Race Relations Act 1976 (Amendment) Regulations 2003** shift the emphasis to the respondent, usually the employer, to prove that they did not carry out acts of racial discrimination or harassment on the grounds of race, or ethnic or national origin. Similar provisions exist in the **Employment Equality (Religion or Belief) Regulations 2003**, the **Employment Equality (Sexual Orientation) Regulations 2003** and the **Sex Discrimination (Indirect Discrimination and Burden of Proof) Regulations 2001.**

Genuine occupational requirement and qualification

It is possible to apply positive action in relation to race and sex. Before using any of the exceptions listed below seek legal advice, or consult the Equal Opportunities Commission or the Commission for Racial Equality.

Under the **Race Relations Act 1976 (Amendment) Regulations 2003**, any job may be restricted to people of a particular race or ethnic or national origin, if one of these characteristics is a **genuine occupational requirement** (GOR) for the job or the context within which it is carried out. This means that employers may lawfully discriminate on these grounds in recruitment, promotion or transfer to a job, in dismissal from a post, and in training for a job.

Employers will need to show that it is **proportionate** to apply the GOR to the job. In other words they will have to show that the job or its context requires the person to be from a particular racial group, for example, and the benefits of employing someone from that racial group are greater than the effects of discriminating against other racial groups.

Colour and nationality are not classed as GORs. If an organisation wants to recruit someone of a particular colour or nationality, it will have to claim that colour or nationality is a **genuine occupational qualification** in one of the following circumstances:
- to achieve authenticity, for example, in a theatre production
- to create a particular mood or ambience
- to provide personal welfare services to people of a particular colour or nationality, and that someone from the same racial group will provide the services most effectively.

Under the **Employment Equality (Sexual Orientation) Regulations 2003** staff can be recruited on the basis of their sexuality where this is a genuine occupational requirement for the post. Likewise under the **Employment Equality (Religion or Belief) Regulations 2003** people can be employed because of their religion or faith where this is a genuine occupational requirement for the post.

Guidelines

ACAS has issued the following guidelines for employers seeking to recruit under a GOR.
- GORS should have been identified at the beginning of the recruitment, training or promotion process, before the vacancy is advertised. Advertisements sent to potential applicants should clearly show that the GOR applies, and this point should be repeated throughout the selection process.
- When claiming a GOR an employer must consider for which duties an exemption is to be claimed. A GOR cannot be claimed unless some of those duties need to be carried out by someone of a specific religious belief or faith, or of a specific sexuality.
- A GOR exemption cannot be claimed in relation to specific duties if an employer already has enough employees who can carry out these duties. Where the organisation has a religious ethos, a GOR exemption cannot be claimed if the nature of the job, or its context, is not of sufficient profile to achieve the overall ethos.
- Each post for which a GOR may apply must be considered separately in terms of the duties of the job and its context.
- A GOR can only be claimed where it is necessary for the relevant duties to be carried out by someone of a particular sexuality, or religion or faith, not just because it is preferable.
- A GOR must be reassessed each time a post becomes vacant.
- The GOR cannot be used to establish a balance or quota of employees of a particular religion or faith, or sexuality.

By 2005 genuine occupation requirements will be introduced in relation to sex discrimination under the **Equal Treatment Amendment Directive 2002**. Currently there are some circumstances in which the Sex Discrimination Act allows **positive action** for one sex:

- if sex is a genuine occupational requirement. This relates mainly to the provision of decency
- schemes established specifically to train people of one sex or designed to encourage people of one sex to apply for specified types of work. The employer must show either:
- that in the past 12 months there were no employees or a very small number of that sex employed in that type of work in the local area, or
- that the training is needed because the potential trainees have not been in full-time employment due to domestic or family responsibilities.

Other race and sex legislation

The **Race Relations Amendment Act 2000** places a positive duty on public authorities to promote racial equality in the provision of services and to improve equal opportunities in employment. Although the Act is primarily aimed at public authorities, voluntary organisations working in partnership with or providing services on behalf of a public authority (either through grant aid or contracts) may need to comply. The Act requires public authorities to promote racial equality in their operations. This means they must:

- take racial equality into account in policy making, service delivery and employment practices
- monitor existing staff and applicants for jobs, promotion and training by ethnic group, and publish the results every year.

Public authorities with more than 150 staff must monitor grievances, disciplinary action, performance appraisals, training and dismissals.

The **Equal Pay Act 1970** makes it unlawful for employers to discriminate between men and women in terms of their contracts of employment, where they are doing the same work or work of equal value. It covers all contractual benefits, not just pay (including holiday entitlement, pension, child care benefits, sickness benefits and car allowances).

The Act covers both direct and indirect discrimination:

- direct discrimination occurs where the pay a woman (for example) receives is less than that of a comparable (see below) man and the reason for the lower pay is because she is a woman

- indirect discrimination in a pay system is where the pay rules may appear fair between men and women but in practice women are at a disadvantage.

Employees do not have to compare themselves to a member of the opposite sex doing exactly the same job for the same organisation. The Act also covers:

- 'like work', for example where men and women administrators work in different departments of the same organisation
- work rated as equivalent through a job evaluation scheme
- work which is of equal value. This is based on the demands of the job, and may include issues such as effort, skill and decision making.

The **Employment Act 2002** introduced an equal pay questionnaire in employment tribunal equal pay cases, making it easier for employees to request key information from their employer when deciding whether to bring a case. Although it is not compulsory to complete the questionnaire, failure to reply (or evasive replies) may be taken into account whenever a tribunal has to decide whether the Equal Pay Act is being infringed. The questionnaire is at available from *www.womenandequalityunit.gov.uk*. The Equal Opportunity's Commission's equal pay kit, which can help employers carry out a pay review, is available at *www.eoc.org.uk*

As there are data protection concerns about the questionnaire, employers are advised to obtain the consent of third party employees (those who may be used as comparators) before disclosing information about their pay. Get legal advice before seeking third party consent or disclosing information.

The Equal Opportunities Commission has published the *Code of practice on equal pay*. Failure to comply with it is not a breach of the law but the Code can be taken into account whenever a court or tribunal has to decide whether the Equal Pay Act is being infringed. Copies are available free from the *Publications and Marketing Unit, Equal Opportunities Commission, Overseas House, Quay Street, Manchester, M3 3HN* or from *www.eoc.org.uk*

Disability discrimination

The law

The Disability Discrimination Act (DDA) states that it is illegal for organisations with 15 or more employees or others working under a contract to discriminate against disabled people. The small employer exemption will be abolished on 1 October 2004 so all employers will then have to comply with the employment provisions of the Act.

In many respects, the law on disability discrimination is similar to those outlawing discrimination on grounds of sex, race, religion and belief and sexuality. For example, the DDA covers the same areas of discrimination, including recruitment, conditions of employment, promotion and training, pay and benefits and dismissal. Job applicants, the self-employed and contract workers, as well as employees, are protected by the Act. From 1 October 2004, indirect discrimination will be outlawed, so that an employer will be required to modify (or even remove) any provision, criterion or practice which puts a particular disabled employee at a disadvantage. Harassment for a reason relating to a person's disability will also be explicitly outlawed.

Changes from 1 October 2004
The important differences are as follows:
- at the time of writing (December 2003) the employment provisions of the DDA only apply to organisations employing 15 or more people (including casual workers and agency workers as well as full and part-time staff); from 1 October 2004 this exemption will no longer apply
- at the time of writing (December 2003) the Act requires employers with 15 or more workers to make reasonable changes to their premises and employment arrangements if these substantially disadvantage a disabled worker or disabled job applicant, in comparison with a non-disabled person. Again the small employer exemption will be abolished on 1 October 2004, when all employers must comply. Changes could include:
- making adjustments to premises
- allocating some of a disabled person's tasks to someone else
- altering working hours
- assigning a disabled person to a different place of work
- allowing a disabled person to be absent during working hours for rehabilitation, assessment or treatment
- providing additional training
- acquiring or modifying equipment, instructions or reference manuals
- modifying testing or assessment procedures
- providing a reader or interpreter
- providing additional supervision.

When deciding what is 'reasonable', account will be taken of the relevant factors, including the extent to which it is practicable for the employer to make the change, the costs of doing so, the resources available to the employer and the ability to raise finance. The duty to make adjustments is especially high if an existing worker has a disability or becomes disabled.

The Act covers agency staff as well as to those employed directly by the organisation. However, unless they are working for an organisation on a long-term basis, it is unlikely that it would be reasonable to expect the organisation to make extensive adjustments.

Good practice
The Act prohibits discrimination against disabled people, and organisations are required to make special arrangements for their benefit. For example, an employer could provide special training, specially adapted equipment or special conditions of service. One source of funding to help with adjustments for an existing or prospective employee is *Access to Work* (see below).

Examine your premises and equipment to make sure they are suitable for disabled workers. Some factors to consider are listed below. Seek advice either from the specific employee or worker for whom the adaptations are being made, or through a proper disability accessibility audit carried out by a trained person.

Factors to consider
- Are there potential hazards for people with restricted sight, for example unmarked pillars, unmarked glass doors, poor lighting, loose mats or holes in carpets?
- Ensure any steps have contrasting edges to make them easier to see.
- Check the parking facilities and whether there are kerb ramps in the vicinity.
- Is there level access, are gradients on ramps too steep, are there lifts accessible to wheelchair users? Don't assume that a goods lift is adequate; a wheelchair user should have the same access as anyone who is able to walk.
- Check the width and weight of doors, make sure there are handrails on steps and WCs with wheelchair access.
- Seek advice from disabled people about the suitability of the premises. Remember that a building suitable for a wheelchair user may be unsuitable or even dangerous for a blind person, so make sure you get advice from people with different disabilities.
- Assess the layout of offices for use by a disabled worker. Wheelchair users require space to manoeuvre their chairs, and visually impaired employees can be seriously injured on sharp edges of desks or filing cabinets sticking out into the room.

- Review office equipment, for example Braille equipment may be required, filing cabinets may have top drawers that are too high for a wheelchair user to reach, and chairs may be too low to get in to or out of easily.

The *Code of Practice for the elimination of discrimination in the field of employment against disabled persons or persons who have had a disability* gives practical examples of the effect of the Act. It is available from the Stationery Office (0870 600 5522) or can be downloaded from the Disability Rights Commission's (DRC) website *www.drc-gb.org*. The DRC publishes a number of other useful booklets and leaflets, many available on the website, including *A good practice guide for managers and employers*, and operates a helpline on 08457 622633 for disabled people and employers who need advice and information on all aspects of disability discrimination.

The local authority may be prepared to help with adaptations, particularly to WCs, if the organisation agrees to make them available for use by the public.

Employment schemes for disabled people
Access to Work
The Department for Work and Pensions runs this scheme to help both employed and unemployed disabled people. This includes providing financial assistance with:
- a communicator for a person who is deaf or has a hearing impairment and needs a communicator with them at an interview
- a reader or assistance at work for someone who is blind or has a visual impairment
- a support worker for someone who needs practical help either at work or in getting to work
- equipment, or adaptation to existing equipment, to suit individual needs
- adaptations to a car, or taxi fares or other transport costs for a person who cannot use public transport to get to work
- alterations to premises or the working environment to enable a specific disabled employee to be employed.

Employers are asked to make a contribution towards the cost if the person concerned is employed. Grants are not available to employers who are only *anticipating* recruiting someone with a disability.

Job Introduction Scheme
This scheme enables employers to give disabled people a 'taster' of a job if they think that the disabled person has the required skills and experience for the job but they may have concerns about practicalities. Employers receive a grant to employ a disabled person on a full or part-time

basis for up to six months. The disabled person receives the 'rate for the job' during this time.

For further details about Access to Work, Job Introduction Scheme and other matters concerning employing and retaining disabled employees contact the Disability Employment Advisor at the local JobCentre Plus office or JobCentre.

Ex-offenders
The **Rehabilitation of Offenders Act 1974** (ROA) gives people the right not to reveal certain convictions after specified periods, which vary according to the sentence and the age of the person when convicted. Such convictions are said to be **spent**. For example, for people aged 17 or over when convicted, a period of imprisonment of between six and thirty months becomes spent after ten years. Sentences longer than 30 months are never spent.

Positions where staff have access to children, vulnerable adults or money are generally exempt from the non-disclosure provisions. In these circumstances, applicants have to disclose spent convictions provided they are told that the posts are exempt under the Rehabilitation of Offenders Act. Application forms for such jobs should ask about criminal convictions and state that the post is exempt under the Rehabilitation of Offenders Act (see *Application forms*, page 68). For further information about these provisions see the Home Office leaflet: *Wiping the slate clean*. For many (but not all) exempt positions there is a statutory duty on the employer to carry out a criminal records check (see page 73). Even where there is no duty to carry out a check, it may be required by funders.

Review of Rehabilitation of Offenders Act
The Home Office has carried out a review of the ROA. The aim was to look at how to minimise the burden of disclosure for ex-offenders, while at the same time maintaining a requirement to disclose where there may be a particular risk of harm, such as work with children. The review recommended that the disclosure scheme should be simplified, with new disclosure periods being the length of the sentence plus an additional buffer period. This buffer period would vary according to whether the sentence was custodial or non-custodial, and the length of any custodial sentence. The buffer period would be one year for non-custodial sentences, two years for custodial sentences under four years, and four years for custodial sentences of four years or more.

Under new sentencing provisions for dangerous offenders in the **Criminal Justice Act 2003**, those passing sentence are able to extend the period on licence for those sexual and violent offenders who pose a particular risk. This will automatically extend the period in which they are required to disclose the conviction. Any job providing the opportunity for considerable harm will continue to be excepted from the disclosure scheme, ie any applicant will be required to disclose all their previous convictions regardless of when they were committed.

The *Report of the Review of the Rehabilitation of Offenders Act* is accessible from the Home Office website (*www.homeoffice.gov.uk*). The government supports most of the review's recommendations and at the time of writing (December 2003) proposed to publish a Bill to reform the 1974 Act as soon as parliamentary time allowed.

Age discrimination

The government must outlaw age discrimination in employment and training by 2 December 2006 to meet its obligations under the European Directive on Equal Treatment in Employment. Until then, the government recommends that employers comply with the voluntary code: *Age diversity in employment: a code of practice*.

Code of practice

The code describes good practice in six aspects of employment. Each section contains guidance, indicators of success and case studies.

Recruit on the basis of the skills and abilities needed to do the job, for example avoid setting unnecessary standards for experience, personal qualities or qualifications; don't include age limits or age ranges in job adverts; and don't use phrases that imply age restrictions, such as 'young graduates'. Consider different ways of advertising posts: younger people are more likely to consult careers services, job centres and newspapers, and older people rely more on community and business networks.

Select the best candidates on merit, for example focus on potential applicants' skills and abilities, form an interviewing panel comprising people of a mixed age range and avoid making age an integral part of the application process. Ensure people on the panel are trained in interviewing techniques and equal opportunities selection.

Promote on the ability, or demonstrated potential to do the job, for example advertise promotion opportunities through open competition.

Encourage everyone to take advantage of suitable training and development opportunities, for example regularly review staff training and development needs, ensure that age is not a barrier to taking up opportunities and ensure that different learning styles and needs are addressed when training is delivered. Monitor participation in training and development to make sure that all age groups are involved.

Base redundancy decisions on objective, job-related criteria, for example look at flexible options such as part-time working, job sharing or career breaks and short-term contracts when considering alternatives to redundancy.

Ensure that retirement schemes are fairly applied, base the policy on business needs; give individuals as much choice as possible; evaluate the loss to the organisation of skills and abilities and plan how to replace these; use flexible retirement schemes; make pre-retirement support available.

Copies of *Age diversity in employment: Code of practice* are available from the Age Positive Team, Department for Work and Pensions, Room W8d, Moorfoot, Sheffield S1 4PQ (website *www.agepositive.gov.uk*)

Government proposals

The following government proposals to implement new age discrimination law are contained in the consultation document: *Equality and diversity: Age matters*, available from *www.dti.gov.uk*

It will be illegal for employers to set **retirement ages** for employees, unless justified. The government is seeking views on whether employers should, in exceptional circumstances, be allowed to set a retirement age, and on whether it should set a default age of 70 at or after which employers could require staff to leave without having to justify their decision. Employers would still be able to employ people aged over 70.

Recruitment, selection and promotion decisions will not normally be based on age, unless this can be justified.

Employers will be allowed to continue to provide **pay and non-pay benefits** based on length of service or experience if they can justify doing so.

Employees would be able to seek redress for **unfair dismissal** at any age apart from retirement at an employer's justifiable mandatory retirement age, or any default age set out in legislation (see above). The government plans to change the way that financial compensation is calculated so that the basic award will no longer be based on the employee's age. The calculation of the award will continue to take account of the employee's length of service, which will still be limited to 20 years.

Some of the age related pay aspects of the **statutory redundancy payments scheme** will be removed (see *Redundancy*, in chapter 4).

Equal opportunities: good practice

Organisations should adopt an equal opportunities policy to ensure that no worker or job applicant, volunteer or trainee suffers direct or indirect discrimination, harassment or victimisation.

Equal opportunities employers will ensure that:
- both paid and unpaid posts are advertised to encourage applications from a wide variety of communities
- applicants for both paid and unpaid work are treated fairly
- no member of staff experiences unfair or unlawful discrimination
- the training needs for specific groups of people are recognised
- disabled people's needs are met through reasonable adaptations to premises, policies and procedures and through the purchase of specific equipment
- the equal opportunities employment policy is regularly monitored and reviewed.

Monitoring effectiveness

It is essential to establish systems to monitor the effectiveness of an equal opportunities policy. Begin by analysing the composition of your workforce to identify posts or departments where people likely to suffer discrimination are overrepresented (in poorly paid jobs) or underrepresented (in more senior posts). The policy should state how often this analysis should be carried out, and require systems to record the composition of:
- those applying for posts
- those being shortlisted
- people being appointed

- employees seeking career training and development
- employees seeking promotion
- employees being promoted
- employees seeking redress under the grievance procedure
- employees against whom the grievance procedure is used
- employees against whom disciplinary action is taken
- employees dismissed
- employees made redundant.

The policy should also require systems to record how people learn about vacant posts, so that the procedures for advertising can be monitored. It is also important to monitor the composition of volunteers, trainees and self-employed workers.

Monitoring should be based on a system of records covering race, gender, age and disability. You may wish to discuss with staff and unions whether to monitor other characteristics, such as religion and sexuality. All this information is defined as 'sensitive' under the Data Protection Act (see chapter 9) and unless it is going to be totally anonymous and not linked to any individual, an employer can collect it only with *explicit* consent from the individual.

Some voluntary organisations adopt a system of self-classification by asking 'How would you describe your race or ethnic origin?' Others have introduced a standard classification system within the organisation to enable them to monitor and compare composition of membership, management committees and service users as well as employees. It is important to involve staff and users in the process of introducing a standard ethnic classification system.

There are many systems for classifying race. The Commission for Racial Equality recommends using the same categories as those used in the 2001 Census (see overleaf). This will enable you to compare the composition of your workforce and users more easily with the local population.

Whatever system is used, people should be told why monitoring is necessary and that participation is voluntary. The names of those being monitored must remain confidential, and information should be stored in a statistical form only, otherwise an employer can collect it only with *explicit* consent from the individual.

2001 Census classification

The question used in the Census was 'What is your ethnic group?', with the instructions: 'Choose one section from A to E, then tick the appropriate box to indicate your cultural background'.

A **White**
British
Irish
Any other White background, please write in

B **Mixed**
White and Black Caribbean
White and Black African
White and Asian
Any other Mixed background, please write in

C **Asian or Asian British**
Indian
Pakistani
Bangladeshi
Any other Asian background, please write in

D **Black or Black British**
Caribbean
African
Any other Black background, please write in

E **Chinese or other ethnic group**
Chinese
Any other, please write in

Data protection

Organisations must be aware of the implications of the **Data Protection Act 1998**. In particular, monitoring for equal opportunities purposes requires the handling of 'sensitive' personal information. See *Data protection*, in chapter 9 for further information. The Information Commissioner's *Employment practices data protection code: Part 2 records management*, available from *www.informationcommissioner.gov.uk*, includes a chapter on record keeping for equal opportunities purposes.

Flexible ways of working

One method of increasing access to work for employees, trainees and volunteers is by introducing flexible working arrangements.

The standard work pattern of an eight-hour day, five-day, 40-hour week discriminates against some people, including parents, other carers, disabled people, people who wish to retrain, and those with other commitments, including for example business, political, religious or social.

Parents of children aged under six or disabled children aged under 18 who have worked for an employer continuously for at least 26 weeks have the right to apply to work flexibly, and their employers have a duty to consider these requests seriously. For further details see *Flexible working*, in chapter 4.

Setting standards and dealing with complaints

The equal opportunities policy should ensure that volunteers, trainees and self-employed people are aware of the standards of behaviour acceptable when dealing with anyone connected with the organisation. Volunteers and trainees guilty of discriminatory behaviour should face disciplinary action.

Contracts with self-employed people should give the organisation the right to terminate their services in the event of proven inappropriate behaviour.

Trainees and volunteers should have access to a grievance procedure if they consider they are being discriminated against, harassed or treated unfairly.

Bullying and harassment

Employers have legal responsibilities to prevent bullying and harassment at work. First, they have a duty of care for all their workers. Allowing sustained bullying or harassment to take place could contravene the **Health and Safety at Work Act 1974**. Under this Act, employers must take reasonable care to ensure health is not placed at risk through excessive and sustained levels of stress arising from the way in which work is organised, and the way people deal with each other at work (see chapter 5). In some cases, employers who fail to tackle harassment and bullying in the workplace may be discriminating under the sex, race and disability discrimination acts and the **Employment Equality (Religion or Belief)** and **Employment Equality (Sexual Orientation) Regulations 2003**. By 2006 there will also be protection against discrimination on the grounds of age. The **Criminal Justice and Public Order Act**

1994 created a criminal offence of 'intentional harassment', whether in the workplace or elsewhere, and harassment may also be a criminal offence under the **Protection from Harassment Act 1997**.

Under recent legislation, not only are the employers liable for any damages arising from types of harassment in the workplace, the perpetrators can also be ordered to pay compensation (see *Discrimination*, page 57).

The **Employment Equality (Religion or Belief) Regulations 2003** and **Employment Equality (Sexual Orientation) Regulations 2003** have provided the following statutory definition of harassment: '... unwanted conduct that violates a person's dignity or creates an intimidating, hostile, degrading, humiliating or offensive environment for them'.

Bullying and harassment are not always face to face activities. They may occur through written communications, e-mail and by phone. Not only are they unacceptable on moral grounds, the activities can severely harm an organisation through, for example, poor performance, absenteeism, high turnover of staff and a damaged reputation and credibility with users.

Many organisations are now developing policies to prevent bullying and harassment and to deal with complaints. As far as possible everyone in the organisation should be involved in the development of the policy, including paid staff, volunteers, the trade union, management committee and users.

Policy checklist

The following checklist provides points to consider when developing a policy:
- a statement of commitment from senior management
- an acknowledgement that bullying and harassment are or may be problems for the organisation
- a clear statement that bullying and harassment will not be tolerated
- examples of unacceptable behaviour. Although it is easy to agree on what constitutes extreme forms of bullying and harassment, it is the more subtle actions that are most difficult to define as unacceptable. ACAS and the TUC provide the following suggestions:
  - spreading malicious rumours or insults (especially on the grounds of race, sex, sexuality, disability or religion or belief)
  - ridiculing or demeaning someone – picking on them or setting them up to fail
  - unfair treatment
  - shouting at someone

- exclusion or victimisation
- overbearing supervision or other misuses of power or position
- unwelcome comments, actions or advances of a sexual nature
- making unfounded threats or comments about job security
- deliberately undermining a competent worker by overloading and constant criticism
- intentionally blocking promotion or training opportunities
- the scope of the policy. It should be made clear that bullying and harassment of users, volunteers, trainees, self-employed workers and members of the management committee as well as paid staff will not be tolerated
- make clear that employees have a duty to comply with the policy and that failure to do so is a disciplinary offence
- the measures the organisation will take to prevent bullying and harassment
- the responsibilities of supervisors and managers
- describe the investigation procedures (including timescales for action)
- describe the grievance and disciplinary procedures (including timescales for action)
- allow people to complain to someone of their own sex, race, age group and, where relevant, experience of a disability
- allow people to be represented throughout the process by a trade union official, an employee representative or friend
- ensure that the person dealing with the complaint is independent of the situation
- guarantee confidentiality and protection against victimisation or retaliation
- ensure that all employees are told about the policy
- ensure that those who have responsibility for dealing with complaints are properly trained
- ensure that an adviser or counsellor is available to support employees suffering harassment or bullying
- allow for regular reviews to monitor the effectiveness of the procedures.

For further details see the ACAS publication *Bullying and harassment at work: a guide for managers and employers* (available from ACAS publications, telephone 01455 852225) and the TUC leaflet *Bullied at work? Don't suffer in silence* (available from the TUC Know Your Rights Hotline on 0870 600 4882).

For further information on sexual harassment see the Equal Opportunity Commission's guidance *Dealing with sexual harassment* (available from *www.eoc.org.uk*).

Making an appointment

The legal requirements

The following sections describe the law and good practice in relation to recruiting staff and then set out possible procedures for appointing self-employed people and volunteers.

During recruitment and selection it is illegal to discriminate against anyone on the grounds of their:

- racial group, sex, religion or other belief or sexuality (unless one or more of these factors is a genuine occupational requirement for the post – see *Discrimination,* page 57)
- disability (unless this is justified) if the employer has 15 or more employees or other workers (this exemption will no longer apply from 1 October 2004)
- membership or non-membership of a trade union.

It is illegal to employ someone who is not entitled to work in the UK.

Under the **Race Relations Amendment Act 2000** voluntary organisations working in partnership with or providing services on behalf of a public authority (either through grant aid or contracts), may have a duty to promote racial equality to improve equal opportunities in employment. This includes examining procedures for staff recruitment (see *Other race and sex legislation,* page 60)

As recruitment may involve collecting 'sensitive' information about candidates, employers should also be aware of the requirements of the **Data Protection Act 1998.** See the Information Commissioner's *Employment practices data protection code: Part 1 recruitment and selection* available from *www.informationcommissioner.gov.uk*

Reviewing posts

As soon as an employee gives notice, review the job description. Its content should be based on the needs of the organisation, not the previous postholder's skills and qualifications.

Examine each vacant post to see whether its requirements fulfil the genuine occupational requirement criteria to limit recruitment to people of a specific racial group, sex, religion or other belief, or sexuality (see page 59). Review the composition of the workforce to determine whether it is appropriate to encourage people of a particular racial group or groups, sex, religion or belief or sexuality to apply (see page 59) – but note that under these provisions, people can *only* be encouraged to apply. Their race, sex, religion or other belief or sexuality cannot be

taken into account in shortlisting or appointing. Consider whether the post is suitable for a flexible working arrangement, see *Flexible working,* in chapter 4. Also see whether it is particularly appropriate for a disabled worker and what adjustments or adaptations could reasonably be made to ensure that disabled people are not disadvantaged. It is not unlawful to say that a particular position is open only to disabled people (as there is no law making it illegal to discriminate against able-bodied people). However it would be unlawful to say that a post was only open to people with a particular disability.

Selection panels

The composition of selection panels depends on the nature of the job and the organisation. They could include people who will be working closely with the new worker, and members of the management committee. Some equal opportunities policies state that each panel must include at least one woman and one black or minority ethnic person, and that if a disabled person applies, should include someone with experience or specialist knowledge of that disability. The policy should require that panel members have training in interviewing techniques and equal opportunities law and good practice. Some organisations invite people from outside the organisation with specialist knowledge of equal opportunities to take part in shortlisting as observers, advisers or participants. Generally in the voluntary sector most panels have between three and five members.

The recruitment process

Making an appointment is a lengthy process. Time will be needed for the panel to:

- finalise the job description and person specification
- decide whether the person specification criteria will be assessed through the application form, interview, tests, examples of work, references or in some other way
- produce an application form (if used) and background information for enquirers
- advertise
- shortlist on the basis of the person specification criteria
- make arrangements for any tests or other assessments
- draw up the interview procedure and questions and decide who will ask them
- prepare for the interview
- interview the candidates (generally allow one day per five or six candidates)
- take up references (this might be done before interview)
- if necessary, carry out medical, criminal records and other pre-employment checks.

From advertisement to starting date could therefore take at least ten weeks:

week 1	advertisement appears
week 4	closing date
week 4/5	shortlisting
week 6	interviews
	offer of appointment made verbally, and accepted
	offer made in writing
	candidate hands in notice to current employer
week 10	employee starts (if four weeks' notice given)

If the job offer is conditional on the employer receiving satisfactory references, medical check and/or criminal records check, the process could take much longer. An employer must be satisfied from evidence that the person is entitled to work in the UK. One method of ensuring that all applicants are treated equally is to ask this of all applicants. Candidates should be asked to provide evidence at interview or before an offer of work is made – because once the offer of work is made and accepted, the employer could be in breach of its duty not to employ a person who is not entitled to work in the UK. See *Restrictions on employing people abroad*, page 56.

Job descriptions

All employees should have a job description outlining the tasks and responsibilities involved in their work. If it forms part of the contract of employment, any change will have to be achieved through a variation of contract procedure, usually this means obtaining the employee's agreement..

The job description should include:
- the job title
- the main purpose of the job
- to whom the employee is responsible
- for whom the employee is responsible
- main working contacts
- the key areas of the job
- the main tasks of each key area
- hours of work, including any requirement to work outside normal office hours*
- main conditions of employment, for example annual leave entitlement.*

These are conditions of employment and will always form part of the contract. They are not necessarily part of the job description, although when producing a job description for recruitment purposes, they may be included with it.

Job sharers

It is essential to include information about how responsibilities will be shared in job descriptions for job sharers (see *Flexible working*, in chapter 4). If some areas are specific to one post, this must be absolutely clear. List shared work areas under a separate heading.

Person specifications

A person specification describes the knowledge, abilities, skills, attitudes and experience needed for the post, and should be based on the tasks outlined in the job description.

All specifications should state the minimum qualifications and experience needed to be eligible, which should have been examined to ensure that they are necessary. For example, is an academic qualification or previous experience in similar employment essential? Other qualities may be just as important, for example personal knowledge of a community, or personal experience of a disability.

Assess all criteria to ensure they are not indirectly discriminatory on the basis of racial group (including nationality and national origin), sex religion or other belief, or sexuality, and to ensure they do not discriminate unjustifiably against people with a particular disability (see *Discrimination*, page 57). For example a requirement to have GCSE maths indirectly discriminates against people who are not from Britain, because other countries do not have GCSE exams. A requirement to have 'maths to GCSE standard' is not discriminatory.

Application forms

Examine the organisation's application form to ensure that it is clear, well structured, and asks only for information relevant to the particular post being recruited.

It is far easier to compare applications without bias if the information is presented in the same way. It may therefore be better to use a standard form for the post rather than asking for a curriculum vitae (CV) and letter of application.

Application forms should include:
- name (ask for 'first name' rather than 'Christian name'. Some organisations ask just for initials, to reduce the possibility of discrimination on the grounds of sex)
- address, home and work telephone numbers and e-mail address (ask whether it is acceptable to contact the candidate at work)
- details of current or most recent employment, duties involved, date of joining and leaving, if appropriate
- details of past employment

- education and qualifications of relevance to the post
- relevant experience (paid and voluntary, and general life experience)
- when the applicant would be able to take up the post
- names and addresses of two referees, one of whom should generally be the current or most recent employer, or college or school (ask whether the current employer may be contacted before interview and whether the applicant wishes to be informed before referees are contacted)
- details of whether the applicant requires a work permit or is otherwise subject to immigration control
- a question asking whether the person is disabled and would require any adaptations to attend for interview or to carry out the work as described in the job
- if the post is exempt under the Rehabilitation of Offenders Act (see *Ex-offenders*, page 62) the form should include the statement: 'This post is exempt under the Rehabilitation of Offenders Act 1974 and you are required to reveal all convictions, even those which are spent'. Because the application may be seen by people who do not have a right to know information about convictions, the applicant should be told to provide details of all convictions separately, in a sealed envelope addressed to the person in charge of the recruitment process
- if the post is not exempt but the organisation is going to ask about convictions, the form should ask whether the person has any criminal convictions and should include the statement 'You should not reveal any convictions which are spent under the Rehabilitation of Offenders Act 1974.' Again, the applicant should be told to provide the information in a sealed envelope.

Allow enough space for employment details and a general statement in support of the application. Make clear that applicants should address their answers to the person specification; an effective method may be to include the headings on the application form. Do not ask irrelevant questions which could lead to discrimination, such as marital status, place of birth or details of dependants.

Questions on date of birth and age may discourage younger and older people from applying. Is such information necessary? For example do you operate a compulsory employees' insurance or pension scheme for which age is a criterion? It may be more appropriate to include these questions on a separate monitoring sheet (see below) to see whether your organisation treats younger and older people fairly. However, in reality it is possible to detect the age of an applicant from education, qualifications and employment history. If questions are asked about age directly or from which age can be identified indirectly, take care not to use age as a discriminatory factor, and remember that age discrimination becomes illegal in 2006.

Take special care to ensure that you are not discriminating against any disabled person who wants to apply. If asked to do so, make reasonable adjustments such as providing an application form in a different format or allowing a candidate to submit an application in a different format, for example typewritten, by telephone, on tape or by e-mail.

Monitoring applications

A form to monitor the breakdown of applicants, in respect of ethnic origin, gender, age and disability should be included in application forms (see *Monitoring effectiveness,* page 64). Some organisations include questions relating to religion and sexuality. All these questions should be on a separate sheet, used only for monitoring purposes. Make clear why you are asking the questions, that the information is confidential, and that completion of the form is voluntary and failure to do so will not affect the success of an application.

If the sheet is not totally separate from the application form (ie there is a possibility an individual could be identified) there are likely to be implications under the **Data Protection Act 1998**. In particular, employers may need the individual's explicit consent when handling 'sensitive' information. Also, it must not be possible to identify the individual from the answers on the sheet, for example if there is only one black applicant for a job, it may be possible to identify who filled in the form. For further information see chapter 9.

Job advertisements

Review the way posts are advertised, to ensure that people from socially excluded groups are likely to become aware of vacancies.

This may involve the use of journals targeted at specific groups, for example *The Voice, Caribbean Times, Asian Times, New Nation* and *the Pink Paper*, local organisations including places of worship and radio stations, and local publications such as a talking newspaper or the local disability organisation's newsletter. The Commission for Racial Equality has a list of newspapers serving the black community on its website. *Disability Now* or the *Disability Times* attract disabled readers as does the website *www.Jobability.com*. It is good practice to inform the Disability Employment Adviser at the local JobCentre Plus, JobCentres and the local careers service of all vacancies.

Also remember the voluntary sector networks including the magazines *Voluntary Voice* (published by the London Voluntary Service Council), *Voluntary Sector* (published by NCVO) and *Third Sector*. Many councils for voluntary service produce newsletters and will include an advertisement.

Adverts should be available in a wide range of formats, for example large print, tape, disk or e-mail.

Think carefully about the wording. It is important not only to attract good applicants, but also to deter unsuitable enquirers and avoid wasting their time and yours.

Advertisements should include:
- name of the organisation
- job title (and department, if appropriate)
- brief description of the job
- brief summary of skills, knowledge, experience and qualifications needed
- whether the post is open only to women or men, or only to a particular racial group or group based on religion or other belief, or only people of a particular sexuality, and if so the section of the relevant legislation under which the post is advertised (see *Discrimination*, page 57). Get legal advice before advertising a post under this legislation, as advertising inappropriately can lead to people who are prevented from applying making claims of discrimination
- salary (and salary scale if appropriate)
- hours, stating whether full or part-time and any flexible working arrangements
- whether the post is open for job sharing
- whether the post is intended to be permanent or fixed-term
- name, address, telephone number and/or e-mail address of the contact for further information and application forms
- closing date for applications
- date (s) when interviews will be held, if this is known
- a statement that an equal opportunities policy is operated
- any further information, for example whether applications are particularly welcome from certain sections of the community (see *Genuine occupational requirement and qualification*, page 59)
- if the organisation is registered with the Charity Commission, a statement to this effect.

Some funders specify that organisations must publish the source of funding in all publicity material, including job advertisements. Check your conditions of grant aid to see whether this requirement applies.

Information for enquirers

Enquirers should be sent a copy of the job description, person specification and a statement of the equal opportunities policy, together with details of the main conditions of service (see *Statement of employment particulars*, in chapter 4) including:
- salary and salary scale, including any cut-off point for starting salary
- method and frequency of pay
- hours of work including any flexible working arrangements
- place of work, and whether this can be varied
- overtime: whether this is paid or time off is given in lieu of pay for extra hours worked
- annual leave in addition to bank holidays
- pension scheme, if any, and whether it is contributory or non-contributory
- the name of any recognised union(s)
- maternity/parental/adoption leave arrangements if these are more favourable than statutory entitlements
- any other points, for example car allowance or removal expenses.

Let candidates know the interview date. Be sensitive when arranging interviewing and selection dates to avoid significant religious times (for example Friday afternoons).

Enquirers should also receive details of the organisation, ideally including a copy of the latest annual report (and charities have to provide at least the statutory annual report(s) to anyone who asks for them, see chapter 6), and details of funding sources (this may be particularly important given the uncertainty of voluntary sector funding).

Shortlisting

Before shortlisting, the monitoring forms should be separated from the application forms and analysed. The results should be stored for future reference.

Shortlist soon after the closing date. All members of the selection panel should have copies of the job description and person specification. It is generally good practice for them to shortlist separately before meeting or holding a conference call to decide on the final shortlist. The decision to shortlist a candidate must be based on whether that person fulfils the knowledge, skills, attitudes and experience requirements detailed in the person specification.

The panel should record why each applicant has or has not been shortlisted. An applicant who feels discriminated against on grounds of race, sex, sexuality, religion or belief or disability, or who has been refused employment on the grounds of membership or non-membership of a trade union has up to three months to complain to an employment tribunal. Shortlisting forms should therefore be kept for a minimum of three months. The tribunal can grant an extension, so it is advisable, as well as good practice, to keep the forms for 12 months.

Invite the shortlisted people to an interview, and let others know they have not been successful. If necessary, ask for the candidates' consent if references are to be taken up before interview, then write to the referees, enclosing a stamped addressed envelope and a copy of the job description and person specification. Even if references are taken up at this stage they should not be read until after the interviews have taken place and a decision has been made, unless the referees have been asked to provide essential information which will be used as a factor in the selection process.

Letters to interviewees should state:
- the date and time of the interview, and its approximate length
- where it is to be held and how to get there
- whether travel expenses will be paid
- who will be on the interview panel
- whether any tests will be included and if so, their nature and length
- whether there is more than one interview stage
- that referees have been contacted (if appropriate)
- that disabled applicants should contact you to discuss any adjustments, or other help they require to attend the interview or take part in testing.

Ask candidates to confirm the time as soon as possible.

Interviews

It is sometimes useful for candidates to visit the organisation before a formal interview. This should generally be entirely for their benefit; the visit should not form part of the selection process unless this is made explicit and all candidates visit.

Planning the interview

It is essential to plan interviews well. If any candidate needs an interpreter or signer arrange this as early as possible; ask the candidate if there is an interpreter or signer they would prefer. The whole panel should agree a list of questions relating to the skills and qualities appropriate to each key task: each member should ask a set of linked questions. Look at the individual forms to see if there are specific questions that should be asked.

You should never ask questions on the following topics in an interview: marital status, sexuality, partner's occupation, number of children and domestic arrangements. Questions about trade union activities should only be asked if explicitly mentioned in the job description. If the job involves evening or weekend work you should ask all the candidates about their availability.

Choose one member of the panel to chair the interviews and decide who will answer candidates' questions on specific topics. Ensure that someone on the panel is authorised to give information about terms and conditions.

Make sure someone is available to welcome applicants, and that there is a suitable waiting area with access to a toilet. If the interviews are running late (which would be bad practice) let the candidates know as soon as they arrive. Have material prepared for any skills being tested (for example bookkeeping, writing or wordprocessing). This should be the same for each candidate, unless they need to be adapted for a disabled candidate.

Organise arrangements for paying expenses, if appropriate.

Tests

A presentation or a test may most effectively assess some aspects of the person specification. If this is the case, make sure applicants are aware of the nature of the presentation or test, how long they will have and what is being tested. If a test involves use of a computer, wherever possible make sure the applicant is able to use a program they know.

Conduct of the interview

The aim of the interview is to assess the applicant's suitability for the job in relation to the person specification.

Ask each candidate the same core questions, give them the same tests and allocate each an equal amount of time for their interview. However, disabled candidates may need more time if, for example, they use an interpreter or signer to communicate with the panel. The chair should inform each candidate of the time allocated and should keep track of time during the interview, intervening if necessary to avoid overrunning. In exceptional circumstances it may be necessary to conclude the interview if it is running significantly beyond the allocated time.

Allow at least ten minutes between each interview for the panel to make notes, but wait until all the interviews have been completed before discussing the candidates. Remember to include a proper break for lunch.

Whoever is chairing the interviews should welcome the candidate, introduce the panel members, outline the structure and say the panel will be making notes. Allow the candidate to do most of the talking and avoid questions that can produce one-word answers. If candidates seem particularly shy, unconfident or unclear about what is being asked, the person asking the question or the chair should restate the question or encourage the candidate to provide more information. Always allow time for the candidate to ask questions and do not let the interviews overrun.

Tell candidates when and how they will be informed of the panel's decision.

Selection

Every member of the panel should make notes on each candidate during and after the interview. One method is to have a list of the skills, qualities and type of experience needed and record whether each has been partly, fully or not met. Candidates must always be assessed on the selection criteria, and not against each other. Each member of the panel must be able to justify individual decisions with evidence. Under the **Data Protection Act 1998** applicants are entitled to view any interview notes which contain personal data about them. Make sure the panel is aware of this and that any defamatory or discriminatory comments could lead to claims of unfair treatment in the civil courts.

Once all the interviews are over, the panel should discuss the applicants. Sometimes one candidate stands out and everyone will agree that person should be offered the job. At other times there will need to be considerable discussion before a decision can be reached. If references have been taken up this is the time to read them.

Contact the successful candidate as soon as possible. A telephone call should be immediately followed by a formal offer in writing. If the offer is subject to any conditions, make this clear in the telephone call and subsequent letter (see *Letter of appointment,* below). Let the unsuccessful candidates know as soon as possible and ask them if they want you to keep their application for future vacancies (if appropriate) or have their details totally removed from file. If they want you to keep their information, tell them how long it will be kept for.

It is important to record why people were not selected, for equal opportunities monitoring. However, you must be able to justify keeping any personal data following the

interviews as being relevant to and necessary for the recruitment process itself, or for dealing with any challenges to the decision by an unsuccessful candidate. Make sure that any personal data kept is securely stored.

As with shortlisting, a candidate who feels discriminated against on grounds of race, sex, sexuality, religion or belief or disability has up to three months to apply to an employment tribunal, (see *Discrimination,* page 57) Interview records should therefore be kept for a minimum of three months. The tribunal can grant an extension, so it is advisable, as well as good practice, to keep the records for 12 months.

If the panel cannot reach a decision, consider why. In some cases there may genuinely be two or more suitable candidates, and it may be useful to re-interview them. Alternatively, the panel may have been unable to gather adequate evidence because of the questions asked, in which case some or all of the candidates could be re-interviewed about those matters, or the information could be obtained by a phone conversation. Perhaps none of the applicants may have been suitable, or the panel may have realised that they disagree about what and who they are looking for. If so it may be necessary to re-advertise. If this is the case, look again at the job description, person specification and advertisement. Would they attract the right candidates?

Letter of appointment

The letter of appointment forms part of the contract of employment (see chapter 4) and should include the following:

- starting date, subject to any conditions being met
- starting salary
- job title
- any conditions of appointment, for example whether it is subject to a satisfactory medical check, references, criminal records check (see below), and the fact that the offer of employment is conditional on these being satisfactory
- the obligation to provide documents required to comply with the **Asylum and Immigration Act 1996** (see *Restrictions on employing people from abroad,* page 56) and the fact that the offer of employment is conditional on the person providing these and having no restrictions on their right to work in the UK (or is conditional on the employer obtaining a work permit to enable the person to take up the post)
- a request for any further information or necessary documentation, for example a P45 (see chapter 4)
- a request for confirmation in writing that the person accepts the offer (and any conditions included in it) and the date they expect to start provided that all conditions have been met.

Criminal record checks

Under the **Protection of Children Act 1999** and the **Criminal Justice and Court Services Act 2000** it is an offence to offer paid or voluntary employment that involves regular contact with children or vulnerable adults to anyone who has been convicted of certain specified offences, or who is included on lists of people considered unsuitable for such work kept by the Department for Education and Skills (DfES) and the Department of Health (DH). The Criminal Records Bureau (CRB) deals with checks under the Acts.

There are three levels of check.

Standard Disclosures are primarily for posts (both paid and voluntary) that involve working with people aged under 18 or vulnerable adults, or some posts involving money or administration of the law. They contain details of all convictions held on the Police National Computer (PNC) including current and spent convictions, as well as details of any cautions, reprimands or final warnings. If the position involves working with children, the Disclosure will indicate whether information is held on lists of those banned from working with children, maintained by the DH and DfES. The Disclosure also includes information held by the DH of those considered unsuitable for working with adults.

An **Enhanced Disclosure** is for posts involving a far greater degree of contact with children or vulnerable adults, for example jobs involving caring for, supervising, training or being in sole charge of such people. It contains the same information as the Standard Disclosure, along with non-conviction information held on local police records if that is seen as relevant to the position sought.

The fees were £24 for a Standard Disclosure and £29 an Enhanced Disclosure in 2003 and £28/£33 from 1 April 2004. There is no charge for checks on volunteers.

At the time of writing (December 2003) **Basic Disclosures** were not available and no date had been set for their introduction. This Disclosure will detail convictions held on the PNC that are 'unspent' under the Rehabilitation of Offenders Act. It will be applied for and issued only to individuals on request. Organisations will be able to ask any applicant who is offered employment to obtain a Basic Disclosure before that job is offered, but the applicant will be under no obligation to show it to a potential employer. The Disclosure will not be job specific and may be used more than once.

Application to the CRB

Application is made to the Criminal Records Bureau by the individual, and applications for Enhanced and Standard Disclosures must be countersigned by a named representative of a body registered with the CRB. Organisations that are likely either to employ people to care for children or other vulnerable groups, or to be countersigning applications by other organisations, which do, are able to register. There is a list of registered bodies and umbrella bodies on the CRB website.

It is a criminal offence to disclose information obtained under these procedures except for specified purposes.

For further information visit the CRB website *www.disclosure.gov.uk* or ring the CRB Information Line on 0870 90 90 811.

Organisations must be aware that screening is not a foolproof way of protecting vulnerable people. Only a minority – around 10% – of the estimated number of child sex offenders has a relevant criminal record. All organisations involved in caring for young people or vulnerable adults should develop policies and procedures to reduce the risk of abuse and increase the likelihood of it being discovered if it does occur. See the Home Office publication: *Caring for young people and the vulnerable? Guidance for preventing abuse of trust*, available from *www.homeoffice.gov.uk*

Probationary periods

Some contracts allow for probationary periods – often of three or six months – to enable the employer and employee to assess how they are getting along in their new employment. An employee has all statutory rights during the probationary period, and all contractual rights unless the contract specifies otherwise. For example the contract might specify a reduced period of notice during the probationary period and/or a simplified disciplinary procedure.

If employment is subject to a probationary period it is usual to make this clear in the letter of appointment, and it must be made clear in the contract. At the end of the probationary period either the employment will be confirmed, the probationary period extended (normally for a further four weeks) or the employment terminated. The probationary period can be extended only if the contract allows for this. If employment is terminated at the end of the probationary period notice must be given as required by statute (see chapter 4) or by the contract, whichever is longer.

For details of managing a probationary period see 'Managing the recruitment process' in *Just about managing?*

Taking on freelance and self-employed workers and consultants

It is important to ensure that your equal opportunities policy includes procedures for appointing freelance and self-employed people and consultants. (A self-employed worker is one who runs their own business. A freelance is someone who does not run their own business, but does work for which they are not your employee. A consultant may be a freelance or self-employed person, or may be a partnership or company.)

Some small pieces of work may not justify the expense of advertising and staff time involved in making an appointment. It may then be necessary to specify the size and type of contracts that do not have to be openly advertised. However, any more informal processes used should be monitored to safeguard against possible discrimination. In any event, always ask freelances, self-employed people or consultancy businesses for examples of previous work and for references.

Contracts

Freelance and self-employed workers are not employees, but they are protected under the employment provisions of the equal opportunities legislation, and those who are not genuinely self-employed people are likely to be included within the definition of 'workers' (see *Some definitions*, page 48). If so they will be entitled to some rights, including those relating to the minimum wage and paid holidays.

A contract with a self-employed worker need not be complicated. It could simply be in the form of an exchange of letters between the organisation and the worker. Some self-employed workers have their own contracts. It is in everyone's interests to ensure that responsibilities are clear.

The following *should* be included in a contract.

Names of the organisation and the worker.
Work to be done. It is imperative that the contract is clear about the work required. This information may be in a separate brief to which you can refer. It needs to be as specific as possible to reduce the possibility of misunderstandings, and for long pieces of work should include provision for regular reviews to ensure the brief remains appropriate and work is being done to the required quantity and quality.
Start and completion dates. Agree a completion date for a specific piece of work. For more open-ended tasks the contract may continue until the work is completed.
The agreed fee, whether the worker is registered for VAT and if so, whether the fee is inclusive or exclusive of VAT.
Expenses. Whether any expenses (for example travel, telephone or secretarial support) are payable in addition to the fee, and if so how they will be calculated. You may want to give a maximum budget, state how expenses will be agreed and ask for proof of how they have been incurred.
Invoicing and payment. Payments can be made monthly or weekly in arrears, at the end of the piece of work, or at specified stages during a longer contract. Sometimes work is paid partly in advance. Ensure that you owe the worker money until the work has been completed to your satisfaction.
Payment terms. Generally that payment is due within 14, 21 or 30 days of invoice date.
Copyright or patent. Clarify who will have the copyright or patent if written material or a new product is produced. If nothing to the contrary is agreed, copyright or patent will belong to the person who produced the work and not to the organisation which paid for it. It is possible to have joint copyright. If a self-employed worker is contracted to produce a publication that may run to a second edition or be translated, the parties' rights and responsibilities in relation to that edition must be clear. Copyright on the design of databases, computer programs, websites etc can be particularly complex and both the organisation and the worker may want to take legal advice.
Self-employment, tax and national insurance. Make clear that the agreement does not create a contract of employment, that the worker is self-employed and remains so, and is responsible for their own tax and national insurance. (Note that in general, organisations are responsible for deducting tax and national insurance from all payments made to individuals. Merely including this statement does not excuse the organisation from this obligation. Only the Inland Revenue can confirm someone's self-employed status and you should take advice from your PAYE office before paying anyone gross rather than deducting tax and national insurance. This is especially important where the person is not genuinely running their own business. Even where the person is running their own business, seek advice from the Inland Revenue if the contract is relatively long-term, is based in your office, or otherwise is more like an employment relationship than a relationship with an outside person.)
Insurance. Depending on the kind of work, it may be necessary for the worker to have public liability insurance and/or professional indemnity insurance (see chapter 7). If so, the contract should state that a copy of the policy or schedule should be submitted as proof of cover. In some situations the policy should also indemnify the organisation for any claims brought against it arising from the worker's negligence.

Equal opportunities. The contract must make clear that the worker is expected at all times to comply with the organisation's policy on equal opportunities and abide by the code of conduct adopted as part of that policy.

Confidentiality. Self-employed workers as a matter of course should always respect confidentiality, but it is useful to include a clause in the contract restricting disclosure of information. This should make clear the worker's duty to comply with data protection law and the organisation's data protection policy.

Variation. The contract should say that it can be varied by agreement with both parties, and should indicate who is authorised to agree variation on behalf of the organisation (and on behalf of the consultant, if it is a consultancy company).

Complaints procedure. The contract should either explain or refer to the procedure to be used if the worker has a complaint about their treatment. Unless the worker is genuinely self-employed, they will have the right to be accompanied by a colleague or trade union official at a grievance hearing.

Dissatisfaction with work. Similarly, the contract should include provision for regular review of the work, and for the steps to be taken if the organisation is dissatisfied with any aspect of the work.

Termination. Clarify the circumstances in which the agreement with the worker could be terminated before the end of the contract, for example if they:

- fail to comply with any aspect of the contract
- cannot complete the work within the agreed timescale or any agreed extension, or
- have brought the organisation into disrepute.

Similarly, the worker should be able to terminate the contract if they are not paid or the organisation fails to supply information or anything else necessary for the work (in such cases the worker must be paid any fees owing).

The agreement. There should be a simple phrase stating that the worker agrees to carry out the work within the timescale (or any agreed variation) and on the terms and conditions included in the contract in exchange for the fee. It should be signed by or on behalf of both parties. The person signing on behalf of the organisation should be explicitly authorised to do so.

The following *may* be included.

Increased time required. It is sometimes difficult to assess accurately the time required for a piece of work. It may therefore be helpful to set out what will happen if the job overruns. You should state whether the worker is expected to complete the work even if more time is required, or allow the option for renegotiation or additional payment.

Other responsibilities on the worker. For longer pieces of work the contract should require regular progress reports on specified dates with details of the time worked and expenses incurred. If the brief demands a policy decision by your organisation during the course of the work, the contract should require the worker to follow your directions. It should also state that the organisation would pay for any additional work arising from the policy decision.

Access to and ownership of documents. You may also wish to clarify whether you have access to or the right to keep any documents paid for by the organisation in connection with the work.

Obligations on the organisation. Always agree to supply any information needed to carry out the work. If you are providing any form of administrative or other support this should be made clear.

Arbitration. You may wish to include an arbitration clause. This should contain a procedure for an arbitrator, agreed by both parties, to be appointed in the event of a dispute, and allow for an independent third party to appoint an arbitrator if the organisation and worker cannot agree.

Taking on volunteers

One of the main attractions of volunteering is its informal nature. Nevertheless, it is good practice to be clear about volunteers' roles within an organisation, and it is important to have some readable and accessible documents in place, such as a volunteer policy, task descriptions and some form of volunteer handbook or induction pack. These can set out:

- screening arrangements, for example criminal record checks
- the tasks volunteers will or could be asked to do and possibly those they will not be asked or expected to do
- details of any induction, training, supervision and support that the organisation will offer and whether the volunteer is obliged to undertake training before being able to carry out certain aspects of the work
- any arrangements for reviewing the volunteer's work and role to ensure both the volunteer and organisation are satisfied
- any arrangements for accrediting the voluntary experience
- arrangements for reimbursement of expenses. This should make clear that only actual expenses can be recovered and set out any limits. Some volunteers may need cash in advance for expenses, and it should be clear that they will be required to provide evidence of expenditure and return any unspent part of the advance
- copyright. Volunteers who are not legally employees will own the copyright or intellectual property rights to any work they create unless they explicitly assign the copyright to the organisation

- a requirement to comply with the organisation's equal opportunities policy, health and safety policy and procedures, data protection policy, confidentiality policy, and other essential policies
- insurance arrangements
- what to do if they are dissatisfied with any aspect of their work or volunteering
- the procedure the organisation will follow if it is dissatisfied with the volunteer's work
- how the organisation can end the arrangement with the volunteer and any rights to appeal
- any minimum time commitment the organisation hopes the volunteer will make.

Having these written down means that both volunteers and volunteer managers know where they stand, and that each case will be treated consistently. As volunteers do not have access to employment rights it is important to give them the security of internal procedures that demonstrate a commitment to them.

The National Centre for Volunteering has sample volunteer agreements. For details ring 0800 028 3304 or e-mail *information@thecentre.org.uk*

It is important that volunteers are aware of their position under tax, benefits and employment legislation. A person who is a volunteer does not need to declare expenses received provided they are direct reimbursement for sums incurred. Any fixed allowances or other payments of any kind may cause difficulties because they could be treated as remuneration and be subject to tax and possibly national insurance. If the volunteer is on state benefits such payments could affect entitlement. They could also potentially create a contractual relationship, entitling the volunteer to workers' rights such as the national minimum wage, or even full employment rights.

People on some state benefits have to notify the relevant office of the mere fact that they are volunteering, even if they are not receiving payment of any type.

Even where a volunteer is not paid, a contractual relationship can be created if they receive training or other benefits or perks which are not necessary for the work. A contractual relationship can also be created even where training or benefits necessary to do the work are provided, if the volunteer is required to make a specified time commitment or is similarly obligated to the organisation.

You must also remember that asylum seekers who are volunteering must only be reimbursed for out-of-pocket expenses, and can receive no income.

The National Centre for Volunteering advises that the following expenses would not classify as taxable earnings and can be claimed without creating a contractual relationship or affecting a volunteer's entitlement to benefit:
- travel to and from the place of volunteering
- travel while volunteering
- meals taken while volunteering
- post and phone costs, and other costs incurred for the volunteering
- care of children or other dependants while volunteering
- the cost of any necessary protective clothing.

Volunteering should not have an effect on someone's right to incapacity benefit or their ability to be available for work in order to claim Jobseeker's Allowance, as long as volunteers still have time to meet the terms of their jobseekers agreement. However, problems can still arise. Individual volunteers who are concerned about their position should seek independent advice. Booklet WK1 *Financial help if you work or are looking for work* is available at JobCentre Plus offices and JobCentres.

The National Centre for Volunteering (0800 028 3304, *www.volunteering.org.uk*) publishes a number of books and information sheets on all aspects of taking on and managing volunteers.

Chapter 4:
Responsibilites during employment

Related chapters
Chapter 3 – Recruitment
Chapter 5 – Health and safety
Chapter 7 – Insurance
Chapter 9 – Data protection

Legally, a contract of employment exists as soon as someone accepts the offer of a job, and it is binding on both sides, as long as the offer or acceptance is not subject to some condition such as satisfactory references, a medical check or a work permit. If such conditions are made, the contract comes into being as soon as they are satisfied or as soon as the person starts work (even if the conditions have not yet been satisfied).

Contents of the contract

Contracts consist of express terms and implied terms. **Express terms** are those which have been specifically stated in the letter of appointment, job description (see chapter 3), terms and conditions of employment, any trade union agreement with that employer, and some other written or verbal statements. **Implied terms** are those not actually stated. These include the employer's duty to pay wages, comply with statutory requirements, provide a safe work environment and treat the employee with respect. The implied terms of an employee's contract include being ready and willing to work, obey reasonable instructions and be honest.

It is important to understand that a contract does not have to be in writing. Any arrangement under which someone receives money or something else in return for work is likely to be a contract, even if nothing is in writing. If the arrangement is for work on an ongoing basis, it is likely to be a contract of employment.

Definition of a worker

Most employment rights apply only to people who are legally employees (see *Some definitions*, in chapter 3). But some employment rights, such as those relating to minimum wage and working time, also apply to 'workers'. An individual is a worker if:
* they work for your organisation under a contract which requires them to provide services personally (ie they cannot sub-contract the work), but
* your organisation is not simply a client or customer of the person's business or professional undertaking.

This means that an individual who runs their own business, for example a plumber, graphic designer, computer consultant or a person who runs a catering business providing sandwiches at your AGM will not count as a worker. However, someone doing a few hours' work typing up the annual report at home or being paid to make sandwiches for the AGM when they do not run a catering business would be a worker. 'Workers' can therefore include agency workers, casuals and some freelances, but does not generally include someone who is genuinely running their own business as a self-employed person. If an organisation's relationship with a volunteer is such that a contract is created, then they would come within the definition of worker, even if they were not normally paid.

NB: Equal opportunities law applies not only to employees and to workers as described above, but also to individuals who are genuinely self-employed.

Statement of employment particulars

The statement of employment particulars describes the main terms and conditions of employment. Under the **Employment Rights Act 1996** all employees whose employment will last or has lasted for at least one month are entitled to a written statement within two months of starting work.

An employer must give written notice of any change to particulars of employment to all affected employees within one month of them taking effect.

Essential

The written statement must cover:
* **names** of employer and employee, and address of the employer
* the **date** when the employment began, and whether any previous employment counts as continuous employment

- **job title or** brief description of the job
- **scale or rate of pay,** including any provision for overtime and bonuses and method of calculating pay, for example an entitlement to increases such as annual increments
- **interval of payments** (ie weekly or monthly)
- **hours of work** (including any terms and conditions relating to normal working hours and overtime)
- the **place(s) of work,** whether an employee is or could be required or permitted to work at other places
- **holiday entitlement** (including public holidays)

The following must be included in the written statement or in another document given to the employee:
- where the employment is not intended to be permanent, the **period for which it is expected to continue** or the **date when it is to end**
- any **collective agreements** that directly affect the terms and conditions of employment and, if the employer is not a party to them, by whom they were made
- where an employee is required to work outside the UK for more than one month:
- the period of work outside the UK
- the currency in which salary will be paid
- any additional pay and benefits to be made while the employee is working outside the UK
- terms and conditions relating to the employee's return to the UK.

The following information must also be provided within two months of taking up the employment, but can be in a separate document made reasonably accessible to employees:
- entitlement to sick leave and sick pay
- pensions and pension scheme(s), or the fact that there is no pension scheme, and whether a pensions contracting out certificate is in force for the employment in question
- details of disciplinary and grievance procedures.

If the document is not provided to each employee, the statement of particulars must say where it is available.

Where the employer has fewer than 20 employees, the document only needs to provide the name or job title of the person to whom the employee should go with a grievance. In organisations employing 20 or more people the statement or another document must:
- specify any disciplinary rules
- specify a person to whom the employee can apply if dissatisfied with any disciplinary decision
- set out the grievance procedure.

It is good practice for all employers to provide this information regardless of size. Under regulations, which at the time of writing (December 2003) were expected to come into force in autumn 2004, all contracts of employment will have to include statutory dismissal, disciplinary and grievance procedures.

The amount of notice the employer and employee must give may be in the statement of particulars, or the statement may refer the employee to the law or to an applicable collective agreement.

An example of a written statement of employment particulars meeting the requirements of the legislation – **PL700A** – is available from the Department of Trade and Industry, *www.dti.gov.uk/er* (click 'Publications'). LVSC's Personnel Employment Advice and Conciliation Service (PEACe) has produced a model contract of employment, which includes examples of good practice, available by e-mail from *publications@lvsc.org.uk*

Some organisations will have a collective agreement between the union and management regarding most aspects of employment, to which employees may refer. Other organisations may have staff handbooks. As indicated above, some employment provisions detailed in such documents must be included in the statement of employment particulars, but for others, the statement can simply refer to the document in which they appear, which need not be the statement of employment particulars.

A document that includes provisions additional to those that must be in the statement of particulars is often called the **terms and conditions of employment**. The statement of particulars and a wider statement of terms and conditions can be the same document, provided it includes everything that has to be in the statement of particulars.

Optional

Employers are not obliged to include the following in the terms and conditions of employment, but may consider it good practice to do so:
- maternity, paternity and adoption leave and pay arrangements, where these are more generous than the statutory entitlements (see pages 83-86)
- arrangements for leave to look after dependants and compassionate leave, where these are different from and/or more generous than statutory parental leave and leave for dependant emergencies (see page 87)
- arrangements for agreeing flexible working, where they are more generous than or different from the statutory requirement (see page 89)

- time off for public duties and trade union activities, where these are more generous than the statutory provisions
- redundancy pay, where this is more generous than statutory entitlement (see *Redundancy*, page 111)
- reimbursement arrangements for travel and subsistence
- religious holidays (under the **Employment Equality (Religion or Belief) Regulations 2003**)
- a provision for extended leave, for example to allow workers to visit relatives abroad, but remember there is a risk of indirect race discrimination on the basis of national origin if people from the UK without relatives abroad are denied comparable opportunities for leave
- childcare: a voluntary organisation may not have the funds to run a crèche, however, it could consider contributing towards the costs of its workers' childminding costs
- probationary periods: if confirmation of employment is subject to a probationary period (see *Probationary periods*, in chapter 3), this should be stated in the contract. During a probationary period the length of notice required from/by either side is normally reduced, and the disciplinary procedure may be simplified
- a clear statement that employees must comply with the organisation's equal opportunities, health and safety, data protection, confidentiality, child protection (if applicable) and other policies
- information about the grievance procedures that exist for staff who feel they are being harassed, bullied or discriminated against and where they may be read.

Employers should also make it clear in a separate equal opportunities code of conduct that:
- harassment, bullying or discrimination by any employee towards another member of staff, committee member, volunteer, self-employed person or service user is a disciplinary offence, and
- anyone who provides information about discrimination, harassment or bullying will not be victimised.

The statement and/or terms and conditions are often called the **contract of employment**. However as indicated above (see page 77), the contract is wider than just the written document(s).

Deciding on terms and conditions

The following sections set out employees' minimum rights under statute (usually the **Employment Rights Act 1996** or the **Employment Relations Act 1999**). Employers may provide more generous terms and conditions, and suggestions are given under some sections. However,

before deciding to offer more generous terms and conditions – particularly in relation to sick pay, maternity, paternity and adoption pay and redundancy pay – consider the financial implications. You need to strike a balance between ensuring the organisation can function effectively with adequate resources and providing good terms and conditions to employees.

You also need to consider the long-term implications. The organisation may be able to afford generous terms and conditions now, but might not be in such a favourable position in future. It may be difficult to reduce contractual terms without making the organisation vulnerable to legal claims and this may become necessary to avoid closure. These are not easy issues for a management committee considering terms and conditions, and it is sensible to get independent advice.

Funding bodies may lay down conditions concerning terms of employment. For example, some local authorities state that grant-aided organisations must offer terms similar to those given to local government employees. Organisations should be very clear about the implications before accepting such conditions, and in particular any obligation to implement pay rises in line with national or regional negotiations over which they have no control. If funders require such linkage, try to ensure the grant or contract requires them to cover the costs of any increases.

Holidays

Under the **Working Time Regulations 1998** all employees, including those on fixed-term contracts, are entitled to four weeks' paid annual leave. They earn this entitlement as soon as they start work. These four weeks may include bank and public holidays but it is common practice to give bank holidays as paid leave in addition to the annual holiday entitlement and to specify this in the statement of employment particulars.

There are statutory rules about the notice the employee has to give before taking statutory leave, and circumstances under which the employer can refuse consent. For details see 'Paid annual leave' in the DTI publication *Your guide to the working time regulations*, available from *www.dti.gov.uk/er*

These rules can be changed through a **relevant agreement** (see below). This is defined as a collective or any other written agreement which is legally enforceable between the worker and the employer. Organisations wanting to be able to recover 'overpaid' statutory holiday pay must explicitly say so in the relevant agreement.

Many voluntary organisations offer at least five weeks' paid annual leave. The leave year is normally the same as the organisation's financial year.

Employees should be encouraged to take all their annual leave entitlement. There is no statutory entitlement to carry over untaken statutory leave. However, some organisations allow workers to carry over a specified amount of statutory and/or contractual leave into the following leave year, for example allowing five days to be carried over provided that the leave is taken within the first three months of the new leave year. Other organisations allow leave to be carried over only at the discretion of the senior officer and/or chair.

Under the Working Time Regulations, workers who have not taken their full statutory holiday entitlement are entitled to pay in lieu of holiday when they stop working for the employer. But the Employment Appeal Tribunal (EAT) has confirmed that if someone has taken more than their statutory entitlement when they leave, the employer may make a pay deduction to compensate for the overpaid days only if there is a relevant agreement under the Working Time Regulations authorising such a deduction.

Contractual holiday taken but not yet earned can be deducted from final pay only if there is provision for this in the contract of employment.

An EAT also ruled that employees on long-term sick leave can continue to accrue statutory and contractual holiday entitlements while off sick. This applies even if they are absent for the whole of the leave year, and even if their statutory and contractual sick pay entitlements have expired. This means than an employee can receive their contractual entitlement to holiday pay when on sick leave, even if he or she is not being paid during that period. The only requirement is for the employee to submit a request for leave.

For further details see the ACAS publication *Holidays and holiday pay available* from *www.acas.org.uk*

Part-time workers

The **Part-time (Prevention of Less Favourable Treatment) Regulations 2000** say that part-time workers have the right to receive proportionally the same amount of holiday as full-timers, including any bank holidays.

Part-time workers are entitled to the same number of working weeks' leave (pro rata) as comparable full-time workers. For example, a full-time worker with five weeks'

holiday would be entitled to 5 weeks x 5 days = 25 days, and a comparable part-timer working three days per week would be entitled to 5 weeks x 3 days = 15 days. In many situations it may be easier to work it out in hours: 5 weeks x 35 hours (or whatever) = 175 hours for the full-timer; 5 weeks x 21 hours = 105 hours for the part-timer.

For further details see the ACAS publication *Holidays and holiday pay*, available from *www.acas.org.uk*

Time off for public duties

Under the **Employment Rights Act 1996** employees are entitled to 'reasonable' time off (which need not be paid), for certain public duties. These include acting as:

- justices of the peace
- local authority councillors
- members of a police authority
- members of any statutory tribunal
- members of a health authority, special health authority or a primary care trust
- members of the managing or governing body of an educational establishment maintained by a local authority or a further or higher education corporation
- members of the General Teaching Councils for England and Wales
- members of the Environment Agency
- members of boards of prison visitors.

The employer must give reasonable time off to attend meetings of the body or any of its committees or subcommittees or to perform duties approved by the body.

The amount of time off must be 'reasonable' for the duties involved and for the employee's needs. An employee who considers an employer has failed to comply with the conditions can complain to an employment tribunal.

For further information see Department of Trade and Industry leaflet *Time off for public duties* (PL 702) available from *www.dti.gov.uk/er*

Hours of work

The **Working Time Regulations 1998** require:

- a 48 hours ceiling on an average working week over a 17-week period (although the employer and employee can agree in writing to a longer working week)
- an in-work rest break of 20 minutes if the working day is longer than six hours
- rest breaks of 11 consecutive hours in each 24 hours
- 24 hours' rest in each seven-day period

- a limit of an average of 8 hours' work in 24 which nightworkers can be required to work.
- free health assessments for night workers.

There are exceptions for some categories of workers. The number of hours young people (aged 16 and 17) can work are more restricted and rest break requirements are longer.

For further details see *Young workers*, in chapter 3.

Sick pay and leave
Statutory sick pay
The aim of **statutory sick pay** (SSP) is to provide a level of earnings replacement for employees unable to work because of short-term sickness. It is paid to employees who are sick for four or more days in a row, for a maximum of 28 weeks. SSP periods with eight weeks or less between them are counted as one period.

Payment is made only for **qualifying days**, usually days on which the employee normally works. No payment is made for the first three qualifying days, referred to as 'waiting days'. SSP is subject to income tax and national insurance contributions.

To be entitled to SSP an employee must:
- have done some work for an organisation under their contract. Liability for SSP can arise if a new employee becomes sick on their first day of employment
- be aged 16 or over but under 65 on the first day of their sickness, although someone already receiving SSP can continue to do so after their 65th birthday as long as entitlement remains
- be sick for at least four consecutive calendar days
- have average earnings in the eight weeks before becoming ill at least equal to the national insurance lower earnings limit (LEL) (£77 in 2003/04, £79 in 2004/05).

Employees cannot get SSP if on the first day of their **Period of Incapacity for Work** (PIW):
- their PIW links with a claim for certain JobCentre Plus or social security benefits
- they are in the 'disqualifying period' relating to their pregnancy
- they have already been paid 28 weeks' SSP from their previous employer
- their average weekly earnings in the eight weeks before becoming sick are below the LEL for national insurance purposes
- they are detained in legal custody
- they are on strike.

The 13% threshold scheme
The employer pays SSP to the employee. Employers always used to be able to recover this from the government, but in most situations this is no longer possible. However if SSP paid in a month exceeds 13% of an employer's total gross national insurance contributions for that month (ie employer's and employees' contributions combined) the employer can recover the amount paid over the 13% threshold. The money is recovered by deducting SSP from monthly payments due to the Inland Revenue National Insurance Contributions Office.

Rates of SSP
There is one flat rate. Up-to-date figures can be obtained from the Inland Revenue National Insurance Contributions Office.

Operating the scheme
Before operating the scheme, the employer needs to:
- agree qualifying days (days for which SSP is paid) with employees. These are usually regular working days but may include weekends
- decide rules for employees notifying absence through sickness
- tell employees what evidence of incapacity is needed. It is normal practice to phone in on the first day of sickness or as soon as possible. Many employers require the employee to send in a completed DSS **self-certification form** (SC 2) for absences of between four and seven days and a doctor's statement for longer periods.

The employer also needs to keep copies of:
- **record sheet** (SSP 2): to calculate the sick pay and record the details required by the Inland Revenue National Insurance Contributions Office
- **employee's statement of sickness** (SC 2): to give details about absences of between four and seven days
- **changeover form** (SSP 1): issued to employees who have received their full SSP entitlement (ie 28 weeks) and would therefore have to be transferred to Incapacity Benefit
- **leaver's statement** (SSP 1(L)): supplied to those who have received SSP within eight weeks before the end of their employment.

It is good practice to give each employee a copy of the leaflet *Statutory Sick Pay – check your rights* (NI 244), available from Benefits Agency/JobCentre Plus offices (addresses in the phone book).

Employers who pay wages or occupational sick pay to employers of a rate equal to, or greater than the rate of SSP for the same days do not have to operate the SSP scheme.

An employer who takes up this option will still need to keep basic records of sickness absence and amounts paid, plus sufficient records to complete:
- form **SSP 1**, to enable employees to transfer to Incapacity Benefit if, for example, they have:
- received their maximum 28 weeks' SSP, or
- run out of their entitlement to contractual sick pay and were not entitled to SSP
- form **SSP 1(L)**, to enable an employee to transfer to another employer.

It is possible to operate a dual system, ie follow the SSP rules for some employees and not for others, or for some periods of sickness. However, an employer who wants to be able to take advantage of recovering SSP if it goes over the 13% threshold (see page 81) will need to keep SSP documentation. It is also good practice (and less complicated) to operate one system for all employees, and for all types of sickness. Employers must be careful not to fall foul of part-timers' rights if operating different rules.

Record keeping
Employers should record payments of SSP on:
- form **P11** – the deductions working sheet – for each week or month that SSP is paid
- form **P14** – the end of year summary – at the end of the tax year transfer the total amount of SSP actually paid
- form **P35** – the employer's annual return – any amount of SSP recovered under the 13% threshold scheme (see page 81).

Records must be kept for at least three years.

For further information see the *Statutory Sick Pay manual for employers* (CA30). Call the Employers' Helpline on 0845 7 143 143 for expert advice on Statutory Sick Pay regulations. People with hearing and/or speech difficulties can call textphone on 0845 7 419 402.

Contractual sick pay
Employers should try to improve on the legal requirements by including additional provisions relating to sick pay in the contract of employment. This contractual sick pay could include:
- payment on sick days for which SSP is not payable, ie the first three days of sickness
- payment at more than the SSP rate (for example a specified number of weeks or months at full pay, and a specified number at half pay in each leave year or in any rolling 12-month period)
- payment for more than the 28 weeks for which SSP is payable.

However, consider the organisation's financial position before incorporating any such provisions. Small organisations can be hit particularly hard by costs arising from staff illness. If a large amount of money is paying sick leave to staff, there may be none available to bring in temporary workers to ensure their work is done.

Sickness/ill health procedures
If someone is often sick, senior managers and the management committee will need to know why. Is there a long-term sickness? Is the illness due to work-related stress, or unhealthy working conditions? If so, what can be done to improve matters? For further information see *Stress*, in chapter 5.

When workers are off sick for long periods this can cause enormous problems for their employers – and this is especially true in the voluntary sector.

These may include financial problems if someone is employed to cover for the sick employee, a decline in staff morale as employees deal with a colleague's workload, work not being done at all, and the management costs of dealing with the person off sick. There are no legal requirements to develop a sickness or ill health procedure but it is good practice for employers to do so. For further details see the ACAS publication *Tackling absence problems*, available from *www.acas.gov.uk*

Such a procedure should include the following.

Methods to measure and monitor absence across the organisation
To identify potential problems employers should keep accurate attendance records to measure:
- how much time is lost across the organisation through absence as a whole and through different types of absence – long-term sickness, short-term certified or uncertified sickness, unauthorised absence and lateness
- when absence occurs most
- whether particular departments are especially affected
- whether some individuals are absent more frequently than others.

Data protection
Remember, it is necessary to get employees' consent to keep details of individual records of sick absence, which are 'sensitive personal data' under the **Data Protection Act 1998**

(see chapter 9). Employees should be assured that this data will be kept only for as long as necessary and accessed only by named individuals.

Full consultation (where possible) with the sick worker

The way an employer deals with sickness can affect an employee's health. Someone can feel worse through anxiety about possibly not having a job to come back to. It is important to ensure that the sick worker is kept in touch with what is going on (including whether anyone has been employed to provide cover) and consulted over actions taken under the sickness procedure.

The right of the worker to representation

Employees should have the right to representation throughout the processes of a sickness procedure.

Consideration of medical reports

An employer can ask for a medical report from an employee's doctor, or from an independent practitioner, but must first obtain written consent from the employee (or have such consent under the contract of employment). Under the **Access to Medical Reports Act 1988** employees have a right to see their medical reports, and it is good practice to ensure that any practitioner is mutually acceptable to the employer, the worker and his or her representative. One option might be to approach a hospital's occupational health unit.

Whoever provides the medical report, the employer should cover the cost (usually less than £100).

Very occasionally the medical report may reveal that the worker is not ill, or not ill enough to justify the amount of absence that has been taken. In such cases the organisation should carry out an investigation and consider action under the disciplinary procedure.

In the vast majority of cases the medical report will reveal the nature of the illness, the worker's likely return-to-work date, and their future capability to carry out their normal job.

In these cases employers have a number of options, depending on the result of the report. Before deciding what action to take, consider whether the worker is a disabled person and covered by the **Disability Discrimination Act 1995** (DDA) (see below) and consult with the person concerned. If in any doubt, seek legal advice.

The options are:
- do nothing – if the worker is likely to return to work within a reasonable period

- make adjustments (which may be required under the DDA) by, for example, allocating some duties to someone else; changing duties or transferring the person to an existing vacancy; altering working hours; transferring to another workplace; allowing absence during working hours for assessment, treatment or rehabilitation; providing training; acquiring or modifying equipment; modifying instructions or reference manuals; providing an interpreter or reader or providing supervision. In some cases you may be able to get assistance to buy special equipment – speak to the Disability Employment Advisor at your local JobCentre Plus/Benefits office
- consider dismissing the worker on the grounds of ill health.

It is illegal to discriminate against anyone on the grounds of health or disability. If it is impossible for a worker to return to their original job, under the DDA organisations with 15 or more employees must see what can be done to enable the employee to carry on working for the organisation. In October 2004 the DDA will apply to all employers.

While a decision is being made, the employee should be fully informed and consulted. Dismissing someone on ill health grounds is a dismissal on the grounds of capability (see *Disciplinary policy and procedures*, page 94) and you must follow the organisation's usual disciplinary procedure (which in this context might be called a capability or incapacity procedure). An appeal must be allowed.

If, following examination of medical reports and consultation with the member of staff, the decision is taken to dismiss a worker on ill health grounds, once notice has been issued the worker is entitled to receive full wages throughout the notice period, or payment in lieu of notice.

If your organisation operates a pension scheme that includes an ill health provision (for example the local government scheme), it is likely that the worker will be entitled to claim a lump sum and a pension. Otherwise workers are only entitled to payment for their period of notice.

Maternity

Women who become pregnant have the following rights, set out in the **Employment Rights Act 1996**, the **Employment Relations Act 1999**, the **Maternity and Parental Leave Regulations 1999** and the **Employment Act 2002**:

- paid time off for ante natal care
- ordinary maternity leave, and in some cases additional maternity leave
- in many instances to receive pay and benefits when on leave
- not to be dismissed or treated unfairly because of their pregnancy
- to return to work after the baby is born.

Paid time off for ante natal care

All pregnant employees, regardless of length of service, are entitled to time off without loss of earnings for ante natal care, including relaxation and parentcraft classes as long as these are advised by their doctor, midwife or health visitor. The employer can ask for an appointment card or a medical certificate, once the pregnancy has been confirmed.

Maternity leave and pay

Length of maternity leave

All pregnant women, regardless of length of service and number of hours worked, have a right to 26 weeks' **ordinary maternity leave**.

A woman who has completed 26 weeks' continuous service by the end of the 15th week before the baby is due is entitled to 26 weeks' **additional maternity leave**. This begins at the end of ordinary maternity leave, bringing the combined total leave to one year. This can be extended by four weeks if the woman produces a medical certificate.

It is also possible to extend maternity leave by four weeks by taking that year's quota of parental leave (see page 87).

Starting maternity leave

Any pregnant employee may start her maternity leave any time after the beginning of the 11th week before the expected week of childbirth (**EWC**). A week begins on a Sunday for this purpose.

By no later than the end of the 15th week before the EWC the woman must tell her employer that she is pregnant, give the date of the EWC and the start date of her maternity leave. An employer can ask for written notification of the start date of maternity leave and can request a medical certificate stating the EWC.

If that timing is not reasonably practicable the woman must give notice as soon as possible, informing the employer that she is pregnant and the EWC or, if the child has been born, the date of birth. If the baby is born before the date given to the employer, or the woman is

absent from work wholly or partly because of the pregnancy at any time after the beginning of the sixth week before the EWC, the maternity leave period will start automatically.

A woman must give her employer at least 28 days' notice (in writing if requested) of the date she wishes to start receiving statutory maternity pay (SMP) (see below). Some women may choose to give notice for SMP at the same time as giving notice for leave. She must provide a medical certificate stating the EWC. A woman may alter her leave dates as long as she gives 28 days' notice.

Within 28 days of receiving the woman's notification the employer must write back to her stating the date her leave will end.

Pay and benefits

Statutory maternity pay

To qualify for statutory maternity pay (SMP) a woman must:
- have been in continuous employment with the employer for at least 26 weeks up to and including the 15th week before the EWC, and
- have average weekly earnings at least equal to the national insurance lower earnings limit (£77 in 2003/04, £79 in 2004/05) in the eight weeks up to and including the 15th week before the EWC, and
- have stopped work because of her pregnancy.

The woman does not have to intend to return to work to receive SMP, but must give her employee proper advance notice of her intention to take leave (see *Starting maternity leave*, above).

SMP can start at any time between the 11th week before the EWC and the week after the birth, for a maximum of 26 weeks. The first six weeks are payable at the higher rate (90% of the woman's average weekly earnings in the eight weeks up to and including the qualifying week) and the remaining 20 weeks at the flat weekly rate of £100 (in 2003/04 – rising to £102.80 in 2004/05) or 90% of her average weekly earnings, whichever is the lower.

The employer pays SMP in the same way, and usually on the same day as normal pay.

Small employers – those paying £40,000 or less annually in gross national insurance contributions – can deduct 100% of SMP from their next payment(s) of PAYE to the Inland Revenue plus an additional 4.5% (in tax year 2003/04) in compensation for the employer's national insurance contributions. Larger employers can deduct 92% of SMP from their next payment.

Maternity allowance

Women who do not qualify for SMP will be entitled to maternity allowance (MA) for up to 26 weeks if:
- they have been employed for at least 26 weeks in the 66 weeks before the baby is due, and
- their average weekly wage is at least £30.

Women will receive a weekly payment of MA worth 90% of their average weekly earnings, up to a maximum of £100 (in 2003/04). MA is payable through the local JobCentre Plus/social security office, from whom further information is available.

A woman is entitled to her normal terms and conditions of employment throughout the 26-week ordinary maternity leave, except those relating to normal wages or pay. She continues to be employed and therefore her leave counts towards her period of continuous employment. Annual holiday entitlements also accrue, these will be either those specified in her contract of employment or the equivalent of four weeks' paid leave under the **Working Time Regulations 1998** (see *Holidays*, page 79). Also, under the **Social Security Act 1989** she will be entitled to pension contributions. A woman returning to work after ordinary maternity leave is also entitled to benefit from any general improvements to the rate of pay (or other terms and conditions) which may have been introduced for her grade while she has been away.

During additional maternity leave, the employment contract continues, and some contractual obligations and benefits remain in force, including contractual redundancy rights and notice, and those related to disciplinary and grievance procedures. Again, the woman continues to be employed during her additional maternity leave, which therefore counts towards her period of continuous employment, and is entitled to benefit from any improvements to rates of pay (or other terms and conditions) which have been introduced for her grade while she was away. However, she has no statutory rights to receive other benefits such as holiday pay.

Right not to be dismissed

No woman, regardless of length of service, can be dismissed or treated unfairly because of pregnancy, or for any reasons connected with the pregnancy or childbirth.

Any woman who is dismissed while she is pregnant or on maternity leave must be given written reasons for her dismissal, without having to request it. She has the right to be offered a suitable alternative vacancy, where available, if she would otherwise have to be made redundant while pregnant or on maternity leave.

Any dismissal in breach of these requirements will automatically be unfair (except in some situations where there are five or fewer — see below).

Returning to work

Under health and safety regulations women are not allowed to work within two weeks of giving birth (or four weeks if the work is in a factory).

Women intending to return to work at the end of ordinary or additional maternity leave do not have to provide employers with further notification. Those who want to return before the end of ordinary or additional maternity leave must give 28 days' notice. This notice does not have to be in writing.

Women returning from ordinary maternity leave have the right to go back to their same job on the same terms and conditions. Those returning from additional maternity leave are also entitled to their same job unless the employer can show that this not reasonably practical. In such cases, the woman is entitled to an alternative, suitable job on pay and conditions no less favourable. However, this right does not exist if the employer has five or fewer employees at the time a woman is returning from additional maternity leave, and has no suitable job available for her.

Women who wish to vary their working pattern on return from maternity leave (or at any time before the child's sixth birthday, or 18th birthday if the child is disabled) have the right to request a flexible working pattern (see *Flexible working arrangements*, page 89).

Improving on the statutory requirements

Employers may want to offer more generous terms than the statutory requirements. This need not incur extra expense, for example the letter writing process could be simplified and the time limits for writing to the woman and her replying could be increased. If funds are available (and are likely to remain available into the future) the employer may offer contractual maternity pay at a higher rate and/or for a longer period than statutory maternity pay.

Whatever improvements are agreed should be included in the written terms and conditions. Both employer and employee should be clear that these improved terms are contractual, not statutory. Contractual maternity pay cannot be recovered from the Inland Revenue. For further information see the DTI publication: *Maternity rights: A guide for employers and employees* (PL958) available from *www.dti.gov.uk/publications*

Paternity leave and pay

Paternity leave

The **Employment Act 2002** introduced new rights of paternity leave and pay. To qualify for paternity leave, employees must:

- have or expect to have responsibility for the child's upbringing
- be the biological father of the child, or be the mother's husband or partner (male or female)
- have worked continuously for the organisation for 26 weeks ending with the 15th week before the baby is due (EWC).

Employees can choose to take either one week or two consecutive weeks' paternity leave, which can start from:

- the date of the child's birth (regardless of whether it is earlier or later than expected)
- a chosen number of days or weeks after the date of birth
- a chosen date later than the first day of the ECW.

Leave can start on any day of the week on or following the child's birth, but must be completed:

- within 56 days of the actual date of birth, or
- if the child is born early, within the period from the actual date of birth up to 56 days after the first day of the EWC.

Employees must inform their employers of their intention to take paternity leave by the end of the 15th week before EWC. They must state:

- the week the baby is due
- whether they wish to take one or two weeks' leave
- when they want their leave to start.

They can alter the date on which they want leave to start as long as they give their employer 28 days' notice. Employers can request notice in writing and ask for a completed self-certificate as evidence of the right to claim paternity leave.

Statutory paternity pay

During paternity leave employees with average weekly earnings above the national insurance lower earnings limit (£77 in 2003/04, £79 in 2004/05) are entitled to statutory paternity pay (SPP). SPP is the same rate as statutory maternity pay (SMP) – either £100 per week or 90% of average weekly earnings if below £100 (in 2003/04, rising to £102.80 in 2004/05).

Employees must give their employer at least 28 days' notice of the date they expect any SPP payments to start

and must provide a completed self-certificate as proof of their entitlement.

Employers can recover SPP in the same way as SMP (see *Statutory maternity pay*, above).

Employees are entitled to their normal terms and conditions of employment during paternity leave, except those relating to normal pay (unless otherwise stated in their contract). They are entitled to return to the same job, and are protected from unfair treatment or dismissal for taking or seeking to take leave.

For further information see the DTI publication: *Paternity leave and pay: a basic summary* (PL514) available from *www.dti.gov.uk/publications*

Adoption leave and pay

Rights to leave and pay for adoptive parents were introduced in the **Employment Act 2002**.

Adoption leave

If a couple jointly adopts, one may be entitled to adoption leave and pay and the other may be entitled to **paternity leave and pay (adoption)**. The parents can choose which one takes which leave and pay. Both entitlements require the parent to be newly matched with a child for adoption by an adoption agency and to have worked continuously for their employer for 26 weeks prior to the week in which they were notified of being matched with a child for adoption.

The parent taking adoption leave is entitled to 26 weeks' **ordinary adoption leave** immediately followed 26 weeks' **additional adoption leave**. Ordinary adoption leave is paid at the same rate as statutory maternity pay (see page 84) and additional leave is unpaid. Provided the other parent has the necessary 26 weeks' continuous employment, he or she is entitled to one week's or two consecutive weeks' paternity leave with paternity pay (see above).

Parents can choose to start their leave from:

- the date of the child's placement, or
- a fixed date, which can be up to 14 days before the expected date of placement.

If the placement breaks down during adoption leave, an employee on adoption leave (but not paternity leave) can continue adoption leave for up to eight weeks after the end of the placement.

Adopters must inform their employer of their intention to

take adoption leave within seven days of being notified that they have been matched with a child for adoption. They must tell their employer:

- when they expect the child to be placed with them
- when they want their leave to start. They can alter the start of the leave date as long as they give the employer 28 days' notice
- the date when they expect any statutory adoption pay to start – at least 28 days in advance.

Within 28 days the employer must write to the adopter setting out the date on which they expect them to return to work if the full leave entitlement is being taken. Employers can ask for documentary evidence from the adoption agency as proof of the entitlement to leave.

Statutory adoption pay

To be entitled to statutory adoption pay (SAP) or statutory paternity pay (adoption) the employee must have average weekly earnings above the national insurance lower earnings limit (£77 in 2003/04, £79 in 2004/05). Both rates are (in 2003/04) £100 per week or 90% of weekly earnings if less than £100 (rising to £102.80 in 2004/05). SAP is payable for 26 weeks and SPP (adoption) for a maximum of two weeks. Employers can recover SAP in the same way as SMP (see *Statutory maternity pay*, page 84).

Adopters must provide documentary evidence from their adoption agency as proof of their entitlement to SAP.

Employees are entitled to their normal terms and conditions of employment throughout their 26-week ordinary adoption leave or two weeks' statutory paternity leave (adoption), except those relating to normal pay (unless otherwise stated in their employment contact). During additional adoption leave, the employment contract continues, with some benefits remaining in force, for example in relation to redundancy notice and compensation. They are protected from suffering unfair treatment or dismissal for taking or seeking to take leave.

Adopters intending to return to work at the end of their full adoption leave do not have to give any further notice to their employers. Those wanting to return beforehand must give 28 days' advance notice.

For further information see the DTI publication: *Adoptive parents: Rights to leave and pay when a child is placed for adoption within the UK* (PL518), available on *www.dti.gov.uk/publications*

Parental leave

The **Employment Relations Act 1999** introduced the right for parents (including birth mothers and fathers, adoptive parents and other legal guardians) who have been continuously employed for one year to take unpaid leave to look after their child. Parents can start taking leave when the child is born or placed for adoption or as soon as they have completed one year's service, whichever is later.

Qualifying periods and leave entitlements

Before parents may take leave they have to satisfy one of the following qualifying periods.

Employees with **children born or adopted on or after 15 December 1999** need one year's continuous service with their current employer. Parental leave can be taken up to the child's fifth birthday, or the fifth anniversary of the placement date for adoption (or 18th birthday if that is sooner).

Employees with children who were **born or adopted between 15 December 1994 and 14 December 1999** must be currently employed, and need one year's continuous service with their current employer or with a previous employer between 15 December 1998 and 9 January 2002. Parental leave must be taken before 31 March 2005 (or, in the case of adoption, up to the child's 18th birthday if that is sooner).

Parents of a disabled child born or adopted on or after 15 December 1994 who is entitled to disability allowance can take parental leave up to their child's 18th birthday.

The main elements of parental leave are:

- Thirteen weeks' parental leave for each child, so if twins are born or adopted each parent will be entitled to 13 weeks' leave for each child.
- Parents of disabled children can take 18 weeks' parental leave for each disabled child born or adopted.
- The leave can only be taken in one-week blocks (except in the case of disabled children, when leave can be taken in daily blocks).

There are statutory fallback provisions for the amount of notice the parent has to give and how the employer can refuse leave. These provisions apply unless the employer has agreed otherwise in a workforce or collective agreement, or in individual agreements (see below).

The employee remains employed while on parental leave with terms such as contractual notice and redundancy terms still applying. In addition:

- where leave is for four weeks or less the parent has the right to return to the same job. For longer periods the parent is entitled to return to the same job or, if not practicable, to a similar job with the same or better status, terms and conditions
- when parental leave lasting four weeks or less follows ordinary maternity leave, the woman can return to the same job she had before the leave (see *Returning to work*, page 85). Where the parental leave follows additional maternity leave, she is entitled to return to the same job if reasonably practicable, or a similar job with similar or better conditions.

At the time of writing (December 2003) the government had said it would look at the case for allowing parents to use their full parental leave entitlement as one block at the end of maternity, paternity or adoption leave.

The fallback scheme

The **Maternity and Parental Leave Regulations 1999** provide for a fallback scheme in cases where no workforce agreement (see below) has been made. Under the scheme:

- parents can take leave only in one week blocks, up to a maximum of four weeks' a year per child. Parents whose child is disabled can take leave in single days or longer periods as they wish
- employees must give 21 days' notice of parental leave with start and end dates (this does not have to be in writing)
- if an employee intends to take parental leave immediately following maternity or adoption leave, they must give notice 21 days before the expected week of childbirth or placement
- the employer can postpone the leave for up to six months where the organisation would be particularly disrupted if the leave were taken at the time requested. The employer should discuss this with the employee and give written notice of the postponement within seven days of receipt of the employee's advance notice, with reasons and new dates for the same period of parental leave as requested
- the employer cannot postpone leave when the employee gives notice to take it immediately after the time the child is born or is adopted.

Workforce agreement

Wherever possible employers and employees should make their own agreements about how parental leave will work in a particular organisation. They may choose to do so through individual, workforce or collective agreements. Individual agreements should be incorporated into the employee's contract of employment; workforce or collective agreements will automatically become part of the relevant employees' contracts.

An agreement can improve upon, but cannot offer less than the key elements set out above. For example, parents must be able to take the equivalent of 13 weeks' leave (or 18 weeks for disabled children). But an employer could allow all parents (rather than parents of disabled children only) to take it in single days. It can also cover matters such as length of notice for parental leave, arrangements for postponing the leave, and how the leave should be taken.

To be valid, a workforce agreement must:

- be in writing
- be shown to all employers to whom it will apply, together with a guide explaining what it means
- be signed when it comes into effect, either by all representatives or most of the workforce where 20 or fewer employees are employed
- last no longer than five years (or until 31 March 2005 for employees of children born or adopted between 15 December 1994 and 14 December 1999).

In the workforce agreement, employers can improve on the legal minimum regulations by:

- extending entitlement to unpaid parental leave to include people with informal responsibility for looking after a child, such as a grandparent, stepparent or long-term foster parent
- waiving or reducing the qualifying period of one year's employment
- disregarding the fact that a child was born or adopted before 15 December 1994 and allow parents of older children to take leave
- increasing the total length of leave to more than 13 weeks (18 weeks for disabled children) or disregard leave taken in a previous job
- ensuring that at least part of the leave can be paid.

There is no statutory duty for organisations to keep records of parental leave taken. But if an employee changes jobs the new employer can ask the previous employer about the amount of parental leave taken, so it is advisable to keep records.

For further information see the DTI publication: *Parental leave: a guide for employers and employees* (PL509) available on *www.dti.gov.uk/publications*

- to deal with an unexpected disruption or breakdown in care arrangements for a dependant, for example if the childminder fails to turn up
- to deal with an incident involving the employee's child during school hours.

There is no set limit to the time off that can be taken; it is a question of what is reasonable. In most cases, the amount of leave will be one or two days at the most, but this will depend on individual circumstances. The employer may allow employees to take a longer period of leave, or to take paid leave, under other arrangements.

Employees should tell their employers as soon as possible about their absence, the reason for it and how long they expect to be away from work.

This right is intended to cover unforeseen situations. If people know in advance that they are going to need time off, they should be able to arrange with their employer to take this time as part of their annual leave entitlement or through contractual entitlement to compassionate or other types of leave.

For further information see the DTI publication: *Time off for dependants: detailed guidance for employers and employees* (URN 99/1186) available on *www.dti.gov.uk/publications*

Flexible working arrangements
Under the **Employment Act 2002** employers must seriously consider requests from parents with young children to adopt flexible working patterns.

Making the request
To be eligible employees must:
- have a child aged under 6, or aged under 18 if the child is disabled
- make a request no later than two weeks before the child's appropriate birthday (ie 6th or 18th)
- have responsibility for raising the child and be making the application to enable them to care for the child
- be either:
- the mother, father, adopter, guardian or foster parent of the child, or
- the spouse or partner of one of the above
- have worked for the employer continuously for 26 weeks at the date the application is made
- not to have made another application to work flexibly under the right during the previous 12 months.

Possible changes
At the time of publication (early 2004) the government was considering a number of further options regarding leave for parents, including:
- allowing parents to take parental leave in one block at the end of the maternity or paternity leave
- extending the period of paid paternity leave and/or introducing unpaid paternity leave
- extending paternity leave in cases of multiple births and disabled children
- allowing unpaid maternity leave to count as being in work for tax credit purposes.

Dependants' leave
Under the **Employment Relations Act 1999** all employees, regardless of length of service, have the right to take a reasonable period off work to deal with an emergency involving a dependant, and not to be dismissed or victimised for doing so.

The right does not include a statutory right to pay, however many employers consider it good practice to give a contractual right to reasonable time off with pay, or to give a senior manager or the management committee the right to agree paid time off on a discretionary basis.

A dependant is defined as the partner (including a same sex partner), child or parent of the employee, or someone who lives with the employee as part of their family, which could include a relative or friend living as part of the household. It does not include tenants or boarders living in the home.

In cases of illness or injury, or where care arrangements break down, a dependant may also be someone who reasonably relies on the employee for assistance. This may be where the employee is the primary carer or the only person who can help in an emergency.

Circumstances where an employee can take time off to deal with an unexpected or sudden emergency and make any necessary longer term arrangements include:
- if a dependant falls ill or has been involved in an accident or been assaulted, including where the person is hurt or distressed rather than injured physically
- to make longer-term care arrangements for a dependant who is ill or injured
- to deal with the death of a dependant, for example to make funeral arrangements as well as to attend a funeral

Examples of working patterns employees can apply for include a change in number of hours worked, a change in times when required to work, or a change in the place of work (including a request to work from home, whether for all or part of the week). For further details of flexible working options see *Flexible ways of working*, opposite.

The onus is on the employee to make an application in writing (which can be by e-mail or fax) well in advance of when the changes would take effect (there is no set time limit, but the guidance suggests at least 14 weeks). The application must be dated and must:
- state that it is an application for flexible working
- describe the relationship to the child (see page 89) and confirm the employee's child rearing responsibility
- set out the changes applied for and the date they would start
- explain any effects the employee thinks the proposed changes will have on the organisation and how these might be dealt with
- state whether a previous application has been made to the employer, and if so when.

Considering an application

Employers must consider all applications and establish whether the organisation can accommodate the work pattern. It is good practice to acknowledge receipt of the request. The employer must, within 28 days, either agree to the changes proposed in writing or arrange to meet the employee concerned to consider the application. The employee can, if they wish, bring a companion, who must be employed by the same organisation, to that meeting. The companion can address the meeting or confer with the employee during it, but cannot answer questions on the employee's behalf. If the companion cannot attend the meeting, the employee should rearrange the meeting at a date convenient for all within seven days of the originally proposed time, or consider an alternative companion. Any companion must be allowed time off with pay to attend the meeting.

The employer must inform the employee of the decision in a dated, written letter within 14 days of the meeting. If the proposal is accepted the letter should include a description of the new working pattern, and its start date. If a trial period or time limited period has been agreed this should also be in the notice. Form **FW(B)*** (application acceptance) can be used to confirm a new working pattern.

If the request is rejected, the notification, which also must be dated, must:
- state the business ground(s) for refusal (see below)
- explain why the business reasons apply in these circumstances
- describe the appeal procedure.

Form **FW(C)*** (application rejection) can be used to reject a request.

The business grounds for refusing an application must be one of the following:
- burden of additional costs
- detrimental effect on the ability to meet demand
- inability to reorganise work among existing staff
- inability to recruit additional staff
- detrimental impact on quality
- detrimental impact on performance
- a lack of suitable work available when the employee proposes to work
- planned structural changes.

Appealing the decision

An employee has 14 days to appeal in writing after the date of a rejection letter/form. The employer must arrange a meeting within 14 days after receiving notice of the appeal. The employee can bring a companion on the same basis as the meeting to discuss the request. The employer must inform the employee of the outcome in writing within 14 days of the meeting. Form **FW(E)*** (appeal reply) is available for this purpose. A written notice of the appeal acts as the employer's final decision and is effectively the end of the formal procedure in the workplace.

Any request accepted under the Act will be a permanent change to the employee's contractual terms and conditions unless otherwise agreed. The employee has no right to revert to the previous working pattern unless this is agreed as part of the original change. It is of course possible to have a trial period before any changes are permanently introduced. Employers should also remember to check that any health and safety requirements have been satisfied, particularly if the employee is to work from home (see chapter 5).

**Copies of the forms can be obtained from the DTI website* www.dti.gov.uk/publications. *For further information see the DTI publication:* Flexible working: The right to request and duty to consider: guidance for employers and employees *(PL520), available from* www.dti.gov.uk/publications

Flexible ways of working

Examples

Flexitime

Many organisations operate a system of flexitime to give people more freedom to work the hours that suit them so far as this is consistent with the needs of the organisation. The key elements of a flexitime scheme are:

- **band width**: the hours over which the system operates, ie the earliest starting and latest finishing times. A limit is usually placed on the number of hours that can be worked in one day – often nine (the maximum under the Working Time Regulations is 13, or 8 for a worker aged under 18)
- **core hours**: the periods when all employees must be present, other than for authorised absence, for example 10.00 am – 12.00 pm and 2.00 pm – 4.00 pm
- **flexible times**: the periods during which starting and finishing times may be varied, subject to the demands of the job. The hours worked during these periods are credited to the employee's total working hours
- **lunchtime**: in general a break of between half an hour and two hours (ie employees have to take at least half an hour) – usually between the core hours
- **accounting period**: the period in which employees must complete their contractual hours – often four weeks. For example, a full-time worker contracted to work a 35-hour week will need to work 4 x 35 (140) hours during a four-week accounting period.

Flexitime allows staff to self-manage their time outside the core hours and can help promote equality of opportunity. It is of particular benefit to employees with caring responsibilities, disabled employees and those wishing to study or pursue outside interests.

Job sharing

Job sharing is where two people share one full-time job. Each sharer does a proportion (often half) of the work and receives that proportion of the pay, contractual and statutory holidays and other benefits. Job sharing does not require any organisational restructuring or changes in establishment levels.

Working at home

Some people may wish to divide their working time between home and the office. Before this happens employers must carry out a risk assessment of the activities undertaken by staff working from home. See *Working from home*, in chapter 5.

School hours working/term time working

These are both specific types of part-time working. School hours working involves someone working only during school hours. Term time working allows an employee to take unpaid leave during the school holidays.

Compressed hours

This allows people to work their total number of agreed hours over a shorter period, for example employees might work their full weekly hours over four rather than five days. It is essential to ensure they do not exceed the number of hours/days permitted under the Working Time Regulations (see *Hours of work*, page 80).

V-time (voluntary reduction in hours)

V-time allows people to trade pay for time off. Staff are given the option of reducing full-time working hours for an agreed period, usually a year, with the right to return to full-time work afterwards. Time off can be negotiated as a reduction in the working week, or as a block of time during the year. They are paid only for the hours they actually work.

Advantages

There are benefits to flexible working. For individuals, the opportunity to work flexibly can improve their ability to balance home and work responsibilities. Employers gain by being able to retain skilled staff, which in turn reduces recruitment and training costs. This is particularly relevant for the voluntary sector, which is often unable to compete in the labour market in terms of salaries and other financial benefits.

Some drawbacks

Introducing flexible working patterns will have implications for management practices, monitoring and staff supervision. The additional management time and costs can be substantial, especially in small organisations – supervising four part-time staff will require far more time than supervising two full-timers. Communication can be more complex, especially if it is not possible to hold staff meetings at a time when everyone can attend. If one job sharer leaves it can be difficult to find an appropriate match. If someone reduces their hours, there may not be a corresponding reduction in workload and/or expectation, and the person can end up being expected – or feeling obliged – to do a full-time job on part-time pay.

For further information on flexible working patterns contact Working Families (*www.workingfamilies.org.uk*).

Retirement

There is no statutory retirement age. However, if an employer has a contractual retirement age, this must be the same for men and women. This is the case even though currently women are eligible for a state pension at 60. Between 2010 and 2020 the state pension age for women will gradually rise to age 65, which means that women born after April 1955 will be entitled to a state pension at 65.

Employees aged 65 or over are not entitled to certain employment rights; for example they do not have the right to redundancy pay if they are made redundant, or to claim unfair dismissal if they are dismissed for an unfair reason or through an unfair procedure.

The government must introduce legislation outlawing age discrimination in employment by December 2006. At the time of writing (December 2003) it was consulting about these provisions, including retirement ages and the right to claim redundancy pay and unfair dismissal after retirement age (see *Age discrimination*, in chapter 3).

Pensions
State pensions
Basic state retirement pension
Everyone who has paid enough national insurance contributions will receive the **basic state retirement pension** when they reach state pension age. This is a flat rate, depending on the number of years the employee has contributed. It is not possible to opt out of the pension; any additional pensions are paid on top.

Second state pension
Second state pension (**S2P**) acts as a top-up pension to the basic state pension, based on the amount earned during an employee's working life. It replaced SERPS (State Earnings-Related Pension Scheme) in April 2002. S2P is financed by a percentage of employees' and employers' national insurance contributions (NICs) and is run by the government.

Contracting out
Depending on their age and earnings, employees could be better off having these NICs rebated into their own stakeholder or personal pension (see pages 93/94). This is known as 'contracting out'. Some pension schemes are contracted out, in which case the choice has, effectively, been made – it is not possible to contract back in whilst you are a member of one of these schemes. People can contract out when they first take out their personal or stakeholder pension, or by asking their existing pension provider to arrange it.

Before contracting out employees need to weigh up whether rebating NICs into a personal or stakeholder pension will give them a better pension than the S2P – it is advisable for employees to seek independent financial advice on this matter.

People who choose to contract out will still be entitled to any SERPS or S2P built up beforehand.

Additional provision
The state schemes do not give a pension on earnings above the national insurance upper earnings limit, a lump sum on retirement or a benefit on death other than a widow's or widower's pension. Many people, therefore, choose to make additional provision for their pension, and employers with five or more employees must provide access to some form of pension arrangement.

Employers cannot advise employees on their pension options. For example, an employer cannot insist that employees join a particular pension scheme or say that they must join the organisation's designated scheme. Every employee must make up their own mind about which option suits them best, but they must have access to information about any scheme(s) offered by the employer, see *Further information*, below.

Occupational pension schemes
There are two main types of occupational pension scheme.

Salary-related (defined benefit) schemes. The pension received depends on the number of years the employee has belonged to the scheme, and how much the employee earns. This is usually earnings on retirement, or when someone leaves the scheme, but could also be related to average earnings over someone's working life. Many employers are no longer allowing employees to join these schemes, because of difficulties in ensuring there will be adequate funds to meet the pension entitlements.

Money purchase (defined contribution) schemes. The money built up in this type of scheme is used to buy an annuity from an insurance company – an agreement to pay a pension for life – when the employee retires. Employees' and employers' contributions are invested, and the pension received is dependent on the level of payments into the fund, how well these investments have done and the cost of purchasing an annuity at retirement.

Under either type of scheme it is possible for both employer and employee to contribute. The maximum the employee can contribute and receive tax relief on is 15% of earnings, although at the time of writing (December 2003) there were proposals to increase this level from April 2005. There is no limit on the amount the employer can contribute. However, the Inland Revenue also imposes limits on the lump sum and pension benefits that can be received from an occupational scheme.

Membership of an occupational pension scheme cannot be restricted to full-time employees; any rights granted to full-time workers must also be granted to comparable part-time workers. Employees on short-term or fixed-term contracts (whether full or part-time) do not have to be given the same pension rights as comparable permanent employees, but if they are not, they must receive higher pay or other benefits to compensate for the lack of access to the pension scheme

Contracted-out schemes
Some occupational pension schemes choose to 'contract out' of the S2P (see opposite). Where this is the case both employer and employee pay national insurance (NI) at a reduced rate. When the employee retires, they should still receive a basic state retirement pension, but will not be entitled to the S2P (although they would receive S2P for any previously contracted-in period).

Any contracted-out scheme must meet certain standards laid down by the Inland Revenue. This can involve a good deal of administration and may not be suitable for a small scheme.

Not contracted-out schemes
If an employee is in an employer's pension scheme which is not contracted out, both employer and employee pay full rate NICs. An employee who wants to contract out of S2P can set up a personal pension scheme (a **rebate-only personal pension**) into which the Inland Revenue will pay some of these NICs. The employee would not be able to pay any contributions other than the NI rebates into the plan. This scheme would be independent of any other arrangements.

Occupational pension schemes can be very complex and, dependent upon the type of scheme chosen, may require an organisation to make a long-term commitment which it may not be able to sustain. So although it is good practice to give some form of pension provision, an occupational pension scheme requires careful thought beforehand.

Organisations funded by local authorities may be able to become admitted bodies to the Local Government Superannuation Scheme. This enables them to provide their employees with occupational pensions without having to set up their own scheme.

Many organisations belong to the Pensions Trust, which is the leading multi-employer occupational pension fund for employees involved in the charity, social, educational, voluntary and not-for-profit sectors. It administers a number of pension schemes especially designed for voluntary groups, including multi-employer schemes. Voluntary sector workers and employers are represented in equal number on the Pension Trust's board of trustees. Further information can be obtained by contacting the New Business Team on 0113 394 2697 or e-mail contact@thepensionstrust.org.uk

Stakeholder pensions
Organisations meeting the following criteria must offer membership of a stakeholder scheme to employees:
- five or more people have been employed by the organisation for at least three months and earn over the national insurance lower earnings limit (£77 per week in 2003/04, £79 in 2004/05)
- no other type of pension scheme is available to employees.

Stakeholder pensions aim to provide access to a low cost pension arrangement for employers who have previously been unable to offer their staff pension provision. They are not intended to replace good occupational schemes, but can make better pension provision available to more people.

Employees can choose whether they wish to join the scheme, and employers can choose whether to make contributions. To offer employees access to a stakeholder pension scheme, organisations must:
- choose a registered stakeholder pension scheme held by the Occupational Pensions Regulatory Authority (OPRA – www.opra.gov.uk)
- discuss the choice of scheme with eligible employees and any trades unions
- formally choose (or 'designate') the stakeholder pension scheme
- give employees the name and address of the scheme. It is good practice to provide information on a named contact, phone numbers, an e-mail address, and any literature about the company. Employers must allow the designated scheme provider reasonable access to the workforce, for example to talk about the benefits of joining the scheme

- arrange to deduct payments from the pay of those employees who have chosen to pay into the designated scheme. Employers are responsible only for making deductions to the designated scheme. If employees choose a different scheme they are responsible for making their own contributions, although the employer could offer to do this on their behalf
- give employees information about payroll deductions. An employee who asks for payroll deductions must be told in writing, with two weeks of their request:
- how to ask for a change in contribution (for example whether it should be in writing or by phone to a named person)
- how often you will accept changes to the deductions (this must be at least every six months)
- how an employee can ask for their contribution to stop at any time
- that you agree to the employee's change in contribution being made no later than the next pay period after the request
- send employee and any employer contributions to the pension scheme provider within the given time limits. For the employee's contribution this must be within 19 days of the end of the month in which the deduction is made so, for example, all deductions made in February must reach the provider by 19 March. The employer can decide when any employer contribution is to be made, but it makes sense to use the same date as for the employee contributions
- keep up-to-date records of the payments made.

OPRA registers and regulates stakeholder pension schemes. It also ensures that employers offer access to such schemes, and that they follow the rules for making contributions (including late and incorrect payments).

For details of registered schemes contact OPRA on 01273 627600 or *www.opra.gov.uk/StakeholderPensions/*

Personal pension plans

An employee can take out a personal pension plan as an alternative to, or to supplement, an occupational pension scheme.

An employer may or may not contribute to a personal pension plan.

Group personal pensions

Some employers organise group personal pensions (GPP) for their employees, to which the employer may or may not contribute. The advantage of this for the employee is

that charges may be lower than for individual personal pensions.

Employers who offer a GPP scheme will be able to continue with the GPP without having to provide access to stakeholder pensions as long as all employees are eligible to join the GPP and:
- the employer agrees to contribute at least 3% of the employee's basic pay into a personal pension on the employee's behalf
- the employer offers a payroll deduction facility to scheme members
- employees who transfer out of the scheme or stop making contributions do not incur any penalties.

Further information

The Financial Services Authority (FSA) has published a useful guide: *Helping your employees with their pension options – a guide for employers offering stakeholder pensions or group personal pensions*, which can be downloaded from the FSA website *www.fsa.gov.uk*. The Pensions Service publishes a range of guides for employers and employees including *A guide to your pension options* (PM1), available free from Pension Guide, Freepost, Bristol BS38 7WA or *www.pensionguide.gov.uk*. Employees can also get information from Pension Advisory Service (OPAS) National Pensions Helpline on 0845 601 2923.

Disciplinary policy and procedures
Defining the scope of the policy

Organisations should agree clear guidelines on what is seen as unacceptable behaviour. Any list should not be exclusive. As well as including obvious offences such as harassment, bullying and petty theft, the guidelines should cover matters such as timekeeping, misuse of telephones and e-mail facilities, misuse of office stationery and postage, carelessness in respect of health and safety and unauthorised absence.

Disciplinary procedures also include a person's capacity to do the work. They will therefore also deal with incompetence, or the inability to perform duties due to illness or disability, and this must be made clear. This part of the procedure is often called a capability or incapacity procedure, to make clear that it covers competence issues rather than discipline *per se.*

Gross misconduct

They should also make clear what type of conduct – often referred to as gross misconduct – might result in dismissal without notice. This will vary between organisations.

Examples include:
- major theft or fraud
- physical violence
- serious bullying or harassment
- bringing the organisation into serious disrepute
- serious incapacity at work brought on by alcohol or illegal drugs
- serious infringement of health and safety rules
- serious negligence which causes or might cause unacceptable loss, damage or injury
- sending abusive or offensive e-mails
- downloading pornographic, racist, sexist or other unacceptable material from the internet.

Developing procedures

When drawing up a disciplinary procedure, follow the *ACAS Code of practice on disciplinary practice and procedures*, or visit its online learning package at *www.acas.org.uk*

The Code says procedures should:
- be in writing
- specify to whom they apply
- be non-discriminatory
- provide for matters to be dealt with without undue delay
- ensure that no disciplinary action is taken until the case has been carefully investigated
- provide for workers to be informed of the complaints against them and, where possible, all relevant evidence before any hearing
- give workers an opportunity to state their case before decisions are reached
- give workers the right to be accompanied (see *Representation*, page 96)
- provide for proceedings, witness statements and records to be kept confidential
- indicate possible disciplinary actions
- specify who has the authority to take the various forms of disciplinary action
- ensure that, except for gross misconduct (see *Gross misconduct*, page 94), no worker is dismissed for a first breach of discipline
- ensure that workers are given an explanation for any penalty imposed
- give a right of appeal – normally to a more senior manager – and specify the procedure to be followed.

A line manager, senior staff member or the chair of the management committee could take an initial disciplinary decision, and the appeal might be made to a subcommittee of the management committee.
Failure to comply with a disciplinary procedure, or

following a procedure which does not comply with the ACAS guidelines or is unfair in other ways, may be taken into account by an employment tribunal, if an employee takes out a claim for unfair dismissal (see page 108).

Always check the facts before embarking on disciplinary action. Employers should take action only if informal discussions and supervision sessions with clear targets for improvement have proved ineffective, or if the misconduct or breach of rules was too serious to deal with informally.

If a problem does arise that cannot be resolved informally then follow the agreed procedure. This will start with an investigation. The contract of employment may allow, in some circumstances, for the employee to be suspended on full pay, reduced pay or even no pay while the investigation is being carried out. The investigation is followed by an interview (often called a hearing) at which the employer gives a full explanation of the situation, and the employee, accompanied by a trade union official or a colleague if they wish, states their case. If the employer considers it appropriate, a disciplinary penalty is given.

No decision should be made until after hearing from the employee. This is usually a verbal or written warning, depending on the seriousness of the matter and the warnings prescribed under the disciplinary procedure. The warning must set out the nature of the problem, the improvement required, the timescale for the improvement, when it will be reviewed, and the consequences of failure to improve. These could be a further warning, a final warning, or dismissal.

When given the warning the employee must be told of any right of appeal and how long the warning will remain on their file. Any record of a disciplinary proceeding, apart from those relating to some serious offences, should be removed from an individual's file after the specified period.

An employee dismissed as the result of a disciplinary proceeding must be given the usual statutory or contractual notice period, whichever is longer (see page 110), or pay in lieu of notice.

An employee who is accused of gross misconduct is generally suspended on full pay while an investigation and disciplinary interview are carried out. However, in some cases the contract may allow suspension on reduced pay. If the gross misconduct case against the employee is proved, the contract may allow for dismissal with no notice and no pay in lieu of notice. If the contract does not provide for dismissal with no notice, statutory or contractual notice or pay in lieu of notice must be given. For further information about dealing with disciplinary problems see chapter 10 of *Just about managing?*

Grievance procedures

Employers use disciplinary procedures; employees use grievance procedures when they want to make a formal complaint about their employer or a fellow employee. Employers should develop a formal procedure to enable employees to bring a grievance to the attention of management. This procedure can also be used to enable an employee to appeal against a disciplinary penalty.

Procedures should be simple, in writing, allow for grievances to be dealt with rapidly and include mechanisms to ensure that proceedings and records are kept confidential. Depending on the organisation's size there should be a two or three-stage procedure, along the following lines:
- the employee raises the matter with their manager or, if the grievance is with the line manager, with that person's manager
- if the matter is not resolved within five working days it goes to the head of the organisation
- if not resolved within a fixed period, say ten working days, it goes to the staffing committee or management committee, who should call a special meeting if necessary. Any decision at this stage is final.
- if the employee is dissatisfied with the final decision and feels their legal rights have been infringed, it may be possible to bring a legal claim against the organisation.

It can be helpful in some circumstances, and with everyone's agreement, to seek external advice and assistance during the procedure. However, dealing with the matter speedily is very important.

Employees have the right to be accompanied by a colleague or a trade union official at any grievance hearing where the grievance concerns the employer's breach of a statutory or contractual duty.

Employers may want to consider having separate procedures for dealing with complaints about harassment and discrimination. If so, it is essential to be absolutely clear about the circumstances in which each procedure is used. It may be better to have one policy that is appropriate and flexible for a range of situations.

The **Employment Act 2002** introduced dispute resolution procedures which are likely to come into effect in October 2004. Employers and employees will have to follow a minimum three-stage process to ensure that disciplinary matters and grievances are discussed and if possible resolved at work. The intention is to reduce the number of cases that go to the employment tribunal.

The statutory process will require:
- the problem to be set out in writing with full details provided to the other party
- both parties to meet to discuss the problem, and
- an appeal to be arranged if requested.

If an employer dismisses an employee without following the procedure the dismissal will be automatically unfair and any award made by an employment tribunal will be increased. If an employee fails to follow the procedure any award made will be reduced.

When the new regulations come in, organisations which have dismissal, disciplinary and grievance procedures will need to review them to ensure they comply with the new procedures. All employers will have to include in their statement of employment particulars the procedures that will apply when an employee is dismissed or disciplined. If the provisions are not in the statement then the statutory provisions will automatically be implied (ie treated as being in the statement even though they are not there).

*Representation**

Under the **Employment Relations Act 1999** workers have the right to be accompanied by a colleague or trade union official when asked by an employer to attend a disciplinary hearing that could result in the following:
- the administration of a formal warning
- other action (including suspension without pay, demotion or dismissal)
- confirmation of a warning issued or some other action taken.

A worker is entitled to the same representation if asked to attend a hearing relating to a grievance that concerns the performance of a duty by an employer in relation to a worker, ie a duty arising from a statute or contractual duty.

The **Employment Relations Bill, published in December 2003, includes measures to clarify the role of the companion in grievance and disciplinary hearings. For further details see www.dti.gov.uk/er*

Monitoring e-mails and internet access

Under the **Telecommunications (Lawful Business Practice) (Interception of Communications) Regulations 2000** an employer can monitor employees' use of e-mail and the internet for a variety of purposes, as long as they are given reasonable notice that such activities will be monitored. Examples of circumstances where monitoring is justified include:

- establishing whether communications are for business or private purposes
- preventing misuse of systems
- monitoring performance standards
- recording transactions.

There is no statutory duty for employers to have an internet/e-mail policy for their staff, but failure to do so could make it difficult to take disciplinary action for misuse of e-mail or the internet. The ACAS leaflet *Internet and e-mail policies* (available from *www.acas.org.uk*) explains that a policy can help an organisation:

- protect itself against liability for its workers' actions (vicarious liability)
- help educate users about the legal risks they might inadvertently take
- notify users of any privacy expectations in their communications
- prevent damage to computer systems
- avoid or reduce time being spent on non-work-related activities.

The policy should establish the following principles and practices:

- covert monitoring is rarely justifiable – workers should generally be told that their communications and activities may be monitored
- employers should carry out an impact assessment before monitoring
- any information collected through monitoring must be treated in accordance with the **Data Protection Act 1998** (see chapter 9)
- there should be clear guidelines explaining how employees may use an organisation's e-mail, telephone and internet systems
- penalties for breaching the guidelines.

Any internet and e-mail use policy should be cross-referenced with other relevant policies, including handling confidential information, use and storage of personal data, equal opportunities and harassment, and discipline and grievances at work.

The Information Commissioner has published a Code of Practice – *Employment practices data protection code: Part 3: Monitoring at work*, available from *www.informationcommissioner.gov.uk/dpr/* – to help employers consider the legal and good practice implications when monitoring their workers' activities, which provides detailed guidance on the circumstances in which it is acceptable to monitor staff. It covers activities such as CCTV, e-mail monitoring software and telephone recording systems.

Components of an internet/e-mail policy

Introduction

The policy could start with a positive statement acknowledging the role of the internet and e-mail facilities in the organisation, for example:

[name of organisation] recognises that internet and e-mail facilities play an important role in enabling us to achieve our objectives by:

- improving communication across the organisation and amongst our stakeholders, and other interested parties
- increasing our access to information and expertise
- promoting our activities through the website.

[name of organisation] encourages staff, volunteers, management committee members and other authorised operators to use these facilities in an appropriate manner. At the same time operators must be aware of the types of internet/e-mail activities that are not permitted.

It is important to specify the legal status of the policy. The rules in this policy are considered part of the terms and conditions of employment, and any breach could have serious consequences and lead to disciplinary action. If illegal material is involved or legislation contravened, breach of the policy could also lead to criminal or civil action.

Some policies also spell out the user's responsibilities to report any incidents of abuse to their line manager or other named person, and for that person to take appropriate action.

Scope

This clarifies exactly who is included in the policy and should cover everyone involved in the organisation with access to your facilities.

This policy applies to all paid employees, volunteers, management committee members and any other authorised person using [name of organisation]'s internet or e-mail facilities.

Responsibilities during employment

Monitoring rights
It is important to be explicit about the circumstances in which an employer would monitor people's use of facilities.

[Name of organisation] reserves the right to monitor and record the volume and cost of each person's internet and e-mail use to ensure efficient and proper use of [name of organisation]'s resources. In the following circumstances [name of organisation] reserves the right to monitor which internet sites have been visited, or to access, retrieve and read e-mail communication:
- when there is a legitimate business need, for example accessing information when the employee is absent or taking action to limit the spread of computer viruses
- where there is reasonable suspicion of criminal activity, misconduct or concern about excessive use of facilities.

Internet use
This section of the policy explains appropriate and forbidden internet activities and could include clauses on the following:
- The extent to which it is acceptable to browse the internet for **professional use,** for example to gather information relating to work or training approved by a line manager.
- If and when it is acceptable to browse the internet for **personal use.** Some organisations may wish to ban personal use altogether; others may choose to accept limited personal use. In the latter case it is important to define the boundaries of personal use, for example there must be reasonable need, it must take place in the individual's own time and use must not contravene the policy's other rules. You may wish to state that the organisation would keep personal use under review.

Prohibited activities
These should include the following:
- Downloading information unless necessary for work or as allowed under the organisation's acceptable personal use policy.
- Downloading material that could infringe copyright laws
- Downloading computer software – such software often needs a licence and there is always a risk of importing a virus.
- Accessing pornographic material, posting messages in sexually explicit newsgroups or similar chat rooms. Any such activities could amount to gross misconduct.
- Accessing material promoting intolerance.
- Accessing games or entertainment software, or playing games over the internet.
- Gambling.
- Accessing sites that encourage criminal activities.

- Accessing chat rooms for personal or private use. Professional and work-related discussion forums, however, may be used.
- Passing off personal views as those of the organisation.

E-mail guidelines
This section explains appropriate and forbidden e-mail activities, and could include clauses on the following:
- The extent to which operators have **personal use of the e-mail facility**. Some organisations may wish to ban personal use altogether but others may choose to accept occasional and reasonable personal use; if so there should be some boundaries attached. These could include:
- there must be reasonable need
- it must take place in the employee's free time
- use must not contravene the other rules in the policy
- e-mails distributed must not contain information that would damage [name of organisation]'s reputation. For example e-mails distributed through work should not be used to advertise a product or for political campaigning
- the system must not be used to distribute chain mail or junk material.
  You may wish to state that the organisation would review the personal use of e-mail facilities.
- The appropriate **use of e-mail in relation to other forms of communication**. For example it is better to use e-mail than posted letters if people need to be reached quickly, and to help reduce paper use. Telephones should be used for urgent messages (but in some cases backed up with an e-mail or letter). E-mail should not be seen as a secure medium, and other forms of communication should be used for sensitive or confidential information.
- **Distribution of e-mails** – only send an e-mail to those who need it; unnecessary distribution wastes time and computer space.
- **Disclosure of status** – e-mails sent outside the organisation are likely to be 'business letters' and must include all the same information about charitable and company status as on any business letter (see *Letterheads*, in chapter 2). If the organisation is registered for VAT, some e-mails may need to include its VAT registration number (see chapter 8).
- **Legal status** – users must be aware that e-mails have the same legal status as any other form of communication and it is possible to make a **legally binding contract via e-mail**. The policy should forbid anyone communicating via e-mails in a way that could lead to a contractual agreement without authorisation from their manager. Alternatively, all e-mails should

contain a statement stating that no contract can be made via e-mail.

- The **penalties** for sending offensive, abusive, defamatory messages or making any improper or discriminatory reference to someone's race, colour, national origin, sex, marital status, religion, age, sexual orientation or disabilities. Any of these activities could be classified as harassment and could amount to gross misconduct. Users should also be aware that libel laws apply to e-mails.
- Warnings to managers **not to use bullying or stressful tactics,** for example sending a request with unreasonable deadlines that is copied to the management committee. E-mails should not be used to rebuke or criticise staff.
- Maintaining **security of the systems,** especially the dangers of importing viruses. Operators should be told, for example, what to do if an e-mail has a suspect attachment or they are sent a chain e-mail, and how to deal with spam messages.
- Awareness that **e-mails are not necessarily confidential;** there is no such thing as a completely secure e-mail system. Under no circumstances should confidential business, personal or sensitive information be transmitted via e-mail.
- Ensuring users are aware of the laws governing **data protection** when recording or obtaining information about individuals.
- **E-mail etiquette** – make sure users are aware of how easy it is to misinterpret the words or tone of an e-mail and how abrupt, inappropriate or unthinking use of language can lead to a bullying tone and possible offence – even harassment. For example, capital letters are sometimes interpreted as shouting. Users should always check the contents of an e-mail before sending it (including spell checking), just as they would a letter.

Good housekeeping practices

These could include clauses on the following:

- All e-mails should include a disclaimer. You may want to add a note saying that under certain circumstances monitoring may take place.
- Managing passwords (for example they must not be shared) and security (for example, connections must not be left unattended).
- Forbidding users to install or download additional internet or e-mail-related software.
- Procedures for dealing with e-mails when absent from the office for extended periods. These could include forwarding e-mails, or granting colleagues access to your in-box.

Paying staff

As soon as you know you will be employing staff for the first time contact the Inland Revenue's New Employer's Helpline on 0845 60 70 143. It will:

- provide help and advice on tax, national insurance contributions, statutory sick pay (SSP), statutory maternity pay (SMP) and tax credits
- register your payroll on the Inland Revenue's PAYE records
- send you a pack containing the tables, forms and information needed to operate a payroll.

Employers are responsible for paying staff and providing them with payslips (see below). They must also make the following deductions:

- national insurance (NI), if the person earns more than the weekly **NI employee's earnings threshold** (see *Primary contributions from employees*, page 102)
- income tax, if the person's tax situation or tax code requires this
- where relevant, repayments of student loans (see page 104).

The employer must pay the worker's income tax and national insurance contributions (NICs), together with the employer's NI contributions, to the Inland Revenue. Employers are also responsible for administering the Working Tax Credit (see page 103).

Employers must complete a **deductions working sheet (P11)**, for each employee. These should be kept for at least three years after the end of the tax year to which they apply.

The **Employment Rights Act 1996** prohibits any deduction from wages unless:

- the deductions are required by statute (for example, tax and national insurance)
- it is a term of the contract of employment that the deduction will be made
- the employee consented before the act which led to the deduction, or
- the deductions are ordered by a court.

There are other exceptions, which include:

- reimbursing an employer's previous overpayment
- deductions made under agreed arrangements for payment to a third party to which the employee has agreed (for example union dues)
- deductions where an employee is on strike or engaging in industrial action
- sums due to the employer under an employment tribunal settlement or court settlement.

Many large organisations have computerised salary payments. Some banks and accountants offer a low cost salary-paying service to small businesses, including voluntary organisations, and some local authorities provide a similar service at low or no cost to organisations they fund. Community accountancy projects and some local councils for voluntary service provide payroll services for a small charge. Many commercial payroll services providers or payroll bureaux offer competitive rates for charities and other voluntary organisations.

Where an employer outsources a service such as payroll management, this organisation becomes a 'data processor' under the Data Protection Act (see chapter 9). The Information Commissioner's Code of Practice (see below) explains how employers should follow the Data Protection Act when managing employee records and includes a section on outsourcing data. Before asking another organisation to manage the payroll system, the Commissioner advises the following:
- ensure that the data processor adopts appropriate security measures both in terms of the technology it uses and how it is managed. When deciding what are appropriate measures the employer must take account of the nature of the data being processed and the harm that might result from a security breach
- have in place a written contract with any data processor that requires it to process personal information only on your instructions, and to maintain appropriate security
- check whether the use of the data processor would involve a transfer of information about a worker to a country outside the European Economic Area (the European Union member states plus Iceland, Liechtenstein and Norway).

For further information see *Employment practices data protection code part 2: Employment records*, available from *www.informationcommissioner.gov.uk*

Payslips
All employees must be given a detailed payslip containing the following information:
- the gross amount of the wages or salary
- the amounts of any fixed deductions and the purposes for which they are made (for example, trade union subscriptions) or the total figure for fixed deductions, when a separate standing statement of the details has been provided
- the amounts of any variable deductions and the purposes for which they are made
- the net amount of any wages or salary payable
- any tax credits

- the amount and method of each part-payment when different parts of the net amount are paid in different ways, for example the separate figures of a cash payment and a balance credited to a bank account.

For further details see the DTI publication *Pay statements: what they must itemise* (PL704) from *www.dti.gov.uk*

Preprinted payslips can be purchased from office stationery suppliers, and compatible versions are available for use with various types of payroll software.

Income tax and national insurance
The method used for deducting income tax is **Pay As You Earn** (**PAYE**). It applies to all employees who receive an earned income exceeding their annual personal allowance or the annually fixed national insurance **lower earnings threshold**. However, if someone has another job you must operate PAYE at the basic rate if they earn more than £1 per week from you.

Each tax month, the employer must pay the Inland Revenue the total amount of tax and national insurance (NI) deducted. The payments will be calculated by:

PAYE
Adding together the tax deducted from employees and any student loan deductions and subtracting any tax credit payments made or tax refunded to employees.

National insurance contributions (NICs)
Adding together all the employees' and employer's NICs due, and subtracting any statutory sick pay, statutory maternity pay/statutory paternity pay/statutory adoption pay (see pages 84-87) and/or NIC compensation you are entitled to recover.

These amounts must be entered onto the **employer's payment record** (P32).

The amount due, together with a **payslip** (P30B) must be sent to the Collector of Taxes within 14 days of the end of each tax month. Tax months always end on the 5th, so the payment must be made by the 19th although a one-day concession applies to those who pay electronically.

Employers whose average monthly payments of tax and NI are likely to be less than £1500 (in 2003/04) may choose to make quarterly instead of monthly payments. The tax quarters end on 5 July, 5 October, 5 January and 5 April and payments must be made within 14 days. Contact your local Inland Revenue Accounts Office to make the arrangements. This has the advantage of reducing paperwork and enabling an organisation to earn interest on the money while it is waiting to be paid, but it also means the organisation builds up a substantial tax/NI liability and must ensure it retains adequate funds to meet this liability when it is due.

The amount of tax deducted from each paid worker depends on:
- the person's tax code
- the amount the person is entitled to earn free of tax (determined by the tax code)
- the amount of gross pay earned since the beginning of the tax year (6 April)
- the amount of taxable pay (gross pay minus free pay – see below)
- the amount of income tax already deducted
- the remaining tax due on the taxable pay.

The amount of NI deducted is determined by using the NI tables provided by the Inland Revenue.

The Inland Revenue provides employers with weekly or monthly tax tables from which tax deductions are calculated. They are divided into two sections:
- **table A** – the **free pay table** – which lists code numbers with the appropriate free pay to date
- **table B** – the **taxable pay table** – which shows the total tax due on taxable pay.

New employees

New employees will normally bring form **P45** parts 2 and 3, giving details of their tax code, NI number, amount of pay received and tax paid to date in the financial year. The employer keeps part 2 and sends part 3 to the tax office.

If the employee does not provide a P45 but will be working more than one week, complete form **P46** and send it to the tax office to obtain the correct tax code. In the meantime, the tax code you use depends on whether the work for you is the person's only or main work (in which case use the emergency tax code) or is not their only or main work (in which case use the basic rate code).

A **P38** must be completed for students working during holiday periods.

Employees leaving

When someone leaves:
- work out their final salary, tax and NI and enter on form P11 in the usual way
- enter the date of leaving on form P11
- make out a P45 for the employee

- send part 1 of the P45 to the tax office (make a photocopy first for your records)
- give the employee parts 1A, 2 and 3 of the P45.

At the end of the tax year

At the end of each tax year (5 April) an employer must complete form P14 for each person taxed under PAYE during the year. This records earnings while in employment, and the tax deducted, less refunds and national insurance contributions, together with any student loan deductions and any tax credits. The first two parts must be sent to the tax office (see below). The third part of form P14 is form **P60**, the employee's certificate of pay, income tax and national insurance contributions. Form P60 must be given to all employees who were employed on 5 April, by 31 May.

Send to the tax office:
- form **P14 – end of year summary** (a summary of the P11) for each employee for whom a P11 has been used at any time in the year, and
- a **P35 – employer's annual return**, listing all employees and their tax and NI contributions.

Form P14 can be obtained from your PAYE tax office; P35 is sent to the organisation by the tax office.

These make up the **end of year return**.

Expenses that have been reimbursed and /or any taxable benefits or perks must be declared to the Inland Revenue on form **P11D** for each employee who has earned over £8500 in the year (in 2003/04) and on form **P9D** for those who have earned £8500 or less. Where employees receive only properly documented reimbursements it is possible to apply to the tax office for exemption from having to file forms P11D and P9D.

Copies of these forms are available from *www.inlandrevenue.gov.uk* or from the Employers Orderline on 0845 7 646 646.

Temporary and casual staff

If anyone is employed on a temporary or casual basis whose wages are not being paid by an agency the employer must keep a record of:
- their name and address
- their NI number
- dates of their employment
- the amount they were paid.

A deductions working sheet (P11) must be completed for

temporary or casual employees in any of the following circumstances:

- the employee gives you a P45, or
- the employee earns more than the lower earnings limit (£77 per week in 2003/04, £79 in 2004/05), or
- the employee works for you for more than one week, or
- the employee is taken on for one week or less but will be working for you again.

If casual workers have more than one job, complete a P46 when they start and use the basic tax rate until you are told the correct amount to deduct.

Sometimes temporary or casual workers want to be paid 'cash in hand', or say they are self-employed and can be paid gross. Cash in hand or gross payments mean the employer does not operate PAYE. This may be unlawful for both the employer and the person receiving the payment. Organisations should always follow the rules above, keeping records of all payments to individuals and operating PAYE if any of the above four bullet points applies. The only situations where PAYE does not have to be operated are where the person works for less than a week, earns less than the NI threshold and has no other taxable earnings, or where the person is genuinely self-employed for the sort of work they are doing for you (running their own business which is registered with the Inland Revenue).

An organisation which fails to operate PAYE when it should can be held liable for the tax and NI it should have deducted for the past six years, plus interest and late payment penalties.

Volunteers

Provided volunteers only receive reimbursement for expenses they actually incur, and do not receive anything else of monetary value in return for their work, they do not count as employees, temporary or casual staff for tax purposes. However, employers must keep records of all reimbursements to them.

For further details of what constitutes legitimate expenses see *Volunteers*, in chapter 3.

National insurance

Class 1 national insurance contributions (NICs) are paid on employees' gross earnings, usually by both the employee and employer. Employers' Class 1A NICs are payable on all taxable benefits-in-kind other than childcare provision.

Class 1 contributions are made up of two elements: **primary contributions** from employees and **secondary contributions** from employers.

Primary contributions from employees

These are payable if the employee is over 16 years and under state pension age and earns more than the earnings threshold (ET) (see below). Contributions are made up of two parts:

- the main primary percentage – paid on earnings above the ET up to and including the upper earnings limit (UEL) (in 2004/05, 11% or 9.4% in contracted-out employment — see *Pensions*, page 92)
- the additional primary percentage – paid on earnings which exceed the UEL (1% in 2004/05).

Secondary contributions from employers

These are payable if the employee is aged 16 or over and earns more than the ET. An employer's contribution is payable on all earnings above the ET, even if the employee is over state pension age or otherwise excepted from paying their employee's contribution. In 2004/05 the rate was 12.8% on earnings above the ET.

Neither the employer nor employee makes contributions for those earning at, or below the LEL. Contributions are also not payable for those earning at or above the LEL, but below the ET, but employees will be treated as having paid contributions to protect their rights to claim contributory benefits.77

Full details of current earnings limits, earnings thresholds and NIC rates are given in *Social security benefits rates* (GL 23), available from *www.dwp.gov.uk* or JobCentre, JobCentre Plus or social security offices.

Employees in an approved personal pension (APP) arrangement (see *Personal pension plans*, page 94) will also be contracted out of the second state pension. However, they must pay NI contributions at the not contracted-out rate and the Inland Revenue National Insurance Contributions (NIC) Office will pay contributions into their APP scheme on their behalf.

The Inland Revenue NIC Office issues contribution tables each year and employers should receive them by mid-March. If they do not arrive by then, contact the local Inland Revenue NIC Office for table **CA38** if you have not contracted out of the state scheme, table **CA39** if you operate a contracted-out final salary scheme, or table **CA43** if you operate a contracted-out money purchase pension scheme (see *Pensions*, page 92).

You can obtain NI numbers for employees who have not worked before from the Inland Revenue NIC Office. People over pensionable age do not pay NI contributions, although the employer's contribution is still payable; anyone to whom this applies should provide the employer with a certificate stating the position. If no certificate is available make the normal deductions and arrange a refund when a certificate is produced.

The Employer's Helpline on 0845 7 143 143 can help with queries about PAYE, statutory sick pay, statutory maternity pay, statutory paternity pay, statutory adoption pay, student loan deductions, tax credits and national insurance. Information about pensions is available from the Pensions Info-Line on 0845 7 313 233.

Employer's childcare contributions*

Employers can claim tax relief for the day-to-day costs of providing or subsidising their employees' childcare. These costs include:
- giving an employee a cash allowance for childcare
- paying the fees of a nursery, childminder or nanny on behalf of an employee
- the running costs of a workplace nursery or playscheme for employees' children, for example rent, rates, heating and lighting.

Employers may also qualify for capital allowances for the cost of equipment for a nursery or playscheme, and tax relief for the capital costs of providing premises to hold a nursery or playscheme.

For further details see *Income tax, national insurance contributions and childcare* (IR115) from *www.inlandrevenue.gov.uk* or the Employer's Helpline on 0845 7 143 143.

New measures for employer supported childcare are to be introduced in April 2005. For details see the 2003 Pre-Budget Report, available from www.hm-treasury.gov.uk

Working tax credit

The working tax credit (**WTC**) is a means-tested allowance for people in paid employment who meet certain financial, personal and family conditions. People aged 16 or over who are responsible for at least one child can claim WTC if they work at least 16 hours a week. People without children can claim if:
- they are aged 25 or over and work at least 30 hours a week

- they are aged 16 or over and work at least 16 hours a week and have a disability which puts them at a disadvantage in getting a job or
- the employee or their partner is aged 50 or more, works at least 16 hours a week and is returning to work after time spent on qualifying out-of-work benefits.

This credit is usually paid through the payroll.

Employees may also qualify for help towards the costs of registered or approved childcare. If they are part of a couple, each partner must work at least 16 hours, unless one is prevented from working by incapacity. Childcare support is paid directly to the main carer.

Employees are protected against dismissal and discrimination on the grounds of their entitlement to receive WTC.

Employers will be told of the date to start paying WTC on the **Start Notice TC700,** and will be given 42 days' notice. To administer the scheme employers must:
- work out the amount payable from the daily rate table supplied on the TC700
- fund the payments through the total deductions made by the employer for PAYE, NICs and/or student loan deductions if deductions will not cover the amount of tax credit payable, the Inland Revenue will fund the difference. To make a claim complete form **TC711**, at least nine working days before funds are needed (the form will be sent to you with the first notice)
- pay the tax credit as an addition to the employee's net pay
- record the amount as a separate entry on the **employee's payslip (P14)** and **End of year certificate (P60)**
- enter the amount paid on the **Deductions working sheet (P11)**
- enter the WTC paid on the **Accounts office payslip (P30BC)**
- record the payments of total WTC paid out and any money received in advance to fund WTC on the **Employer's annual return (P35).**

Records of payment must be kept for at least three years after the end of the tax year to which they relate.

For general advice and information about WTC phone the Employers Helpline on 0845 7 143 143 (textphone 0845 602 1380) or read the Inland Revenue booklet: *Working tax credit paid with wages,* available from *www.inlandrevenue.gov.uk*

Student loan deductions

The Inland Revenue is responsible for collecting repayments of student loans. If you receive a Start notification to begin making student loan deductions from an employee:

- 'tick' box headed 'student loan deductions case' on the employee's form P11
- keep the Start notification in your wages records
- work out the employee's gross pay for student loan deduction purposes
- use the **Student Loan Deduction Tables SL3**, to work out the deductions.
- record the amount on:
- the employee's P11 at the appropriate week or month
- the employee's payslip
- the P14/P60 and P35.

If you receive a Stop notification:

- stop making deductions from the employee's pay – you will get 42 days' notice
- keep the Stop notification in your wages records.

For further information see the Inland Revenue booklet: *Collection of student loans: employer's guide*, available from the Employer's Orderline on 0845 7 646 646.

Keeping records

Employers have a legal duty to keep records of:

- gross pay
- tax and national insurance deductions or refunds
- any tax credits
- any student loan deductions
- statutory sick pay
- statutory maternity leave and statutory maternity pay
- statutory paternity leave and statutory paternity pay
- absence due to adoption and statutory adoption pay.

It is also useful to keep information about employees such as:

- personal details – including addresses, NI numbers, next of kin
- employment details – application form, references received, job descriptions, a signed copy of the employment contract
- employment particulars
- annual leave taken and details of any parental and/or dependants' leave
- contractual maternity, paternity and adoption leave
- sickness and other authorised absence
- any unauthorised absence
- any disciplinary action, unless it has been agreed that this will be removed from the employee's file
- training and development courses
- copies of references written (see *Providing references*, page 112).

Personnel records should be kept in a locked cabinet. Under the **Data Protection Act 1998** employees are entitled to access their personal details whether held on computer or manually. The **Access to Medical Reports Act 1988** gives employees the right to see medical reports supplied by their medical practitioner for employment purposes.

The Data Protection Act lays down eight principles relating to the collection, storage and management of personal data. It is essential that voluntary organisations understand and follow these principles, including those in relation to personnel records. For further details see chapter 9.

Confidentiality

Confidentiality is a complex subject, but both workers and managers must understand and respect the need for confidentiality in relation to their roles.

Confidentiality and workers

Most organisations have some information that could be considered confidential, for example concerning clients or users, or about the organisation itself. It is essential to give workers clear guidance as to what is, and what is not, confidential. Make sure that everyone understands any rules about confidentiality – it is clearly unfair to discipline workers for revealing 'confidential' information if they have never been told it is confidential. Neither is it acceptable to have a policy that says 'everything is confidential unless you are told otherwise'.

The **Data Protection Act 1998** applies to both computerised and manual records. The Act restricts the circumstances in which you can use or disclose personal information even by sharing it within your organisation. Employers should therefore ensure that their confidentiality policy and procedures and staff guidance incorporate the requirements of the Act. Advice is available from the Information Commissioner, from any national umbrella group for your organisation, a specialist in data protection or your local council for voluntary service or rural community council. For further information see chapter 9.

The Information Commissioner has produced a Code of Practice which explains how organisations can follow the Data Protection Act in the context of keeping employee records: *Employment practices data protection code part 2: Employment records*, available from *www.informationcommissioner.gov.uk/dpr/dpdoc.nsf Data protection for voluntary organisations*, by Paul Ticher, published by the Directory of Social Change, is also very useful.

Public interest disclosure – 'whistleblowing'

The **Public Interest Disclosure Act 1998** protects staff from being dismissed or victimised as a result of 'blowing the whistle' on any breaches of the law or dangerous activities carried out by their employer. To qualify for protection the worker must have a reasonable belief that the employer is guilty or is likely to be guilty of at least one of the following:

- a criminal offence
- a failure to comply with any legal obligation
- a miscarriage of justice
- endangering the health and safety of any individual
- damage to the environment
- deliberately concealing information showing responsibility for any of the above.

The Act defines two categories of people to whom protected disclosures can take place. The first – the 'first level' – is the employer in question. The category of 'second level' disclosure would include an 'appropriate person' such as a professional body, regulator, MP or trade union. Disclosures to the media are not protected.

Protection is only provided to a second level disclosure if an employee:

- makes the allegation in good faith
- has no personal profit motive
- believes the allegation to be true
- feels that they cannot raise it with the employer through fear of victimisation, or has a belief that there will be a cover up, or that the matter has already been raised but insufficient steps have been taken to deal with it.

It is good practice for all employers to introduce their own whistleblowing procedures.

For further information see the Department of Trade and Industry's booklet *Disclosures in the public interest: protections for workers who 'blow the whistle'* (PL502 Rev 2), available from *www.dti.gov.uk*

Unions

Employees' rights

Employees have the right to belong to a trade union and to take part in union activities outside working hours, and during working hours if this is agreed by the employer. They have the right not to be victimised or discriminated against because of trade union membership, and the right to take part in lawfully organised industrial action.

Employees also have the right not to belong to a union, and not to be discriminated against because of non-membership.

Union recognition

Under the **Employment Relations Act 1999** an organisation employing 21 or more people must recognise an independent trade union if there is support for one by the majority of the workforce. Recognition will allow unions to represent employees over matters such as pay and conditions of employment.

To start the process, a union applies for a ballot when it can show a 10% membership within the **bargaining unit** (the group of workers to be covered by the recognition agreement) and that a majority of the employees in the bargaining unit are likely to support recognition.

The employer must respond within ten days. The immediate possible options are that the employer agrees to union recognition straight away or enters into a 20-day period of negotiation.

If the employer still refuses recognition the Central Arbitration Committee is called in. There is then a 20-day period for the employer and union to agree on the bargaining unit – which must be compatible with 'effective management'. If there is no agreement at the end of that period the Committee will make a decision after a further ten days.

If the union can prove it has a majority of membership in that bargaining unit, it gains recognition. If it cannot, a ballot is called within the next 20 days – either at the workplace or through the post – with costs being shared. After a ballot is called, the employer has to allow facilities for campaigning, which could include, for example, noticeboards and e-mail.

To win and gain automatic recognition, the union must gain 50% in the ballot and have 40% of employees within the bargaining unit voting. If the union loses it must wait for three years before applying again.

Union recognition in smaller organisations

The above regulations apply only to larger organisations. Staff in smaller organisations – ie with fewer than 21 staff – may want to have their union officially recognised. Although under no legal obligation, it is good practice for employers to respond positively to any such requests.

Union agreements

If a union is recognised the employer can draw up agreements with the union.

Collective agreements

A 'collective agreement' is an agreement between one or more employers and one or more union covering:

- terms and conditions of employment or physical conditions of employment
- provisions which are different from the statutory default provisions, for example for parental leave
- recruitment or non-recruitment or termination or suspension of staff
- the duties of one or more staff member
- allocation of work to teams or staff
- matters of discipline
- membership or non-membership of trades unions
- facilities for officials of trades unions
- procedures for negotiation or consultation.

Workforce agreements

A 'workforce agreement' is an agreement between an employer and its workers. It must be in writing and apply to all employees who are not covered by a collective agreement, and be signed by properly elected employee representatives. If there are 20 or fewer employees it may be signed by the majority of employees rather than by elected representatives. All employees covered by the agreement must be given a copy before it is signed on their behalf.

If the organisation and its staff agree, a workforce agreement can override the statutory rights to parental leave and working time.

If employees belong to more than one union, the employer may decide to recognise the union with the greatest number of members in a collective agreement and recognise the others for discussing individual rights only. An alternative is to ask the representatives of the various unions to form a joint committee, with whom the employer will negotiate.

Contact ACAS for further information about union recognition and agreements.

The rights of recognised trades unions

Once an employer has given a union official recognition it acquires the rights to:

- receive information for collective bargaining purposes. ACAS lists the following as possibly relevant for collective bargaining: pay and benefits; conditions of service; staffing; performance; finance (see ACAS' *Code 2: Disclosure of information to trade union officials for collective bargaining purposes*)
- appoint safety representatives
- be consulted over redundancy if this is included in the collective agreement (see *Redundancy*, page 108)
- reasonable paid time off for union officials to perform union duties and undertake relevant training
- paid time off for trade union learning representatives (see below).

Union representatives

The union should notify management of the names of the elected representatives, who will have been given **credentials** (papers authorising them to act for their union). Representatives have a right to some facilities, and it is good practice to provide others, including:

- a desk and a lockable filing cabinet
- use of a phone to make calls in private
- a union notice board
- use of a computer
- if appropriate, access to electronic communications such as e-mail and intranet/internet
- use of a photocopier and mailing facilities
- meeting space.

An employer can encourage people to join the union by:

- negotiating with the union rather than with individuals
- enabling union representatives to talk to all new employees as soon as they start
- arranging for union contributions to be deducted direct from pay ('check off') if members agree.

The main unions in the voluntary sector are Amicus, Transport and General Workers' Union (T&G) and Unison.

Time off for trade union learning representatives

Under the **Employment Act 2002** trade union learning representatives (ULRs) have a right to reasonable paid time off work to ensure that they are adequately trained to carry out their duties, including:

- analysing learning or training needs
- providing information and advice about learning or training matters
- arranging learning or training opportunities
- promoting the value of learning or training
- consulting the employer about these issues
- preparation to carry out any of the above activities
- undergoing training relevant to their functions.

To qualify for paid time off the member must be sufficiently trained to carry out the duties of the learning representative, either when the trade union gives written notice to the employer that they have been appointed as the ULR, or within six months of that date. In the latter case the union must state in writing that the ULR will undergo relevant training, and confirm in writing when this has taken place.

Employees who belong to a recognised trade union are allowed reasonable time off work to access their ULRs.

For further information see the ACAS publication *Time off for trade union duties and activities.*

Employee representatives

Employers must consult with **appropriate representatives** when 20 or more staff are to be made redundant in a 90-day period, or are to be transferred to another employer. 'Appropriate representatives' are either officials of recognised trades unions or elected representatives of employees. Employers who have a collective agreement (see above) covering redundancy must, under the agreement, consult the trade union. They can then choose whether to consult employee representatives as well. It would be good practice to consult both.

Employee representatives have the same rights to reasonable time off with pay to carry out their duties as union officials.

All employees have the right not to be dismissed or suffer adverse treatment for taking part in the election of an employee representative.

Where there is no recognised trade union, employees can also elect safety representatives (see chapter 5).

Employment Relations Bill

The **Employment Relations Bill,** published in December 2003, includes measures to improve the operation of the statutory recognition procedure. It:

- clarifies issues surrounding the determination of the appropriate bargaining unit
- clarifies the topics for collective bargaining
- allows unions to communicate with workers at an earlier stage in the process
- clarifies and builds upon current legislation relating to supplying information to the Central Arbitration Committee and the Advisory Conciliation and Arbitration Service (ACAS).

For further details see *www.dti.gov.uk/er*

Taking on other organisations' staff

The **Transfer of Undertakings (Protection of Employment) Regulations 1981 (TUPE)** say that an organisation taking over work previously done by another organisation (including contracted-out work from a public body such as a local or health authority) may automatically become the new employer of the other organisation's staff. The staff may automatically retain virtually all their old terms and conditions (apart from occupational pension rights, although see below).

The government has issued a code of practice that extends these employment rights to new employees who are subsequently employed to do the same work as staff transferred from a local authority. Any new employee must be offered terms and conditions which are, overall, no less favourable than those of transferred employees. The local authority must monitor compliance through its best value reviews. New employees must also be offered access to the local government pension scheme, an alternative employer pension scheme, or a stakeholder pension scheme.

The code of practice is an annex to the ODPM circular *Best value and performance improvement* (03/2003), available from *www.local-regions.odpm.gov.uk*

The law in this area is complex, and subject to ever-changing interpretation by both the UK and European courts. One example is the decision in 2003 of the Employment Appeal Tribunal which suggests that if a transferring employer does not consult employees affected by a TUPE transfer, the new employer can be liable for this failure to consult. Before committing to taking over work previously done by another organisation it is essential to get legal advice on whether TUPE applies and what effect it may have.

It is also essential to consider the financial implications. For example, under TUPE an organisation will be taking on employees who have accrued rights dependent on length of service, such as redundancy pay, and will have to be able to meet these commitments. This may significantly increase the amount of reserves it has to hold to meet potential redundancy liabilities.

Organisations taking on work previously done by local authorities can now join the local government pension scheme. This enables them to provide any workers transferred from the local authority with the same pension rights as they enjoyed in local government. For further advice, contact the section within your local authority that deals with pensions.

For further information see the DTI booklet: *Employment rights on the transfers of an undertaking* (PL699).

Reorganisation

Voluntary organisations, like other employers, sometimes have to reorganise. This may involve changes to conditions of employment, for example a change in workplace, different jobs and, in some cases, different terms and conditions of employment. Well written contracts will allow for flexibility, for example by saying the place of work is '56 Viking Street or such other place within Greater London as the employer may require'. However, some changes and reorganisations will require a change to the contract of employment.

If the contract does not allow for variation (changes), any change should be made with the consent of the employee, if possible. Early and full consultation is important to get agreement for change. If there is a recognised trade union involve it in discussions at the earliest opportunity. If agreement cannot be reached on changes to the contract of employment it is advisable to get specialist legal advice before going ahead. This is because if the employee does not agree to a change in their contract of employment, the only way to achieve the change is to terminate the old contract and re-employ them on a new contract containing the new terms and conditions. The employee must be given the required notice to bring the old contract to an end.

Unfair dismissal

The **Employment Rights Act 1996** states that employees are dismissed fairly if they are dismissed 'for some substantial reason which justifies dismissal'. The courts have ruled that a necessary reorganisation by the employer may count as a 'substantial reason'. Provided there are good reasons for a reorganisation, an employee who has been dismissed, or who has been offered reasonable alternative terms and conditions and refused them, is unlikely to be able to claim unfair dismissal.

Offering reasonable alternative terms of employment

Employees who consider they have a valid redundancy or unfair dismissal claim on reorganisation can take the complaint to an employment tribunal. The tribunal will decide whether the offer of alternative employment was suitable and whether the refusal of the offer was reasonable. Organisations should therefore take account of the effects on each employee of any revised terms and conditions, pay, job description or place of work. Changes may need to be adapted to take account of staff members' particular circumstances.

Procedures for reorganisation

Organisations mostly go wrong by failing to follow their own procedures (if they have a set procedure) and failing to properly consult with staff before making any final decision. In order to protect itself from claims for redundancy payments or unfair dismissal, an organisation should ensure that:

- it has seriously considered the need for reorganisation so that it can be carefully and objectively justified
- all the possible alternatives to reorganisation have been examined
- negotiation has taken place with recognised trade union and/or employee representatives (see *Employee representatives*, page 107)
- all employees affected by the potential reorganisation have been consulted and reasons for the proposed changes have been explained
- views expressed by those employees or on their behalf have been considered, and suggested alternative strategies examined
- the final decision has not been made until employees' views have been taken into account
- even in the light of employees' views it is decided that there is no reasonable alternative but to reorganise
- in amending the terms of the contract of employment, each employee's needs have been considered

If the reorganisation involves the deletion of posts and the creation of new ones then there is a redundancy situation. A redundant employee could be offered the choice of the new post or a redundancy payment and may even be entitled to the offer of a new position (see *Offers of alternative work*, page 110). In this situation an organisation should seek specialist legal advice.

Redundancy

By law an employee is dismissed because of redundancy if any of the following apply:

- the employer has ceased or intends to cease carrying on the activities for which the employee was employed
- the employer has ceased or intends to cease carrying on the activities in the place where the employee was employed
- the need for the employee to carry out particular work has ceased or diminished or is expected to do so
- the need to carry out particular work in the place where the employee was employed has ceased or diminished or is expected to do so.

Change of place of work: Whether a move of offices or workplace involves redundancy will depend on the circumstances, including the contract of employment. If the contract specifies where someone is employed, for example a particular address, then any shut down of the workplace and a move to a new address will be a redundancy situation. This is because the employer will have stopped carrying out the activities in the specific place 'where the employee was employed'. Even if the contract allows a different location, a redundancy situation will still occur if there is a major relocation that would entail significant inconvenience for the employee, for example having to move house or buy a car. If employees are opposed to a move and you are in doubt whether a redundancy situation exists, seek legal advice.

Change in the work required: There will only be a redundancy situation if the work the employee was doing under their contract of employment has ceased or diminished. In practice this may mean that if another member of staff is going to be asked to do that work then there is no redundancy.

Other changes: Other changes to terms and conditions are likely to be caused by a financial crisis or a grant or contract ending. Whether this constitutes a redundancy situation depends on whether the organisation is scaling down its activities.

'Suitable alternative employment': An employee who is offered 'suitable alternative employment' on new terms and conditions, at a new place of work, or with a slightly different job, will not receive a redundancy payment if they refuse the offer. It may be necessary to get legal advice about whether the alternative employment is 'suitable', see *Offers of alternative work*, page 110.

Notifying those involved

Consultation with those affected by redundancy provides an opportunity to discuss the problem and identify possible solution. Consultation is also a legal requirement.

The unions and employee representatives

Under the **Collective Redundancies and Transfer of Undertaking (Protection of Employment (Amendment)) Regulations 1999**, if 20 or more employees are to be made redundant within a 90-day period or are to be transferred to another employer:

- employers who recognise a trade union must inform and consult that union
- if there is no recognised trade union the employer must inform and consult other appropriate representatives of the affected employees

- the representatives may be elected specifically for the purpose, or form part of an existing consultative body. If existing representatives are to be used, their remit and method of election must be suitable for the employees affected by the proposals. If new representatives are to be appointed for the consultation process the regulations clearly state how they are to be elected
- representatives of *all* employees who may be affected by the redundancies or transfer must be consulted – not just those under threat of redundancy
- representatives have the right to paid time off for training and to be provided with facilities to fulfil their role, for example a room, phone and copying facilities
- where no representatives are elected, the employer must pass information to all affected staff.

Case law has established that in most redundancies employers have a duty to consult the individuals who are or might be affected. A tribunal case in 2002 indicated that even where fewer than 20 employees were affected, the employer should inform and consult a recognised union or workplace representatives.

For further information see the ACAS booklet *Redundancy handling*.

Minimum periods for consultation

The employer must begin the process of consultation in good time and in any event at least:

- 90 days before the first dismissal takes effect if the employer proposes to make 100 or more workers redundant in one workplace within a 90-day period
- 30 days before the first dismissal takes effect where between 20 and 99 redundancy dismissals are proposed within a 90-day period.

The union or employee representatives must be told in writing:

- the reasons for the proposed redundancies
- the number of workers affected and their job titles
- the total number of employees at the location
- the proposed method of selecting people for redundancy
- the proposed method of carrying out the dismissals
- the proposed method of calculating redundancy payments in addition to statutory payments.

The consultation must consider ways of avoiding or reducing the number of dismissals and mitigating their consequences, and must aim to reach agreement with the union or representatives.

It is also good practice to consult or, where appropriate, negotiate on some or all of the following:

- the effect on earnings if transfer or downgrading is accepted in preference to redundancy
- arrangements for travel, removal and related expenses, where work is accepted in a different location
- whether a redundant employee may leave during the notice period, or postpone the date of expiry of notice, without losing entitlement to statutory redundancy payment
- any retention of company benefits where an employee is made compulsorily redundant
- any extension of the length of the statutory trial period in a new job.

Department of Trade and Industry (DTI)

The employer must notify the DTI in writing of any proposal to make 20 or more people redundant within a 90-day period. This is to enable government departments to develop measures to help or retrain the employees in question. The notice requirements are the same as those for consultation with the unions or other representatives (see above). A copy of the notice to the DTI must be given to the union or other representatives.

Employers may notify the DTI by letter or use form HR1, obtainable from any Redundancy Payments Office or JobCentre Plus Office. For further information, see the DTI booklet *Redundancy consultation and notification* (PL833) available from *www.dti.gov.uk*

The employees

Under the **Employment Rights Act 1996** each employee being made redundant must be given an individual written notice of a redundancy dismissal – notice cannot be given collectively. Workers on fixed-term contracts have all the same rights as permanent employees and must be given notice of dismissal in the same way as any other employee. (Until 1 October 2002 workers on a fixed-term contract of two years or more could waive the right to redundancy pay. Any waivers inserted into contracts agreed, renewed or extended after that date are no longer valid. A waiver in a fixed-term contract of two years or more entered into before 1 October 2002 remains valid, but applies only to the right to redundancy pay. The employee has all other redundancy rights, including the right to notice of redundancy dismissal.)

Notice of redundancy dismissal should be either the statutory minimum period or the period agreed in the contract of employment, whichever is the longer. Employers who do not give advance notice must pay wages for the period of notice. This is separate from any obligation to give the employee redundancy pay (see below). The statutory minimum notice required is:

- one month to two years' service – one week's notice
- two to twelve years' service – one week's notice for each complete year
- 12 or more years' service – 12 weeks' notice.

Offers of alternative work

Under the **Employment Rights Act 1996** employers must offer an employee threatened with redundancy suitable alternative employment, if a suitable post exists within the organisation or with an associated employer or a successor employer that takes over the organisation. Any new job must start within four weeks of the old employment contract ending. A redundant employee who unreasonably refuses a suitable offer of alternative work may lose their entitlement to redundancy payment.

If the terms and conditions of the new job are different or the work itself is different, the employee is entitled to a four-week trial period before accepting the arrangement. This period can be extended by agreement if retraining is necessary. The right to redundancy pay is preserved during the trial period, but once the new job is accepted redundancy rights are lost.

Time off to look for work

Employees under notice of redundancy who have a minimum of two years' service are entitled to reasonable paid time off work during working hours to look for another job or make arrangements for training for future employment.

There is no legal definition of 'reasonable', but it is good practice to allow as much time off as the person needs.

Selection for redundancy

The employer has a legal duty to select people for redundancy in a fair and reasonable manner. Someone selected for redundancy for any of the following reasons could automatically claim unfair dismissal:

- because of trade union membership or non-membership
- for carrying out duties as an employee representative
- for taking part in an election of an employee representative for collective redundancy purposes
- for taking action on health and safety grounds as a recognised health and safety representative
- for reasons relating to the national minimum wage, working tax credit or Working Time Regulations

- for making a 'protected disclosure' (whistleblowing) within the meaning of the **Public Interest Disclosure Act 1998**, or in breach of a previously agreed procedure.

An employer must not discriminate on the grounds of race, sex or pregnancy, religion or belief, sexual orientation, or disability. This currently only applies if there are 15 or more employees or others working under a contract, but this exemption will disappear on 1 October 2004.

Review procedures and criteria for selection for redundancy to ensure that they do not indirectly discriminate. For example, arrangements whereby part-time workers should be laid off first could affect women disproportionately, and 'last in first out' arrangements could potentially discriminatory on the basis of age.

Redundancy pay

The **Employment Rights Act 1996** governs statutory redundancy pay. To be eligible under the Act an employee must be:
- continuously employed for more than two years (a period of employment before the age of 18 does not count towards the two years*)
- dismissed for reasons of redundancy
- aged over 18 years*
- aged under 65 or the normal retirement age; if this is lower than 65 it must be the same for men and women.

The level of statutory redundancy pay depends on the employee's age,* length of service and weekly pay. The rates are:
- half a week's pay for every complete year of service in which the employee is aged between 18 and 21 years
- one week's pay for every complete year of service in which the employee is aged between 22 and 40 years
- one and a half weeks' pay for each complete year of service in which the employee is 41 years or over but below 65. Employees aged 64 have their redundancy pay reduced by one-twelfth for each complete month they are over 64.

The maximum number of years to be counted is 20. The government sets an upper limit each year on the amount of weekly pay that can be counted (£270 from February 2004). The employer is responsible for paying this lump sum. There is a redundancy calculator on the DTI's website *www.dti.gov.uk/er*

The government plans to remove some age-related criteria in the statutory redundancy payments scheme when it introduces legislation to outlaw age discrimination in employment and training in 2006. The calculation will *be on the basis of one week's pay per year of service, subject to the current maximum of 20 years, regardless of age. Under the proposals, service below the age of 18, which is currently ignored, will be taken into account. See Age discrimination, in chapter 3.*

Good practice

The law provides a safety net for employees who are made redundant. However, the provisions outlined above are far from generous. Employers should look at ways of introducing better terms into employees' contracts.

Improvements on the legal minimum include:
- helping people find alternative work
- allowing all employees facing redundancy, even those who have worked less than two years, time off to look for work or for training
- arranging for redundancy counselling
- extending the period of redundancy notice given to employees
- providing contractual redundancy pay entitlement above the statutory minimum, for example by extending the number of weeks' redundancy pay, increasing the maximum figure for 'weekly' pay, or reducing the qualifying period.

Consider the organisation's financial position carefully before agreeing to better financial provisions. The decision to make staff redundant will often be made when an organisation's assets and income do not cover its costs. The contractual liability to employees is a debt. If these liabilities are increased, an organisation may have to close earlier, which is against the interests of service users. Also remember that the management committee of an unincorporated organisation (unincorporated association or trust) may become personally liable if the organisation cannot pay its employees the amount stated in their contracts.

Claiming money owed

If an organisation becomes insolvent and goes into voluntary liquidation and is unable to pay salaries and redundancy pay, the employees can claim some of the money owed to them from the government's **National Insurance Fund** (0500 848 489).

Employees may claim:
- statutory redundancy pay
- statutory maternity pay
- a basic award of unfair dismissal compensation, made by an employment tribunal (but only if no redundancy payment is made)

- a compensatory award for the employer's failure to give statutory notice of redundancy
- up to eight weeks' arrears of pay, to a maximum limit
- up to six weeks' holiday pay
- unpaid contributions to an occupational pension scheme
- pay for the statutory period of notice.

An employee of an incorporated organisation (company or industrial and provident society) who is still owed money after receiving these awards (for example for any additional arrears of wages) would have a claim for some priority debts against the employer. The employee would therefore become a **preferential creditor** (see *The liquidation*, in chapter 10). An employee of an unincorporated organisation (unincorporated association or trust) may be able to bring a claim against some or all members of the management committee. Employees are always advised to seek help, for example from their union or a law centre.

Providing references

An employee who leaves or applies for another job will often request a reference. It is good practice to provide a reference wherever possible. To ensure that future managers or management committee members can do this, it is good practice to maintain enough information in the employee's file to enable accurate references to be written in future.

All references provided must be fair and accurate. If unfairly critical, an employee could make a financial claim against your organisation. Ensure you stick to the facts. You can, for example, say that 'Allegations have been made that the employee has stolen property belonging to a colleague. Disciplinary proceedings are pending and we cannot at this stage say whether the allegations are true.' That is a pure statement of fact and does not say that the employee is guilty of theft. If you are proposing to write a critical reference for a former employee and are worried about being sued, send the employee a draft and ask them to agree the reference before it is provided. Also beware of writing artificially good references; there is a danger of being sued by the new employer for misrepresentation.

The Information Commissioner has produced a Code of Practice which explains how organisations can follow the Data Protection Act in the context of keeping employee records. The Code contains a section on references, which provides the following benchmarks:

- Set out a clear policy stating who can give references on behalf of the organisation, in what circumstances, and how references are accessed. Make sure that anyone who is likely to become a referee is aware of this policy.
- Do not provide confidential references about someone unless you are sure this is their wish.
- When someone's employment ends, establish whether the person wishes references to be provided to future employers or to others.

In relation to receiving references:
- When responding to a request from a worker to see their own reference which enables a third party to be identified, make a judgement as to what information it is reasonable to withhold.

Employment practices data protection code part 2: Employment records is available from *www.informationcommissioner.gov.uk*

Post-employment discrimination

It is unlawful to discriminate against someone on the basis of their race, sex, disability, religion or belief, or sexuality after the termination of their employment, providing the act of discrimination is closely connected to the employment relationship.

Examples of post-employment discrimination would include failure to provide a reference or providing a bad reference on the grounds that a person had claimed or threatened to claim discrimination while they were employed, and possibly matters such as not pursuing a grievance post-termination.

Employment tribunals

Employees who consider their employment rights have been infringed usually have the right to apply to an employment tribunal. Amongst other matters, employment tribunals can deal with the following:
- claims for unfair dismissal (including the right to return to work after maternity, paternity and adoption leave)
- claims for unpaid redundancy payments
- complaints of race, sex or disability discrimination in employment, and for equal pay
- failure to receive the national minimum wage
- complaints under the Working Time Regulations
- whistleblowing
- being denied parental leave

- being denied dependants leave
- an application for employment particulars to be determined if they have not been given by the employer
- an application for pay details to be determined if the employer has not provided an itemised pay statement
- unauthorised deductions from wages
- a complaint that time off has not been given in line with statutory requirements
- a complaint that ante natal leave has not been provided
- breach of contract.

Most complaints to an employment tribunal must be made within three months, although those related to redundancy and equal pay must be made within six months. Redundancy and equal pay complaints can sometimes be extended (if the employer deliberately concealed relevant facts or if the individual concerned was under the age 18 or mentally incapable).

An employment tribunal has the power to award compensation for unfair dismissal within a statutory limit (£55,000 from February 2004). There is no financial limit to compensation that can be awarded in cases involving discrimination on the basis of sex, race, disability, religion or other belief or sexual orientation.

Generally employment tribunals do not award legal costs. However, following changes in the rules, which widen the scope of when costs can be awarded, this is now happening more frequently. Any award will probably only be a small part of an organisation's actual legal costs. Employees may be represented by trades unions or receive financial assistance from the Equal Opportunities Commission, the Disability Rights Commission or the Commission for Racial Equality. This can place employers at a disadvantage because they will have to pay for their own legal representation and probably will not recover any of the legal costs even if successful. Employers therefore often decide it is less costly to settle a complaint to an employment tribunal by making a payment to the employee even if they consider the complaint is unjustified. ACAS can help draw up an agreement settling a tribunal case. Employers often insist on any settlement being made in the form of a **compromise agreement**, which can settle all claims, settles the employment tribunal claim and prevents any other claim being made to the tribunal. The employer draws up the compromise agreement and an employee must obtain legal advice on the effect of signing a compromise agreement, which is usually paid for by the employer.

Unified tribunal service

The **Employment Act 2002** includes provisions to incorporate the employment tribunals and employment appeal tribunals into a unified tribunal service that will be created over the next few years. The aim is to provide a more streamlined service for users as well as a more efficient service through sharing costs and resources across other tribunals. There will be a full consultation on the detailed proposals.

Claims brought in court

Breach of contract claims can be brought in the courts rather than the employment tribunal and must be if the employment is ongoing. There may be an advantage for the employee in doing this, because there is no limit to awards in the court, and the winner is generally awarded their legal costs. However, if the claim is for under £5000 this will be dealt with in the small claims court, which has fixed costs.

Chapter 5:
Health and safety

Related chapters
Chapter 3 – Harassment
Chapter 4 – Employment
Chapter 6 – Premises
Chapter 7 – Insurance
Chapter 9 – Public activities; data protection

Legislation

The **Health and Safety at Work Act 1974** (**HSW Act**) provides a comprehensive framework for health and safety in the workplace. The Act covers the health and safety of employees (whether working on the premises or remotely) and others using an organisation's premises and equipment, including the public, trainees, volunteers, committee members, self-employed workers and contractors.

Regulations

Details of how employers must comply with their responsibilities under the HSW Act are given in regulations, approved by parliament following proposals from the Health and Safety Commission (HSC). They include:

- the management of health and safety
- health, safety and welfare in the workplace
- personal protective equipment
- provision and use of work equipment
- manual handling, for example lifting
- control of asbestos at work
- display screens
- fire precautions.

Guidance

The Health and Safety Executive (HSE) publishes guidance on a range of subjects, to help people understand and comply with the regulations. Much of this is available free of charge at *www.hse.gov.uk*

Approved codes of practice

Approved codes of practice (ACoPs) give advice on how to comply with the law and have a special legal status. If an employer is prosecuted for a breach of health and safety law, and it is proved that they did not follow the relevant provisions of the ACoP, a court can find them at fault unless they can show they have complied with the law in some other way.

Enforcement

The HSE through its inspectors, and local authority environmental health officers are responsible for enforcing the responsibilities under the HSW Act. They have wide powers to enter and inspect premises, test equipment, take measurements, photographs and samples, and, if necessary, remove equipment for testing or preserving. They can also require staff and committee members to answer questions on health and safety matters.

If an organisation is not complying with the law, inspectors can serve an **improvement notice** or a **prohibition notice** or they can prosecute the organisation. An improvement notice sets out measures the organisation must take, with a timescale, to comply with the law. A prohibition notice will be served only if there is or will be immediate risk of serious personal injury (including any disease or physical or mental impairment), and can require the organisation to stop one or all of its activities until health and safety measures are implemented. Failure to comply with either type of notice is a criminal offence.

The inspector can also prosecute an organisation for failing to carry out its responsibilities. This is likely to happen only if an accident occurs in which someone is seriously injured or killed, or if an organisation:

- has failed to address health and safety issues
- is considered to be unwilling to implement health and safety measures or is believed to be deliberately delaying them
- has ignored obvious and imminent risks.

Anyone injured because of an organisation's failure to comply with health and safety law can claim compensation. Organisations employing staff must, by law, take out **employers' liability insurance** to cover claims by employees, and display the certificate. They should also take out **public liability insurance** to cover claims by others, including service users, members of the public, volunteers, trainees and self-employed workers (see chapter 7 for further information on insurance).

Responsibilities of committee members and staff

Management committee (committee) members have a legal duty to ensure that the organisation complies with health and safety legislation. The HSW Act states that where an organisation has failed to comply with the law and has committed an offence, then that offence has also been committed by anyone who has failed in their individual responsibilities. This will always include committee members, and may also cover senior staff who have health and safety responsibilities.

Committee members and senior staff should therefore be aware that if they do not individually ensure the organisation carries out its responsibilities, they could be committing a criminal offence and be prosecuted and fined. The committee cannot rely on staff to ensure their own health and safety nor on safety representatives to alert them to dangers. The legal responsibility rests with the committee. HSE guidance recommends that every committee should appoint a member to take on particular responsibility for health and safety.

For further details see *Directors' responsibilities for health and safety* (INDG343), available from *www.hse.gov.uk*, which explains how committee members can ensure their organisation has an effective approach to managing health and safety risks, and sets out a number of action points.

Registering

Under the **Offices Shops and Railway Premises Act 1963** organisations which employ staff in shop or office premises may need to register with the HSE or the local authority. For further information contact the local authority or telephone the HSE InfoLine on 08701 545500.

General duties under the HSW Act

The HSW Act imposes general health and safety duties on both employers and employees.

Duties to employees

Employers owe a duty 'so far as reasonably practicable' to ensure their employees' health, safety and welfare at work.

This duty includes:
- providing and maintaining machinery, equipment, appliances and work systems that are safe and free from health risks

- having arrangements for ensuring articles and substances are safely used, handled, stored and transported, without any risk to health
- providing appropriate information, instruction, training and supervision to ensure the health and safety of staff
- maintaining any place of work in a safe condition and without risk to health
- maintaining workplace access and exit so that it is safe and without risk to health
- providing and maintaining a safe, risk-free working environment with adequate arrangements for staff welfare.

An employer cannot charge staff for any measures required for health and safety.

'Reasonably practicable'

The general obligations on employers do not extend to guaranteeing total protection against accidents or ill health, as this would be impossible. Essentially, the organisation has to balance the needs to achieve its objectives and the cost of safety measures against the risks staff face and measures that can be taken to reduce or avoid those risks.

Home-based workers

Most of the regulations under the HSW Act also apply to home-based workers. For further details see *Homeworking: Guidance for employers and employees on health and safety* (INDG226), available from HSE Books or *www.hse.gov.uk* and *Telework guidance*, available from *www.dti.gov.uk*

Duties to non-employees

Employers also have a duty to manage the organisation in such a way as to ensure 'so far as reasonably practicable' that people who are not employees but who might be affected by its activities are not exposed to health or safety risks.

Such people would include trainees, volunteers, committee members, self-employed workers, users, members of the public and people temporarily working in an organisation's premises. Contractors appointed by the organisation will also have a duty of care, and it is important to discuss with them how they will limit risks (for example minimising noise or fumes resulting from their work).

Technically the HSW Act does not apply to an organisation without employees. But it is good practice to take all reasonable steps to comply with the requirements of the Act even if there are no employees.

Duties to users of premises

Anyone responsible for non-domestic premises has a duty to people who are not their employees but who work or use equipment or substances provided on the premises. They must ensure 'so far as reasonably practicable' that the premises, the means of access and exit, equipment and materials are free from health and safety risks. People considered responsible for premises include anyone who is an owner or tenant, has responsibility for repairs, or has responsibility under a licence or tenancy for the health and safety of people using the premises.

This duty will be owed to trainees, volunteers, committee members and self-employed workers who use the premises, to anyone sharing the premises and, in some cases, to anyone hiring the premises.

Duties of employees

The HSW Act imposes a duty on each member of staff to take reasonable care for their own health and safety and that of any person who may be affected by anything they do or fail to do. Staff must also cooperate with employers to fulfil their responsibilities.

Employers may wish to include a clause about employees' responsibilities within the statement of terms and conditions of service. However, remember that the strength of duty is greater for the employer than the employee.

Other general requirements of the HSW Act

Health and safety policy

An organisation with five or more employees (including temporary, sessional and part-time employees) must have a written health and safety policy, which must:
- state the general policy on health and safety
- describe responsibilities for health and safety management
- outline systems and procedures for ensuring appropriate standards of health and safety
- be brought to the attention of all employees
- be revised whenever appropriate, and every revision must be brought to the employees' attention
- be signed and dated by the employer.

It is good practice for all employers (and organisations which only use volunteers) to have a written policy.

The policy should cover issues such as:
- managers' and supervisors' responsibilities
- employees' and volunteers' duties (both statutory and organisational)
- consultation arrangements (for example safety committees), including name(s) of any employee representative(s)
- training arrangements (including induction and job specific training)
- hazard identification
- findings of general risk assessments
- findings of specific risk assessments for employees aged under 18 (see *Young employees*, page 120) and fire risks (see *Fire safety*, page 127)
- fire evacuation arrangements
- location of health and safety poster or leaflets
- accidents, first aid and work-related ill health
- monitoring arrangements
- emergency procedures.

The HSE booklets *An introduction to health and safety: Health and safety in small businesses* (INDS259(rev1)) and *Stating your business: Guidance on preparing a health and safety policy document* (INDG324) and *The health and safety handbook for voluntary and community organisations*, published by the Directory of Social Change (DSC), include example health and safety policies. The DSC policy covers volunteers as well as staff.

Health and safety poster

All employers must display the statutory poster *Health and safety law – what you should know,* or distribute a copy of the equivalent HSE leaflet *Your health and safety – a guide for workers to all employees.* Updated versions of both are available from HSE Books.

Safety representatives

Any recognised trade union (see *Unions*, in chapter 4) may appoint safety representatives. Wherever possible, the representatives should have worked for the organisation for at least two years or have had at least two years' experience in similar work.

Employers must consult safety representatives in good time when drawing up their health and safety policies.

Safety representatives appointed by recognised trades unions have the right to:
- investigate potential hazards and dangers and examine the causes of any accidents

- investigate complaints by staff relating to health, safety and welfare
- submit proposals to the employer on any health and safety matters at work and in particular suggestions relating to complaints, hazards and accidents
- carry out workplace inspections and inspect relevant documents (see below)
- represent employees in discussions with the employer on health, safety and welfare and with health and safety inspectors
- receive information from inspectors about matters identified by them during inspections
- attend meetings of safety committees where these have been set up (see *Safety committees*, page 118).

An employer must allow safety representatives to take reasonable paid time off to carry out their responsibilities and for health and safety training. *Safety representatives and safety committees* (L87), available from HSE Books, sets out the rules relating to time off for training.

Employers must allow union safety representatives to inspect the workplace or any part of it:
- at least once every three months, or
- where there has been any substantial change in the conditions of work, for example when new machinery has been introduced, or the HSC has issued new guidance relating to that type of work or workplace, or
- where there has been a serious accident, a dangerous incident or a notifiable disease.

The safety representative must give the employer reasonable notice before carrying out the inspection. In turn, the employer must give the safety representative reasonable assistance, including facilities for independent investigation and private discussion with employees.

An employer must also let the representative inspect and take copies of any health and safety documentation.

There are exceptions, which include:
- an employee's health records where the individual can be identified
- information which cannot be disclosed by law (for example under the **Data Protection Act 1998** – see chapter 9)
- information relating to any individual unless they have consented
- other information that would cause 'substantial injury' to the employer's business.

Consultation with employees who are not represented by a recognised trade union

Under the **Health and Safety (Consultation with Employees) Regulations 1996** employers must consult employees who are not represented by trade union safety representatives about health and safety.

Employees must be consulted on the following:
- any change that may substantially affect their health and safety, such as introducing new equipment or ways of working
- arrangements for getting competent people to help them satisfy health and safety laws (see *Getting advice*, page 119)
- the content of health and safety information to be provided to employees
- planning and organisation of health and safety training
- health and safety consequences of introducing new technology.

Employees may be consulted either directly or through the staff who have been elected to represent them on health and safety matters (**Representatives of employees' safety – ROES**).

The regulations do not specify the election procedure for ROES.

Elected ROES have the right to:
- receive information needed to participate fully and effectively in any consultation when carrying out their functions
- receive information included in any records of accidents, injuries and diseases kept by the employer, with the same exceptions that apply to trade union representatives (see *Safety representatives*, page 116)
- make representations to the employer on potential hazards and dangerous incidents at the workplace that affect the employees they represent
- make representations to the employer on general matters affecting the health and safety at work of the group of employees they represent and, in particular, the matters on which employers are obliged to consult (see above)
- represent their colleagues in consultations with inspectors at the workplace
- receive a reasonable amount of training, with the costs, including travel and subsistence, being paid for by the employer
- use any other facilities or receive reasonable assistance needed to carry out their function

- take paid time off during working hours necessary to perform their functions and to stand as candidates in an election as a ROES.

Although ROES have many of the same rights of representation as trades union representatives, they do not have the right to inspect or investigate, and will not have access to trade union resources such as legal help and advice.

Safety committees

Any two safety representatives can require an employer to set up a safety committee to review measures taken to ensure the health and safety of staff, within three months of the request. The employer must consult the safety representatives and recognised trades unions when setting up the committee and let staff know the members' names. Membership could include volunteers and users, as well as paid staff and management committee members and should be balanced between management and others.

Regulations under the Act
The management of health and safety at work

The **Management of Health and Safety at Work Regulations 1999** cover the matters listed below. Full details can be found in *The management of health and safety at work. Approved code of practice and guidance* (L21), from HSE Books. The HSE InfoLine 08701 545500 or hseinformationservices@natbrit.com can help with many queries.

Risk assessment

The regulations require that every employer must:
- assess the health and safety risks employees are exposed to at work
- assess risks to the health and safety of others (for example users, volunteers, committee members, self-employed workers and members of the public) arising from the organisation's activities
- take action to eliminate the hazard (ie something with the potential to cause harm) or if that is not possible, to reduce the risk as far as possible
- review and revise the assessment whenever necessary
- carry out a specific assessment of the risks to the health and safety of young employees before employing anyone aged under 18 (see *Young employees*, page 120)
- carry out a separate fire risk assessment (see *Fire safety*, page 127).

The regulations require a systematic examination of an organisation's activities. This must involve:
- identifying hazards arising from activities (whether from the type of work, fire hazards or other factors, for example the condition of the premises)
- deciding who might be harmed, and how
- evaluating the extent of the risks, taking into account any existing precautions, including fire safety arrangements
- identifying what is already being done to minimise the risk, or to minimise the negative effects if it does happen, and what the organisation could or should be doing
- producing a health and safety policy for reducing risks, with named responsibilities and deadlines (see *Health and safety policies*, page 131)
- putting the plan into action.

Employers are also required to do a risk assessment of work activities carried out by home-based workers. This may involve visiting their homes, although people working from home can also help in identifying hazards. For more information see *Homeworking: Guidance for employers and employees on health and safety* (INDH226), available from HSE Books and *www.hse.gov.uk* and *Telework guidance*, available from *www.dti.gov.uk*

Reviews

Employers should regularly review their assessment of risk as well as continually monitoring health and safety. If they develop a new area of work, move into new premises or buy new equipment, they must carry out further risk assessments.

Carrying out the assessment

In small organisations with few hazards, the assessment can be carried out by non-specialist staff or a committee member as long as that person has undertaken appropriate training. In larger organisations or where there are special hazards, an overall assessment can be carried out by a non-specialist followed by a specialist assessment of particularly hazardous activities. In organisations with several workplaces, some risks will be common and can be included within an overall assessment, but each site and the equipment within it has to be assessed separately.

It is important that the risk assessment takes account of what actually happens in the workplace rather than what is supposed to happen. If staff ignore safety or other instructions, for example on the use of equipment or keeping fire doors closed, this should be noted within the risk assessment and a decision made on what action to take.

Employers should pay particular attention to those who may be especially at risk, for example inexperienced or new staff or volunteers, disabled people, people who work unusual hours, such as cleaners and security staff, and those who have difficulty understanding written or spoken English.

The risk assessment should examine existing precautionary measures, the extent to which they are actually being used, and their effectiveness.

Organisations with five or more employees must produce a written record of the significant findings of the assessment. It is good practice for all organisations to do so. The record should include:
- significant hazards identified
- the people who are at risk
- existing control measures and the extent to which they control, minimise or eliminate the risks
- risks which are not adequately controlled and the action taken.

The form should be signed and dated by both management and safety representatives.

Getting advice

Employers must appoint at least one competent person to help them carry out the risk assessment and take necessary preventative and protective measures. The assessor, who may be a member of staff, must have appropriate training, experience and knowledge, including knowledge of fire safety, and must be given all the necessary information, including details of anyone working on short-term contracts. Assessors must also have enough time and the means to fulfil their functions.

Where possible, an employee must be appointed as a competent person in preference to someone not in the workforce.

Guidance on how to carry out risk assessments is included in the *Management of health and safety at work. Approved code of practice* (L21), available from HSE Books. *An introduction to health and safety: Health and safety in small business* (INDG259(rev)), from HSE Books, and *Five steps to risk assessment* (INDG163(rev1)), from *www.hse.gov.uk*, include a sample recording form. *Five steps* is particularly useful for small organisations.

Publications and other information

Employers and employees should read health and safety publications. Publications mentioned in this chapter (many of which are free) and many others are available from HSE Books on 01787 881165 or *www.hsebooks.co.uk*. Other information is available from *www.hse.gov.uk* and the HSE InfoLine 08701 545500, minicom 02920 8085537 (8am-6pm) or *hseinformationservices@natbrit.com*

Preventative and protective measures

The regulations require that every employer must have arrangements for effective planning, organisation, control, monitoring and review of preventative and protective measures and, where there are five or more employees, must record these arrangements in writing. It is good practice to put these in writing even where there are fewer than five employees, or no employees.

The regulations state that an employer must use the following hierarchy of preventative measures:
- it is best to avoid risk altogether if possible
- risks should be tackled at source rather than mitigated, for example it is better to design equipment so there is no risk than to put up a warning notice
- wherever possible work should be adapted to the individual, for example in workplace design, choice of work equipment and work methods
- the employer should take advantage of any technological and technical progress that enables work to be done more safely
- risk prevention measures need to be part of a coherent policy and approach and aim progressively to minimise risks that cannot be prevented or avoided altogether
- priority should be given to those measures that affect the whole workplace and so yield the greatest benefit
- all workers, including trainees and volunteers, must understand what they need to do in relation to health and safety
- avoiding, preventing and reducing risks to health and safety should be an accepted part of the approach and attitude at all levels of the organisation, ie there needs to be a 'health and safety culture'.

Health surveillance

Apart from the responsibilities for health surveillance under specific regulations, for example relating to asbestos and other dangerous substances, this regulation requires all employers to introduce health surveillance where it is needed. The Health and Safety Commission recommends it is introduced where the risk assessment shows that:
- there is an identifiable disease or some health condition relating to the work carried out
- techniques are available to detect indications of the disease or condition
- there is a reasonable likelihood that the disease or condition may arise in the work environment

- surveillance will improve protection for the staff against the disease or condition.

Emergency procedures

All employers must have appropriate procedures to follow in the event of serious and imminent danger to people at work, and nominate enough competent staff to implement the procedures to evacuate premises in an emergency.

The procedures must ensure that all staff exposed to serious and imminent danger are informed of the nature of the hazard and of the steps to be taken to protect them. They must also enable people to stop work and leave the danger area if exposed, and not to return until it is safe to do so.

The risk assessment should identify the likely events that will lead to the implementation of emergency procedures, for example a fire, bomb alert or building collapse.

The procedures should set out the limits of actions required of employees in an emergency, for example when to fight a fire and when to evacuate, whether to notify emergency services, shut down machinery or secure essential documents, and how the emergency procedures will be activated.

Information to employees

Employers must provide all employees with understandable and relevant information on the risks identified, preventative and protective measures, emergency procedures and the names of those responsible for evacuation. Employees must also be told about risks, including fire risks, identified by any other employers using the same workplace.

It is important to recognise the needs of staff who have difficulties with communicating in written or spoken English, for example by producing information in different languages, in Braille or on tape, or in a simplified or pictorial format for workers with learning difficulties.

Cooperation between employers

If two or more employers share a workplace, they must cooperate on health and safety matters. If there are risks arising from one employer's activities, that employer must provide information about these risks to the other employers' staff. Wherever possible, employers must coordinate their health and safety measures, including those they take to ensure fire safety in the workplace. Cooperation may involve carrying out a joint risk assessment for the whole premises as well as a more limited assessment for each employer's activities. The Health and Safety Commission recommends that either one employer, for example the owner or tenant, takes responsibility for the premises, or that a health and safety coordinator is jointly appointed.

Visiting employees

Employers have a responsibility to visiting employees (for example someone coming in to fix the photocopier or to attend a meeting) and self-employed people working within the organisation or on its premises. They must notify self-employed people and the employer of anyone working on their premises of any health and safety risks and of the precautionary measures taken. They must also provide instructions and understandable information about any risks to the self-employed person or visiting employee.

Examples where this rule will apply include cleaning and service contracts and the use of agency staff.

Staff capabilities and training

Employers must ensure that staff capabilities regarding health and safety are taken into account when allocating work, and provide adequate health and safety training when staff are recruited and if they are exposed to any new or increased risks. Training should be repeated periodically and take place during working hours. Employers have a specific responsibility to consider the extent of the health and safety training for people aged under 18 before any such person is employed.

Temporary workers

Agency staff and anyone employed on a temporary or fixed-term contract must be given understandable information about any special qualifications or skills required to carry out work safely and any necessary health surveillance before they begin work.

Young workers

Before employing anyone aged under 18, employers must carry out a risk assessment of the work hazards specific to that individual (see *Risk assessment*, page 118).

The assessment must take particular account of:
- the young person's inexperience, immaturity and lack of awareness of risk
- the fitting out and layout of the workplace and workstation
- the nature, degree and duration of exposure to physical, biological and chemical agents
- the form, range and use of work equipment and the way it is handled

- the organisation of processes and activities
- the extent of the health and safety training to be provided to the young person and special risks set out in health and safety guidance.

People aged under 18 must not be employed for work:
- which is beyond their physical or psychological capacity
- involving harmful exposure to agents which are toxic or carcinogenic or cause genetic damage or harm to unborn children or chronically affect human health
- involving harmful exposure to radiation
- involving the risk of accidents which would not be recognised or avoided by young people because of insufficient attention to safety or lack of experience or training
- in which there is a risk to health from extreme cold or heat, noise or vibration.

This does not prevent 16 or 17 year olds being employed for work which is part of their training if they are supervised by a competent person and where any risk will be reduced to the lowest level reasonably practicable.

Before employing someone who is under the school leaving age, their parent or guardian must receive comprehensible and relevant information on:
- the health and safety risks identified by the risk assessment (see *Risk assessment*, page 118)
- the preventative and protective measures (see *Preventative and protective measures*, page 119)
- any risks notified by other employers using the same premises.

Work experience trainees
Work experience trainees have the same status as employees under the HSW Act.

Further guidance and a table on hazards, risks and ways of avoiding them are included in *Young people at work: A guide for employers* (HSG165), available from HSE Books.

New and expectant mothers
Employers who employ women of child bearing age must take particular account of any risks to a new or expectant mother or her child when carrying out the risk assessment (see *Risk assessment*, page 118). A 'new' mother is one who has given birth within the previous six months, or who is breastfeeding.

Where a risk to a new or expectant mother or her child(ren) cannot be avoided by other measures, the employer must alter the woman's working conditions or

hours of work if it is reasonable to do so and would avoid the risk.

If it is not reasonable to alter the woman's working conditions, the employer should identify and offer her suitable alternative work, and if that is not feasible, suspend her from work. The **Employment Rights Act 1996** requires that this suspension be on full pay.

Where a new or expectant mother normally works at night and presents a medical certificate from a doctor or midwife which shows that she should not continue to do so, the organisation must offer her suitable alternative work during the day, on the same terms and conditions, or if this is not feasible, suspend her on full pay for the period specified in the certificate as long as this remains necessary for health and safety reasons.

No action need be taken until the employee has provided written confirmation that she is pregnant, has given birth within the previous six months, or is breastfeeding. It is good practice not to require this information in writing, but the employer should record the date they were told.

Further guidance is contained in *New and expectant mothers at work: A guide for employers* (HSG122, 2nd edition), from HSE Books. The leaflet *A guide for new and expectant mothers who work* (INDG373) can be downloaded from *www.hse.gov.uk/mothers*

Workplace health, safety and welfare
The **Workplace (Health, Safety and Welfare) Regulations 1992** apply to all workplaces. Full details can be found in *Workplace health, safety and welfare. Approved code of practice* (L24) and are summarised in *Workplace health safety and welfare: A short guide for managers* (INDG244). *Welfare at work: Guidance for employers on welfare provisions* (INDG293) includes suggestions for good practice. All are available from HSE Books.

Premises and equipment
Premises and equipment must be kept in a good state of repair and in proper working order, and must be properly maintained. Employers should rectify defects immediately or take steps to protect anyone who might be at risk, for example by preventing access. Where a defect makes equipment unsuitable for use but causes no danger it can be taken out of service until repaired. The organisation should have a suitable servicing and maintenance system that identifies potentially dangerous defects and ensures they are remedied, and should keep a record of any defects and maintenance carried out.

Ventilation

There must be effective and suitable provision for ventilation. This may simply involve windows that open. Any air conditioning or mechanical ventilation must be cleaned, tested, maintained and serviced, and must operate effectively. Recycled air must be filtered.

Temperature

The workplace must be neither too hot nor too cold, with enough thermometers to enable people to establish the inside temperature. Unless there are special reasons for lower temperatures, in most cases the minimum acceptable temperature is 16°C. Although not a legal requirement, the World Health Organisation recommends 24°C as a maximum.

Lighting

Every workplace must have suitable and sufficient lighting. As far as practicable, this should be natural light. There must also be emergency lighting if anyone working in any part of the premises would be in danger if normal lighting became defective. The light should be sufficient for people to work and move safely around without eye strain. Stairs should be well lit and without shadows on treads. Where necessary, individual workstations and places of particular danger should be lit separately. Windows and skylights should be cleaned regularly if possible.

Cleanliness and rubbish disposal

Workplaces, furniture and fittings must be kept clean and there should be additional cleaning if there is a spillage or soiling. Rubbish should not be allowed to accumulate except in rubbish receptacles. The standard of cleanliness should be adapted according to the workplace or area use.

Workspace

There must be enough space in workrooms to enable staff to get to and from their workspaces and move easily and safely. This will depend on the layout and how much space furniture and fittings take. A worker should normally have an absolute minimum of 11 cubic metres of space (approximately two metres square, including workstation and chair, but excluding filing cabinets), discounting any height above three metres. This may be insufficient if a high percentage of the space is taken by furniture.

Workstation design

A workstation is the place where an individual works, for example a desk, chair, computer, immediate shelving and drawers. It must be suitable for the individual or individuals concerned as well as for their work. It should be protected from the weather and be designed so that someone can leave it quickly in an emergency. The design should also ensure that an individual will not slip or fall. A suitable seat and footrest should be provided where necessary. Work equipment and materials should be within easy reach without undue bending or stretching. The workstation should take account of the specific needs of disabled members of staff.

There are specific workstation requirements for computer use (see *Display screen equipment,* page 126).

Floors and internal traffic routes

Floors must be suitable for their purpose without any dangerous holes or slopes or slippery or uneven surfaces and should have drainage where necessary. Handrails should be provided on all staircases except where they would obstruct a traffic route.

Preventing people and objects from falling

Employers should take suitable and effective measures to prevent anyone being injured through falling or being hit by a falling object. Any area where there is a risk should be clearly indicated. Wherever possible any place where someone could fall and injure themselves should have fencing.

Storage units should be strong and stable enough for their task and not be overfilled. The height of stacking should be limited and checks made on the safety of stored objects.

Windows

All windows and other transparent areas should be made from material which does not cause danger, for example making them robust enough not to break, or using shatter-proof glass. Transparent surfaces should be marked so that they are apparent.

It should be possible to reach windows, skylights and ventilators so that they can be safely opened and closed. There should be controls to prevent people falling out of any window.

It should be possible to clean windows and skylights safely, for example through having pivoting windows or using ladders.

Vehicles

There should be measures to ensure that pedestrians are not put in danger from vehicles. Traffic routes for pedestrians and vehicles should be clearly marked, and if possible separated. Pay particular attention to the safety of wheelchair users and people with visual disabilities.

Doors and gates

Doors and gates should be suitably constructed. Sliding doors should have a device to prevent them from being derailed, and upward opening doors a device to prevent them from falling back. Powered doors must have features preventing them from trapping anyone, and enabling them to be overridden if power fails. It should be possible to see through doors that open both ways.

WCs

WCs must be suitable, adequately ventilated and lit, and kept clean and tidy. There should be separate facilities for men and women unless each WC is in a separate room with a door that can be locked from the inside. There must be at least one women-only WC for every 25 women and one men-only WC for every 25 men. Exact requirements are shown below.

Number of employees	Minimum number of toilets/washrooms
1-5	1
6-25	2
26-50	3
51-75	4
76-100	5

There must one additional WC and one additional washing station for every 25 people (or fraction of 25) above 100.

Washing facilities

There must be suitable and sufficient washing facilities if needed because of the nature of the work or for health reasons. These must also be by each WC and changing area, with hot and cold running water, soap or other washing agent and a means of drying hands, for example towels or a hot air dryer. The rooms must be ventilated and properly lit and be kept clean and tidy. Men and women should have separate facilities unless they are provided in a room with a lockable door and the facilities in each room are used by one person at a time.

ACAS guidance notes that some religions and beliefs do not allow individuals to undress or shower in the company of others. If staff need to change their clothing or shower in the interests of health and safety, it is good practice to discuss with staff how such needs can be met. Insisting on communal shower and changing facilities could constitute indirect discrimination or harassment.

For further details see *Religion and belief in the workplace: Putting the Employment Equality (Religion Or Belief) Regulations 2003 into practice*, from ACAS.

Drinking water

Drinking water must be easily accessible from marked places. Taps and containers must be clearly and correctly labelled as drinking water, and cups provided unless the water comes in a jet.

Storage and changing facilities

Staff who need to change for work must have secure storage facilities for home and work clothes – two areas if the two types of clothes need to be kept separate for hygiene or health reasons. There should also be facilities for drying clothing.

If changing requires privacy, there should be separate facilities for men and women.

Rest and eating facilities

Workplaces should have suitable rest facilities at convenient places, which must include suitable arrangements to protect non-smokers from discomfort caused by tobacco smoke. There must be enough tables and seating with backs for the number of people likely to use them at any one time and enough suitable seating for the number of disabled people at work. If food eaten in the workplace is likely to become contaminated, there should be separate eating facilities. Facilities should also be provided to enable pregnant women and nursing mothers to rest.

Remember that some religions or beliefs have special dietary requirements. If staff bring food to work they may need to store and heat it separately.

Smoking

There must be suitable arrangements to protect non-smokers from dangers caused by tobacco smoke (including in rest rooms, see above). Many organisations now enforce a no smoking policy and the Health and Safety Executive recommends that all employers have a written policy on smoking in the workplace, which should give priority to the needs of non-smokers. For further information see the HSE leaflet *Passive smoking at work* (INDG63) or contact ASH or Quit.

Personal protective equipment

Full details of the **Personal Protective Equipment at Work Regulations 1992** can be found in the HSE's *Personal protective equipment at work. Guidance on regulations* (L25). The regulations do not apply if there are more specific regulations relating to the use of cutting machinery.

Personal equipment and clothing must be provided to protect staff against the weather and risks to their health and safety, unless risks are controlled by other equally effective means.

The regulations include, for example, providing helmets, gloves, rainwear, high visibility jackets, aprons, eye protectors, life-jackets and safety harnesses.

Protective equipment and clothing must:
- be appropriate for the risks involved, the conditions at the place where the risks may occur, and the period for which it is worn
- take account of the practicality of its use and the state of health of the person wearing it, and of the characteristics of each person's workstation
- be capable of fitting the wearer correctly
- be effective in preventing or controlling the risks involved.

The equipment provided must be readily available.

Employers must carry out an assessment of the general suitability of protective equipment before they supply it. They must also assess the needs of individual workers and whether the equipment meets those needs. If more than one piece of personal protective equipment is required, employers must ensure the equipment is compatible.

Unless there is a suitable cleaning process, only one person may use equipment that needs to be hygienic and otherwise free of risk to health.

Employers must also ensure that equipment is well maintained, in good working order and replaced when necessary, and that there are storage facilities for equipment not in use.

Employers must give staff clear information, instruction and training to enable them to know:
- the risks avoided or limited by the equipment
- what the equipment is for and how to use it
- steps they should take to maintain the equipment.

Employers must take reasonable steps to ensure that protective equipment is used. In turn, employees must use the protective equipment and report any defects or loss.

Work equipment

Details of the **Provision and Use of Work Equipment Regulations 1998** (**PUWER**) can be found in the HSE's *Safe use of work equipment. Approved code of practice and guidance* (L22) and in the *Simple guide to the Provision and Use of Work Equipment Regulations 1998* (INDG 291).

The regulations impose a duty both on an employer and on any organisation controlling premises where people work and where machinery is used. An organisation that shares its premises and equipment will owe a duty to the employees of those sharing the premises as well as to its own staff.

Mobile work equipment

Under Part III of PUWER mobile work equipment used for carrying people must be suitable for this purpose. Employers should take measures to reduce the risks (for example from it rolling over) to the safety of the people being carried, the operator and anyone else.

Suitability and maintenance of equipment

Employers must ensure that work equipment is suitable for the purpose for which it is used and for those who use it. This includes taking into account any special needs. When selecting equipment, employers must take into account working conditions, existing risks and any additional risk posed by the equipment. There are also requirements in relation to maintenance of equipment relevant to fire safety (see *Fire safety*, page 127).

Employers must also ensure that equipment is in good repair, and its maintenance should be recorded in a log book.

Specific risks

If any equipment is likely to involve a specific risk to health or safety, its use must be restricted to specifically authorised and suitably trained staff.

Information and instruction

Employers must ensure that all those who use work equipment, and their managers, have adequate, understandable health and safety information and, where appropriate, written instructions on its use. Instructions should include details of:

- how the equipment should be used
- possible problems, for example likely faults, and the action to be taken if they occur
- comments from those with experience of using the equipment.

Training

Employers must ensure that everyone using equipment, together with their managers, has received adequate health and safety training which includes:

- ways to use the equipment
- possible risks from its use
- precautions to be taken.

Other requirements

More specific requirements apply to machinery, covering:

- dangerous parts of machinery
- protection against specific hazards
- high or very low temperatures
- stop controls
- isolation from sources of energy
- stability
- lighting
- maintenance operations
- markings
- warnings.

For further information on reducing risks from work equipment see *Using work equipment safely* (INDG229), available from *www.hse.gov.uk*

Manual handling
General duties on employers

Employers should, wherever possible, avoid the need for staff to undertake manual handling which involves a risk of injury. Manual handling covers physically lifting, lowering, holding, pushing, pulling, carrying or moving an object or load ('load' includes a person). This would include helping people in and out of vehicles, lifting wheelchairs, moving furniture and other equipment, pushing trolleys, clearing rubbish and gardening. If a task cannot be avoided, employers must assess the risks involved against a series of factors set out in the regulations, including those listed below.

Tasks involved in the handling

Do they involve:
- working with loads at a distance from the body
- awkward body movements
- excessive lifting or lowering distances
- excessive carrying distances

- excessive pushing or pulling
- risks of loads moving suddenly
- frequent or prolonged physical effort?

Type of load

Is it:
- heavy
- bulky or unwieldy
- difficult to grasp
- unstable?

Working environment

Are there:
- space constraints, preventing good posture
- uneven, slippery or unstable floors
- variations in floor levels or work surfaces
- extremes of temperature or humidity
- poor lighting conditions
- conditions causing ventilation problems or gusts of wind?

An individual's capability

Consider the following:
- strength
- height
- physical suitability
- clothing, footwear or other personal effects the person is wearing
- whether the activity requires a certain level of stamina or fitness
- experience, knowledge and training
- results of a risk assessment, in particular whether the employee is within a group of employees identified by the assessment as being especially at risk
- whether the activity creates a hazard for pregnant women
- age
- information or training needed.

Other factors

These could include, for example, whether movement or posture were hindered by personal protective equipment or by clothing.

Full details of the **Manual Handling Operations Regulations 1992** can be found in *Manual handling. Guidance on regulations* (L23). The guidance provides a model checklist that can be used for making the assessment.

The HSE has developed an online *Manual Handling Chart Tool* to help identify high risk workplace manual handling activities – see *www.hse.gov.uk/msd/*

Managing asbestos

From 21 May 2004 Regulation 4 of the **Control of Asbestos at Work Regulations 2002** creates a new duty to manage asbestos in non-domestic premises. Anyone responsible for maintaining and repairing all or part of a property, or who has control of the building (the duty holder) must:

- find out whether the building contains asbestos, and what condition it is in
- presume materials contain asbestos, unless there is strong evidence that they do not
- assess the risk, for example if it is likely to release fibres
- make a plan to manage that risk
- provide information on the location and condition of the material to anyone who is liable to work on or disturb it.

Anyone who controls or has information about the building must cooperate with the duty holder. For example, landlords must pass on relevant information to new tenants, and leaseholders must allow access for inspection by managing agents.

For further details see *Managing asbestos: Your new legal duties* C4000 and *A short guide to managing asbestos in premises* (INDG223), available from *www.hse.gov.uk*

Display screen equipment

Full details of the **Health and Safety (Display Screen Equipment) Regulations 1992** can be found in *Display screen equipment. Guidance on regulations* (L26). This provides useful guidance on safe methods of using display screens (VDUs), including diagrams of seating arrangements. *Working with VDUs* (INDG36(rev2)) includes a summary of the regulations, gives suggestions for simple adjustments users can make to workstations and screens and lists sources of further advice. It also draws attention to the role of employees and safety representatives in risk assessments. Both publications are available from *www.hsebooks.co.uk*

The regulations impose duties on employers only in relation to 'users' – employees who use display screen equipment as a significant part of their normal work. The code of practice gives examples of staff who are likely to be included and excluded by the regulations.

Analysis of workstations

Employers must carry out a thorough analysis of workstations to assess the health and safety risks. The assessment must be updated as often as necessary.

Identified risks must be reduced to the lowest reasonably practicable extent. All display screens – not just those used by 'users' (see above) – must comply with the regulations.

Requirements for workstations

Workstations should be set up to ensure the following:

- the display screen is adequate for the type of work, with legible characters and adjustable brightness and contrast
- the screen is detachable and adjustable, in height and swivel, to allow for the operator's individual preferences
- the screen is properly and regularly cleaned to ensure dirt and grime do not affect legibility; there should be wipes at each workstation
- the keyboard is adjustable
- each workstation has a wrist rest and a footrest
- each workstation has an anti-static mat, a lamp and a document holder
- direct light does not fall on the screen, and where possible, the screen should be at a right angle to the window
- the work desk is non-reflective
- there is adequate space on work surfaces surrounding computer equipment
- the work chair is adjustable for both height and back support, and stable
- there is sufficient space at each workstation for each user to alter their position comfortably.

Daily work routine for users

It is important to consider the organisation of VDU work:

- jobs should be designed to allow for changes in activity
- staff should take regular breaks (at least ten minutes away for every hour at the screen). Short, frequent breaks are better than occasional longer breaks. Individuals should have some discretion over when to take breaks – some people prefer to take frequent 'micro' breaks.

Portable computers

The design features necessary to make portables easy to carry, such as small keyboards, can make prolonged use uncomfortable.

The HSE advises that it is best to avoid using a portable computer on its own if full-sized equipment is available. People who use portable computers should be trained in how to minimise risks. This includes sitting comfortably, angling the screen so it can be seen clearly with minimal reflections, and taking frequent breaks. Wherever possible, portables should be used on a firm surface at the right height for keying.

Eye and eyesight tests

The employer must pay for all staff defined as 'users' (see *Display screen equipment,* page 126) to have eyesight tests. These should take place at regular intervals – including before someone starts using the equipment, if they request this – and at any time they may be experiencing difficulties attributable to their work with VDUs. The definition of a 'user' is quite restrictive, so an employer may wish to pay for eye tests for all staff who regularly use computers.

When a test shows that, as a result of work with VDUs, a member of staff needs to purchase special corrective appliances (usually glasses) the employer should pay for these. This excludes those normally used for purposes other than work with VDUs.

Upper limb disorders

Work related upper limb disorders (ULDs) are often associated with keyboard work and mouse use. The term **repetitive strain injury (RSI)** is often used to refer to pain resulting from working with computers (although 'ULD' covers more than 20 medical conditions). The employer, by following best advice, should provide VDU, keyboard and mouse equipment and furniture which help prevent the development of these musculoskeletal disorders. Staff, however, can contribute to their own safety and welfare by:

- avoiding sitting in the same position for long periods
- adjusting equipment and furniture to appropriate/comfortable positions
- taking short pauses from mouse work to relax their arm
- taking rests from VDU work (at least ten minutes away every hour or frequent 'micro' breaks).

Using a mouse

Because use of a mouse, trackball or similar pointing device concentrates activity on one hand and one or two fingers, users may experience more problems with their fingers, hands, wrists, arms and shoulders than with keyboard work. Users can reduce risks by adopting a good posture and technique, and taking their hand away from the mouse when they are not using it.

The HSE booklets *Aching arms (or RSI) in small businesses* (ING171) and *Working with VDUs* (INDG36(rev2)) give advice on reducing disorders such as RSI.

Pregnant women

The level of electromagnetic radiation emitted from VDUs is well below the safe levels set out in international recommendations, and employers are not obliged to check radiation levels or provide any special devices, such as screens or aprons. Taken as a whole, research does not show any link between miscarriages or birth defects and working with VDUs. However, a pregnant woman who believes she is at risk, however much she is reassured, should not be forced to work with VDUs, and wherever possible employers should arrange alternative ways of working.

Training

All users of display screen equipment must receive health and safety training, before they start using the equipment. Further training must be provided if a workstation is modified.

Information

Staff must be given information on all aspects of health and safety relating to their workstations, together with the measures taken to analyse risks and comply with the regulations. Employers must also provide information about the steps they are taking to ensure breaks in equipment use and the training they are providing.

Fire safety

Fire certificates

Under the **Fire Precautions Act 1971** some buildings used by the public require a fire certificate, issued by the fire authority. Check with the local fire brigade if in any doubt. Strict rules apply to such buildings. The main requirements cover:

- means of escape
- fire alarms
- fire fighting equipment
- access for fire-fighters.

Fire precautions

All employers must comply with the **Fire Precaution (Workplace) Regulations 1997** (as amended) for each workplace under their control (even if a fire certificate has been issued). Where premises are leased, the person or organisation with responsibility for maintenance, repair or safety in the workplace under the terms of the lease is treated as being in control.

Health and safety

Risk assessments

All employers must:

- carry out a fire risk assessment of the workplace (and record the findings in writing if there are five or more employees)
- provide and maintain adequate fire precautions and safeguard those who use the workplace
- provide employees with information, instruction and training about fire precautions.

Employees must cooperate with the employer to ensure the workplace is safe from fire and not do anything that would place themselves or others at risk.

The regulations also require that:

- a workplace must be equipped with appropriate fire fighting equipment and with fire detectors and alarms
- any non-automatic fire fighting equipment must be easily accessible, simple to use, and indicated by signs.

Employers must also:

- take measures for fire fighting in the workplace appropriate to the organisation's activities and size, taking into account everyone who may be present (ie not just employees)
- in consultation with employees (or their representatives) nominate sufficient, adequately trained employees to implement those measures, taking account of the workplace size and hazards
- inform other employers with workplaces in the building of any significant risks identified which might affect their employees' safety, and cooperate with them about the measures proposed to reduce or control those risks
- arrange any necessary contacts with external emergency services.

Employers must ensure that, in case of fire, there are emergency exit routes from a workplace, which are kept clear at all times.

Taking account of the extent of the risk, employers must ensure that:

- in the event of danger employees can evacuate the workplace quickly and safely
- emergency routes and exits lead as directly as possible to a place of safety
- emergency routes and exits are clearly signed
- the number, distribution and dimensions of emergency routes and exits are adequate
- emergency doors open in the direction of escape
- emergency doors can be immediately opened in an emergency, ie they should not be locked or fastened
- sliding or revolving doors are not used as emergency exits

- routes and exits have emergency lighting in the case of failure of the normal lighting (in smaller workplaces this could take the form of battery-operated torches placed in suitable positions, for example along the emergency exit routes).

Employers must ensure that all workplace equipment and devices are regularly and efficiently maintained to avoid risk of fire.

When designing evacuation procedures remember to take into account the needs of those who may be especially at risk, for example physically disabled people and those who have difficulty understanding written or spoken English.

For guidance on the implementation of the regulations see *Fire safety: an employer's guide*, from HSE Books or *www.archive.official-documents.co.uk*

Fire alarms

It is a legal requirement to provide a fire alarm in many premises. The type of system needed depends on the size of the building and how easy it would be to hear an alarm; for example in premises with only a few rooms, a handbell would be enough so long as everyone could hear it. Employers should also consider installing alarms with flashing lights to alert deaf and hearing impaired people. The Disabled Living Foundation (*www.dlf.org.uk*) has details.

Larger buildings must have an electric fire alarm, with call points at exit door. If there are more than six call points or if people sleep on the premises, the electric system must have a secondary power supply so that if the power fails during a fire the alarms can still go off (modern systems will have battery back ups). Fire alarms must be tested regularly. Smoke detectors may also be required. Fire prevention officers will advise on different fire alarm systems.

The Office of the Deputy Prime Minister (which has responsibility for fire safety) is currently developing proposals for modernising fire safety legislation, in consultation with the HSE. A new Regulatory Reform Order is expected to come into force in mid-2004.

Fire fighting equipment

Premises must have adequate means of fighting fires, including fire extinguishers and possibly fire blankets (these are particularly important if there is a kitchen with a risk of a fat fire), and sprinklers or foam inlets. Fire extinguishers should only be used by people who have been trained. They must be recharged as soon as they have been let off and must be inspected annually. Fire prevention officers can advise.

Other health and safety laws and regulations

Electrical apparatus

The **Electricity at Work Regulations 1989** set out requirements for the construction, use and testing of electrical systems in all workplaces. For further information see the HSE's *Memorandum of guidance on the Electricity at Work Regulations* (HSR25).

The regulations impose a general duty on employers to ensure that, so far as is reasonably practicable:
* systems are constructed to prevent danger
* systems are maintained to prevent danger
* systems are used in a manner to prevent danger arising.

The regulations also have specific requirements about earthing and types of connectors, and state that users must be properly trained and supervised to avoid injury.

Maintaining portable electrical equipment in offices and other low risk environments (INDG236), available from *www.hse.gov.uk*, sets out precautions that can be taken in premises where risks are generally low, for example offices.

Hazardous substances

The **Control of Substances Hazardous to Health Regulations 2002 (COSHH)** require employers to identify hazardous substances and assess risks to employees and others who may be affected. Hazardous substances could include, for example, photocopier toner and cleaning fluids. The assessment must be reviewed whenever necessary. Exposure to substances identified must then be prevented or controlled, or protective equipment issued. Employers must prepare plans and procedures to deal with accidents, incidents and emergencies involving hazardous substances, and must ensure employees are properly informed, trained and supervised. Any protective equipment or control methods must be regularly monitored and reviewed.

The employer must record both the assessment and the maintenance tests, keep these records safely and make them available for inspection.

Further guidance on COSHH can be found in *A step by step guide to COSHH assessment* (HSG97), available from HSE Books and *COSHH: a brief guide to the regulations* (INDH136(rev2)), available from *www.hse.gov.uk/coshh*

First aid

Under the **Health and Safety (First Aid) Regulations 1981** workplaces must have adequate and appropriate equipment, facilities and personnel to enable first aid to be given to employees if they are injured or become ill at work. The level of provision will depend on the circumstances at the workplace, identified through the risk assessment (see *Risk assessment*, page 118).

At the time of writing (December 2003) the regulations were being reviewed, and new legislation was likely.

The minimum requirements are:
* a suitably stocked first aid box
* an appointed person to take charge of first aid arrangements.

The HSE booklet *First aid at work* (L74) contains an approved code of practice and guidance.

First-aiders

Organisations with fewer than 50 employees in a 'very low risk' environment (such as an office) have no legal obligation to have a trained first-aider on the premises, but it is good practice to have at least two people with first aid training (even if there are no employees).

Training

First-aiders must have undertaken training and obtained qualifications approved by the HSE. First aid certificates are valid for three years. Refresher courses must be started before certificates expire, otherwise a full course will need to be taken.

Appointed person

Organisations with no trained first-aiders must ensure there is an appointed person authorised to take charge of the situation (for example to call an ambulance) if there is a serious injury or illness. Consider providing emergency first aid training for all appointed persons.

First aid boxes

First aid boxes and kits should contain only the items that a first-aider has been trained to use. They should not contain medication of any kind.

Information

Employees should be told about first aid arrangements, for example through notices giving the names of the first aider(s)/appointed person and the location of the first aid box. Remember to take into account the needs of people with reading or language difficulties.

For further information about first aid, including contents of first aid boxes, see the HSE leaflet *First aid at work: your questions answered* (INDG214), available from *www.hse.gov.uk/pubns/firindex.htm*

Occupational road risk

The HSW Act places a legal duty on employers to adopt a proactive approach to **managing occupational road risk** (**MORR**) and do all that is reasonably practicable to protect any staff (including volunteers) who may be on the road as part of their job. This applies whoever owns the vehicles.

When assessing risks associated with any transport services the organisation provides, remember older or disabled service users may have particular difficulties escaping from a vehicle in the case of an accident.

Managing occupational road risk in voluntary organisations: a pilot study, published by RoSPA, includes a sample policy statement on road risk, frameworks for interviewing employee and volunteer drivers and doing random vehicle checks, and lists of information requirements and control measures. It is available from *www.rospa.com* or 0870 777 2171.

Working hours

The **Working Time Regulations 1998** include requirements for leave, rest breaks and maximum working weeks to protect workers' health and safety (see chapter 4). The regulations contain specific provisions for night workers.

Duties relating to premises

The **Occupier's Liability Act 1957** states that reasonable care must be taken to ensure that anyone using the premises with permission will be reasonably safe. This includes users of services and activities, staff, committee members, guests and people delivering goods or mending appliances.

The **Occupier's Liability Act 1984** also applies to trespassers (for example burglars, or children who come on to a site when closed). There is in all circumstances a duty to take reasonable care to avoid the risk of people being injured or killed; for example a site that is dangerous to unsupervised children may have to be securely fenced, particularly if children are coming on to the site without permission.

Public health laws

Public health legislation is very detailed and broad in scope, and includes many local bylaws. It is therefore important to meet the local authority's environmental health officer, preferably on site, to discuss the organisation's obligations. The main scope of public health legislation is detailed below.

The quality of the air

Any building in which people work or meet must have proper ventilation. The property must be free from pollution, for example from a badly maintained boiler or the burning of rubbish. Noise pollution and vibration are also controlled by law.

The quality of housing

If a group is running hostel accommodation or has a resident worker, further public health laws, concerned with housing, come into force. Environmental health officers have powers to insist on standards of cleanliness, fire precautions, the provision of lavatories, hot and cold water supplies, heating, rubbish disposal and proper repairs. Their exact powers will depend on whether the building is classified as having a single tenant or as being a 'house in multiple occupation'.

Contact the local authority environmental health department for advice.

Drainage and refuse disposal

Any faults in drainage and refuse disposal systems can create serious health risks, and the environmental health officer will look carefully at the systems provided.

Organisations that burn rubbish or allow it to accumulate can be prosecuted. It may be necessary to pay for trade refuse to be removed.

Pests and vermin

If pests such as rats, mice or cockroaches are found on the premises, contact the local authority's environmental health department immediately. After an outbreak, review the arrangements for cooking, cleaning, and storing food. Regularly inspect the premises, especially behind boilers and pipe runs and under floors. Call in a specialist firm to carry out a complete spring clean if necessary.

If there are young children on the premises look out for head lice and bugs and if any are found contact the health visitor or nurse from the health authority.

The quality of food
The **Food Safety (General Food Hygiene) Regulations 1994** cover the provision of any food served on the premises, for example pensioners' lunches and refreshments at socials. Many local authority environmental health departments publish guides to the regulations.

Public entertainment
Premises used for public entertainment have to meet particular conditions, especially on fire precautions, ventilation and sound insulation. A group will usually need a licence (see *Entertainment licences*, in chapter 9); the licensing authority will provide details.

Accidents and diseases
All employers (regardless of the number of employees) must keep a record of all accidents (an **accident book**). Records must be kept for at least three years.

The HSE published a new version of the official accident book in May 2003 (available from HSE Books), which employers must now use. It has 50 pages that can be removed and stored separately (under data protection law personal data in accident books must be kept confidential), as well as information about first aid regulations and rules for reporting injuries, diseases and dangerous incidents.

Under the **Reporting of Injuries, Disease and Dangerous Occurrences Regulations 1995** (RIDDOR) employers must report deaths, major injuries, accidents resulting in more than three days off work (not counting the day of the injury itself), diseases and dangerous occurrences. The report must be made to the enforcing authority, generally the local authority's environmental health officer.

If there is an accident connected with work and an employee or a self-employed person working on the premises is killed or suffers a major injury (including as a result of physical violence) or a member of the public is killed or taken to hospital the enforcing authority must be notified immediately, either by telephone or by completing form F2508, available on the website *www.riddor.gov.uk* or in *RIDDOR explained* (HSE31(rev1)), available from *www.hse.gov.uk*

Any accident connected with work (including an act of physical violence) that results in an employee or a self-employed person working on the premises being unable to work for more than three days must be reported within ten calendar days. The three days include any days they would not normally be expected to work such as weekends, rest days or holidays.

The enforcing authority must be informed if the organisation is told by a doctor that an employee suffers from a reportable work-related disease.

If something happens which does not result in a reportable injury, but which clearly could have done, then it may be a dangerous occurrence which must be reported immediately.

For further information see *RIDDOR explained* (HSE31(rev1)), available from *www.hse.gov.uk*, or *www.riddor.gov.uk*

Health and safety policies
Good practice
The highest duty under health and safety legislation is to protect employees. However, voluntary organisations must also develop health and safety policies to protect volunteers, trainees and users. Volunteers, trainees and service users could be invited to join the safety committee.

Implementation
Implementing a health and safety policy may appear daunting and, certainly in larger organisations, involves substantial work. One way of producing information in a manageable form is to use a series of headings, following the format used in the risk assessment (see *Risk assessment*, page 118), which could be:
- **hazard identified**, for example shelves overloaded, floor slippery
- **risk**, for example items may fall, person may slip
- **priority**, for example high, medium or low
- **preventative or protective steps** required, for example new shelving in neighbouring room, new floor covering
- **committee or staff member responsible** for implementing preventative or protective steps
- **costs** involved
- **timescale for completion of steps** identified
- **information and training** required for staff
- **timescale for completion of training and information.**

A similar format can be used to identify the steps required to comply with the workplace, personal protective and work equipment, manual handling, display screen equipment and fire safety regulations. Details of new hazards, for example from new equipment, can be added as necessary.

Information presented in this way enables the organisation to carry out monitoring and reviews easily. It can be simple to see whether the steps and training required have been delivered within the agreed timescale. If a particular hazard has become more urgent, for example if it proves to be more dangerous than envisaged, the priority can be changed and the timescale revised.

Also see the implementation checklist at the end of the chapter.

Stress

Stress at work is a serious problem: workers can suffer severe medical problems, which can result in severe under-performance at work, and cause major disruptions to an organisation. The HSE defines stress as 'the adverse reaction people have to excessive pressure or other types of demand placed upon them'.

According to HSE-commissioned research, in 2001/02 13.5 million working days were lost as a result of stress and related conditions, and every year work-related stress costs society between £3.7 and £3.8 billion.

Stress is a workplace hazard that must be dealt with like any other. Thus the responsibility for reducing stress at work lies with both employer and employee.

The primary causes of stress at work, as identified by the Health and Safety Executive, are shown on page 134.

To reduce problems relating to stress at work employers should:
- ensure close employee involvement, particularly during periods of change
- provide opportunities for staff to contribute to planning and organising their own jobs
- be approachable
- ensure variety in work
- make sure workplace hazards, including noise and the threat of violence, are properly controlled
- ensure staff have reasonable work targets
- make sure individuals are matched to jobs, provide

training where necessary and increase the scope of jobs for those who are over-trained
- provide training in interpersonal skills
- implement effective systems for dealing with bullying and for racial, sexual or other harassment (see chapter 3)
- encourage good communication between staff and management
- instil a supportive culture in the workplace
- be understanding about the pressures on staff with personal problems
- encourage a healthy work-life balance
- identify opportunities for flexible work schedules
- ensure employees don't work long or anti social hours
- regularly examine all policies, working practices and conditions of employment and remove components that may lead to stress
- ensure employees are made aware of the causes of stress, and that they do not work in ways that increase their own stress or that of their colleagues.

Employers and employees should not make unrealistic demands on other workers by imposing impossible deadlines and/or increasing others' workloads to a level they cannot cope with.

An organisation as a whole should develop an atmosphere of mutual respect amongst staff and ensure that interpersonal conflicts are avoided or dealt with sensibly.

In order to deal with stress if it does occur, there must be appropriate procedures and support for affected staff. Managers should investigate the cause(s) of any stress, and take appropriate action to remove them. Organisations should neither discriminate nor tolerate discrimination against employees suffering from stress.

Work-related stress: a short guide (INDG281(rev1)) addresses some common questions and includes details of sources of general advice, advice on all aspects of mental health and a list of related publications. *Tackling work-related stress: A guide for employees* (INDG341) includes guidance for employees on identifying and managing work-related stress. Both are available from *hse.www.gov.uk*

At the time of writing (December 2003) the HSE was working on producing management standards on work-related stress. Draft standards and a draft process for piloting these in your organisation are shown on *www.hse.gov.uk/stress/stresspilot*

Checklist
Health and safety policy

Organisation

- Ensure that the management committee decides who is responsible, and if necessary delegates decision making powers. Even if powers are delegated, the management committee as a whole is ultimately responsible and potentially liable, and must be aware of this.
- Appoint staff members to be given overall responsibility for health and safety and for implementing the policy on a day to day basis, for example the director may take overall responsibility and an administrator could be given day to day responsibility.
- Set up a safety committee including those management committee members and staff members with responsibility for health and safety, together with trades union representatives and/or employee representatives and other staff and volunteers.
- If premises are shared, cooperate with other employers in all health and safety matters, but especially in carrying out a fire safety risk assessment and appointing a coordinator.

Ensure the costs of health and safety requirements are included in the annual budget.

Information and training

- Obtain necessary advice and publications, for example from the Health and Safety Executive, the local authority and trades unions, and guidance from the Office of the Deputy Prime Minister on fire safety.
- Identify the training needs of committee members and staff with health and safety responsibilities and design a training programme.

Risk assessment

- Carry out a preliminary risk assessment of the workplaces and activities in consultation with staff and trades unions. Before starting, list the headings covered by the health and safety regulations. Assess the risks to users and members of the public as well as to staff. Include homeworkers if appropriate.
- Carry out a thorough inspection of workplaces to identify the steps required to comply with the workplace and fire safety regulations.
- Carry out a thorough inspection of work and display screen equipment to identify any steps required to comply with regulations.

- Assess any manual handling operations using the checklist in *Manual handling. Guidance on regulations* (see page 125).
- Carry out a fire safety risk assessment.
- Before employing anyone aged under 18 ensure a risk assessment is carried out specific to that person and the work they will be doing (see *Young employees*, page 120).
- Arrange external expertise if needed to complete the assessment.
- Make a written record of the assessment and discuss the findings with the members of the safety committee and other staff.
- Decide on a review date for the assessment.

For further details see *5 steps to risk assessment*, published by the Health and Safety Executive.

Preventative and protective measures

- Identify preventative and protective measures to reduce or avoid any risks. These may include providing personal protective equipment, health surveillance, eye tests and regular servicing of equipment.
- Identify any necessary changes to new or expectant mothers' working hours or conditions to reduce risks to them and their child(ren).
- Identify the modifications to display screen and work equipment and the workplace necessary to comply with the regulations.
- Establish the costs of preventative and protective measures and any necessary modifications and draw up a timescale for their implementation in consultation with the safety committee.

New premises and equipment

Ensure a risk assessment is made before acquiring new premises or equipment and that the costs of removing any risks are identified.

Emergency procedures

Draw up emergency procedures to deal with risks identified during the assessment and identify those responsible for evacuation and other tasks in the event of an emergency. These must include what to do in the event of fire.

Training, instructions and information for staff

- Inform staff of the risks identified, the steps they should take to reduce the risks and the steps you (as employer) will be taking.
- Ensure that all staff are properly trained and instructed in the use of all protective equipment, work and display screen equipment and on safe manual handling techniques.
- Ensure that staff who work outside normal working hours, at home or in isolation are given necessary health and safety information.
- Ensure new and temporary staff are given necessary health and safety information.
- Pay particular attention to staff who may be more vulnerable to accidents, for example inexperienced or young staff and disabled people.
- Include the cost of staff induction, training and instruction in the annual budget.

Accidents

- Establish a policy requiring all accidents and near accidents and their causes to be reported and recorded, and reported to the safety committee.
- Establish procedures for dealing with accidents and ensure that there are sufficient staff with first aid training.
- Ensure all reportable accidents under RIDDOR (see *Accidents and diseases*, page 131) are reported to the relevant authorities.

Monitoring and review

- Ensure that those responsible for health and safety regularly receive updated information and training.
- Regularly monitor the implementation of the policy in consultation with the safety committee, and revise the assessment and targets as necessary.
- Consult with employees and safety representatives in good time.
- Revise the assessments and the steps required whenever circumstances change, including new kinds of work, new premises, new equipment or changes in good practice.

Work-related stressors

Culture
Lack of communication and consultation
A culture of blame
Denial of potential problems
Expectation of excessively long working hours or taking work home

Job demands
Too much to do, too little time
Too little or too much training for the job
Boring or repetitive work
Too little to do
Poor working environment

Control
Lack of control of work activities

Relationships
Poor relationships with others
Bullying, racial or sexual harassment

Change
Uncertainty about what is happening
Fears about job security

Role
Conflicting demands
Confusion about how everyone fits in

Support and the individual
Lack of support from managers and co-workers
Conflicting demands of home and work

Chapter 6:
Premises and environmental concerns

Related chapters
Chapter 1 – Legal status; trading
Chapter 5 – Health and safety
Chapter 7 – Insurance
Chapter 9 – Public activities

Buying or renting property is a major step and involves considerable responsibilities for both staff and management committees.

When an **unincorporated association** or a trust buys property or holds a lease, the property will often be put into the names of two or more individuals as trustees (often called **holding trustees**). Although legally there need only be two holding trustees, you should consider having three or four. In such cases it is usually advisable to draw up a separate trust deed setting out holding trustees' and management committee members' respective rights and obligations and the position of holding trustees in relation to the committee. This is discussed later in the chapter.

Another option for unincorporated associations or trusts is to put the property in the name of a corporate body (such as a bank) authorised to act as a **custodian trustee,** or the **Official Custodian for Charities** (a member of the Charity Commission's staff appointed to hold land on behalf of charities).

If the organisation is **incorporated** (registered as a company limited by guarantee or an industrial and provident society) the deed or lease will be in the name of the organisation itself, rather than in the name of holding trustees or a custodian trustee. This is because incorporated organisations can own property in their own right (see chapter 1).

Always get legal advice before taking on property.

Forms of tenure

There are three main forms of tenure: **buying** a freehold or a long leasehold, **renting** on a lease (or tenancy), or taking property on a **licence**. The options are discussed below. Make sure the management committee understands the implications of whichever form of tenure it is considering.

Regardless of the form of tenure, the way in which the property is held will depend on whether the organisation is unincorporated or incorporated (see chapter 1).

Buying property

There are two ways of purchasing property: buying a **freehold** or buying a **long leasehold**. As a freehold gives absolute ownership of both the building and the land it stands on, the only controls on the property are the rules on **planning permission** and **building regulation approval** that apply to all buildings. Some properties may also be subject to special restrictions known as **restrictive covenants** or special rights known as **easements**, which a solicitor will identify.

A **leasehold interest** in a property involves paying a capital sum to acquire a long lease, for example 99 years, together with an annual, and usually small, rent. Such a lease provides long-term security of tenure. Because long leases generally have fewer restrictions than short leases, they offer a certain amount of freedom in managing the property.

It is crucial to obtain advice from a solicitor and surveyor before signing a lease or mortgage agreement. Remember that one or more named individuals may have to stand as a guarantor for any mortgage an organisation raises. Guarantors, and their estate after they die, remain liable until the lease ends or the mortgage is paid in full. No one should ever stand as a guarantor without taking independent legal advice.

Under **Section 38** of the **Charities Act 1993** a charity considering taking out a mortgage must get 'appropriate' advice before doing so. This advice can be from anyone the management committee believes has the necessary experience and practical ability.

A company that takes out a mortgage must notify Companies House on form 395 and must enter specified details in a register of charges (a list of mortgages and other loans secured on the organisation's assets). There is no such requirement for industrial and provident societies.

Advantages and disadvantages

The advantages of buying a freehold or a long leasehold are long-term security and independence, although leaseholders are subject to some controls and have to pay a small rent. However, these options are available only to organisations that can raise a substantial capital sum or obtain a mortgage.

Leasing or renting premises

Leasing or renting premises for a short period usually involves paying a market (or near-market) rent and always grants the tenant an exclusive right to occupy a property. A lease (or tenancy) imposes obligations on both the landlord and tenant.

'Exclusive possession' means the tenant has the right to exclude everyone else from the premises, including the landlord (although leases often include exceptions, such as allowing access for emergency works or to do work on adjoining properties).

Before signing a lease, make sure everyone involved fully understands the meaning and implications of all the clauses, the costs of complying with the obligations, and the risks if the obligations are not met. It is essential to get independent advice from a solicitor and, where necessary, a surveyor when negotiating the terms of a lease. see *Points to check in a license or lease,* page 138).

Advantages and disadvantages

The **Landlord and Tenant Act 1954** gives security to tenants in business premises in England and Wales; property rented by voluntary organisations usually falls within this category. If a business tenant breaches a term of the lease, a landlord may seek repossession. Otherwise, landlords can serve notice only under terms of the Act and even if they do so, tenants may be able to ask a court to grant a new tenancy if they are unable to agree terms (but see below). Landlords can oppose such applications on certain specified grounds, for example that the rent has not been paid, or that they need the premises for themselves. If the landlord does not oppose the application, the court will grant a new tenancy if the tenant wants one.

Some business tenancies do not have renewal rights. These include:
- those granted for less than six months, where either the tenant has been in occupation for less than 12 months or there is no provision for extension or renewal

- those where both parties have agreed, before entering into the lease, that renewal rights should not apply. At present, this requires court approval. However, a new procedure comes into force on 1 June 2004, under the **Regulatory Reform (Business Tenancies) (England and Wales) Order 2003**. The need to get court permission will be replaced by a 'health warning' notice, served on the tenant. The notice must explain the loss of rights and the importance of getting professional advice. The tenant must sign a declaration that they have read the health warning and have accepted its consequences. The landlord must give the tenant at least 14 days' notice. For further information see *www.odpm.gov.uk* Many landlords will only lease premises to organisations that are prepared to agree to exclude security of tenure. As some funders will only grant aid refurbishment or redecoration if an organisation has adequate security of tenure, think carefully before agreeing to this.

The property industry has introduced a voluntary code of practice for business leases. It contains recommendations for landlords and tenants when they negotiate new business leases, in particular rent reviews. The code can be viewed at *www.commercialleasecodeew.co.uk*

Holding a licence

Unlike a lease, which gives an exclusive legal interest in a property, a licence grants only a permission to occupy the premises, is generally a temporary agreement, and the Landlord and Tenant Act does not apply.

A licence will spell out the landlord's and licensee's obligations more simply than a lease. Before signing a licence, get legal advice and ensure the organisation has the financial resources to meet its obligations under the terms of the licence.

If the occupier has exclusive use of the property, an agreement is likely legally to be a lease even if described as a 'licence'.

Advantages and disadvantages

The main advantages of holding a licence are that the licensee generally has no obligation for repairs, maintenance or buildings insurance and it may be easier to terminate the agreement, by 'surrendering' (ie returning) the licence to the landlord. Also, because many local authorities do not consider licensees to be occupiers for the purposes of non-domestic rates, it may be cheaper to have a licence than a lease. However, it is likely that the landlord will charge the licensee all or part of the rates, so check this before signing. Licensees may still be responsible for water charges.

As properties held under licence are not protected by the Landlord and Tenant Act the licensee has very little security. A licence will usually be either for a fixed period (for example one year) or will continue indefinitely but have a fixed notice period. Once notice has been given and expired the occupant must leave. If the licence continues on a weekly or monthly basis and no notice period is mentioned, the law would imply that the licensee would be entitled to 'reasonable notice'.

The advantages of a licence must be set against the lack of security. The ultimate decision may depend on the organisation's finances.

Finding premises

Organisations may rent their premises from local authorities, other voluntary organisations, commercial landlords and, occasionally, private individuals.

One place to start looking for new premises is the local authority. The property department or the department responsible for economic and business development keeps a record of vacant council premises which will be available either under a lease or a licence.

The local authority may charge a commercial rent but include an equivalent amount in an organisation's grant, or it could charge a **peppercorn** (nominal) rent. It may state as a condition of tenure that an organisation must use the premises only to carry out the activities for which it is being funded. If the organisation changes its activities without permission, it could then be evicted.

Local estate agents have lists of property belonging to commercial and private landlords, who will charge market rents. Landlords may be willing to negotiate the terms of a lease. For example it may be possible to persuade them to reduce the rent, agree to a rent free period, redecorate the premises or pay for repairs. Any concessions need to be balanced against the possibility of future rent increases.

The local council for voluntary service, churches, community centres and housing associations may know of vacant premises. London Voluntary Service Council sometimes advertises offices wanted and to let in its magazine *Voluntary Voice* and on its website *www.actionlink.org.uk*

When looking for premises, consider:
- proximity to public transport and access on foot and bicycle

- access for disabled people (including car parking) and those with children
- local facilities for staff, for example basic lunch time shopping, a bank, a supermarket
- the immediate locality and whether members would be happy attending activities in the premises and how people would feel if they had to work late or attend evening meetings. For example a building down a dark alley would not be suitable for some activities, as service users or staff might feel unsafe going home
- time restrictions on access
- the neighbours, for example noisy activities may not be popular next door to residential accommodation
- whether goods can easily be delivered. This is particularly important if an organisation receives regular deliveries of heavy items
- any planning permission granted on a property.

There may be legal obligations to ensure that there is access for disabled people (see below).

Disabled people

Employers

Under **Part II** of **the Disability Discrimination Act 1995** (**DDA**) organisations employing 15 or more staff (whether full or part-time) must make 'reasonable' changes to any 'physical features' of their premises which may put a disabled employee or prospective employee at a disadvantage. Physical features include a building's design and construction, approach and exit, fixtures, fittings, furnishings, equipment and materials. 'Reasonable' will be defined by a number of factors, including the practicality and cost of making the change, the resources available to the employer and the ability to raise finance. Even organisations that employ fewer than 15 people should follow good practice guidelines. On 1 October 2004 the small employer's exemption will be removed.

For further information see *The Disability Discrimination Act 1995: What employers need to know* (DL 170), from the Disability Rights Commission.

Service providers

Under **Part III** of the **DDA** all providers of goods, services or facilities, regardless of number of employees, must take reasonable steps to change practices, policies or procedures that make it impossible or unreasonably difficult for a disabled person to access a service. This could mean providing extra help to a disabled person, changing the way a service is provided, or adapting the service to make it accessible.

From 1 October 2004 all service providers will also have to make reasonable adjustments to their premises' physical features (see above) for disabled people. If a physical feature makes it unreasonably difficult, or impossible for a disabled person to use a service, the organisation will have to take measures, where reasonable, to:
- remove the feature, or
- alter it so that it no longer has that effect, or
- provide a reasonable means of avoiding the feature, or
- provide a reasonable alternative method of making the service available to disabled people.

The Disability Rights Commission recommends considering removing or altering physical features wherever possible, ie taking an 'inclusive approach', so that disabled people receive services in the same way as other customers.

The DDA does not override planning or historic buildings legislation. Organisations making adaptations to buildings should therefore ensure they get all necessary planning permissions, and occupiers of listed buildings or buildings in conservation areas should take specialist advice.

The organisation should take these requirements into account in its equal opportunities policy and procedures.

Access audit

It is useful for both employers and service providers to carry out an access audit, taking into considering the following:
- approach and parking areas
- routes and external level change, including ramps and steps
- entrances, including reception, and exits
- corridors, internal doors and internal ramps
- lifts, stairlifts and internal level changes
- toilets and washing facilities
- facilities for cooking or refreshments
- fixtures and fittings
- lighting and ventilation
- emergency exits
- public facilities, such as telephones and service desks
- providing information.

Further information

The Disability Rights Commission (DRC) operates a helpline on 08457 622 633 (textphone 08457 622 644) and produces a number of publications including *Making access to goods and services easier for disabled customers: A practice guide for small businesses and other small service providers* and *2004 – What it means for you – service providers*. Other useful publications include *Code of practice: Rights of access – goods, facilities, services*

and premises, published by the Stationery Office and *Access audits: A guide and checklists for appraising the accessibility of buildings*, published by the Centre for Accessible Environments.

Making the decision

The management committee may wish to delegate some decisions about premises to a subcommittee which could, for example, collect information and make recommendations. Before doing so check whether the constitution will allow this. In any case, the full management committee must take any final decisions about taking on or giving up premises.

In an unincorporated association or trust individual committee members or trustees may be personally liable for complying with the terms of any lease or licence. The whole committee should therefore participate in the final decision once it has all the relevant information.

When negotiating to take on premises allow enough time for getting appropriate advice and informed decision making. Although organisations may want to move into premises quickly, it is important to consider the risks of taking on an inappropriate lease and to ensure committee members understand their responsibilities and potential liabilities.

Points to check in a lease or licence

Listed below are some of the main points to consider when negotiating a lease or licence. Where a landlord is eager to rent out premises, the organisation may be in a strong negotiating position. Always get a lease checked by a solicitor before agreeing to anything or signing.

NB: For the sake of brevity 'lease' is used to refer to both leases and licences throughout this section. Any differences between leases and licences are noted.

The duration

Leases can be weekly, monthly, annual or for a fixed period. There may be an option to renew a fixed-term lease at the end of a specific time. The duration of a lease is particularly important because an organisation must meet its obligations for the whole period of a fixed-term lease, even if it no longer uses the building. The committee members of unincorporated associations and trusts will be personally liable for the rent for the full term of a lease even if the organisation has run out of funds and no longer operates.

To avoid this situation, the lease should include a **break clause** (see below) to allow the organisation to surrender or assign the lease. **Surrendering a lease** means handing it back to the landlord or giving notice to quit. **Assigning a lease** means selling or giving it to new tenants.

Under the **Landlord and Tenant (Covenants) Act 1995** a tenant is normally released from future liabilities for a lease once it is assigned. However, in many cases the landlord may only agree to the assignment on the condition that the original tenant remains liable for the rent. This has the effect of overriding the provisions of the Act.

If this is the case, an organisation must ensure that the new tenants are financially viable, otherwise it could be responsible for their debts. Take legal advice on this point when assigning a lease. Charities have to go through certain formalities before surrendering or assigning a lease (see *Disposing of premises*, page 146).

Committee members can avoid or reduce their personal liability by making sure that the organisation can assign or surrender the lease and by ensuring that if the lease is assigned they are no longer liable for the rent. They can avoid liability completely if they can persuade the landlord to include a clause in the lease which excludes any personal liability for the rent. However, experience shows that few commercial landlords are prepared to accept such a clause.

Some funders specify the minimum duration of a lease they will accept when considering applications for building or refurbishment, for example the Community Fund will only consider leases of five years or more (depending on the capital cost of the work involved).

Break clauses

Some landlords will want to include a landlord's break option if the lease includes such a clause for tenants. Be cautious about accepting this condition. If the landlord exercises the break option the organisation would have to find new premises, with all the resources – in terms of both staff and finance – this implies. A right to a break clause for the landlord can rarely be justified in practice.

Rent levels and payment periods

Always check whether the rent is inclusive or exclusive of VAT. Most leases give landlords the option to introduce VAT at any stage during the period of the lease. Also, note the payment period; leases often require rent to be paid quarterly in advance.

Rent review

Longer leases often include a clause allowing the landlord to review the rent periodically. In such cases, it would be wise to negotiate a break clause so that the organisation could surrender the lease (see above) if it could not afford the higher rate.

Service charges

Many leases of shared premises include a clause requiring the tenant to pay a service charge in addition to the rent. Check the lease carefully to see how this is calculated and what it will cover. If for example a building needs a new roof, a tenant could end up having to pay a proportion of the cost even if the lease is short term.

Although it is appropriate for organisations taking on short-term leases to pay a contribution, for example towards heating and lighting of communal parts, they should ensure that they do not have responsibility for paying service charges towards long-term maintenance and repair obligations.

There are two ways in which a lease may be amended to protect a tenant:
- ensure the service charge provision makes clear that it cannot include maintenance and repair costs or major structural repairs and maintenance costs
- specify a fixed amount for service charges or impose a top financial limit on repair and maintenance costs during any financial year. A fixed sum could be written in as the contribution for repairs and maintenance or added to the rent.

Responsibility for repairs

Tenants have to maintain property to a reasonable standard. It is important to define this responsibility and clarify any other obligations for repairs. The usual arrangement is for the landlord to have responsibility for the building's exterior and structure and the tenants to have responsibility for the interior (including decorating) and fixtures and fittings. Where possible, have the property inspected by a surveyor and discuss the likely costs of minor repairs and the possibility of encountering major ones. The surveyor should also draw up a schedule of condition describing the state of the property before the tenant moves in, which must be agreed by the landlord and tenant – check who will be paying for this. Make sure someone in the organisation knows exactly what was included in the original schedule and keeps track of any changes made.

When a tenant moves on, the landlord may ask for another survey and expect the tenant to pay for any repairs needed to put the property back into the original state. Just as the organisation or its trustees are responsible for the rent throughout the duration of the lease, they will also be responsible for putting the property back into the original condition once the lease expires.

Take particular care to check whether the landlord is proposing a **full repairing lease,** as this makes the tenant responsible for putting the property back to good condition whatever its state when the lease was taken on. An organisation will want to avoid being legally obliged to hand back the property in a better condition than when it took on the lease.

Insurance

Most leases require either that the tenant insures the premises or, more usually, pays the premium to the landlord, who will arrange insurance. If the landlord makes the arrangements the lessee has to be able to inspect the policy. A lease will require the tenant to have public liability insurance and, where relevant, insurance for fixed glass, for example shopfronts. Insurance is discussed further in chapter 7.

Rates and water charges

Tenants will usually be responsible for non-domestic (or 'business') rates and water charges. Always check with the local authority the exact amount of rates payable on occupation (see *Paying rates*, page 146). However, most premises used by charities have a mandatory 80% exemption from business rates and the local authority has discretion to exempt the other 20%. The local authority can also grant discretionary relief of up to 100% of the business rates for non-charitable voluntary organisations.

Regardless of its size, an organisation will have to pay water charges in full unless the landlord agrees to meet these under the terms of the lease.

The costs of drawing up the lease

Most commercial leases impose a requirement that the tenant pays the landlord's legal costs in drawing up the lease. Landlords' solicitors often charge substantial amounts for this. Before entering into detailed negotiations ensure there is a top limit placed on the landlord's legal costs.

Permitted activities

Check whether any activities are restricted under the terms of the lease. Some leases state permitted uses; make sure these cover the organisation's intended activities. There may be other restrictions, for example on dancing or alcohol consumption. Try to ensure that the lease allows a sufficiently wide range of uses to enable it to be assigned if necessary, but remember that a wider range of uses may also mean a higher rent. Also check whether the property has planning permission for the intended use.

Subletting and use by others

Most leases do not allow subletting. However, hiring out rooms or sharing the premises with other organisations would not normally amount to a subletting. If the organisation plans to hire out rooms or anticipates sharing its premises (see *Sharing premises*, page 142) make sure the lease allows this, and if necessary negotiate an amendment.

Alterations to the structure of the building

Most leases do not permit structural alterations without the landlord's consent (although a well drawn-up lease should allow minor alterations). If alterations are necessary, try to get the landlord's permission before signing the lease – do not assume that if an organisation takes on a property in poor condition that it is free to make improvements.

When the requirements under the Disability Discrimination Act for service providers to adapt premises come into force in October 2004 (see *Disabled people*, page 137), this will automatically imply the inclusion of provisions in leases to enable organisations renting premises to make necessary alterations with the landlord's consent. Landlords will not be able to withhold their consent unreasonably.

Is the lease or licence right for you?

Before making a decision to take on a lease or licence:
- get independent advice (from a solicitor and/or surveyor) about the organisation's obligations and likely expenditure
- understand all the provisions of the agreement and its obligations, particularly those that will incur expense and those that involve long-term obligations
- have funds to meet the likely expenditure, including rent, VAT, insurance, service charges, non-domestic rates, water charges, repairs, decorations and structural alterations, and to cover health and safety requirements (see chapter 5) and any alterations that may be needed to comply with the Disability Discrimination Act (see *Disabled people*, page 137)

- make sure there are no covenants (restrictions) in the lease which prevent the organisation using the property how it wants
- obtain planning permission for use of the premises, where relevant (see *Obtaining planning permission*, page 145)
- have building regulation approval for any intended alterations (see *Planning and building regulations*, page 144)
- have the landlord's consent for proposed adaptations
- ensure there is a way of terminating the lease if the organisation wants to move or runs out of money; this is particularly important for unincorporated associations and trusts
- consider the implications if individuals are being asked to guarantee the lease (see page 135) and encourage potential guarantors to seek independent legal advice.

Signing the lease or mortgage agreement

Check the organisation's constitution for any provisions relating to signing leases or other documents.

Incorporated organisations

The organisation itself (as opposed to individuals) can be a named party to a lease. For companies, a lease can be sealed with the company seal (if it has one) in the presence of two committee members, or the company secretary and one committee member. If the company does not have a seal, the lease must be signed on behalf of the company by two committee members or one committee member plus the company secretary. An industrial and provident society must attach its seal* in the presence of the secretary and two committee members.

Under the Co-operatives and Community Benefit Societies Act, 2003 (see chapter 1), IPSs will no longer need to have a seal. If an IPS chooses not to have a seal, the lease will have to be signed by two officers or two members of the society or a member and the secretary. At the time of writing (December 2003) the Act had not yet been enacted.

Unincorporated associations and trusts

There are a number of ways in which unincorporated associations and trusts can enter into legal arrangements relating to premises.

Appoint holding trustees. The constitution of an unincorporated association may either require or allow holding trustees (see *Forms of tenure*, page 135) to be appointed by the committee. If this option is used, the committee should agree a trust deed with the holding trustees clearly setting out their responsibilities and obligations and the position of the holding trustees in relation to the committee. A model trust deed is given at the end of this chapter. Although not all the provisions in the model may be necessary they should still be considered.

It is important to realise that if the premises are owned or held on a long lease, it may be necessary to change the holding trustees and enter into new legal documents if holding trustees die or wish to withdraw from the arrangement. In the case of a lease, the landlord's consent may be required.

If the organisation is a trust, the property can be held in the name of the trustees. In this case it is not necessary to have a separate trust deed. All the trustees can sign or, unless prohibited by the trust deed, the trustees can pass a resolution which authorises at least two members of the committee to enter into legal documents on behalf of the committee under **Section 82** of the **Charities Act 1993** (see below). However, whenever the trustees change, the property will need to be transferred to ('vested in') the new trustees.

Apply to the Charity Commission for the appointment of the **Official Custodian for Charities** as a trustee: see the Charity Commission booklet *The Official Custodian for Charities' land holding service* (CC 13). The advantage of a charitable unincorporated association or trust using the Official Custodian is that there will be no need to change trustees.

Appoint a bank or other incorporated body as a custodian trustee to hold the property on behalf of the organisation. The custodian trustee will provide a trust deed setting out its relationship with the organisation. There is likely to be a charge for this. As with the Official Custodian (see above), there is no need to change trustees. This option may be appropriate for non-charities, which cannot use the Official Custodian.

Pass a resolution which authorises at least two members of the committee to sign legal documents on behalf of the committee under **Section 82** of the **Charities Act 1993**. Any such document must then contain a specific clause stating that it has been executed in pursuance of Section 82 of the Charities Act 1993 by people signing on behalf of the charity, who are then deemed to have signed on behalf of the whole committee. This method has two advantages. There is no need to draw up a separate deed of trust between the committee and the holding trustees, and it does not place two or three individuals in a more risky position than the whole committee. Check the constitution to see if it includes any restrictions on passing such a resolution.

Apply to the Charity Commission for **incorporation of a charity's trustee body** (management committee) under **Section 72** of the **Charities Act 1993**. This will enable the committee to hold the property in the same way that an incorporated organisation (company or industrial and provident society) does, and avoids the need to appoint separate holding trustees or a custodian trustee or have the property held by the trustees in a charitable trust. It is important to note that this type of incorporation does not provide limited liability for management committee members. They still remain personally liable for any liabilities under the lease that cannot be met by the organisation. For further information see *Incorporation of charity trustees* (CC43). Applications must be made on the form in the application pack *How to apply to the Charity Commission for a Certificate of Incorporation* (CHY 1093), available from Charity Commission offices.

Checklist of formalities

Before entering into a lease or licence or before buying property:

- check the constitution to see if the organisation has powers to lease or buy property
- check the constitution to see whether holding trustees need to be appointed or whether there is the option of passing a resolution under Section 82 of the Charities Act 1993 (see *Signing the lease or mortgage agreement*, page 141)
- pass a resolution appointing holding trustees or a custodian trustee if they are to be appointed, or appointing signatories if the property is to be held by a charity's trustees
- if appointing holding trustees agree the terms of any trust deed.

Sharing premises

Belonging to another organisation

One way of obtaining premises is to share property belonging to or rented by another organisation, as either a subtenant or (more likely) a licensee. The arrangements between the two organisations must be clear from the

start and so the following points need to be clarified in writing:

- the areas that will be for exclusive use (for example an office) and those to be shared (for example kitchen, WCs and meeting rooms)
- how use of shared facilities will be organised
- that insurance companies will be notified of plans to share premises
- whether furniture or equipment will be provided
- use of resources such as a photocopier and fax, and charging policies
- whether adaptations to the premises are permitted (this is unlikely in a licence) (also see *Alterations to the structure of the building*, page 140)
- responsibilities for safety and security arrangements
- responsibilities for cleaning
- other rules and regulations, for example regarding non-smoking.

Belonging to your organisation

Renting out or licensing parts of the premises either short or long term can be a useful way of raising funds. The points made later in this section about security and safety when hiring out premises apply equally to any sharing arrangements. In addition, the following points need to be considered.

Subletting: Always check the terms of the lease before entering into any arrangement with another organisation: it may prohibit subletting.

If an organisation sublets any part of the premises it may create a business tenancy and be unable to regain the right to use the whole premises. Just because a document is called a 'licence' rather than a 'tenancy' or 'lease' does not prevent it creating a subtenancy.

In order for a tenancy or lease to be created, an occupant must have exclusive use of some part of the premises. An organisation can avoid this situation by retaining the right of access for regular cleaning or to use equipment or property held in that part of the building, or by providing the organisation with the right to share the whole premises.

Restrictions in the lease: Check whether other restrictions in the lease might prohibit sharing premises with other organisations. For example some leases contain a provision allowing only the tenant to use the premises. A landlord may be prepared to waive that requirement provided it is clear that no subtenancy is being created.

Avoiding disputes: It is advisable to draw up a formal agreement that clarifies the relationship between the two organisations. The points made under *Sharing premises belonging to another organisation*, above, and some of the provisions in the model hiring agreement at the end of the chapter could form the basis of such an agreement.

Legal advice: Always take legal advice before making any arrangement for the continuous use of any part of the premises by another organisation.

Hiring out parts of premises

Hiring out rooms for meetings and functions can be a useful way of raising funds as well as providing a community facility.

The key points to consider when other organisations are using your premises are:
- complying with the law
- security
- safety
- retaining control.

Legal requirements

The relevant legal requirements to consider include:
- restrictions imposed by the lease or licence, for example some leases state that the premises cannot be used by other organisations, or that music must not be played
- licensing laws if alcohol is to be sold, or if the premises are to be used for public entertainment or for dancing or the playing of music (see chapter 9)
- planning laws, for example a condition may be that the building cannot be used after 11 pm
- noise limits under the **Environmental Protection Act 1990**
- whether corporation tax is payable: even charities may be required to pay corporation tax on rents and licence fees, if in doubt check with the Inland Revenue or an accountant.

It is worth stating in the hiring agreement that alcohol can only be provided on the premises in circumstances which require a licence if one is obtained by the hirer (for details see chapter 9).

Security

The organisation should consider the following security precautions when the building is in use by the hirer:
- checking the identity of those entering (in large buildings identity passes may be necessary)

- locking internal doors to private areas (but remember that fire doors must remain unlocked)
- warning staff to take special care of their belongings when other people will be in the building
- providing secure storage for personal belongings
- locking away cash, cheques and other valuables
- securing expensive office equipment.

Remember that security includes protecting staff from possible attack by intruders who may gain access to offices or other parts of the premises unchallenged. This is especially important if staff work in the evening or if multiple activities are taking part in the building.

Take the following precautions after people have left the building:
- clarify responsibility for locking up. This could involve appointing a caretaker, worker or management committee member to lock up after use and set the burglar alarm or ensure the hirer has done so
- adopt procedures for ensuring that everyone has left the building before it is locked up.

Insurance

It is essential to inform the insurance company that the premises will be hired out. It may impose additional conditions on the policy which must be met if the insurance is to be valid.

Safety

An organisation letting out a building is likely to be responsible for any injury or damage sustained by visitors caused by the state of the premises. It may also be responsible if someone is injured because the fire fighting apparatus is not functioning or a fire escape is blocked. Specific clauses in the hiring agreement may require the hirer to take certain precautions. The agreement should certainly require the hirer to ensure that fire escapes are not blocked (see the model at the end of the chapter).

The hiring agreement should make clear that the hirer must take all reasonable steps to ensure the safety of the people taking part in their activities.

The organisation should take out public liability insurance to cover injury or loss sustained by visitors and others (see chapter 7). Again, make sure the insurance company is told that the building will be hired out. The cost of this can be passed on to the hirer(s) through the hiring charges. The hirer may also need to take out its own public liability insurance, as the landlord's insurance will not cover claims brought against the hirer.

Planning and building regulations

Planning laws govern many aspects of a building and its surroundings and can restrict an organisation's activities, regardless of tenure. The primary legislation is found in the **Town and Country Planning Act 1990**. The local planning authority, through granting or refusing planning permission, enforces its detailed planning regulations, often called development control.

The planning system can be extremely complicated. Check with the local planning authority if in doubt. You may also wish to contact Planning Aid, which provides free, independent and professional advice on planning matters to voluntary organisations and individuals who cannot afford to employ a planning consultant.

Development

Some minor developments are given automatic permission by the **Town and Country Planning (General Permitted Development) Order 1995,** which also allows certain changes of use (see *Use of buildings and land*, below). Some temporary developments are possible without planning permission, for example land used for certain activities for 28 or fewer days in any calendar year.

Planning permission is needed for:
- certain changes in the use of buildings and land
- major changes to the external appearance of a building
- changes to the internal or external appearance of listed buildings (listed building consent)
- erection of new buildings.

Use of buildings and land

The **Town and Country Planning (Use Classes) Order 1987** sets out 16 classes of use for land and buildings, collected into four groups. To change from one use to another within the same group does not amount to development and does not require planning permission.

The four basic uses are:
- **class A:** retail shops, financial and professional services and food and drink shops
- **class B:** offices, industrial and commercial uses
- **class C:** residential, including houses, hotels, hostels, hospitals and residential institutions
- **class D:** public places, including churches, schools, libraries, art galleries, cinemas, nurseries and arts centres.

The subclasses particularly relevant to voluntary organisations include:
- **class A1:** shops, including charity shops
- **class A2:** financial and professional services – this could apply to advice centres
- **class A3:** food and drink – relates to the sale of food or drink to be consumed on the premises or hot food to be taken away
- **class B1:** business – includes office premises used by charities; could cover small manufacturing processes such as making poppies or Christmas cards
- **class B8:** storage and distribution – includes warehousing and storing the products of small manufacturing processes (see class B1, above)
- **class C1:** hotels and hostels – charities providing hostel accommodation would be included where there is no significant element of care provided
- **class C2:** residential institutions – residential accommodation with care
- **class C3:** dwelling houses – includes houses providing accommodation for not more than six residents living together as a single household, including those where care is provided for residents
- **class D1:** non-residential institutions – for example day centres, crèches, halls, arts centres and educational uses
- **class D2:** leisure use.

The appearance of a building

In the majority of cases (apart from buildings in some conservation areas), it is not necessary to get planning permission for painting or repairs. However, permission is needed for a major change in a building's appearance, for example:
- installing a shopfront
- building an extension (although certain extensions to a house may, subject to certain restrictions, be classed as permitted development)
- erecting a garage.

The **Town and Country Planning (Control of Advertisements) Regulations 1992** govern planning permission for advertisements. Illuminated and hanging signs usually need planning permission, but non-illuminated signs do not. Check with the local authority's planning department if in doubt.

Listed property and buildings in conservation areas

There are extra restrictions imposed on buildings in conservation areas or listed as being of special architectural importance. These apply to both external and internal alterations to listed buildings and to certain works to buildings in conservation areas. Conservation area consent is required to demolish any building in a conservation area. Again, if in doubt check with the local authority.

Tree preservation orders

Local authorities have the power to make a tree preservation order, applicable to individual or groups of trees and woodlands. Such an order can prohibit cutting down, topping or lopping trees without the consent of the local planning authority. The local authority will confirm whether a tree is covered by such an order.

New buildings

Most new non-domestic buildings need planning permission, which is a two-stage process. Firstly you must submit an outline application, and the local planning authority will decide whether the development is acceptable 'in principle'. If so, permission will be subject to the approval of the details ('reserved matters'), which include siting, design, external appearance, access and landscape. Building work cannot begin until the local planning authority has approved all these details.

Obtaining planning permission

If your organisation is buying or moving into a building, your solicitor should check the need to apply for planning permission as part of the searches. Organisations wishing to make alterations to a building they already occupy should contact the local authority's planning department. The staff there will need to know:
- the address of the premises
- the floors being occupied, if applicable
- what the premises are (or have been) used for
- what new activity is intended
- any alterations being considered.

Making an application

All planning applications must be submitted on a form provided by the planning department, together with plans showing the location of the premises and the details of the proposed development such as external appearance, siting, car parking and layout and a certificate of ownership. The fee payable depends on the nature of the application. If the applicant does not own the land or buildings in question to make an application, they must serve notice on the owner and any other parties with an interest in the land, informing them that an application has been made.

The local authority has to notify neighbours of an application, through an advertisement in the local press, a site notice and/or a letter. Check whether this is going to happen and, if an application might be seen as controversial, explain to the neighbours what is involved.

When considering alterations to the building you must take the needs of disabled people into account. This applies both to individual members and potential members of staff and to members of the public using the building.

The British Standards Institution's *Design of buildings and their approaches to meet the needs of disabled people* (BS 8300) explains how the built environment can be designed to anticipate and overcome restrictions that prevent disabled people making full use of premises and their surroundings. It includes recommendations for the design of new buildings and their approaches to meet disabled people's needs.

If permission is refused

Permission could be refused altogether, or conditions imposed, such as restricting the hours of certain activities. There is a right of appeal to the Secretary of State against refusal or the imposition of conditions. An appeal must be made within six months of a local authority's decision, and decisions can take a long time. It is however possible to agree to lease or buy subject to obtaining planning permission.

For further information see *www.planningportal.gov.uk*

Building regulations

Building regulations made under powers in the **Building Act 1994** apply to new buildings and extensions or major structural changes to existing property. In general the regulations control:
- structure
- fire safety
- site preparation
- toxic substances
- sound insulation
- ventilation
- hygiene
- drainage and waste disposal
- fuel storage systems
- protection from falling, collision and impact
- conservation of fuel and power
- access and facilities for disabled people
- glazing.

The regulations are enforced by the local authority's building control service, who must check the work as it progresses. It will usually be the builder's responsibility to make the arrangements, but it is important to confirm this before work starts. Also remember that the building's owner, not the builder, will be served with an enforcement notice if work doesn't comply with the regulations. It may also be necessary to consult the environmental health department and fire brigade.

For further information see *Building Regulations: explanatory booklet*, available from *www.odpm.gov.uk*

Paying rates

The occupiers of premises must pay **non-domestic rates** and **water charges**. Although non-domestic rates are usually referred to as **business rates** or the **uniform business rate** they are payable on any premises which are not used as a dwelling and so will include most premises occupied by voluntary organisations. Organisations that occupy premises under a lease will normally be the occupiers and will therefore be liable for both non-domestic rates and water charges. However, a licence to occupy premises may state that the landlord is still in occupation and is therefore responsible for non-domestic rates.

In unincorporated organisations the management committee will be the occupier, and members will be personally responsible for paying rates and water charges if the organisation fails to do so.

Mandatory rate relief

Under **Section 43(5)** of the **Local Government Finance Act 1988** registered charities, and charitable organisations which are exempt or excepted from registering with the Charity Commission (see chapter 1), are entitled to 80% relief on non-domestic rates. The same rate relief applies to registered community amateur sports clubs, under the **Relief for Community Amateur Sports Clubs (Designation) Order 2002**.

There is no statutory requirement for charities to submit applications for rate relief but it is advisable for all voluntary organisations to inform the rating authority immediately they begin to occupy premises. Also, as charity law requires trustees to safeguard the organisation's assets, spending them unnecessarily on rates could be seen as a breach of trust.

Discretionary rate relief

Under **Section 47** of the **Local Government Finance Act 1988** local authorities have the discretion to grant additional relief to charities on all or some of the remaining 20% of non-domestic rates. Local authorities also have the discretion to grant additional relief to registered community amateur sports clubs.

They also have the discretion to grant rate relief of up to 100% where properties are occupied wholly or partly by non-profit making bodies which are not charities. All voluntary organisations should therefore consider applying for relief from non-domestic rates.

Discretionary relief can only be backdated to the beginning of the rating year in which the local authority agrees to grant relief (1 April to 31 March). Once relief is given it can continue automatically each year, but this decision is up to the local authority.

If the end of the rating year is close it may be necessary to ask for relief in advance.

Disposing of premises

Organisations can dispose of their premises in a number of ways including:
- selling
- leasing or creating subtenancies
- transferring a lease
- giving the lease back to the landlord (surrendering the lease or giving notice to quit).

Always take legal advice before disposing of premises and, if appropriate, consult the Charity Commission (see below).

Requirements for charities

The **Charities Act 1993** sets out certain requirements that must be followed by charities in some cases before they can dispose of their premises. The rules apply both to the disposal of premises to an outside person or organisation or to a non-charitable subsidiary of the charity. However, if a charity wishes to sell or lease its premises to another charity at a lower than market price, and this is permitted under the terms of its constitution, it may be possible to:
- assign the lease to another charity at no cost
- transfer property it owns to another charity free or for a reduced price
- lease or sublet its premises to another charity at a peppercorn or reduced rent.

Apart from those relating to documentation, the provisions discussed below do not apply to industrial and provident societies with charitable rules.

Leases

If a charity plans to let or sublet premises for seven years or less, before entering into the lease the committee has to obtain advice about property values from someone with the necessary ability and practical experience. The committee then has to be satisfied that, having considered that person's advice, the proposed terms are the best that can be reasonably obtained in the circumstances. This also means that a charity must charge a market rent if it leases any premises to a trading subsidiary (see *Trading*, in chapter 1).

Other disposals

A charity's management committee has to obtain written advice from a qualified surveyor (ie a member of the Royal Institute of Chartered Surveyors – see *www.rics.org*) if it proposes to do any of the following:
* sell its property
* enter into a lease for more than seven years
* transfer its property or lease to another organisation
* surrender its lease to the landlord.

Again, the committee has to be satisfied that the proposed terms are the best that can reasonably be obtained. In addition, the property for sale or lease must be advertised publicly unless the surveyor has advised that this would not be in the charity's best interests. The Charity Commission has the authority to waive the requirements.

Premises held on trust

If premises were given or sold to a charity to fulfil a specific purpose, certain restrictions apply on their disposal. The trustees must give at least one month's public notice of their intention to dispose of the premises, so that people who may be affected can give their views.

These rules do not apply if:
* the property disposed of will be replaced with other property, or
* the premises are being let for two years or less, or
* the Charity Commission has said that the rules should not apply to the charity generally, or to the particular disposal in question.

Documentation

The Charities Act sets out requirements for specific clauses that must be included in any document disposing of a charity's property. The organisation should take legal advice when these documents are drawn up.

For further information see *Disposing of charity land* (CC28).

Equipment contracts

Many organisations enter into leasing contracts for equipment, including computers, photocopiers and vehicles.

Leases are often for a fixed term and then continue automatically unless the lessee gives the required notice to terminate them. A lessee who wants to dispose of equipment before the term has finished must either pay off all the charges until the end of the contract, or acquire other equipment from the owner.

Before signing any equipment lease make sure that you understand the full terms and conditions of the lease, and in particular note:
* any routine charges made
* whether any limits are attached to what is provided, for example the lease may exclude maintenance or servicing
* when servicing or maintenance is provided, whether this is for the full period of the lease (this is often not the case, and in order to encourage the purchase or hire of a new machine it can cost a substantial amount to take out a maintenance contract when the service period has finished)
* whether the owner can increase the charges and if there is a maximum limit on any increases
* whether the maintenance contract is limited, for example if it excludes breakdown if the lessee is at fault or whether certain expensive parts of the machine are excluded
* whether the owner guarantees to continue servicing and maintenance throughout the contract or if they can decide to discontinue the service. Also note the position if the owner goes out of business: will anyone who acquires the ownership still have an obligation to maintain the machine?
* whether the hirer is responsible for insuring the equipment against loss, theft or damage
* whether VAT is charged on top of the basic charges.

All equipment contracts should be discussed and agreed by the management committee.

The green office

Voluntary organisations were amongst the first to research and publicise the damage being inflicting on the environment by human activity. The sector now has a key role to play in developing environmental policies and procedures:

- it has become a significant employer of paid staff and volunteers and as such is a major consumer of resources
- voluntary organisations have a responsibility to promote good practice
- developing environmental policies can make economic sense as green fiscal measures such as taxes on energy consumption and congestion charging become more widespread
- environmental policy and practice may be expected in any quality standard accreditation.

This section starts by looking at the law in relation to the environment, and then goes on to discuss how organisations can develop environmental policies.

Environment law

Most voluntary organisations will have limited contact with environmental legislation, which in the main is focused on industrial, extractive and agricultural processes. However, voluntary bodies, like all other organisations, must comply with the **Environmental Protection Act 1990**, and with other legislation and regulation which governs how waste from business premises is handled, collected and disposed of.

In practice this means making arrangements with a landlord, council or waste management company to have waste removed, and complying with their instructions on the types of waste to be collected and on collection arrangements.

Special arrangements, which may attract charges, cover the safe and legal disposal of hazardous items such as batteries, paint, waste oil, pesticides and asbestos.

Voluntary organisations may also face charges for the legal disposal of used vehicles because scrap values no longer cover costs of compliance with stringent environmental standards on, for example, brake fluids, oil and heavy metals. From 2007 however, the implementation of EU regulations will transfer costs of disposal to vehicle manufacturers.

Tightening regulations could also mean charges for the legal disposal of computers, mobile phones and other electrical and electronic goods such as fridges. Charges can sometimes be avoided or reduced where products or components can be reused or recycled (see *Reducing, reusing and recycling waste*, page 149).

For advice on the legal disposal of hazardous items, vehicles and electrical and electronic goods contact the local authority refuse department or environmental health officer.

Simply dumping or fly-tipping waste items is illegal.

Organisations must also comply with statutory and local by-laws on noise pollution, the use of smokeless fuels and emissions from any vehicles they own or operate. They must also comply with planning law, make appropriate risk assessments and follow health and safety procedures where staff or volunteers work with hazardous materials or in potentially hazardous situations (see chapter 5).

Voluntary sector environmental organisations

A major growth area for voluntary sector activity is the environment itself. Organisations involved in activities such as waste recycling and reuse, wildlife and landscape conservation, allotments and food growing, city farms, cycling, walking and community transport will be subject to more specialist environmental law.

For example, handling, storing, processing and distributing waste materials and products for recycling or reuse is subject to detailed regulation. There may be assessment, planning and site management obligations for environmental conservation projects. Regulations governing the composting or treatment of organic waste, particularly kitchen waste, have recently been made more stringent. The management of animals and animal waste is strictly regulated, and the management of transport is subject to regulations relating to emissions, waste oil and fluids and vehicle disposal.

The Community Recycling Network (CRN), the national umbrella organisation for community-based, not-for-profit and cooperative waste management organisations can help with developing a reuse or recycling initiative. Phone CRN on 0117 942 0142 or visit *www.crn.org.uk*

For new voluntary organisations involved in developing an environmental conservation or community transport project, the best sources of advice on legal and planning matters are established organisations already active in the same field. Such organisations are often part of national networks, most of which offer advice freely to new entrants. See the *NCVO Voluntary agencies directory* or contact the NCVO helpdesk on 0800 2 798 798.

Environmental policy

The impact most voluntary organisation activities make on the environment will be determined more by policy and practice decisions than by environmental law. Organisations can develop their own environmental policies relatively easily by drawing on the following.

The purpose of an environmental policy is two-fold:
- to help conserve resources
- to help reduce pollution.

At the minimum most voluntary organisations should be able to meet these by:
- finding ways of reducing, reusing and recycling waste
- making sure they use energy efficiently and do not waste water and other scarce resources
- looking at environmental considerations when acquiring supplies and other equipment for offices and other purposes
- minimising the environmental impact of transport use.

Reducing, reusing and recycling waste

For many voluntary organisations, adopting a reduce, reuse and recycle policy (the so-called **3Rs**) may happen almost automatically because funds to buy new equipment and services are limited. Whatever your financial circumstances, there are some simple and effective measures which can help to reduce the environmental impact of generating waste.

Reducing waste

Measures to reduce waste include:
- using washable crockery and cutlery rather than disposable kitchenware
- using bottled milk deliveries and avoiding disposable containers
- disciplined reuse of file hangers, lever arch files and other office stationery items
- introducing simple but effective paper saving policies, for example:
- reusing single sided or discarded paper for scrap, internal memos, drafts, file, fax and e-mail copies (but be aware of the data protection and confidentiality implications of reusing paper that contains personal or sensitive information – see chapter 9); e-mailing rather than printing documents
- printing only necessary pages from documents

- running a spell check before printing
- putting up memos in communal areas rather than distributing them to all staff
- developing e-filing systems rather than printing file copies
- ensuring all staff and volunteers know how to use a photocopier's double sided function
- putting public information on a website.

Reuse of materials and items

There are voluntary organisations that resell or, in some cases, give away the following used items:
- IT equipment
- office furniture
- white and other electrical goods
- leftover paint.

For details of organisations that refurbish and redistribute IT, furniture and electrical goods contact the Waste Watch Wasteline on 0870 243 0136 or *www.wasteonline.org.uk* Waste Watch Wasteline is operated by Waste Watch, the national charity promoting action on waste reduction, reuse and recycling.

There may be small removal charges, and it may not be possible to refurbish very out of date equipment or items in poor condition.

Surplus paint can be offered to a Community Re›Paint scheme. For information on the nearest scheme visit *www.communityrepaint.org.uk* or phone SWAP on 0113 243 8777. You may need to take paint to the scheme rather than have it collected.

Unused, surplus building or decorating materials as well as unused stationery items, cloth, card, plastic sheeting might be of interest to a scrapstore for reuse by a school or children's project. Details of scrapstores can be found from Waste Watch Wasteline (see above).

Recycling in the office

Provided there is enough space to store sufficient quantities to make collection viable, waste paper recycling is the simplest way of participating in practical environmental improvement (but shred any documents with information about individuals, the organisation's internal business, or other sensitive information). Details of local office waste paper recycling schemes can be obtained from Waste Watch Wasteline (see above).

Many waste paper recycling initiatives are themselves non-profit or small community enterprises. Some schemes make a charge for collections to help cover costs, but these are usually small, and may be reduced for voluntary organisations. If there are charges for waste disposal, it could be cheaper to join a recycling scheme. Most waste paper collectors specify a minimum quantity that they will collect and most collectors also prefer to take unshredded paper for space reasons. Collectors usually provide an accredited security shredding service to meet confidentiality requirements. Your confidentiality policy (see chapter 4) should be compatible with whatever arrangements are made for recycling waste paper.

Other office items that should be recycled include toner cartridges (many of which can be returned to the supplier), mobile phones, fluorescent tubes and vending cups. For details contact Waste Watch Wasteline (see above).

More efficient use of energy, and conserving water

Using energy efficiently is a matter of common sense and prudent budgeting. Try to create a culture in which everyone in the organisation uses simple checklist measures. These include:

- ensuring someone is responsible for switching off equipment and lighting at the end of the day
- ensuring there are effective systems for reporting faults and maintaining and repairing equipment
- switching off lights when rooms are not in use (making sure neither security nor health and safety are compromised)
- only switching on computers, copiers, printers and other powered equipment when you need them. Switch off monitors (VDUs) if they are not in use. Most of the energy needs in a desktop PC are in the VDU. Where possible share printers through a network rather than having standalone printers. Set PCs to go on stand-by after ten minutes of inactivity or, better still, put the monitor to sleep. Avoid using energy consuming screen savers
- replacing conventional light bulbs with low energy equivalents (although these cost more to buy, they will save money in the long run, as they last much longer)
- locating desks and workstations to derive maximum benefit from natural light
- ensuring any thermostats or other heating control systems work, are maintained and used. Turn radiators down rather than open windows
- in buildings with air conditioning, ensuring that the cooling is not running at the same time as the heating or when people are not in the building, keeping doors and windows closed in air conditioned areas, and switching off lighting and office equipment where possible to reduce heat gains
- ensuring that any lighting control systems work properly

- adopting obvious but often overlooked good housekeeping measures such as not overfilling kettles, using a plug or bowl when washing dishes and keeping fridges sensibly defrosted
- adopting water conservation measures, for example installing a water meter to monitor consumption, fixing dripping taps, keeping any water saving devices such as automatic taps and urinal flushers in good working order, installing a water saving device in the cistern, putting up signs reminding staff, volunteers and visitors not to leave taps running, and installing water butts to water any garden or lawn areas.

Other measures will depend on the control or influence organisations can exercise over their premises or their landlord, and on their budget. These include:

- installing draughtproofing, roof space insulation and hot water system lagging
- specifying a green tariff from an electricity supplier, under which the supplier buys energy from renewable sources such as wind, solar and hydro (although the cost may be higher). For information about different tariffs see the Green Electricity Marketplace website at *www.greenelectricity.org*. To find out more about renewable energy visit *www.energy21.org.uk*
- when planning to replace heating or lighting systems, getting good advice on energy saving installations from the Energy Saving Trust (020 7222 0101 or *www.est.org.uk*), the Environment and Energy Helpline (0800 585 794), or a local energy efficiency advice centre (for details ring 0800 512 012 or visit *www.saveenergy.co.uk*).

Green procurement

It is fairly easy for voluntary organisations to participate in 'green procurement' – buying products and services that will reduce their environmental impact. Waste Watch's *Recycled products guide* provides a comprehensive list of recycled products as well as advice on green purchasing. For details visit *www.recycledproducts.org.uk* or ring 020 7089 2100. The London Sustainability Exchange (*www.lsx.org.uk*) runs the *Green Offices Group*, an e-mail discussion forum where members can find advice, share good practice and learn from each others' experience.

Simple steps include:

- buying recycled stationery. The quality of recycled paper has improved in recent years and its price has come down. The critical factor in terms of environmental impact is the proportion of post-consumer waste content in the product, which should be greater than 70%. (Post-consumer waste means that it has been used, collected and reprocessed.) All major

stationery suppliers offer good quality recycled paper. Some waste paper recycling companies also sell recycled paper, sometimes at a discount
- buying remanufactured or refilled toner cartridges for printers and copiers. These are now high quality products, some supplied by original manufacturers at the same time as used cartridges are returned for remanufacture (but check to be sure that use of these products does not invalidate the warranty on the equipment)
- buying refurbished computer and other office equipment and furniture, which can also save money
- Waste Watch Wasteline has details of IT and office suppliers, ring 0870 243 0136 or visit *www.wasteonline.org.uk* The non-profit organisation Green-Works supplies recycled office furniture to community organisations across the country at low cost, phone 020 7981 0450 or visit *www.green-work.co.uk*
- Community Re›Paint schemes (0113 243 8777) and local scrapstores (details on the Waste Watch Wasteline) may also be able to supply some materials to voluntary organisations that would otherwise be unable to afford redecorating costs
- London-based organisations could consider signing up to the Mayor's Green Procurement Code, which promotes recycled goods, including office stationery and IT consumables. For more information visit *www.londonremade.com*
- when buying new equipment or other products consider environmental information about energy consumption and harmful emissions. Buy new furniture from accredited suppliers that can confirm the sustainability of the source.

Minimising the environmental impacts of travel

You can help to reduce the environmental impact of travel by encouraging staff, volunteers and visitors to use public transport, cycle or walk and minimise the use of cars for journeys connected with your work. You can do this by developing a simple green transport plan or policy, which might include the following points:
- Make sure you take into account the quality of local public transport when considering the location of new premises.
- Advertise for staff and volunteers locally.
- Encourage public transport use by:
- giving staff, volunteers, committee members and visitors up-to-date information on public transport. All UK rail and many bus timetables are available through the UK Public Transport Information Network at *www.pti.org.uk*

- offering interest-free or low-interest loans to buy season tickets. Staff do not have to pay tax or national insurance contributions (NICs) if they repay the cost of the loan in full and the total outstanding amount of all individual loans is less than £5000.
- Encourage staff and volunteers to cycle by:
- providing secure facilities for bicycles at the office and at project locations
- instituting a mileage allowance for bicycle use on work related journeys. The Inland Revenue allows a tax free mileage allowance of up to 20p per mile (2003/04) for work-related bicycle journeys*
- providing bicycle and safety equipment for use by staff*
- holding designated 'cycle to work days' and providing refreshments for participating staff. Up to six cyclist 'breakfasts' a year per employee are exempt from tax and NICs
- providing information on local cycle routes and cycle training schemes from the local authority.
Employees do not have to pay tax or NICs on any of these benefits (though the cycles must be used mainly for travelling for work). Employers can claim tax relief for capital expenditure for cycles bought as part of a travel plan.
The London Cycling Campaign can advise on how to encourage people to cycle to work, phone 020 7298 7220 or visit *www.lcc.org.uk*
- Where car use is necessary (for example, journeys by those for whom public transport is inaccessible, travelling to multiple or remote locations, transporting equipment or materials, late night travel or where personal security might be compromised) reduce its impact by:
- encouraging staff and volunteer car sharing for work-related journeys
- selecting fuel efficient, low emission models when buying, leasing or renting vehicles
- investigating whether there is a local car share scheme when vehicles are only required occasionally or for very short periods. Participants are charged only for the costs of what can be very short hire times. For further information contact the Community Car Share Network: 0113 234 9299 or visit *www.carshareclubs.org.uk*
- Reduce the need to travel by:
- encouraging flexible working arrangements and allowing staff to work from home wherever possible (see *Flexible ways of working*, in chapter 4)
- making use of telephone, electronic or virtual conferencing (see *Virtual or electronic meetings*, in chapter 2).

For further details on tax and NIC concessions see the Inland Revenue's guide: *Green travel: a guide for employers and employees on tax and national insurance contributions* (IR176).

When encouraging bicycle or alternative transport it is important to be sensitive to the needs of disabled people and others who for various reasons may need to use cars.

Going further: voluntary organisations and sustainable development

Adopting the measures listed above and keeping them under review will allow most organisations to make a reasonable contribution to reducing harmful environmental impact. The measures may also help to save money – modest amounts now, but greater sums in future if green fiscal measures such as weight-based waste charging and congestion charges are extended throughout the country, and office car park charges are introduced.

Environmental auditing and environmental management A comprehensive environmental policy would help an organisation play a more systematic part in reducing its environmental impact. Global Action Plan carries out environmental improvements strategies for organisations. For further details phone 020 7405 5633 or visit *www.globalactionplan.org.uk*

If a full-scale audit and strategy is inappropriate, self-help programmes are available. Friends of the Earth Scotland, for example, has developed an online audit to help organisations gather basic information about current green office practices, take further action and track progress – see *www.green-office.org.uk* The publication *The green office manual – A guide to responsible practice* (Wastebusters/Earthscan, 2000) is available from Waste Watch on 020 7089 2136.

Shaping environmental policy
The voluntary sector may have a much wider contribution to make to environment policy. Since the early 1990s many community and local environmental organisations have been involved in **Local Agenda 21 (LA21)** initiatives,

which were developed in response to the challenges of the UN Environment Programme Earth Summit in Rio in 1992.

The sector's role in contributing to local sustainable development has been recognised in the new duties placed on local authorities under the **Local Government Act 2000**. In particular, councils must now prepare community strategies which 'improve or promote the economic, social and environmental well-being of their areas and contribute to the achievement of sustainable development'.

Local authorities must form local strategic partnerships (LSPs) to bring business, health, police and voluntary and community organisations together with the council to develop community strategies, (and in the 88 most deprived areas of England, also to oversee the Neighbourhood Renewal Fund).

Voluntary organisations have an opportunity to influence environment policy at local level and make linkages between social policy, economic policy and sustainable development. The potential of the community strategy to bring about local sustainable development goes well beyond the non-statutory basis of the LA21 movement.

Two publications from the Community Development Foundation (*www.cdf.org.uk*) provide a useful overview of the potential contribution to sustainable development and environmental improvement which the voluntary sector might make: *A better place to live: A guide for community groups to local action on sustainable development* (Chris Church, June 2003) and *Changing where we live: A guide to working with community groups to create green and sustainable communities* (Chris Church and Charlie Garratt, September 2003).

Other resources include the websites: *www.sustainable-development.gov.uk*, which reports upon progress towards sustainable development and *www.defra.gov.uk/environment/business/*, which describes government environmental protection policy and initiatives.

Deed of trust setting out terms of appointment of holding trustees

NB: *The model deed makes clear that anyone who is acting as a holding trustee (whether or not they are a committee member) is entitled to financial information and has the right to be heard at any meeting that makes decisions affecting the trustee's responsibilities. This provides a safeguard for holding trustees in respect of the additional responsibilities they are taking on.*

This is a Deed of Trust made on the (*day, month, year*) BETWEEN:

1. The Committee of Management of the XYZ Community Association acting by (*enter names and positions of two people to sign on behalf of the Committee, for example the Chair and Treasurer*).

   and

   (names and addresses of holding trustees)

Background to this Agreement

2. (*name of organisation*) is an unincorporated association (or charitable trust) with a constitution (or trust deed).

3. (*name of organisation*) proposes to enter into a lease of premises at (*address*).

4. Clause (*enter number*) of the constitution (or trust deed) states that the title of all real and personal property which may be acquired by or for the purposes of (*name of organisation*) may be vested in Holding Trustees appointed by the Committee of Management. That clause also requires that such Holding Trustees shall enter into a Deed of Trust or such other document as may be appropriate.

5. At a duly convened meeting of the Committee of Management of (*name of organisation*) held at (*place*) on (*date*) it was resolved that the Holding Trustees named above should be appointed to hold the title to the premises at (*address*) for the purposes of the (*name of organisation*) and (*enter names of persons authorised to sign on behalf of the Committee*) was/were authorised to sign this Deed on behalf of the Committee of Management.

AGREEMENT
The following is agreed:

1. (*name of organisation*) appoints the Holding Trustees to act as Holding Trustees of (*name of organisation*) for the purposes of holding the lease due to be completed in respect of (*premises*).

2. The Holding Trustees jointly and individually agree to hold the said lease in trust for the purposes of (*name of organisation*).

3. The Holding Trustees agree to act in respect of (*premises*) only in accordance with the lawful and reasonable instructions of the Committee of Management of (*name of organisation*).

4. The Committee of Management hereby jointly and individually indemnifies the Holding Trustees against all the costs, claims and liabilities incurred or to be incurred under the terms of the proposed lease.

5. (*name of organisation*) will use its best endeavours to obtain the release of the Holding Trustees or any of them from the terms of the lease in the event that any Holding Trustee wishes to resign from their post prior to the termination of the lease.

6. Whether or not the Holding Trustees are members of the Committee of Management of (*name of organisation*), they shall have the following rights during their term of office as Holding Trustees, or until such time as the lease has been determined and all the obligations of the Lessee under the lease have been discharged, whichever is the longer:

   a. the right to receive notification of any meeting of the Committee of Management of (*name of organisation*) as if they were members of that committee

   b. the right to receive notification of any general meeting of members of (*name of organisation*) as if they were members

   c. the right of access upon demand to inspect the books of account of (*name of organisation*) including cash books, vouchers, bank statements, cheque books and other similar documents (including the right for their advisers to inspect such books) and the right to take copies of those documents upon payment of a reasonable fee

d. the right to attend and speak at any meeting of the Committee of Management or any general meeting of the members of (*name of organisation*) on any matter relating to the proposed lease or finances of (*name of organisation*)

Signed and delivered as a Deed by (*names – at least two*)

e. the right to receive from time to time the names and addresses of all members of the Committee of Management of (*name of organisation*) and to be kept informed of any changes

on behalf of the Committee of Management of (*name of organisation*)

f. the right to receive copies of any internal memoranda, financial reports or assessments and accounts and balance sheets produced for the treasurer, Committee of Management or any subcommittee of (*name of organisation*)

acting under their authority by resolution on (*date*)

g. the right to require immediate payment of any liability outstanding under the terms of the proposed lease.

in the presence of:

7. The Holding Trustees agree:

Signed as a Deed
by (first Holding Trustee)

a. to notify the Secretary or Treasurer of the Committee of Management of (*name of organisation*) of all correspondence or other communication in respect of (premises)

in the presence of:

b. to act in accordance with all lawful and reasonable decisions made by the Committee of Management of (*name of organisation*) in respect of (premises) but not otherwise

Signed as a Deed
by (second Holding Trustee)
in the presence of:

c. that they have no powers of management except such as are expressly conferred on them by this Deed

(and so on for each Holding Trustee)

d. that they have the custody of all documents of title relating to the Property, but the Committee of Management or any of them have free access thereto and are entitled to take photocopies of them

e. that the powers of appointing new or additional Holding Trustees and of discharging Holding Trustees are exercisable by the Committee of Management alone, but the Holding Trustees have the same power of applying to the court for the appointment of a new Holding Trustees as has any other trustee under law.

Conditions of hire of XYZ Community Association's meeting hall

1. The person named in the application shall be the Hirer and shall be personally responsible for ensuring that these conditions are complied with in all respects.

2. The management committee of the organisation referred to in the hiring application shall be jointly and individually liable with the Hirer for complying with this agreement.

3. The premises to be hired are part of the premises of XYZ Community Association and consist of the meeting hall, kitchen, bar area, toilets and entrance hall. Tables, chairs, cooker, fridge and sound equipment are provided by the XYZ Community Association.

4. **THE HIRER AGREES:**
   a. To pay a deposit of 25% of the hiring charges upon the acceptance of the hiring application by the XYZ Community Association.

   b. To pay the full hire charge (of £ ...) and a cleaning deposit of £25 not less than two weeks before the date of hiring.

   c. That he or she has inspected the premises and they are suitable for the purposes for which they are hired.

   d. That no public announcement or advertisement of any function proposed to be held shall be made until the application is accepted by the XYZ Community Association and the deposit has been paid.

   e. To ensure that any licences required for the function, including liquor or entertainment licences, are obtained from the relevant authority and are displayed as required, and that the premises are not used for any activities that require a licence unless the appropriate licence has been obtained and a copy provided to XYZ Community Association.

   f. That employees and members of the committee of the XYZ Community Association are not authorised by the XYZ Community Association to assist the Hirer in the organisation of any function held on the premises or to accept responsibility for the safe custody of any money or goods.

   g. To ensure that they or some other person authorised in writing by them (the 'responsible person') is present throughout the period of hire.

   h. To ensure that the responsible person does not leave the premises at the end of the period of hire until the caretaker attends to secure the premises. *Note: The Hirer must provide the XYZ Community Association in advance with a list of those persons who will be responsible during the period of hire.*

   i. To ensure that the premises are not used for any purpose other than that stated in the hiring application.

   j. To ensure that authorised members of the committee or staff of the XYZ Community Association are allowed access to the premises at all times during the period of hire.

   k. To accept full responsibility for and to indemnify the XYZ Community Association against all costs, charges and claims in respect of injury to any person using the premises except such as may be caused by the negligence of the XYZ Community Association or its staff or agents.

   l. To compensate the XYZ Community Association for any damage caused during the period of hire or as a result of any breach of this agreement to the building or to any apparatus, fittings or appliances belonging to the XYZ Community Association or its staff.

   m. To compensate the XYZ Community Association or any member of its staff should any theft occur of any items during the period of hire or as a result of a breach of this agreement.

   n. To ensure it has sufficient insurances to enable the hirer to meet these indemnities.

   o. To ensure that the fire apparatus and other equipment required for health and safety on the premises is not interfered with.

   p. To ensure that at no time during the period of hire is any emergency exit from the premises locked or obstructed.

   q. To allow no more than *xxx* people to attend the premises at any one time.

   r. To ensure that the responsible person and at least *xxx* other people are aware of the site of fire appliances, emergency exits and evacuation procedures (as detailed on the attached map).

s. To take all proper precautions for the prevention of accidents to any persons on the premises during the period of hire.

t. Not to issue tickets or tokens to any function on the premises less than two hours prior to the commencement of the hiring.

u. Not to issue tickets or tokens on the premises or in the area of the premises during the period of hire.

v. To take proper steps to control admittance to the function and ensure that there is no intrusion or hindrance to any other event or function taking place elsewhere in the community centre.

w. To ensure that no music is played on the premises after 11 pm.

x. To ensure that all noise, including music, is kept within the level set by the local authority, details of which can be obtained from the environmental health department.

y. To ensure that the noise level during the arrival or departure of people attending the premises is not such as to cause a nuisance or inconvenience to occupiers of neighbouring property.

z. To ensure that the activities for which the premises are hired cease in sufficient time before the time stated for completion of the hire in the application form to enable all people to leave the premises and all apparatus concerned with the hire to be removed and the premises are cleaned and tidied by the time for completion of the hire.

zz. To ensure that all facilities used are left clean and tidy.

5. The XYZ Community Association reserves the right of entry of authorised members of its committee and staff to the premises at all times during the period of hire.

6. The XYZ Community Association shall not be responsible or liable for any damage to or loss of property, articles or objects placed or left on the premises by the Hirer or any other person.

7. The XYZ Community Association reserves the right to allow the use of other parts of the community centre during the period of hire and to allow the common use of the entrance hall and toilets.

8. The XYZ Community Association will provide cleaning materials.

9. The XYZ Community Association will retain the £25 deposit for cleaning charges if condition 4.z is not complied with.

10. The 25% deposit paid on acceptance of the hiring is payable in addition to the hiring charge and shall be held by the XYZ Community Association as security for any damage to property belonging to the XYZ Community Association during the course of the hiring or any other breach of this agreement. Any portion not required for these purposes will be returned within four weeks of the event.

11. In the event of any breach of the above conditions or in the event of any misstatement in the form of application or any material omission from the form whenever discovered, the hiring may be cancelled without prior notice at the absolute discretion of the XYZ Community Association, and any charges paid, including the hiring charge, may be forfeited.

12. If the full hiring charge is not paid as required by condition 4.b, the XYZ Community Association may, without prior notice, cancel the hiring and keep the deposit unless the XYZ Community Association is satisfied in its absolute discretion that there is good reason why the full charges were not paid. If the XYZ Community Association is satisfied there was a good reason, or it receives another application for hire covering the same period and suffers no loss of income, it will retain 5% of the deposit to cover administrative costs.

13. (Name of staff and/or committee member(s)) of the XYZ Community Association has/have delegated authority from the XYZ Community Association to act on the XYZ Community Association's behalf in relation to matters under this agreement.

14. The XYZ Community Association reserves the right to cancel this agreement for any good reason beyond its control and in that event to return all fees and deposits paid to the Hirer.

15. The Community Association's Hiring Agreement and these conditions of hire represent the complete contract between the Hirer on behalf of the management committee of the organisation referred to in the hiring application and the XYZ Community Association. No variation or amendment to the conditions shall be valid unless they are in writing signed by one or more of the person(s) named in Clause 13.

Chapter 7:
Insurance

Related chapters

Chapter 1 – Breach of trust
Chapter 5 – Health and safety
Chapter 9 – Defamation
Chapter 10 – Wrongful trading

This chapter describes general rules about insurance contracts and looks at compulsory and discretionary insurance that organisations need to consider.

The organisation's governing body is responsible for ensuring all insurances are taken out, paid and kept up to date. It is advisable to get several quotes before taking out any insurance policy. Insurance can be purchased directly from an insurance company or through a broker. The British Insurance Brokers' Association has a list of registered brokers for each area (available online at *www.biba.org.uk*) and can also identify those of its members with a particular interest or specialism. It may also be worth asking other local voluntary organisations, particularly the local council for voluntary service or rural community council, who they use. Some umbrella bodies can arrange insurance for members at a lower rate than commercial companies.

A number of organisations have negotiated specialist insurance packages for voluntary organisations, including the London Voluntary Service Council, Wales Council for Voluntary Action, Scottish Council of Voluntary Organisations, the National Association of Councils for Voluntary Service and Community Trading Services.

General rules

In insurance contracts, an application for insurance is a **proposal** and the person or organisation taking out the insurance the **proposer**.

When taking out insurance the proposer owes a duty of the **utmost good faith** to the insurance company. This means that the company can refuse to pay out on any insurance claim if, when making the proposal (usually by completing an application form or giving details over the phone or internet) the proposer has failed to disclose or has misrepresented a **material fact** (see overleaf).

The extent of the duty

The proposer must disclose all material facts until the proposal is accepted, and must inform the insurance company if additional material facts arise after submitting the application.

The obligation to disclose material facts includes providing information which could be discovered by making reasonably prudent enquiries. The insurance company should be told if any material fact changes during the course of the policy.

Who should be covered

Any action, or the failure to perform any action by an organisation is, in practice, the responsibility of one or more individuals within that organisation. These would usually be employees or management committee members but could also be volunteers or members. It is therefore advisable to cover employees, management committee members, volunteers and members for any liability they may incur carrying out the organisation's work. This would include cover by professional indemnity insurance (see page 161), public liability insurance (see page 160) and road traffic insurance (if they are driving the organisation's vehicles).

Most insurance companies design their policies for individuals or businesses. Their standard policies may cover staff (in terms of both staff protection and third party liability) but usually do not cover volunteers or unpaid management committee members, so it may be necessary to get specific extensions to standard policies A specialist policy designed for the voluntary sector may therefore be preferable and cheaper (see above), as it will probably give volunteers protection under the employer's liability section, and include their third party liability under the public liability section.

Incorporated organisations

Incorporated organisations (companies and industrial and provident societies – and charitable incorporated organisations when established – see chapter 1) can take out insurance in the name of the organisation.

Unincorporated organisations

Unincorporated organisations should take out insurance in the name of the committee members but the proposal form should be signed by one individual who is specifically stated to be taking it out on behalf of the other committee members. If that person leaves the organisation the insurance must be transferred to someone else's name.

Material facts

A material fact affects the degree of risk the insurance company is accepting. Examples are given below.

All insurance

- Previous refusals of similar insurance
- Special conditions imposed on previous insurance
- Unspent criminal convictions of staff or management committee members. The type of conviction and time limits vary between insurance companies and between types of policies
- Previous claims on similar insurance

Theft insurance

- Use of the premises by other organisations or the public

Fire insurance

- Defective fire fighting equipment
- Internal blocking of fire exits
- Regular blocking of fire access, for example by cars
- Use of the premises by other organisations or the public

Motor insurance

- Drivers' age
- Drivers' road traffic convictions
- In the case of minibus drivers, lack of necessary training
- The use of vehicle(s)

Public liability insurance

- Use of the premises by other organisations or the public
- The organisation's activities and the extent of any associated risks

Professional indemnity insurance

- The organisation's professional services (for example, giving information or advice about legal, financial, health or similar matters or providing medical treatment)

Renewals

The proposer must disclose all material facts each time the insurance is renewed even though there is no need to complete an additional proposal form. These include changes or additional material facts that have arisen since the last renewal. The proposer must volunteer additional information even if not specifically asked to do so.

Exclusions

All insurance policies include a list of circumstances excluded from cover (the **small print**). It is important to be clear about them before taking out a policy.

Amount of cover

In all types of insurance it is essential to be covered for the right amount.
- **Contents** would normally be insured for the cost of replacing the lost or damaged goods.
- **Buildings** would normally be insured for the reinstatement cost, including VAT, all professional fees and site clearance.

Other insurance

For other types of insurance, the proposer will need to work out the likely maximum claim that might be made against the organisation. Take advice from a reputable insurance broker who understands the organisation and its work.

Underinsurance

A policy usually states that the organisation must insure for a sufficiently large sum to cover any claim. If it is underinsured, some policies allow the insurance company to reduce the claim payment or refuse to pay out at all.

Other policies operate an **average clause**. This means that the insurance company pays out only a proportion of any loss. For example if a building valued at £200,000 is insured for £50,000, the insurance company would pay only one quarter of any claim made, however small. So if the organisation claimed for £4000 worth of damage to a roof during a storm the insurance company would only pay £1000.

Completing the proposal

Whoever is responsible for completing a proposal on behalf of an organisation (whether staff or committee member) must be aware of the consequences of making a mistake. Leaving a blank space on a proposal form is taken to mean that no material fact exists in reply to that particular question: if in any doubt give the insurance company too much rather than too little information.

If an insurance broker completes the proposal form, make sure all the information recorded is accurate, all the necessary information has been recorded and that the organisation receives a copy. As a matter of good practice, all insurance proposals should be read and signed by a committee member.

Some insurers now issue a **statement of facts** in place of a proposal form when insurance is arranged over the phone or on the internet. The insurer will send the proposer a copy of the statement with the insurance policy. It is essential to check the statement carefully – some can be very detailed – and send the insurer an amended statement of facts if necessary.

If a material fact is not disclosed or the application form is inaccurate, the insurance company may refuse payment of a claim. If the insurance company refused to pay a claim against an unincorporated association, the management committee members could be personally liable to pay compensation to the person making the claim.

Keep at least two copies of all information supplied: keep one copy away from the premises so that it can be referred to if other papers are lost through fire or theft.

Making a claim

As soon as there is a possible insurance claim check the conditions to ensure that the organisation complies with them. There may be preconditions, for example reporting the matter to the police, or submitting a claim within a specific period.

Contact the insurance company as soon as possible, giving full details and quoting the policy number. If a claim involves a question of legal liability and the organisation is insured for this type of claim, the insurer will deal with the other party.

Never admit responsibility for an accident, however obvious it is that the organisation is at fault, because this could prejudice an insurer's position.

Types of insurance

Organisations should consider obtaining cover above the legal minimum for all types of insurance.

Compulsory insurance

Two types of insurance are required by law.

Employer's liability insurance

Under the **Employer's Liability (Compulsory Insurance) Act 1969** all employers have a duty to insure against claims by workers for injury or illness caused by the employer's negligence or failure to comply with a statutory duty such as health and safety. The insurance must be for at least £5 million to cover any one claim, and the current insurance certificate must be displayed in all workplaces and be retained by the employer for 40 years.

This insurance does not usually cover injury or illness caused to committee members, trainees, consultants, self-employed people working for the organisation, volunteers or service users, although some specialist policies (see page 157) automatically cover volunteers. Public liability insurance is needed to cover these categories of people (see page 160). Nor does employer's liability insurance cover an employee being injured through an accident rather than through the employer's negligence (for this, see *Insurance for accidents, medical care and assaults*, page 163) or claims brought by an employee for breach of employment or equal opportunities law (for this, see *Legal expenses insurance*, page 163).

Road traffic insurance

Under the **Road Traffic Acts** all organisations that use vehicles on the road must insure the drivers against **third party risks** – injury or death caused to other people (including passengers) and damage caused to other people's property. The certificate of insurance must be readily available.

Third party insurance does not cover theft of or damage to a vehicle. It is therefore worth extending the insurance either to **third party, fire and theft** (which covers theft and fire damage to the vehicle) or **comprehensive**, which covers all damage. Some comprehensive policies may cover death or injury of the driver, but cover will be very limited. Such circumstances need to be covered by personal accident insurance (see page 163).

The insurance company must be informed about use of the vehicle and who is likely to be driving it. Insurance may be cheaper if the number of named drivers is limited.

If employees and/or volunteers use their own vehicles to carry out the organisation's work it is essential to ensure that their insurance policies cover journeys made for these purposes, otherwise they will be uninsured when using their vehicles for these journeys. Use of a vehicle for work purposes is called 'business use' even if the organisation is a charity or other voluntary organisation and even if the person is using the vehicle as a volunteer rather than an employee.

An organisation may be liable for personal injury or damage to property as a result of a traffic accident in the course of work, so it is essential to ensure adequate cover. Check the following:
- the insurance is current
- it covers the employee and/or volunteer for use in connection with their work (including voluntary work)
- the nature of the work has been accurately disclosed to the insurance company
- the insurance company has been notified of any particular risks associated with how the vehicle will be used, for example to carry service users, or for unusual activities such as off-road driving.

The above also apply if the employee or volunteer uses a car owned by someone else, for example their partner.

Some specialist policies will cover the costs incurred by an employee or volunteer through loss of a no claims discount and/or having to pay the excess on a claim.

Insurance that may be required

There are a number of other types of insurance that, although not required by statute, may be required by, for example, a landlord or funder or under the terms of a contract, or may be in the organisation's best interest.

Buildings insurance

An organisation that leases a building may, under the terms of the lease, have to reimburse the landlord for the cost of insuring the building, the rent, property owner's liability, and possibly the glass.

The building should be insured for its reinstatement cost as new, allowing for all professional fees and site clearance costs. Under the lease, the tenant should have the right to inspect the policy.

In the few cases where the landlord does not organise the buildings insurance, the tenant would insure the building, normally as a condition of the lease, thus protecting the landlord.

Organisations are under no statutory obligation to insure premises they own. However, as there is a duty under charity law to protect a charity's assets, charities have a duty to take out buildings insurance. A committee that left a building uninsured would be negligent in their duty to the charity, and therefore in breach of trust.

It is usual to insure for the cost of rebuilding the premises (including VAT) if completely destroyed, and to include all professional and site clearance fees. It is also worth considering cover for the cost of alternative accommodation while the rebuilding takes place. The organisation may also want to consider 'business interruption insurance' – see *Discretionary insurance*, page 142.

Insurance for plate glass windows

Leases of properties with shopfronts often require tenants to insure any plate glass windows against breakage, either accidentally or through criminal damage. Check the lease to see whether taking out the insurance is the responsibility of the landlord or tenant.

Public liability insurance

This covers claims made against the organisation (or committee members of an unincorporated body) for injury, loss or damage caused to any person as a result of an organisation's negligence. It would include injury suffered by someone using the organisation's premises as a result of a breach of the duties under the **Health and Safety at Work Act 1974** or **Occupier's Liability Act 1957** (see chapter 5). It does not cover injury, damage or loss caused by the provision of professional services (see *Professional indemnity insurance*, below) or the supply of goods (see *Product liability insurance*, page 161). It also does not cover situations where the committee has been negligent in its duty to the organisation (see *Trustee and directors' indemnity insurance*, page 161).

When taking out public liability insurance, ensure that the insurance policy or schedule includes liability for damage, injury or loss caused by anyone who carries out work on behalf of the organisation. In other words, it should cover not only the organisation itself but also members of staff, trainees, committee members and volunteers. Most policies will automatically cover paid staff, but insurance companies may not be used to dealing with voluntary organisations and so would not automatically provide policies covering the acts of committee members or volunteers. Specialist policies for voluntary organisations (see page 157) will usually cover volunteers and committee members.

It is important to inform the insurance company of the nature of the organisation's work and the fact that it uses volunteers, trainees, outside workers and/or secondees.

Examples of situations covered by public liability insurance include injury to a person (other than an employee) who trips on loose carpet or lino or is injured by faulty equipment, damage to clothing caused by failure to put up 'wet paint' signs, or food poisoning caused to people attending a lunch club.

Although this insurance is not compulsory, it would be extremely unwise for an organisation not to have some form of public liability insurance if it has premises and/or provides activities or services. It may be a condition of a lease or grant aid, and is required by some local authorities.

Organisations providing services under contract with a public body or funder will almost always be required to have public liability insurance as a condition of the contract. Check the value of insurance required.

Professional indemnity insurance

Public liability insurance will not cover injury or damages arising from negligence in the course of providing any type of professional service, for example information, advice or health treatment. It will therefore be necessary to take out professional indemnity insurance to cover any claims resulting from incorrect advice or negligent services (even if the service is free) which cause damage, injury or loss to a service user. It is sometimes included in trustee indemnity insurance (see below).

Examples of situations covered by this insurance include a person injured by a massage therapist, someone losing out on housing or welfare benefits because they are given incorrect or misleading information, or an organisation facing an employment tribunal claim because it was given incorrect advice about employment law.

Self-employed people or others who are not employees or volunteers who carry out work on behalf of the organisation will not be covered by the organisation's public or professional indemnity insurance. It is therefore essential to ensure that such workers are adequately insured themselves where there is any element of risk, and to make this a condition of appointment. Check that their insurance is in force, covers the work they are doing for the organisation, and indemnifies (repays) the organisation if it faces any claims because of the worker's negligence. At the same time check that the organisation's own public liability or professional indemnity insurance covers it for any liabilities incurred as a result of the worker's activities.

Professional indemnity policies can be expensive, as some insurers have high minimum premiums, but this cover can be included in specialist policies for voluntary organisations (see page 157).

Some national umbrella or support organisations have negotiated lower rate policies for members. For example adviceUK, the umbrella body for independent advice-giving organisations, arranges insurance for members on a block policy.

Defamation and unintentional breach of copyright

Insurance against defamation (slander or libel, see chapter 9) or unintentional breach of copyright can often be included with another type of cover, for example public liability insurance, professional indemnity or trustee liability insurance.

There are always risks of either of these occurring if an organisation represents people, writes letters on their behalf or publishes any kind of material, including in e-mails or on the internet.

Both insurances are also available separately.

Product liability insurance

If your organisation manufactures, sells or supplies any goods, it is advisable to take out product liability insurance to cover any illness, injury, death or damage that may arise from faulty goods.

Trustee and directors' indemnity insurance

Indemnity insurance protects trustees or directors against the risk of personal liability arising from their breach of trust and negligence to the organisation itself (see *Breach of trust*, in chapter 1) or, in the case of a company or industrial and provident society, for liability for wrongful trading in some situations. However it will not protect again deliberate wrongful trading (see *Who is liable?*, in chapter 10).

Some insurers include other types of insurance with trustee/directors' indemnity, for example, professional indemnity, defamation, fidelity (theft by staff or committee members) and/or loss of documents. If this is the case, make sure it doesn't duplicate cover already held.

Some people are not prepared to serve as committee members unless they are protected by this kind of insurance, and some local authorities require it before making nominations to management committees. People often believe that this insurance covers far more than it actually does. Many think, for example, that it covers committee members for personal liability for the organisation's debts, or that it covers negligence to third parties. However, this is not the case.

Before considering buying trustee/directors' indemnity insurance, committee members should focus on putting in place procedures and policies to help reduce any potential risk.

There are restrictions on the circumstances in which an organisation can take out this form of insurance. Because it covers committee members rather than the organisation, there is a potential conflict of interest between the individuals and the organisation they are managing.

Charities

Charities must have explicit constitutional power to take out and pay for trustee indemnity insurance (TII). If a charity wants to amend its constitution to include the power, it must obtain written permission from the Charity Commission to use the charity's funds for this purpose.

The Charity Commission will not accept the purchase of TII that covers:

- fines
- costs of unsuccessfully defending criminal prosecutions for offences arising out of a committee member's fraud, dishonesty or reckless misconduct
- liabilities resulting from conduct which committee members knew, or must be assumed to have known, was not in the charity's interests, or which committee members did not care whether it was in the charity's interests.

Given these exclusions, the only circumstances likely to be covered by TII are where committee members entered into an arrangement which turned out to be in breach of trust, having made an honest but reasonable mistake. But as explained in chapter 1 (see *Breach of trust*), charity committee members who have acted reasonably in good faith and made an innocent mistake can be excused personal liability, so are unlikely to be held liable for such inadvertent breach of trust.

The Charity Commission must be satisfied that it is in the charity's interests to buy the policy, but will accept a structured but minimal level of justification. Under a self-certification procedure, committee members certify (on a specific form) that they have identified the risks to which they are exposed and have decided that the purchase of TII is in the charity's best interests.

The Commission allows charitable companies to take out insurance cover to protect committee members against claims for 'wrongful trading' (see *Incorporated organisations*, in chapter 10), provided it does not cover deliberate insolvent trading or doing so recklessly. It would cover committee members only if they made an honest and reasonable mistake.

The Commission will give authority to purchase TII on the condition that the committee members' declaration is materially accurate and true. Committee members are therefore responsible for ensuring they have completed the declaration form correctly. It is an offence, under **Section 11** of the **Charities Act 1993**, to mislead the Commission deliberately.

For further details see *Operational Guidance trustee indemnity insurance* (OG 1001 A1), and *Charities and insurance* (CC 49), available from *www.charitycommission.gov.uk*

Trustee or directors' liability insurance does not cover committee members for losses or debts arising from contracts, negligence or other obligations to third parties. It does not, for example, cover inability to pay bills or meet redundancy costs.

Discretionary insurance

Organisations should also consider the following types of insurance, depending on the nature of their activities and the extent of their property.

Contents insurance

This normally covers the contents of a building for theft or damage, for example by fire, but will usually exclude theft by the organisation's employees or volunteers (for this, the organisation would need theft by employee insurance, see *Fidelity or theft by employee insurance*, below). Many policies also cover **accidental damage** – damage caused directly by individuals (for example by spilling coffee over a keyboard) – if the policy doesn't include this, it may be worth extending the cover. The insurance may or may not cover property while it is out of the organisation's building (and may or may not cover property during a move to other permanent premises, see *All risks insurance*, below).

NB: For the same reason that charities should insure their buildings – because of the charity law duty to protect a charity's assets – there may also be a charity law duty to insure contents.

The organisation must tell the insurance company about the building's likely users. The insurer may impose conditions on the policy, for example restrict cover to loss after a break-in or insist on additional locks or an alarm. If the policy is to cover theft of cash, the insurance company may require the cash to be stored in a safe, set a limit for how much cash can be kept on the premises, and/or place conditions on the transit of cash (for example the number of people who have to be involved in carrying cash – say, two for up to £5000, three for £5000-£10,000, a security firm for larger amounts).

It is especially important to inform the insurance company if volunteers carry out any work or the premises are used by other organisations.

All risks insurance

This is usually an extension of the contents insurance, extending cover to property when it is outside the building (for example laptops and presentation equipment). It is especially useful for organisations that shift around expensive equipment to different venues, for example theatre or music groups, or where staff take the organisation's laptops home or to conferences.

Business interruption insurance

It is possible to get cover for the cost of interruption of business if it is necessary to move premises because of damage. Examples include losing income from a fee paying service the organisation was unable to provide for a period, or incurring extra costs through additional rent, installing phone lines and advising service users of a change of address.

Equipment failure insurance

It is possible to insure major equipment, such as boilers and lifts, against damage and breakdown. Most policies then require regular maintenance checks and servicing.

Engineering inspection insurance

This provides an inspection and reporting service for major equipment such as passenger lifts, stairlifts and tailboard lifts that have to be inspected to comply with relevant legislation (for example the **Factories Act 1961** and the **Offices, Shops and Railway Premises (Hoists and Lifts) Regulations 1968**). Such insurance could cover all major equipment failure.

Fidelity or theft by employee insurance

Organisations dealing with large amounts of cash or holding high value stock or equipment should consider insuring against employees' dishonesty. The insurance company would want details of any convictions.

Some organisations may wish to consider insuring against dishonesty by members of the management committee and/or other volunteers. This is not a standard type of insurance, but an insurance company might supply it as an extension to a policy covering employees' dishonesty, and a specialist insurance policy (see page 157) may also cover volunteers. Again, members and volunteers would have to disclose any previous convictions.

Computer insurance

Specially tailored insurance for computers can be arranged which, as well as covering loss or damage to the computer and/or its peripherals (such as a printer or scanner), also covers reinstatement of data and the increased costs of working as a result of the damage (for example a manual system has to be run at the same time as a computerised system).

Insurance for accidents, medical care and assault

It is possible to insure against staff sickness, to cover the cost of sick pay. Other policies are available that pay out standard sums to staff for specific injuries at work, for example loss of a limb. It would also cover staff who had suffered injuries through being assaulted. The organisation may want to negotiate extending this to cover volunteers and committee members.

Insurance for outdoor events

It is possible to take out cover against losses arising from cancellation of outdoor events due to bad weather. This is commonly known as **pluvius** (rain) **insurance.** It usually involves strict time limits and arrangements for measuring rainfall, and organisations should take professional advice before considering such cover.

Legal expenses insurance

This could cover legal expenses incurred in:
- employment and equal opportunities disputes
- defending prosecution against the organisation under legislation such as the Health and Safety at Work Act and Trade Descriptions Act
- property damage and nuisance against third parties
- in depth investigation by the Inland Revenue into the organisation's tax affairs

- disputes with Customs and Excise regarding VAT
- contract disputes for amounts over £1000.

In case of a claim or potential claim, the insurer usually requires the organisation to comply with its advice, and failure to do so may invalidate the insurance. This can reduce the organisation's scope for dealing with a claim in other ways (for example, the insurer may recommend making an out-of-court settlement in a situation where the organisation might prefer to go to court in order to clear its name).

Legal advice helplines

Some legal expenses and other insurance policies include free access to legal advice, usually via a telephone helpline. This can be a useful service if an organisation requires immediate advice about a problem that might develop into a loss or claim.

Risk management

Insurance premiums have increased significantly, and this trend is likely to continue. Also, some insurers no longer offer insurance in what they consider to be high-risk areas, because of their experience of increased claims. At the time of writing (December 2003) insurers and the government were considering measures in an endeavour to ensure the cost of insurances did not become prohibitive.

These factors are significant for voluntary organisations. Before taking out insurance committee members need to consider a number of questions, including the following:

- does the nature of the organisation's activities and services present a risk of a particular form of loss or liability?
- how much would it cost to insure against such risks?
- is there any way to reduce this cost, for example:
  - by taking steps to reduce the likelihood of a claim
  - by instructing an insurance broker to seek competitive quotes
  - by collaborating with other organisations when buying insurance
- how can the organisation ensure it can afford to meet the insurance costs?
- should the organisation reduce or abandon the activity that gives rise to the risk?
- should the organisation stop (or not take out) that type of insurance? What are the potential implications of this if something goes wrong and the organisation is not insured for it?

For further information see *Charities and insurance* (CC 49), available from *www.charitycommission.gov.uk* This Charity Commission booklet includes information that would be useful for any voluntary organisation.

Chapter 8:
Financial management

Related chapters
Chapter 1 – Legal status
Chapter 4 – PAYE
Chapter 7 – Insurance
Chapter 9 – Gift Aid
Chapter 10 - Insolvent organisations

All voluntary organisations should keep accounts and in most cases are legally obliged to. Properly kept accounts will help to show funders, members and the public that an organisation is operating effectively. Keeping well-organised records will also help an organisation manage its activities by showing how actual income and expenditure compare with budgeted figures.

Legal requirements – accounts

Regulations governing accounting records, statements of account and auditing requirements vary according to an organisation's legal status (see chapter 1), whether it is charitable (see chapter 1), and its annual income and expenditure.

Charities

Charities Act 1993

Part VI of the **Charities Act 1993** (as amended) and associated regulations govern accounting, reporting and auditing rules for unincorporated charities. All charitable associations and charitable trusts, and charities established under acts of parliament or by Royal Charter are required to:

- prepare and maintain proper financial records
- prepare annual accounts and, in most cases, a report on the accounts (see *Annual reports on the accounts*, page 168), and
- make their most recent annual accounts and report available to any member of the public on request.

The obligations for charitable companies (under company law), and charitable industrial and provident societies (under IPS law) are virtually identical.

Charitable associations and trusts whose **annual income and expenditure are £10,000** or less are subject to less onerous accounting requirements than other charities, sometimes referred to as the 'light touch regime'.

All registered charities with an **annual income or expenditure of more than £10,000** have to submit annual accounts and reports to the Charity Commission; those whose annual income and expenditure are £10,000 or less need only submit annual accounts and reports on request.

Charities SORP

For charities with annual income or expenditure over £100,000, or for charities with lower income or expenditure that prepare accrual accounts (see page 167), the requirements for charity accounts and annual reports are laid down in Accounting and Reporting by Charities: Statement of Recommended Practice (the **Charities SORP** or **SORP 2000**). Although the SORP is not a legal requirement, it is backed by the **Charities (Accounts and Reports) Regulations 2001**, and the Charity Commission expects charities to comply. Any significant divergence from its recommendations must be explained in the charity's accounts. SORP 2000 is available from the Charity Commission's contact centre on 0870 333 0123 or its website *www.charitycommission.gov.uk*.

Accounting records

Committee members of all charities have a duty to ensure the charity keeps accounting records that record the financial transactions – money spent and received – on a day-to-day basis, and show the nature and purpose of each transaction. The records must also show all **assets** (what the organisation owns and is owed) and **liabilities** (what it owes).

Although records do not have to be updated each day, accounts must be able to show the charity's financial position on any particular date in the past.

Unincorporated charities must keep accounting records for at least six years from the end of the financial year to which they relate. This applies even if the charity folds before the end of six years.

Companies limited by guarantee, whether charitable or non-charitable, must maintain records to the same standard, under the Companies Act 1985. Although companies need only keep records for three years, funders may require that records be kept for longer periods and it is good practice to keep them for at least six years from the end of the financial year.

Annual accounts

The Companies Act 1985 governs the requirements for preparing charitable and non-charitable companies' annual accounts and the committee's report on the accounts; industrial and provident societies are governed by the Friendly and Industrial and Provident Societies Act 1968, and unincorporated charities by the Charities Act 1993. For further information on charity accounting see *Charity accounts: the framework* (CC61).

Companies limited by guarantee

All companies – whether charitable or non-charitable – are required, under company law, to prepare a set of accounts. Commercial companies prepare a profit and loss account and balance sheet. Companies set up on a not-for-profit basis must prepare an income and expenditure account and balance sheet and notes to the accounts, and submit them to Companies House within ten months of the end of the financial year. Small and medium companies (see below) can submit abbreviated accounts.

Proposals in the companies law white paper simplify accounting requirements for small and medium-sized companies, but remove the option to submit abbreviated accounts and reduce the time for submitting the accounts to seven months.

Small companies

To be a small company, at least two of the following conditions must be met:
- annual turnover (ie income or expenditure) must be £5.6 million or less
- the balance sheet total must be £2.8 million or less
- the average number of employees must be 50 or fewer.

Small companies need only submit an abbreviated balance sheet and a special auditor's report (unless exempt from audit – see *Auditing or examining accounts*, page 167) and modified notes to the accounts to Companies House.

Medium companies

To be a medium company, at least two of the following conditions must be met:
- annual turnover must be £22.8 million or less

- the balance sheet total must be £11.4 million or less
- the average number of employees must be 250 or fewer.

Medium companies need only submit an abbreviated profit and loss account, a full balance sheet, a special auditor's report, the directors' report and notes to the accounts.

Charitable companies whose income is £10,000 or over must submit accounts to the Charity Commission as well as to Companies House. Those whose income and expenditure are £10,000 or under must submit accounts to Companies House, but to the Charity Commission only if requested.

Industrial and provident societies (IPSs)

IPSs must prepare an annual revenue account and balance sheet. The revenue account can cover the whole society, or there can be two or more revenue accounts dealing with specific aspects of the society's work. The balance sheet must cover the whole society. The accounts and balance sheet must be submitted to the Financial Services Authority.

Unincorporated charities

Income £100,000 or less

Unincorporated charities with gross annual income of £100,000 or less may prepare either a receipts and payments account and a statement of assets (what the charity has, for example money in the bank or equipment) and liabilities (for example, unpaid bills), or a full set of accounts. If the latter, they must be prepared in accordance with the Charities (Accounts and Reports) Regulations 1995 and the Charities (Accounts and Reports) Regulations 2000 (see *Income over £100,000*, below).

The *Receipts and payments accounts pack 2001* (CC 64), available from the Charity Commission (0870 333 0123 or *www.charity-commission.gov.uk*), includes a receipts and payments form that, when completed, will meet the legal requirements and guidance in SORP 2000, and gives detailed guidance on completing the form.

Income over £100,000

Unincorporated charities with gross annual income over £100,000 must prepare a full statement of accounts for each financial year on what is known as the accruals basis, in accordance with the Charities (Accounts and Reports) Regulations 1995 and the Charities (Accounts and Reports) Regulations 2000.

Accounts prepared on the accruals basis must contain the following:

- a **statement of financial activities** (**SOFA**) (see below)
- a **balance sheet,** showing the charity's assets (what it has, for example money in the bank, property and equipment) and liabilities (for example, unpaid bills and other outstanding debts)
- **notes to the accounts,** which detail the accounting policies adopted, explain or expand on the information in the SOFA and balance sheet, and give further useful information.

The SOFA is basically an income and expenditure account, divided into columns for different types of fund:

- **unrestricted** (ie money that can be used for any purpose within the charity's objects)
- **restricted income** (money with some condition which has been agreed with or imposed by the donor, for example funds raised specifically to buy a minibus, or a grant to cover a particular salary)
- **capital** or **endowment** (money given to the charity with the restriction that the capital be invested, and only the income from the investment (ie not the capital) can be spent).

It includes a column showing the total income and expenditure for each type of fund, and a column comparing these with the previous year's total for each type of fund. Income and expenditure must be presented under headings designated by the SORP (see *Charities SORP*, page 165). The SOFA must include a line showing any transfers between funds.

The layout of the SOFA and balance sheet, and the content of the notes are covered in the regulations and the SORP.

For guidance on preparing a full set of accounts see the *Accruals account pack* (CC65), available from the Charity Commission (0870 333 0123 or *www.charitycommission.gov.uk*).

Auditing or examining accounts

Legal requirements are given below; the audit process is described in the final section of the chapter.

Non-charitable companies

Non-charitable companies with a turnover of more than £5.6 million, or with assets of £2.8 million or more, must have a full audit by a registered auditor. 'Registered auditor' means someone eligible under the **Companies Act 1989,** including members of the Institute of Chartered Accountants in England and Wales and many members of the Chartered Association of Certified Accountants (registered auditors use the initials CA, ACA, FCA, ACCA or FCCA after their name).

Non-charitable companies with a turnover of £1 million or less do not need an audit if they qualify as a small company (see page 166) and have assets of £5.6 million or less, unless required by the membership, the articles of association (constitution) or funders. But if their turnover is more than £90,000 they have to produce an audit exemption report (see below).

Charitable companies

Charitable companies whose gross income is £250,000* or above must have their accounts audited.

Charitable companies whose gross income is more than £90,000 but less than £250,000* must have an audit or produce an **audit exemption report**. An audit exemption report involves a less detailed examination of the accounts by a qualified practising accountant, and the accountant's certificate need not certify that the accounts give 'a true and fair view' of the company's financial position. An audit exemption report is therefore cheaper than a full audit.

*The draft Charities Bill will propose raising this threshold, to at least £500,000. It may also introduce an asset threshold, requiring charities with sizeable assets but low income to have a full audit.

Charitable companies whose gross income is £90,000 or less need not have an audit or produce an audit exemption report unless required to do so by their articles of association (constitution), the membership (see below) or funders.

All companies

Regardless of turnover, a company's articles of association or its funders may require an audit. Members of a company can also request one. To exercise this right at least 10% of the membership has to give notice in writing to the registered office, no later than one month before the end of the financial year in question.

Industrial and provident societies (IPSs)

A non-charitable IPS whose annual turnover is in excess of £350,000 must have a full audit. For charitable IPSs this limit is £250,000.

An independent report on the accounts is required where the turnover is above £90,000 but below the limit over which a full audit is required (£350,000 for a non-charitable IPS and £250,000 for a charitable IPS). No audit or report is required where the turnover is £90,000 or less.

Unlike companies, the presumption is that there will be a full audit unless the members decide they do not want one. This decision will need to be made each year. In some cases, the rules under which the IPS is registered may require an audit. If so, the IPS may wish to consider changing its rules.

If the receipts and payments in respect of a year do not exceed £5000, the assets do not exceed that sum and the membership is less than 500, an audit can be carried out by an unregistered person unconnected with the organisation.

Unincorporated charities
The **Charities Act 1993** lays down the following requirements for charitable associations and trusts.

Charities with an annual income and expenditure of £10,000 or less need not have their accounts audited or examined, unless required by the constitution or by funders.

Charities with gross income *or* **total expenditure over £10,000** *and* with **gross income and total expenditure under £250,000** in the current financial year and each of the two previous financial years need to have their accounts examined by an **independent examiner** – 'an independent person who is reasonably believed by the trustees to have the requisite ability and practical experience to carry out a competent examination of the accounts'.* This includes people such as bank managers. They must, if the constitution or funders require, have a full audit. For guidance see the Charity Commission booklet *Independent examination of charities* (CC 63).

The draft Charities Bill will introduce a requirement for independent examiners to be professionally qualified, probably only for examining accounts above a specified amount.

Unincorporated charities with a gross income or total expenditure of more than £250,000* in the current financial year or either of the two previous financial years must have their accounts audited by a registered auditor (see *Companies limited by guarantee*, above).

The draft Charities Bill will propose raising this threshold, to at least £500,000. It may also introduce an asset

threshold, requiring charities with sizeable assets but low income to have a full audit.

If the audit is not carried out within ten months of the end of the financial year, the Charity Commission has the right to order an audit and make the trustees jointly and individually liable for the costs, or recover the costs from the charity's funds. The Commission also has the power to order an audit by an eligible auditor if it is not satisfied with an independent examiner's report.

Exempt and excepted charities
Exempt charities and unregistered excepted charities (see chapter 1) need not have their accounts audited or examined under the Charities Act but may have to under other legislation, for example if they are an industrial and provident society (see page 166).

Annual reports on the accounts
Registered charities
Charity trustees (management committee members) of registered charities have to prepare an annual report on the accounts, and send it to the Charity Commission, with the annual accounts, within ten months of the end of the financial year. This is not necessarily a glossy publicity document, but a straightforward report that must include certain information. A publicity document can serve as the legally required report, provided it includes all necessary information.

The contents of annual reports are detailed in the *Charities (Accounts and Reports) Regulations 2000* and the *Statement of Recommended Practice – Accounting and Reporting by Charities* (*the Charities SORP*).

Income £250,000 or under
All annual reports must include the following:
- financial year covered
- registered name* (and any other names by which the charity is known)
- charity registration number (if registered) and principal address (and company number and registered address if a company)
- particulars of the constitution
- description of the charity's objects
- a brief summary of the main activities and achievements during the year in relation to the charity's objects
- names of anyone who has been a trustee during the financial year covered by the report**
- names and addresses of other principal advisors

(including bankers, solicitors and auditor/independent examiner)

- any external person or body entitled to appoint charity trustees, and a description of how such appointments are carried out
- a statement about the relationship between the charity and related parties and with other charities/organisations with which it co-operates in pursuit of its charitable objects
- names of anyone holding, or who has held property on behalf of the charity during the financial year covered by the report**
- a description of any policies adopted in relation to:
- reserves
- investments
- grant-making.

The report must be dated and signed by one of the trustees (management committee members) who has been authorised to do so.

An excepted, unregistered charity must use the name as set out in its constitution and any other names by which it is known.

**The Charity Commission will grant special dispensation if disclosure of any trustee's name could endanger their safety.*

Income over £250,000

Larger charities' reports must contain the same information as that of smaller charities (see above) but must also include:

- a review of all activities (instead of a brief summary of achievements and activities), including:
- significant developments and achievements in relation to the charity's objects
- any significant changes in activities
- any important event affecting the activities since the end of the year
- future plans
- steps taken to eliminate any deficit in place at the beginning of the financial year
- the charity's organisational structure
- details of assets held and any special arrangements with respect to the safe custody of such assets
- a risk management statement (see *Risk management*, below).

For further details see *Charity accounts and reports: core guide* published by the Home Office and available from the Stationery Office, and the Charity Commission publications *Charity accounts – the framework* (CC61),

Receipts and payments account pack (CC64) and the *Charities SORP*.

The trustees' report, together with the statement of accounts or audited/examined accounts and auditor's/examiner's report (see *The auditing or examining process*, page 178) must be submitted to the Charity Commission within ten months of the end of the charity's financial year. The Charity Commission will make the report available to members of the public on request. Charities with income and expenditure of £10,000 or less do not have to submit their report and annual accounts unless requested.

Exempt charities and excepted, unregistered charities

Exempt charities and excepted, unregistered charities need not prepare a trustees' annual report unless they are required to do so under other legislation or, in the case of excepted, unregistered charities, if required to do so by the Charity Commission.

Charitable companies

Charitable companies have to prepare a trustees' annual report according to the above requirements. Although this is not the same as a company directors' report (prepared under the Companies Act 1985, see below) it is possible to combine the two by ensuring the report fulfils the requirements of both Acts. Companies must include a copy of their accounts prepared under **Part VII** of the **Companies Act 1985**, together with the auditor's report or audit exemption report if required (see *Charitable companies*, page 167, with the trustees' report.

The directors of a company limited by guarantee (the company's committee members) have to prepare a directors' annual report and send it to Companies House, with the accounts, within ten months of the end of the financial year.

Under proposed company law changes, the time for submission to Companies House would be reduced to seven months.

Small companies

Small companies' (see page 166) reports must include:
- names of directors who held office during the year
- the company's principal activities during the year, and any significant changes
- political and charitable contributions above £200
- a statement that the company has taken advantage of

exemptions for small companies, if it does not include the additional information required for the reports of medium companies (see below).

Medium and large companies

Additional information required by medium (see page 166) and large companies includes liability insurance paid by the company for its directors, senior managers or auditors and specified information about the health, safety and welfare of the company's employees.

If the average number of employees exceeded 250 during the year, the report must also include information about:

- the company's policy on employing, training and advancing disabled people
- how the company is involving employees in decisions about its policies and performance.

For further information contact your accountant or auditor.

Risk management

Under SORP 2000 the trustees' annual report for charities with income or expenditure over £250,000 must include a risk management statement, confirming that the trustees have identified and reviewed the major risks to which the charity may be exposed, and have set up systems to mitigate those risks. The Charity Commission encourages smaller charities to do the same. Possible financial risks include accuracy of financial information, adequacy of reserves and cashflow, diversity of income sources and investment management. There are also a number of other areas of risk, often classified into governance, operational, external, and compliance with law and regulation. For more details on identifying, reporting and managing risk see *Charities and risk management*, published by the Charity Commission, available from *www.charitycommission.gov.uk*

Public access to accounts

Anyone can ask any charity for a copy of its most recent accounts and report. This must be provided within two months of a written request. The charity can charge a reasonable fee.

Legal requirements – other financial records

PAYE

Organisations employing staff must keep records of income tax deductions under Pay As You Earn (PAYE), national insurance contributions, statutory sick pay and statutory maternity, paternity and adoption pay payments, tax credit payments and student loan repayments (see chapter 4).

An organisation must register with the Inland Revenue for PAYE if it pays workers, even on a casual basis, who:

- earn more than the earnings (PAYE) threshold (£89 a week in 2004/05), or
- have a second job (even if they earn less than the earnings threshold in either or both jobs).

The employer must deduct tax and national insurance (NI) from the earnings of workers who earn more than the thresholds, and pay tax, NI (both employees' and employer's contributions) and other deductions to the Inland Revenue every month, or in some cases on a quarterly basis. PAYE records must be kept for at least three years, although it is advisable to keep them for at least six (for further details of PAYE see chapter 4).

Value Added Tax (VAT)

Contrary to popular belief, the law on VAT applies to charities. An organisation whose turnover from sources other than grants, donations, investments and other sources defined as 'non-business' under VAT law exceeds the annual threshold (£56,000 in 2003/04) may need to register for VAT, charge VAT on its goods and services, and keep detailed records complying with VAT law. Once registered, it will be able to recover the VAT it pays when purchasing some or all goods and services.

An organisation charging for goods or services (even if the services are charitable) or contracting to provide services should check with Customs and Excise whether it may be liable to register. If so, it must include the VAT element when pricing the contract.

An organisation will need to register for VAT if:

- at the end of any month, the value of **taxable supplies** (goods or services provided which are liable to VAT either at the standard rate or at the zero rate) in the past 12 months has exceeded the annual threshold, or
- at any time, there are reasonable grounds for believing that the value of taxable supplies in the next 30 days will exceed the annual threshold.

For further details see *Should I be registered for VAT?* (VAT700/1), available from the Customs and Excise National Advice Service (0845 010 9000) or *www.hmce.gov.uk*

There is one month in which to register, by completing registration form **VAT1** (available from the National Advice Service or *www.hmce.gov.uk*). Customs and Excise will stipulate a date from which an organisation is registered and provide a VAT number. It is unlawful to charge VAT before being registered. Once registered the organisation must provide and keep VAT invoices. Quarterly returns will be sent automatically and must be completed and returned within one month of the end of the quarter. Organisations which have been registered for at least a year and whose annual taxable supplies excluding VAT are £600,000 or less may be able to submit annual returns.

There are substantial penalties for failing to register for VAT or registering late. It is therefore essential to be fully aware of which of the organisation's supplies are subject to VAT and to keep a regular check on the level of turnover for those supplies to see whether the organisation will reach the annual threshold. Remember that income from grants, donations, legacies and certain other sources does not generally count towards the threshold.

Customs and Excise will provide details of the current threshold, advise on registration and record keeping and help with the assessment of taxable turnover.

VAT registration may bring some benefits and an organisation may be able to register even if its taxable turnover is below the threshold. Although the organisation would have to charge VAT on some goods or services provided, it can recover VAT on some goods or services purchased, and this may result in an overall saving. It is essential to take professional advice before considering voluntary registration.

VAT is a complicated subject, particularly for charities, and cannot be covered in full in this book. For further details contact your accountant or auditor or the joint Inland Revenue, Customs and Excise and Charity Commission helpline (08453 02 02 03).

Income tax and corporation tax

Corporation tax is a tax on the profit of associations and incorporated bodies, and income tax (in this context) is a tax on the income of charitable trusts. Grants and donations are not subject to income or corporation tax.

For other income, charities are generally exempt from income tax and corporation tax provided that the income is used only for charitable purposes, subject to certain conditions and activities. However, income from other sources, such as trading or property rents, may be subject to tax. Charities are not allowed to pay tax on their trading or similar profits, as this would be a misuse of charitable funds. They must therefore carry out any taxable trading or similar activities in a subsidiary non-charity that donates its profits to the charity under the Gift Aid scheme.

Non-charities may be subject to income or corporation tax on any income other than genuine grants and donations, and should take advice from their accountant or auditor.

Gift Aid

Charities that reclaim tax on Gift Aid donations (see chapter 9) must keep sufficient records to show that their tax reclaims are accurate. Further information is available from IR Charities (08453 02 02 03).

Duties of the committee

All committee members have a duty to see that the organisation is properly managed and that funds are spent correctly. Under charity law committee members of charities (trustees) have a statutory duty to ensure that funds are being spent appropriately for charitable purposes within the charity's objects and powers. Although the treasurer oversees the finances on behalf of the committee, the trustees have overall responsibility for the charity's money and property and cannot delegate their responsibility. Trustees who fail to carry out their duty properly may be in breach of trust (see chapter 1) and personally liable for any losses caused.

Committee members of companies must conform to the Companies Acts' requirements; IPS committee members must conform to those of the **Friendly and Industrial and Provident Societies Act 1968**.

The committee's main financial responsibilities are to:
- comply with legal requirements – these will vary according to the organisation's legal structure and whether it is charitable, but the basic principles are the same for all
- approve and monitor budgets
- ensure proper financial records are kept
- ensure proper control is exercised over income and expenditure
- oversee fundraising policy and activities, and trading activities

- ensure tax affairs – and VAT if applicable – are managed properly
- ensure the organisation's funds are used in accordance with its constitution, committee decisions and funders' conditions
- ensure proper financial reports are provided to the committee, funders, and others who have a right to see them
- ensure annual accounts and reports, audited if required, are produced.

The committee members of any organisation must make sure the treasurer and finance staff are carrying out their jobs properly. This means being satisfied that the treasurer and all staff who handle money, whether paid or voluntary, are honest and competent.

There are several ways in which the committee can minimise risks. For example, it can:
- make sure that anyone who stands for election as treasurer has experience of handling money and accounts
- arrange additional training for the treasurer if necessary
- appoint a finance subcommittee to oversee day-to-day management of finances and regularly examine the accounts
- require the treasurer to make regular financial reports to the committee
- have careful procedures for handling cash, involving at least two people (see *Looking after cash*, page 175)
- require two signatures on cheques and ensure that blank cheques are never signed, for any reason (no cheque should ever be signed without documentation, for example an invoice, explaining the expense)
- ensure that the treasurer, manager or other authorised person authorises all expenses, that no one can authorise expenses paid to themselves, and that all expenses are paid by cheque rather than in cash
- ensure that no one can sign a cheque to themselves or to a close relative
- employ a bookkeeper to carry out day-to-day transactions.

Charities and risk management, available from *www.charitycommission.gov.uk*, includes a list of potential financial risks, with their potential impact and steps to mitigate the risk.

Specific duties of the treasurer

In a small organisation, the treasurer may deal with all aspects of financial management including keeping records. Larger organisations with paid staff may delegate day-to-day financial management to a paid finance worker or another staff member, who would report to the treasurer or senior staff member.

However, final responsibility for financial matters always rests with the committee as a whole.

The treasurer's responsibilities may include the following:
- general financial oversight
- managing income – funding, contracts, fundraising and sales
- financial planning and budgeting
- financial reporting
- banking, bookkeeping and record keeping
- control of fixed assets and stock
- investments
- insurances (see chapter 7)
- premises, if there is no premises subcommittee (see chapter 6).

Use the following checklist to decide which tasks should be carried out by the treasurer or finance staff and which need the involvement of the finance subcommittee or whole committee.

General financial oversight

This covers broad responsibility for the organisation's financial decision making and may include:
- ensuring workers and committee members know enough about financial administration, bookkeeping and the accounts to make appropriate decisions
- advising on financial policies, for example what expenses can be claimed and the procedures for claiming them, financial implications of new activities, or the organisation's policy on charging for its services
- advising on employment and other contracts
- making day-to-day financial decisions on behalf of the committee, if given delegated authority, and reporting such decisions to the committee
- liaising with the bank and other financial institutions
- preparing accounts for audit or independent examination and liaising with the auditor/independent examiner
- recommending to the committee measures to ensure security of cash and cheques.

Financial planning and budgeting

This includes:
- preparing budgets and cashflow forecasts (see page 178) in consultation with workers and funders
- presenting budgets to the committee for approval
- keeping track of how actual income and expenditure

compares with budgeted income and expenditure and adjusting financial forecasts as appropriate

- in the case of cashflow problems, deciding priorities for paying bills, pursuing any money owed to the organisation and negotiating for late payment if necessary.

Managing income

This involves ensuring the organisation has enough money to carry out its activities. Income sources can be divided into funding (grant aid), contracts or service agreements (to provide activities or services – see chapter 9), fundraising (for example membership drives, appeals, jumble sales or special events) and sales of goods or services.

Responsibilities include:
- developing and implementing an income-generating strategy
- coordinating fundraising activities
- running fundraising activities
- collecting information on funding sources
- completing, submitting and coordinating funding applications
- liaising with funding agencies
- ensuring money received for a special project is spent for that purpose and if necessary is separately accounted for
- drawing up tenders or proposals for contracted services
- ensuring appropriate pricing of goods or services.

Financial reporting

The treasurer is responsible for ensuring the committee has enough information to make decisions. This means:
- providing the committee with regular written reports on the organisation's financial position
- preparing and presenting financial reports and accounts when required
- presenting the end of year financial report (draft annual accounts) to the committee
- presenting the audited or examined accounts to the annual general meeting (AGM) or other general meeting
- ensuring members at the AGM or other general meeting understand the annual accounts and the budget for the current year.

Banking, bookkeeping and record keeping

The treasurer is responsible for:
- advising which banks or other financial institutions the organisation should use and the type of bank accounts it should have (note that every decision to open, close or change bank or other accounts must be approved by the committee)

- serving as a signatory for the organisation's bank accounts (all changes of signatory must be approved by the committee)
- ensuring proper systems are in place for receiving and paying out cash and cheques
- setting up appropriate bookkeeping and petty cash systems, and ensuring related documentation is kept
- ensuring membership records are kept and subscriptions collected
- ensuring other money due to the organisation is collected, that there are procedures for non-payment and that such action is taken if required
- ensuring all bills are paid and receipts are received for all payments
- ensuring payment of wages, income tax, national insurance, statutory sick pay, pensions, statutory maternity, paternity and adoption pay, tax credits and student loan repayments, and that records are kept of these payments
- ensuring everyone handling money for the organisation keeps appropriate records and documentation.

Control of fixed assets and stock

The treasurer has broad responsibility for ensuring proper control of fixed assets (major equipment, vehicles, buildings and other property owned by the organisation), its materials or supplies (goods required for running the organisation) and its stock (goods such as publications waiting to be distributed or sold). This responsibility includes:
- ensuring the organisation keeps records of materials and supplies used
- establishing systems for stock control and reorders
- undertaking or overseeing regular stock checks
- ensuring the organisation keeps records of its equipment and vehicles, including date of purchase, supplier, value, model and serial number (sometimes called an inventory)
- ensuring the organisation has all necessary insurances and keeps them up to date (see chapter 7).

Investments

The treasurer will:
- ensure the organisation takes proper financial advice in relation to any investments
- ensure the organisation complies with its constitution and charity law in relation to investments
- ensure all decisions about investments are properly made and minuted
- monitor the progress of investments and report regularly to the committee.

The budget

Each year an organisation needs to draw up a budget – an estimate of how much it expects to pay out and receive during the financial year – which should be used to monitor income and expenditure. Many organisations produce a longer term financial plan covering, for example, three years, which will include any planned new developments.

It is essential to estimate costs as accurately as possible and include these in any funding application. Funders are realistic and want to see a viable proposal. The shift from grant aid to service level agreements or contracts between voluntary organisations and statutory authorities (see chapter 9) makes accurate estimates even more important. An organisation that contracts to provide a service for a fixed price could be in breach of contract if it cannot complete the work because it has inadequate funds. It is particularly important to get proper advice about VAT when contracting for services.

When preparing a budget allow for the following:
- salaries and future salary increases, including annual increments, overtime if paid, and use of temporary staff
- statutory and contractual sick pay (see chapter 4)
- contractual maternity, paternity and adoption pay and any portion of statutory maternity pay that cannot be recovered (see chapter 4)
- cover during staff holidays and sickness, and maternity, parental, paternity, adoption and dependants leave
- employer's national insurance contributions
- employer's pension contributions, if paid
- recruitment costs
- staff, volunteer and committee induction and training
- insurance (see chapter 7)
- travel costs
- capital expenditure
- heating, lighting, water, telephone, fax and online access
- office expenditure such as stationery, post and printing
- auditor's/examiner's fees, legal fees, bank charges and bookkeeping costs
- building costs, including rent, rates, repairs, service charges, maintenance and insurance
- equipment costs, including rent, repairs, maintenance and insurance
- costs of providing services
- cost of health and safety requirements (see chapter 5)
- any costs associated with quality assurance
- marketing and publicity costs
- any other costs.

Other matters to take into consideration are:
- inflation
- how staff and the treasurer will be involved
- timing – allow time for presenting the budget to the committee.

Think carefully about the headings used in the budget, as the same headings should be used in financial records and accounts (see *Record keeping*, page 175).

The budget must be presented to the full committee for approval. Members must ensure they understand what is being presented and ask the right questions:
- Do I understand where the income comes from?
- Do I understand the headings used for expenditure?
- Do the figures balance?
- Are estimates and assumptions reasonably justified?

A **balanced budget** is one in which anticipated income equals anticipated expenditure. If anticipated income is greater than anticipated expenditure the excess may be shown as 'surplus transferred to reserves' to balance the budget. If the reverse is true, the difference will be shown as a deficit. If this is the case, the committee needs to know how the organisation will cover it. It is not appropriate to 'balance' a budget by saying the money will come from fundraising (or whatever) unless it is likely that the money will genuinely be raised.

The treasurer should report at least quarterly on the organisation's income and expenditure and whether it is in line with budget. If the organisation has more than one project the report should cover these separately. Such reports are called **management accounts** (see *Financial reports*, page 177) and are the best way to enable organisations to anticipate any financial problems.

General rules on handling money

Always issue receipts for money received and obtain receipts for all expenditure. Ensure that all money received is entered into the account books (or computerised accounts) before it is used to pay outgoings. Pay money into the bank as soon as possible.

Keep detailed records and notes of all transactions, whether by cash, cheque or bank transfer (BACS).

Bank accounts

To open an account in the name of an organisation the committee needs to pass a resolution, the wording of which is set out on a form supplied by the bank (the **Form of Mandate**), which must be completed by officers of the organisation. A copy of the organisation's constitution should be attached. Individuals authorised to draw cheques on behalf of the organisation must be named on the form. Banks will often require detailed information about the individual signatories.

The constitution may include rules on cheque signatories. Many organisations choose to have three or four and state that cheques must be signed by at least two. If an organisation has paid staff it may be convenient for one or more of them to be a signatory. As most organisations need to withdraw small amounts for cash, it is possible to arrange that cheques below a certain figure require only one signature, but above that amount two signatures would be necessary. The organisation might have rules saying that for cheques above a certain amount one or both signatories must be committee members, rather than staff. Blank cheques should never be signed; any individual who signs a blank cheque might have to pay the organisation back for any loss that resulted.

It is important to have proper controls over how and by whom expenditure is authorised. Although a control at the cheque signing stage is necessary it may be too late to do anything about the payment if the goods or services have already been ordered.

Organisations with extra cash should consider opening a deposit account. Registered charities do not have to pay tax on interest earned in a deposit account.

Bank charges vary and can add a significant amount to an organisation's expenditure. It is worth spending some time talking to a number of banks in order to get the best deal. Always get written details of how charges are calculated.

Looking after cash

Organisations that handle cash should take extra precautions, to safeguard against theft by outsiders, staff, volunteers or committee members. This could include taking out fidelity insurance (see chapter 7).

Wherever possible ensure that two people are involved in cash management. This could include opening the post together if money is likely to be sent to the organisation, and whenever cash is collected, for example at events, ensuring two people collect and count it. All cash received should be paid into the bank, and the amounts required for cash expenditure should be drawn out separately. Use as little cash as possible to make payments – most should be made by cheque or bank transfer (BACS).

An insurance company may require certain precautions for cash insured, for example keeping it in a safe (see chapter 7).

Never keep more cash than is necessary on the premises, pay any surplus into the bank as soon as possible. Only authorised people should have keys to the safe, with a duplicate copy kept at the bank.

Remember that staff may be more vulnerable to attack if there is cash on the premises.

Record keeping

Financial responsibility involves keeping records ('accounts' or 'books') of how much money has come into the organisation, where it has come from, and how it has been spent. This process is called **bookkeeping**. Along with the books the organisation must keep documentation, such as invoices and receipts, to prove the money was spent in the way shown. The books and proofs will be used to draw up regular accounts (monthly and/or quarterly), financial reports (**management accounts** – see *Financial reports*, page 177) and the annual accounts.

Unincorporated charities are legally required to keep the books and financial documentation for six years: it is good practice for all voluntary organisations to do so. Companies must keep their records for three years, but again, it is good practice to keep them for longer.

You should aim to keep books or computerised accounts necessary to maintain adequate financial control and the information the committee needs. Two books may be sufficient for small organisations:
- the **cash analysis book**: to record money paid in to and out of the bank (this includes cheques, standing orders, direct debits and bank transfers)
- the **petty cash book**: to record incidental expenses made in cash.

Subsidiary records are used to record additional detailed information that may be difficult to enter into the cash analysis book (for example full details of membership subscriptions).

Analysis books can be purchased from large stationers. They are available with different numbers of columns, so check how many you need before making a purchase.

Alternatively, the organisation could use a computerised accounts package such as *Sage Instant, Sage Line 50, Sage Line 100, MYOB, Microsoft Money* or *TAS Books.* Computerised accounts programs use the same basic formats as paper accounts.

Brief descriptions of these books are given below; for more detailed information, including examples, see *The charity treasurer's handbook*, by Gareth G Morgan, published by the Directory of Social Change.

Cash analysis book

The cash analysis book, often known as the cash book, is an organisation's most important financial record. Make entries as soon as possible after every transaction (for example, cheques received, cash or cheques paid into the bank, cheques written, bank transfers, standing orders or direct debits paid or received).

If an organisation receives income from a number of sources it may be advisable to have two books – one to record income and one to record expenditure. An alternative is to use one book and record income and expenditure on alternate pages, or in different parts of the book.

Cash analysis books use a number of columns to analyse each transaction. Each column is given an appropriate heading, for example, 'grants', 'fundraising activities', 'stationery', 'rent', 'travel', but it is up to the treasurer and committee to decide what these should be. It is convenient to use budget headings to compare actual and anticipated expenditure. Codes may be used in computerised accounts to identify each heading.

For each transaction you should record:
- the date
- cheque number, SO (standing order), DD (direct debit) or BACS (bank transfer) if a payment; receipt number if income
- to whom the payment was made and for what, or where income came from and what it was for
- the full amount of the transaction (less VAT if registered for VAT)
- the transaction divided into the appropriate column heading(s)
- the VAT element of the transaction and the VAT rate (standard, reduced, zero, exempt) if registered for VAT.

It is good practice to issue receipts to those who give money to the organisation. Receipt books, in duplicate, can be purchased with numbered pages. The receipt number should be entered in the cash book.

When setting up accounts on computer you should use the same basic approach to headings and information.

Petty cash book

A common method for recording small cash transactions is the **imprest** or **float** system. You estimate how much you are likely to need each month (say £100) and draw that amount from the bank account to start up the float. When most of the money has been spent (say £85), it is topped up by drawing cash from the bank equal to the expenditure (ie £85).

Keep cash transactions to the minimum; use cheques and BACS payments wherever possible. Record all petty cash transactions on petty cash vouchers and in the petty cash book, and analyse them under appropriate headings (for example 'travel expenses', 'postage'). Whenever possible obtain a receipt and staple it to the petty cash voucher, which should be numbered. Enter details of the transaction – the amount, what it was for and the voucher number – into the petty cash book.

The amounts entered in each of the cash book columns should be entered into the main cash book every month.

Bank statements and bank reconciliation statements

A **bank statement** is the bank's record of the organisation's finances. This record may not agree exactly with that in the cash book(s) because it can take a few days for credits and debits to appear in a bank account.

Bank statements should be checked immediately against the cash book(s), and a **bank reconciliation statement** prepared along the following lines and kept with the bank statement.

Bank reconciliation statement

If the two figures do not balance, check the entries in the cash book:
- Have all payments and receipts been entered (standing orders, direct debits, bank transfers and bank charges might be on the statement but not yet in the cash book)?
- Have they been entered correctly?
- Has a cheque been issued but not been cleared?
- Has the cash book be added up correctly?
- Are there any unexplained items in the bank statement?

Restricted funds

If the organisation receives a grant or donation for a specific purpose, for example a summer playscheme, it is not necessary to open a new bank account unless required by the funder. Extra bank accounts only complicate bookkeeping and can create additional bank charges. All that is usually needed to be able to account for restricted funds (grants or donations received for a specific purpose) is an additional analysis column on both the income and expenditure sides of the cash book. A brief comment should be made in the details column explaining the entries (for example 'playscheme').

When drawing up the annual accounts or possibly even the financial reports (management accounts) you may need to allocate a proportion of salary, rent, photocopying and other costs to various restricted purposes (for example, a proportion of the manager's salary to cover the time spent managing the playscheme, a proportion of phone and stationery costs for the playscheme). This can be complex and you may need an accountant's advice.

Other financial records

Other necessary records include those relating to PAYE and VAT (see *Legal requirements – other financial records, page* 170), a sales invoice book, purchase order book, purchase invoice book and income covered under Gift Aid declarations (see chapter 9).

Financial reports

A **financial report** or **management account** is any statement that informs committee members or staff with responsibility for budgets of the current financial situation. For most small organisations an appropriate financial report would be presented at least quarterly and would include:

* receipts and payments for the period, showing income received, expenditure made, and the balance in hand (amount left at the end of the period)
* a statement showing where the balance is held (for example current account, deposit account, petty cash, cheques not yet paid in)
* a statement of how much money is owed to the organisation at the end of the financial period, and for what
* a statement of how much money the organisation owes and for what
* a comparison with the budget to date showing variances and a projection to the end of the financial year
* an indication of any actual or potential financial problems or situations needing a decision by the finance subcommittee or full management committee.

Receipts and payments account

This is the form of report favoured by most small voluntary organisations, because of its simplicity. A summary of the cash book, it presents a simple statement of money received and paid out.

The system does have its drawbacks. Although a receipts and payments account gives an accurate statement of money received and paid out by an organisation it does not show its true financial position. It does not include expenditure committed but not yet paid, payments made in advance, income due but not yet received or income received in advance.

Income and expenditure account

An income and expenditure account (also called an **accruals account**) is based on the receipts and payments account but is adjusted to include money owed to and by the organisation, and payments made or income received in advance. It gives a more accurate surplus/deficit position but requires records that show not only what has been spent and received, but also the period to which that expenditure or income applies.

Balance sheet

A balance sheet is designed to show how much the organisation is worth on a particular day (normally the last day of the financial period). It includes **assets** (everything the organisation owns and is owed) and **liabilities** (what it owes). A balance sheet shows the organisation's **net worth** at a particular point; it does not show what happened over a period. It shows the solvency of the organisation.

For further information, including worked examples, see *The charity treasurer's handbook*, by Gareth G Morgan, published by the Directory of Social Change.

Forecasts

A forecast revises the organisation's anticipated income and expenditure by considering developments since the budget was drawn up and helps the committee make financial decisions. Ideally forecasts should be produced every quarter, and at least every six months. They can also be built into the financial reports/management accounts (see above).

When examining forecasts, committee members should consider the following:

* does the budget for income or expenditure need to be adjusted, either upwards or downwards
* what are the implications of any adjustments
* do they take account of inflation or interest rate changes

- does the organisation need to take steps to ensure future budgets are more accurate?

Cashflow forecasts

Cashflow means just that – the flow of money (cash and cheques) in to and out of the organisation. A cashflow forecast shows, usually on a monthly basis, when in the year payments are made and income is received. It is therefore a useful method of warning committee members or senior staff when there may be a cash shortage.

Cashflow and other financial problems

If an organisation has a short-term cashflow problem, an arranged overdraft will ease the crisis, but constant overdrafts are not a good form of financial control. They are expensive, which can make the financial situation even worse, and the bank will probably want security, in the form of **collateral** (the organisation's assets) or personal guarantees from committee members. Overdrafts can also be called in at any time. An organisation which does not have a constitutional power to borrow may not be able to take out an overdraft.

Committee members who give personal guarantees become personally liable for the overdraft if the organisation cannot pay it. In unincorporated organisations the committee members will always be responsible whether or not they provide personal guarantees.

If the organisation does not have a reasonable prospect of being able to meet its financial obligations it needs to get advice urgently from a qualified accountant or auditor. If the organisation is unincorporated, committee members could be held personally liable for its debts.

If the organisation is a company limited by guarantee it may be unlawful under the **Insolvency Act 1986** to carry on operating. It should contact the company's accountant or auditor immediately. If the organisation carries on despite being in such financial difficulty, individual committee members could lose their limited liability and be held personally liable for the organisation's debts (see chapter 10).

Charities' reserves

A charity's trustees (committee members) have a legal duty to use charity funds within a reasonable time of receiving them unless they are being held for a specific future purpose. However, charities need to be able to secure their future, absorb setbacks and take advantage of change and opportunities. Many provide for this by putting aside, when they can afford to, some of their current income as a reserve for future plans or against future uncertainties.

To overcome the possible perception that a charity is hoarding its money – and asking the public for funds that are not immediately needed – it is essential to be able to justify and explain the position on reserves. Responsibility for this lies with the charity's trustees.

When applying for funds you should establish funders' policies on reserves.

The Charity Commission's publication *Charities' reserves* (CC19) provides guidance on what a charity should do to develop a reserves policy and justify its reserves.

The auditing or examining process

Each year the annual accounts may have to be audited or examined (see *Auditing or examining accounts*, page 167). Industrial and provident societies (IPSs) must submit these accounts to an annual general meeting (AGM). Limited companies must present their accounts to a general meeting within ten months from the end of the financial year to which they apply, unless the company has passed a resolution to dispense with this requirement. The general meeting is usually the AGM, but does not have to be unless specified in the articles of association (constitution). Some unincorporated organisations' constitutions require an audit to be carried out and financial reports to be presented at an AGM.

Limited companies must circulate annual accounts at least 21 days before the general meeting at which they are presented. Under the **Companies Act 1985 (Electronic Communications) Order 2000** companies can send accounts to a member's nominated e-mail address. There are strict rules regarding electronic communications, which must be followed, and companies are recommended to refer to guidance produced by the Institute of Chartered Secretaries and Administrators. For further details see *www.icsa.org.uk*

Other organisations' constitutions may require annual accounts to be circulated to members a specified period before the meeting at which they are presented; in IPSs the time limit is usually 14 or 21 days. It is good practice for all organisations to do the same.

The requirement for conducting an annual audit will often be laid down by a grant giving body, which may also state that a registered auditor must be used.

Responsibilities of the auditor

An auditor's main duty is to ensure that there is reasonable certainty that the accounts are free from material misstatement. To do this the auditor may:

- check that the organisation has spent money within the terms of its constitution or aims and objectives, committee decisions, agreed accounting policies and funders' requirements
- check that all money received and spent has been entered in the books
- verify that vouchers (such as receipts, used cheques or cheque stubs) and subsidiary records exist to back up the entries in the cash book
- verify that the treasurer, staff and others with financial authority have followed instructions from the committee and officers
- verify that the receipts and payments account (or statement of financial activities plus balance sheet) gives a true picture of the organisation's financial position and transactions
- advise on how to improve controls and record keeping systems, if necessary
- report the findings to the organisation's members and issue a written statement saying that proper books of accounts have been kept (assuming this is the case).

Appointing an auditor

Many constitutions include a clause stating that the auditor must be appointed by the AGM. Some also state that the AGM must set the fee or delegate responsibility for this task.

Before employing a professional auditor get quotations. It may be useful to seek advice or recommendations from your local council for voluntary service or rural community council, community accountancy project, other charities or bank manager.

Records the auditor needs

The items the auditor or independent examiner will require to carry out an end of year audit are:

- a copy of the constitution
- cash analysis books
- petty cash book
- any subsidiary records kept
- PAYE records
- VAT records
- bank statements
- bank reconciliation statements
- bank paying in book
- cheque book stubs, and used cheques if returned by the bank
- written confirmation by the bank of the balance in the bank account (the auditor will normally request this)
- purchase invoices
- all vouchers, including receipts obtained for money paid out and the duplicate receipt book (which should contain carbon copies of receipts for money received)
- details of wages and salaries, and written evidence of salary changes
- conditions of grants from funders
- the annual accounts and statement of assets and liabilities or balance sheet for the previous year
- the draft receipts and payments account (or statement of financial activities and balance sheet) for the period being audited
- all legal documents signed during the year
- a copy of the organisation's written financial procedures, if any
- list of debtors (people who owe money to the organisation) and creditors (people to whom the organisation owes money)
- list of opening balances
- list of liabilities including items contracted but not yet paid for and unpaid purchase invoices
- committee minutes.

Summary of accounting regulations for charities

See chapter 4 for definitions of legal status

Unregistered very small charities (under £1000 income*)

❏ Have to prepare annual accounts
❏ Do not have to submit accounts to the Charity Commission
❏ Do not have to prepare a trustees' annual report
❏ Must provide a copy of their accounts to any member of the public within two months of a written request and may charge a reasonable fee

*The draft Charities Bill will propose changing this threshold to £5000

Registered very small charities

Very small charities which are voluntarily registered must comply with the requirements for unincorporated charities with income up to £10,000.

Unincorporated charities

Annual income and expenditure £10,000 or below

❏ Must prepare annual accounts, which can be either a receipts and payments account and a statement of assets and liabilities, or a full set of accounts
❏ Do not need to have their accounts audited or independently examined unless required by their constitution, funders or the Charity Commission
❏ Must prepare a trustees' annual report
❏ Do not have to submit annual accounts or a trustees' report to the Charity Commission, unless specifically required to do so
❏ Must provide a copy of their accounts within two months of a written request by a member of the public and may charge a reasonable fee

Annual income above £10,000 but no more than £100,000

❏ Must prepare annual accounts, which can be either a receipts and payments account and a statement of assets and liabilities, or a full set of accounts
❏ Must have their accounts examined by an independent examiner or audited by a registered auditor
❏ Must prepare a trustees' annual report
❏ Must submit the trustees' report, together with the examined/audited accounts and examiner's/auditor's report to the Charity Commission, within ten months of the end of the charity's financial year
❏ Must provide a copy of their accounts within two months of a written request from a member of the public and may charge a reasonable fee

Annual income above £100,000 but no more than £250,000 and expenditure £250,000 or under

❏ Must prepare a full set of accounts
❏ Must have their accounts examined by an independent examiner or audited by a registered auditor
❏ Must prepare a trustees' annual report
❏ Must submit the trustees' report, together with the examined/audited accounts and examiner's/auditor's report to the Charity Commission, within ten months of the end of the charity's financial year
❏ Must provide a copy of their accounts within two months of a written request from a member of the public and may charge a reasonable fee

Income or expenditure over £250,000

❏ Must prepare a full set of accounts
❏ Must have their accounts audited by a registered auditor*
❏ Must prepare a trustees' annual report
❏ Must submit the trustees' annual report, together with the audited accounts and auditor's report to the Charity Commission, within ten months of the end of the charity's financial year
❏ Must provide a copy of their accounts within two months of a written request from a member of the public; a reasonable fee can be charged

*The draft Charities Bill will propose raising the audit threshold to at least £500,000. It may also introduce an asset threshold, requiring charities with sizeable assets but low income to have a full audit.

Charitable companies

Income or expenditure under £90,000

❏ Must prepare a set of accounts in accordance with company law
❏ Do not need to have their accounts audited or an

audit exemption report prepared unless required by the articles of association (constitution) or funders

❏ Must prepare a directors' annual report as required under company law and a trustees' annual report as required under charity law (these reports can be combined, but must fulfil both sets of requirements)

❏ Must make their accounts and reports available to the public as required under company law

❏ Must submit the directors' annual report and annual accounts to the Registrar of Companies within ten months of the end of the charity's financial year

Charitable companies whose income or expenditure exceeds £10,000 must also submit the trustees' annual report, together with the full accounts and auditor's or other report to the Charity Commission, within ten months of the end of the charity's financial year

Charitable companies whose income or expenditure is £10,000 or below must submit the above to the Charity Commission if requested

Income or expenditure £90,000 or above but below £250,000

❏ Must prepare a set of accounts in accordance with company law

❏ Must have their accounts audited or an audit exemption prepared*

❏ Must prepare a directors' annual report as required under company law and a trustees' annual report as required under charity law (these reports can be combined, but must fulfil both sets of requirements)

❏ Must make their accounts and reports available to the public as required under company law

❏ Must submit the trustees' annual report, together with the full accounts and auditor's or other report to the Charity Commission, within ten months of the end of the charity's financial year

❏ Must submit the directors' annual report and annual accounts to the Registrar of Companies within ten months of the end of the charity's financial year

The draft Charities Bill will propose raising the audit threshold to at least £500,000. It may also introduce an asset threshold, requiring charities with sizeable assets but low income to have a full audit.

Income or expenditure £250,000 or above

❏ Must prepare a full set of accounts in accordance with company law

❏ Must have their accounts audited

❏ Must prepare a directors' annual report as required under company law and a trustees' annual report as required under charity law (these reports can be combined, but must fulfil both sets of requirements)

❏ Must make their accounts and reports available to the public as required under company law

❏ Must submit the trustees' annual report, together with the full accounts and auditor's or other report to the Charity Commission, within ten months of the end of the charity's financial year

❏ Must submit the directors' annual report and annual accounts to the Registrar of Companies within ten months of the end of the charity's financial year

Proposals in the companies law white paper simplify accounting requirements for small and medium-sized companies (see page 167 for definitions), but reduce the time for submitting the accounts to seven months.

The draft Charities Bill will introduce a new form of incorporated charity – the charitable incorporated organisation (CIO – see chapter 1). CIOs will only have to register with the Charity Commission, not with Companies House, and so their accounting and auditing requirements will come under charity, but not company law.

Chapter 9:

Services and activities

Related chapters
Chapter 1 – Charity law
Chapter 2 – Equal opportunities
Chapters 3 and 4 – Employment
Chapter 5 – Health and safety
Chapter 6 – Premises
Chapter 7 – Insurance
Chapter 8 – VAT

This chapter looks at the law and good practice governing a range of services and activities carried out by voluntary organisations. It starts by describing how organisations should review their activities in light of equal opportunities legislation. Following sections outline the law and good practice relating to contracting with public authorities to provide services, handling information, meetings, marches and protests, fundraising, human rights, freedom of information and looking after people.

Equal opportunities in service delivery

The voluntary sector is a major provider of services and activities. It is essential that everyone knows what is available, feels confident about seeking help or asking to participate, and believes the services are appropriate and sensitive to their needs. Organisations should therefore examine their services and how they are delivered, and take positive measures to make sure that they comply with the law and are accessible and relevant to all those entitled to use them.

Legal requirements

Sex discrimination
The **Sex Discrimination Act 1975** generally prohibits discrimination against men or women in the supply of goods or services. There are two major exceptions for voluntary organisations. These are:
- where an organisation's main object is the provision of services to one sex
- where a non-charitable organisation restricts membership to one sex and provides services only to its members.

Race discrimination
The **Race Relations Act 1976** generally prohibits discrimination in the provision of goods and services on the basis of race. There are the following exceptions:

- Organisations with fewer than 25 members may use racial group as a factor in selecting members.
- Organisations of any size can limit their membership and services to people of a specific racial group (not defined by reference to colour) if the main object of the organisation is to enable the benefits of membership to be enjoyed by people from that group.
- Charities can limit their services to a particular racial group if their constitution explicitly allows this, provided the group is not defined by reference to colour.
- A charity may restrict access to some services or allocate services first to members of a specific racial group if:
- it can be shown that members of the group have a need which is different in kind from, or is the same as but proportionately greater than, the other population of the area covered by the charity
- the need is attributable to and distinguished by a characteristic specific to the racial group, and
- the special need relates to education, training, welfare or ancillary benefits.

If in any doubt take advice from the Commission for Racial Equality on 020 7939 0000.

The **Race Relations Amendment Act 2000** places a duty on public authorities to promote racial equality in service provision. Although the Act is primarily aimed at public authorities, voluntary organisations working in partnership with or providing services on behalf of a public authority (either through grant aid or contracts) may need to comply. In any event it is good practice for voluntary organisations to adopt the measures listed below.

Authorities are required to take proactive measures to eliminate unlawful racial discrimination and promote equality of opportunity and 'good relations' between people of different racial groups.

Specific duties include:
- preparing a publicly stated policy on race equality
- setting out arrangements for assessing and consulting on proposed policies
- monitoring how their policies impact on the promotion of race equality
- publishing the results of assessments, consultations and monitoring
- ensuring public access to information and services
- training staff on relevant issues.

The Commission for Racial Equality has published a statutory code of practice and a range of non-statutory guidance: *Code of practice on the duty to promote racial equality, Ethnic monitoring – a guide to help public authorities in England and Wales meet their duty, A guide for public authorities* and *The Law, the duty and you*. For further details see *www.cre.gov.uk*

Disability discrimination

The **Disability Discrimination Act 1995** (DDA) generally prohibits discrimination in the provision of goods, facilities and services on the basis of disability.

Service providers must treat disabled people no less favourably than others when providing a service or facility unless different treatment is justified under one of the exceptions set out below. The Act applies to all service providers – whatever their size – and whether the goods or services are free or paid for.

Unless different treatment is justified under one of the exceptions, service providers must also:
- **review policies, practice and procedures**, and take reasonable steps to amend any that make it impossible or unreasonably difficult for disabled people to access goods, services or facilities
- **take reasonable measures to provide auxiliary aids and services** to enable disabled people to use a service or to use it more. Examples would include:
- producing information on audio tape, in Braille and in large print
- providing induction loops, textphones and sign language interpreters
- using simplified text
- designing accessible websites (see *Accessible web design*, page 185)
- having well designed signage, portable ramps and designated car parking
- **take reasonable steps to provide services by alternative means** where the design or construction of, or access to, a building makes it impossible or unreasonably difficult for disabled people to use a

service. Examples include providing services that normally require a person to come into an office at other locations, at home, by telephone or by video link.

From 1 October 2004 providers must take reasonable measures to remove or alter any physical features in their premises that make it impossible or unreasonably difficult for a disabled person to use a service, or provide a reasonable means of avoiding the feature.

Exceptions

Organisations should not look for reasons to discriminate against disabled people wishing to use their services. The following reasons might justify less favourable treatment, but cannot be used as an excuse to exclude all disabled people:
- The health or safety of the disabled person or someone else may be endangered if the same service or facility is provided. Do not use safety requirements as an excuse for discrimination based on generalised assumptions about disabled people. If possible ask the person about their disability before making a decision.
- The disabled person is not capable of understanding the terms of a contract, ie the nature of the agreement or their obligations. However, without clear evidence to the contrary organisations should assume that the disabled person is able to enter into a contract. This exemption does not apply if another person is legally acting on behalf of the disabled person.
- Providing the service to the disabled person would stop the service being provided at all. Organisations would have to show that other users would be prevented from using the service, and not just inconvenienced.
- Organisations can charge a disabled person more for a service if that charge reflects the additional cost of meeting their specification, ie the service is individually tailored to the disabled person's requirements.
- Organisations do not have to make any adjustments that would fundamentally alter the nature of their service, profession or business.

For further details of these requirements and examples of their effect, see the *Code of Practice: Rights of access, goods, facilities, services and premises* or *Making access to goods and services easier for disabled customers: A practical guide for small businesses and other service providers* (code SP5) from the Disability Rights Commission's website *www.drc-gb.org/drc*, or see *Rights of access to goods, facilities, services and premises. Disability Discrimination Act 1995*, available from *www.disability.gov.uk*

Good practice

Organisations should draw up an equal opportunities policy relating to service provision which extends beyond the legal requirements.

The policy should prohibit all discrimination on grounds of race, sex, disability, HIV or other medical status, age, religion or belief, trade union membership or activity and sexuality – unless there is a specific reason for providing services to particular groups, and it is lawful to limit services in this way under the organisation's constitution and equal opportunities law. The policy should also identify ways in which services can be monitored and, if necessary, adapted so that they are relevant to all sections of the community. Measures to consider are given below.

Think about the image of the organisation. If it is seen as predominantly made up of or controlled by people from one sex, racial group or social class, many people may be deterred from using its services. One way of changing this image is to ensure the organisation's management committee, any subcommittees and working parties reflect the diversity of the local community (see *Equal opportunities*, in chapter 2). Another way is to seek to ensure that the composition of staff, at all levels of the hierarchy, and volunteers reflects the make up of the community (see *Equal opportunities*, in chapter 3).

Identifying needs

Find out about the needs of people facing discrimination and how services could be adapted to meet these needs by arranging conferences, open days and visits. Make recommendations from this consultation process publicly available so that organisations can monitor and demonstrate progress in making changes.

Assessing services

An organisation can provide services for one racial group or sex if:

- under its constitution it is set up specifically to work with that racial group or sex, or
- it can prove that the group has a need which is greater than or different from the needs of other racial groups or the other sex.

Examine the organisation's services to make sure that they do not discriminate against any group unless this is allowed. Also consider how they could be adapted to tackle discrimination in a proactive way.

Introduce the promotion of equal opportunities in new and existing programmes and policies and with targets where appropriate. The management committee should regularly discuss and record progress.

Before planning a new project to meet the needs of particular people, consider whether the organisation is the most appropriate one to deliver the service. It may be better to help the people concerned to set up their own service, or to establish a joint project with an existing group.

Monitoring

Organisations should examine their services to judge their effectiveness in meeting the needs of everyone in the community. However, the following principles apply in relation to collecting data about service users:

- people cannot be forced into providing information about themselves for monitoring purposes, and you should never guess the answer if they don't provide the information themselves. You can only explain why it matters to you and encourage them to respond
- if you do not need to know the identities of service users, it is best to monitor anonymously. This must be 'genuine' anonymity (not just that you will only release the information anonymously or as statistics): there must be no way of linking the information back to the person
- if collecting monitoring information which is not anonymous,* you must:
- tell people that you will be using the information for that purpose
- make it clear that they don't have to provide it
- inform people clearly about how you will handle the data (for example, that you will only release it as statistics, that you won't keep the individual forms after the statistics have been compiled), and
- make it clear that they do not have to consent to personal details given in order to receive the service, being used for monitoring purposes.

The purpose must be genuine monitoring: the information must not be used to make decisions about the individual.

These rules apply in particular to monitoring on the basis of race or ethnicity, disability or religion. They are good practice when monitoring on the basis of age, gender or less contentious criteria (such as postcode or ward). Monitoring on the basis of other 'sensitive' data – including sexuality, criminal record or political views – can only be done with consent (again unless it is anonymous). In other words even if you already have the data for other reasons, you must still check that it is acceptable to use it for monitoring.

The rules also apply to monitoring information collected over the phone. You must use a standard script that explains everything properly before asking any questions.

For further information see *Equal opportunities*, in chapter 2.

Publicity

All written material should be free of jargon so that it can be more easily understood by people whose first language is not English and by those who have not had the opportunity to learn the jargon. Consider translating information into other languages, recording onto tapes, publishing in Braille and producing it in pictorial or other form for people with learning difficulties. Also look at the possibility of producing material in large print, and ensure the organisation's website is accessible to people with sight impairment (see below). Many organisations will not be able to afford to translate all their written material. However, translating a pilot run may demonstrate to funders the need for translation.

Examine how the organisation promotes itself. Ask organisations representing people who are socially excluded to publicise your services. Make sure such groups are invited to the annual general meeting, open meetings, courses, conferences and all other public events.

Add newspapers and journals written for people facing discrimination to your press list. The Commission for Racial Equality has a list of the black and minority ethnic press. The *Writers' and Artists' Yearbook* has a comprehensive list of all magazines and newspapers published in the UK. Copies are generally available in local reference libraries.

Accessible web design

RNIB has produced useful guidance on designing a website that is accessible to disabled people, including those with visual impairment. Key questions to ask are:

Is the text legible? Good colour contrast is central to accessible site design. Choose combinations of text and background colour that offer maximum contrast, for example a pastel shaded background with strongly contrasting, dark text. It is important to use crisp clearly defined typefaces. There are literally thousands to choose from but sans serif typefaces (those without small lines at the top and bottom of the letters) such as Helvetica, Univers, Arial and Verdana are amongst the clearest.

Is the design flexible? There is no 'best colour scheme' for partially sighted web users, as everyone has individual needs. Instead, web designers are encouraged to create flexible designs that enable the person using the site to control the text size and colour scheme. Is it easy to change the colour scheme and text size by adjusting the local browser settings?

Does every image include a verbal description? The web designer should use an 'alt-text' attribute within the image tag to provide a plain English description of an image, so that blind people accessing the site using speech synthesis software know what the image contains (for example alt = London skyline). For images that are purely decorative, the tag should read alt = "".

Is there a text site map? This helps people understand the layout of the website quickly and makes it easier to navigate.

Do links make sense out of context? People relying on synthesised speech technology to 'hear' websites use alternative ways of scanning screens of information quickly to get to the items that interest them. Access software for blind people generally provides a list of all the links on the page to give a flavour of the content. If a link contains only the words 'click here' , its function will not be obvious if presented out of context. All links should therefore contain enough information about their destination, for example 'this link will take you to the Department of Trade and Industry's website'.

Do frames have titles, and is 'noframes' used? Some software packages used by blind people cannot read frames. It is therefore vital to use the NOFRAMES tag, to offer alternative frames-free versions of the pages. Make sure that any frames used are titled, otherwise a blind visitor may hear only 'link to a frame' without any indication of its content.

Are alternative scripts offered for JavaScript, applets, Flash or plug-ins? Pages written in anything other than HTML (hypertext mark up language) may exclude some people from a site, as not everyone can download and use all the scripts and plug-ins. However, companies such as Macromedia are working towards making their technologies fully accessible. Refer to Macromedia's guidance at *www.macromedia.com/macromedia/accessibility/*

Are the PDF (portable document format) files accessible? Many websites include the option to download documents as PDF files, which can be opened by any computer that has the free program *Acrobat Reader*, regardless of which program they were created in. It is possible to create accessible PDF files in Versions 5 and 6 of *Acrobat*. Refer to Adobe's guidance at http://access.adobe.com The World Wide Web Consortium (W3C) Web Accessibility Initiative (WAI) has produced guidelines for the creation of websites that anyone can use (*www.w3.org/wai*). A free CD, *Websites that work*, is available from RNIB via *webaccess@rnib.org.uk* or 020 7391 2178.

For further information on accessible web design visit RNIB's Web Access Centre at *www.rnib.org.uk/webaccesscentre*

Public events

Think about where and when services are available, and the location and timing of special events. Consider how to make premises and other meeting places more accessible to disabled people (see chapter 6). Whenever possible provide crèche or childminding facilities at public events, conferences and training courses. Arrange for drivers to bring people with limited mobility to these events; the local dial-a-ride group may be able to provide transport. Remember that people with children or other dependants often find it difficult to attend evening meetings, and some people may not like travelling after dark. If meetings are held in the evening, find out whether participants would appreciate an escort to and from the meeting, or to and from public transport. Don't forget to take into account dates of all faiths' festivals when arranging events (see the *Shap calendar of religious festivals*, published by the Shap Working Party, available from *www.shap.org*).

Affiliation

Before deciding to affiliate with or become a member of another voluntary organisation examine its commitment to equal opportunities. It may be necessary to help other organisations develop an equal opportunities strategy.

Complaints

Introduce a complaints procedure for people who feel that they have been discriminated against. Make sure that it is well advertised on your premises. Direct and indirect discrimination, victimisation and harassment by a member of staff against any user should be a disciplinary offence (see chapter 4).

Contracting to provide services

Many voluntary organisations enter into legally binding agreements to provide defined services for local authorities, health authorities and government departments. These could be called **contracts** or **service levels agreements** and include conditions attached to grant aid. The management committee must be aware of its responsibilities and commitments made under such agreements.

Entering into an agreement to provide a defined service raises many questions for voluntary organisations, some of which are set out below.

Should the organisation take on the service?

Before taking on a contract consider the following questions:

- are the proposed activities consistent with the organisation's aims and objectives and are they allowed for within its objects and powers? Remember organisations cannot operate outside their objects or powers (see chapter 1)
- is it advisable to become a company limited by guarantee before entering into a contract (see chapter 1)
- does the organisation have the financial and staff resources for any consultancy or legal advice needed to prepare a bid and take on the contract
- is it ready to take on a new role and does it have the capacity to manage the growth this may involve
- do staff and committee members have sufficient training and expertise to manage contracts
- can the required service quantity and quality be provided under the contract arrangements
- will the organisation have to charge VAT and/or pay corporation tax on profits if it enters into contracts? Check this with your accountant and Customs and Excise. Fees charged by or paid to a charity for carrying out a service can be subject to VAT
- does the organisation have adequate insurance cover for any additional services and if not, can this be afforded (see chapter 7)
- does the organisation have adequate health and safety procedures to manage the service (see chapter 5)
- will taking on a new service affect other providers, for example those in the statutory sector or other voluntary organisations active in the field
- how will the organisation's other activities, for example campaigning or community development, be affected by a contract to supply services

- will the organisation be obliged to take on the authority's staff if the contract is for services previously provided by the authority?

The **Transfer of Undertakings (Protection of Employment) Regulations 1981 (TUPE)** mean that if an organisation takes over activities from another employer, that employer's staff are likely to be automatically transferred on the same terms and conditions.

The government has issued a code of practice on the transfer of services from local authorities to private and voluntary sector contractors. It states that employees who join the new organisation after the transfer must be offered terms and conditions which are at least equal to those of employees who have transferred from the local authority. Also make sure that any staff have been adequately consulted about the changes affecting them – the obligation to consult is not just with transferred staff but all staff of both employers who might be affected by the transfer. The new employer can be held liable if a transferring employer does not consult its employees affected by TUPE. The law in this area is complex and organisations should always take independent legal advice on this, and on the potential tax, VAT, health and safety and insurance implications of taking over services.

Costing the service

Any agreements should be costed in the same way as other services, see *The budget*, in chapter 8.

Assessing the contract

Before signing the contract make sure you and your legal advisor are satisfied with the terms, and in particular the following points:
- duration
- arrangements for renewal
- insurance obligations, including any indemnity clauses where the organisation agrees to cover any claims made against the local authority or other purchasing body
- whether payments are in arrears or in advance, their frequency and whether interest will be charged for late payment. If there is no contractual agreement organisations can charge interest on late payments at the rate specified under the **Late Payments of Commercial Debts (Interest) Act 1998**, which is dealing rate plus 8%. The dealing rate is set twice yearly, on 31 December and 30 June
- provision for VAT if applicable

- the extent to which payments are guaranteed and the circumstances in which they can be withheld
- the extent to which payments are dependent on outputs or outcomes
- increases in payments to cover inflation and annual increments
- provisions for changes to payments if the service required alters, and arrangements for dealing with disputes in such cases
- the mechanism for dealing with complaints and disputes, including arbitration where other measures fail
- rules on confidentiality
- reviews of the contract and the services provided
- monitoring of the service provided (organisations themselves should monitor services using both qualitative and quantitative measures)
- penalty and termination clauses if either party defaults, and protection against termination by the authority in unwarranted circumstances
- clauses guaranteeing equal opportunities in recruitment and services delivered under the contract, including a complaints procedure for users
- the right for the organisation to have the final say on who uses the service
- the rights of service users in relation to both the organisation and the authority: this is often not included in contracts
- whether service users or others who benefit under the contract, but who are not parties to it, have the right to take legal action if they do not receive the service as specified. Take legal advice before excluding or including this right. Under the **Contract (Rights of Third Parties) Act 1999**, third parties who benefit from the contract have a right to sue unless their right to take action is explicitly excluded. A voluntary organisation would need considerable amounts of insurance to cover the potential risk of litigation.

Where possible draw up a contract in partnership with the authority requiring the service and in consultation with service users.

For further details see the Charity Commission booklet *Charities and contracts* (CC37) and *Mutual obligations – NCVO's guide to contracts with public bodies*, published by the National Council for Voluntary Organisations.

Equipment contracts are covered in chapter 6.

Handling data and information

Data protection

Organisations that record and use personal information about recognisable, living individuals will almost certainly be **data controllers** and must comply with the **Data Protection Act 1998**. Personal data includes both facts and opinions about an individual.

The following is covered by the Act:
- information held on computer (including in e-mail systems) about an individual who can be identified from the data (even if the person's name is not used) or from a list of codes that includes the person's name
- information held in manual (paper) filing systems where it is possible to access information about particular people, for example in an alphabetically organised filing cabinet or card index files
- information collected with the intention of storing it on a computer or in a manual system.

Data protection principles

Anyone processing personal data must follow the eight data protection principles. 'Processing' covers everything that could be done to data including collecting, recording, storing, organising, consulting, using, disclosing and destroying it.

The principles say that data must be:
- processed fairly and lawfully
- collected only for specified purposes and any further processing must be compatible with these purposes
- adequate, relevant and not excessive
- accurate and up to date
- not kept longer than necessary
- processed in line with the data subject's rights under the Act
- secure (against loss, destruction or unauthorised use)
- not transferred to countries outside the European Economic Area without adequate protection (publication on the internet is automatically regarded as an overseas transfer).

Data can usually only be processed if one of the following circumstances apply:
- the **data subject** (ie the person the information is about) has consented to the processing, knows who is using the information and why, and whether it will be made available to anyone else. Explicit consent is needed for 'sensitive' personal data (see below)
- it is needed in connection with a contract involving the data subject

- it is necessary to protect the data subject's 'vital interests' or to carry out public functions
- there is a legal obligation to process the information (for example, for sick pay records)
- it is in the legitimate interests of the data controller or certain third parties to process the data except where such processing is unwarranted because of the prejudice to the data subject's rights. This requires a balancing exercise to decide if processing is appropriate.

Sensitive personal data

Special rules apply to sensitive personal data, which includes information about someone's racial or ethnic origin, their political opinions, trade union membership, religious beliefs, health, sex life and any criminal proceedings and convictions. For protection, the data controller should get such consent in writing.

There are special rules permitting the processing of sensitive personal data needed for monitoring racial or ethnic origin to ensure equality of opportunity. This information can be collected and used for monitoring purposes provided there are adequate safeguards for the data subject's rights and freedom. Regulations can specify the safeguards required, but at the time of writing (December 2003) none had been made. It would be wise to check with the Commission for Racial Equality and Office of the Information Commissioner before carrying out a monitoring exercise. Also, the Information Commissioner's *Employment practices data protection code: Part 2 records management* includes a chapter on record keeping for equal opportunities purposes.

Data subjects' rights

Under the Act, data subjects have the right to see information about themselves held on computer and in some manual records (see above). In response to a **subject access request** the data subject must receive:
- a copy of the information held about them and any available information about its source
- a description of why the data is being processed
- details of anyone who may see it or to whom data may be passed or disclosed.

Data controllers may ask for subject access requests to be made in writing and can charge a fee of up to £10. They must deal with requests within 40 days of receiving the written request and fee (if charged). If the data subject needs to be asked for further details to help find their data, or to confirm their identity, the 40 days will begin when this extra information is received.

The court can make the data controller correct inaccurate data. However, if you accurately recorded the information given to you, and had done your best to ensure the information was accurate, you may have to add a statement of the true facts.

Individuals also have the right to object to their data being used for direct marketing by post, fax, telephone, e-mail, text message or other electronic means. This includes fundraising and could also include volunteer recruitment or similar communications.

Implementation
The majority of the Act is now in force. The only exception is manual systems in place immediately before 24 October 1998, which don't have to comply with the Act until 23 October 2007.

Registering
Although all data controllers must comply with the Act, some may not have to **notify** (register with) the Information Commissioner. Data controllers do not need to notify if they keep only the following data:

- manual systems (ie no personal data on computer, microfilm or other electronic media except as specified below)
- computerised accounts and payroll activities
- computerised membership records, where members have consented to the records being kept and those records are used only for sending information to all members. Organisations that record preferences to enable certain categories of members to receive different mailings must register.

Further information is available from the notification helpline 01625 545740 and in *Notification exemptions: a self assessment guide*, available from *www.dpr.gov.uk*

Developing a data protection policy
The following action points could form the basis of an organisational policy on data protection, perhaps linked to the confidentiality policy (see *Confidentiality*, in chapter 4). They are taken from the *Guide to the 1998 Data Protection Act* written by Paul Ticher and produced by Lasa (*www.lasa.org.uk*).

- **Ensure that everyone about whom the organisation holds information knows it is held**, what it is used for, and to whom it might be passed. Often a short statement on forms and leaflets, or a notice in the waiting room, will be sufficient.
- Wherever possible get **consent** for holding people's

information, and get explicit consent, in writing if possible, for any 'sensitive' information the organisation wants to hold (see above).
- Make sure people have the chance to **opt out** of any direct marketing.
- **Modify the organisation's systems** to record, where necessary, consent, direct marketing opt-outs and opt-ins.
- **Design or modify the systems** so that the organisation can easily comply with any request by data subjects (see above) to see the records held on them.
- **Make appropriate security arrangements,** for both manual and computer systems, depending on the sensitivity of the information.
- **Train or brief staff** in what they are and are not allowed to do with people's information, and whom they have to ask if they are unsure.
- **Notify the Information Commissioner** about any data processing activities which are not exempt.
- **Appoint a member of staff as data protection compliance officer,** so that part of their job is to find out about data protection in more detail and keep the organisation within the law.
- **Appoint a member of the management committee to oversee data protection** on behalf of the committee, and to liaise with the staff data protection compliance officer.

Further information
The Information Commissioner has published a data protection code on employment practices. At the time of writing (December 2003) three parts had been published, relating to recruitment and training, record management and monitoring at work (see chapters 3 and 4 for further details), and a draft of part 4, covering workers' health information, was out for consultation.

If you handle any kind of personal data you should obtain further information about the effect of the 1998 Act. For further information and guidance contact the Information Commissioner's enquiry/information line (01625 545 745), visit *www.informationcommissioner.gov.uk* or see *Data protection for voluntary organisations* (2nd edn), by Paul Ticher, published by the Directory of Social Change.

Electronic marketing
Under the **Privacy and Electronic Communications (EC Directive) Regulations 2003**, it is an offence to send individuals and unincorporated organisations unsolicited marketing e-mails (spam), text messages or faxes unless they have given prior consent. E-mail and text message marketing to existing customers is permitted if the

marketing relates to similar goods or services, being offered by the same organisation.

Organisations should therefore use an opt-in statement on any publicity, fundraising and membership materials, along the lines of 'We may want to send you information about our work and products by e-mail, text, fax or other electronic means. Please tick here to give your consent', rather than the currently widely used 'tick here if you don't want to hear from us' opt-out. If you send direct marketing e-mails, you must make clear in the subject line what they are and make clear how people can opt out.

The regulations also prohibit phone marketing if the subscriber's line is on the Telephone Preference Service register, unless an individual gives specific consent to the contact. For further details see *www.tpsonline.org.uk*

Freedom of information

Under the **Freedom of Information Act 2000** members of the public will be able to apply for access to information held by bodies across the public sector. By June 2004 all public authorities, and those providing services for them, will have to set up schemes for publishing information which specify the classes of information to be published, the manner of publication and whether they will make a charge. Rights of access under the Act will come into force on 1 January 2005.

Under **Section 5** of the Act it is possible that the legislation could apply to voluntary organisations carrying out work on behalf of a public authority. However, there will be full consultation before this happens.

For further information see *www.informationcommissioner.gov.uk*

Copyright

Essentially the copyright on any material belongs to the person who originally produced it, unless:
- they have assigned (transferred) that copyright, or
- it has been produced by an employee as part of their work, in which case the copyright will normally belong to the employer.

Organisations that intend to publish their own material should ensure that any contracts of employment make clear who owns the copyright if employees may write books or articles outside of their normal work. Normally the employer would own the copyright of anything written by an employee as part of their job but the employee would own the copyright of anything written outside the normal course of work.

It is also essential to clarify who will own the copyright of material or documents produced in contracts with self-employed workers, designers and consultants, and in volunteer agreements. Unless agreed otherwise, copyright will belong to the person who created the work – even if a self-employed worker, designer or consultant has been paid for it. It is possible to have joint copyright, between two or more parties, but you should take legal advice to ensure the provisions are fair to all parties and are workable. They should state, for example, what happens if one party dies (if an individual) or is wound up (if an organisation).

If the organisation is planning to publish material written, designed or produced by anyone other than an employee who did the work as part of their employment, check that the copyright holder has given permission, or that the work is copyright free. This applies to illustrations, photographs and logos as well as written material and material on the internet. There are some exceptions, which include publishing for the purposes of criticism or news reporting provided the source of the material is acknowledged and only a limited amount is reproduced. It is possible to insure against unintentional breach of copyright (see chapter 7).

Electronic copyright

There is no real difference between copyright and electronic copyright. Material published in electronic format (such as CD-ROMs or online databases) has the same protection as its printed equivalents.

Copyright material sent over the internet or stored on a website is protected in the same way as material in other media. If the organisation has a website, it is advisable to mark each page with the copyright symbol (©) (although this has no legal meaning in the UK), and include a statement explaining the extent to which content may be used without permission.

If in doubt take legal advice.

For further information on handling data and information see chapter 38 of *The voluntary sector legal handbook*.

Reproduction of copyright material for visually impaired people

Under the **Copyright (Visually Impaired Persons) Act 2002** voluntary organisations can make multiple accessible copies of publications and literary, dramatic, musical or artistic work for use by visually impaired people, where the material exists only in an inaccessible form. This exception does not apply where making the accessible copies would involve recording a music performance or would infringe copyright in a database.

Defamation

Defamation covers both **libel** (involving the written word or any other permanent record such as a photograph, tape recording or video) and **slander** (involving speech in a non-permanent form, including a conversation between two or more people). For example a verbal statement made in a speech at a meeting could be slander, and if recorded in the minutes or on tape, reported in a newsletter or on a website or repeated in a letter or e-mail could be libellous.

Anyone suing for defamation has to prove that their reputation has been damaged. This means that an untrue statement has been made to a third party, which tends to:
- lower the victim in the estimation of society, or
- make people view them with feelings of hatred, fear, ridicule, dislike or contempt.

Simply making one of the following accusations is likely to be defamatory:
- saying that someone has committed a criminal offence serious enough to be punished by imprisonment
- alleging something calculated to disparage the person as to their office, trade or profession.

A general comment could be defamatory if:
- someone's name is mentioned in conjunction with damaging circumstances, for example 'Only criminals go to the XYZ club. Pat was seen there last week.'
- someone could deduce a meaning by implication or innuendo, for example 'A person not a million miles away from Pat was seen handing money over to a police officer'.

Anyone defaming an unnamed member of a small identifiable group could be sued by each person in that group. So if, for example, six members of a management committee are accused of being dishonest, one or all of them could take action.

The five means of defence against an accusation of defamation are:
- proving that the **statement was true**
- showing that the words were **fair comment**: correctly stated facts giving an opinion, not malicious, about a matter of public concern. This defence cannot be used against defamation of a person's moral character

- **privilege**, this would include statements made by MPs in parliament or judges in court
- **qualified privilege**, which covers people reporting fairly and accurately court cases, parliamentary proceedings and, in some cases, public meetings. It also includes reporting an allegation, when under a legal or moral duty, to an enforcement authority, for example social services or the police
- **innocent defamation**, which claims that the statement was unintentional and reasonable care was taken to avoid making the mistake. An offer of amends, such as publishing a correction and an apology in a newsletter, should be made as soon as possible.

It is possible to insure against unintentional defamation (see chapter 7).

Activities
Meetings and marches
Meetings on private premises
Owners, and tenants with leases, can usually refuse to let a hall without giving a reason, as long as they do not discriminate on the grounds of race, sex or disability (unless, in the latter case, it is justified, see *Disability discrimination*, page 183). Similarly, those organising a meeting have the right to refuse admission, regardless of whether an entry fee is charged, without stating why. The only exception to these rules arises during elections, when some publicly funded organisations may have to allow a meeting room to be used for a public election meeting. Contact the Returning Officer at the town hall (and the Charity Commission, if your organisation is charitable) if asked to allow such use.

People who force their way into a meeting are trespassing and can be evicted using reasonable force. If there is no admission charge, someone can be asked to leave at any time without warning. However, people who have paid an entrance fee can only legally be asked to leave if they are acting in such a disorderly way that the meeting cannot continue. Under the **Public Meeting Act 1908** it is illegal to break up a meeting.

The police can attend meetings on private premises only if invited by the organisers or if they believe that there is likely to be a breach of the peace.

Hiring out rooms
In legal terms, rooms are let on licences, and owners can lay down conditions for their use. If these are broken, the licensee may have to compensate the owner or can be asked to leave.

Conditions that may be imposed include:
- a ban on alcohol – this is quite common in church halls and some charity buildings
- restrictions on music
- a finishing time
- a limit on the number of people allowed on the premises – this is likely to have been set under fire regulations and must be strictly adhered to
- the responsibility for any accidents or damage during the let of the hall is taken by the hirer. It is possible to insure against this (see chapter 7).

For further details on hiring out premises see chapter 6.

Meetings in a public place

The **Public Order Act 1986**, amended by the **Anti-Social Behaviour Act 2003**, gives a senior police officer the power to impose conditions on 'public assemblies' – meetings of two or more people held in a public place in the open air. The officer has to believe that members of the public are being, or could be, harassed or intimidated by the behaviour of the group. Conditions relate to:
- the location of the meeting
- its duration
- the maximum number of people who may attend.

The provisions do not apply to people taking part in peaceful picketing by trade union members at their place of work.

In addition, several local bylaws and Acts of Parliament control public meetings in parks and open spaces and in some streets. Details are available from your local authority. Local laws may require notice to be given to the council's chief executive or local police.

It is an offence to try to break up a public meeting, although anyone has the right to heckle within reasonable limits. Stewards may not ask people to leave a meeting held on public property.

Marches and processions

The **Public Order Act** also governs marches and processions. Seven days' notice must be given to the local police of any public procession that is intended to:
- demonstrate support for, or opposition to any views or actions
- publicise a cause or campaign, or
- mark or commemorate an event.

The police must also be notified of any changes to a planned march. If the procession is organised within seven days, you must give as much advance notice as is reasonably practicable. There is no need to give notice if it is not reasonably practicable or if the procession is regularly held in that area.

The police can direct the route of a march or prohibit a march from entering a specific public place.

If you are organising a march take advice from a solicitor or the police about the detailed legal requirements for notice. Marches and processions may also be governed by local bylaws or Acts of Parliament. Ask the local authority for details of the requirements.

In London the police have additional powers under the **Metropolitan Police Act 1839** to prevent traffic congestion caused by demonstrations or meetings. While parliament is in session, open air meetings and processions on the north side of the Thames within a mile of Parliament Square are banned. Carrying banners and placards, and handing out leaflets, are also prohibited within this area.

For information about meetings held in Trafalgar Square and Parliament Square contact the Square's Management Team in the Greater London Authority, for meetings in Royal Parks, the Royal Parks Agency, and for other parks, the relevant local authority. For other information and guidance contact the Public Order Branch of the Metropolitan Police Service on 020 7230 1212.

Protests

The police have some powers under the **Criminal Justice and Public Order Act 1994**, as amended by the **Anti-Social Behaviour Act 2003** to control organised protests. It is a criminal offence to trespass on land (which now includes buildings) with the intent of intimidating other people engaged in lawful activity, or to obstruct or disrupt them. This would include, for example, the disruption of a hunt or the building of a new road, or entering and intimidating people conducting medical research on animals.

A senior police officer who reasonably believes that an offence has been committed or is planned, and that at least two people are trespassing with the intent to intimidate people or disrupt their activity, can require them to leave the land. It is then a criminal offence to stay on the land or to return within three months.

The police can also apply to the local authority for an advance ban on any organised protest that is likely to involve trespass on private property if they believe protest would result in serious disruption to community life or would damage any historic monument or building.

Loudspeakers

Local bylaws govern the use of loudspeakers, the details of which may be obtained from the local authority. It is usually necessary to give 48 hours' written notice to the police before using a loudspeaker for non-commercial purposes. Under the **Control of Pollution Act 1974** loudspeakers are not allowed in public places between 9 pm and 8 am.

In London the **Metropolitan Police Act 1839** governs what can be said through a loudspeaker.

Festivals and parties

Festivals and raves

The **Criminal Justice and Public Order Act 1994**, as amended by the **Anti-Social Behaviour Act 2003**, applies to open air festivals and parties involving 20 or more people where amplified music is played at night and which are likely to cause serious distress to local residents. It also covers raves in buildings, if those attending are trespassing. A senior police officer can require people preparing for, or turning up to, a festival to leave the land and remove any vehicles or property they have with them. It is then an offence to stay on the land or return within seven days. The provisions do not apply when an entertainment licence has been obtained (see below).

The police also have powers within five miles of a festival to prevent people from reaching the festival after they have been directed to leave. It is also an offence for anyone to make preparations for or attend a rave within 24 hours of being told to leave the land.

Street parties

The police and local authorities may close streets only in an emergency or by going through a lengthy statutory procedure, which is not designed to cater for street parties or festivals. But if you are planning to hold an event on publicly owned space or in the street you should inform the police, as well as the engineer's and housing departments of the local authority, to make sure there are no objections. The police can advise on certain aspects of organising an event such as safety, access and traffic problems. The engineer's department can advise on services such as gas, electricity and toilets. You have to arrange any temporary water supplies through the water company, which will ask you to sign an indemnity form absolving it of any responsibility. Make sure your organisation is adequately insured (see chapter 7).

Selling and storing food

Rules of food hygiene are contained in the **Food Safety (General Food Hygiene) Regulations 1995**. The regulations cover events where food or drink is stored or supplied either on a temporary basis, for example stalls at a fete, or regularly, for example a café in a community centre, and apply whether food and drink is sold at a profit, sold at cost or less, or is given away.

Under the regulations organisations must have effective food safety management measures (or 'controls') in place, to ensure that food is produced safely and that the health of consumers is not put at risk.

The Food Safety (Temperature Control) Regulations 1995

Under these regulations certain foods must be kept either at or above 63°C or below 8°C, except for short periods. They apply to all types of food premises (which includes out of doors).

For further information contact the local environmental health department and see Community Matters' information sheet 11 *Food safety and food hygiene*, or the *Guide to food hygiene* and *The Food Safety Regulations*, from the Food Standards Agency, Aviation House, 125 Kingsway, London WC2B 6NH, 020 7276 8000, *www.food.gov.uk*

Licensing laws

Current licensing laws

Current licensing laws will be replaced by the **Licensing Act 2003**, but are expected to be in force until early 2005.

Under the **Licensing (Occasional Permissions) Act 1983** it is possible for charitable and other voluntary organisations to get an occasional permission to run a bar, by applying to the local licensing magistrates at least three weeks before the function. An organisation can have no more than 12 occasional permissions during each 12 month period in one licensing area. For further information see *Providing alcohol on charity premises* (CC27), from the Charity Commission.

The organisers can refuse to admit or may eject people who are drunk, and can refuse to serve anyone, providing that they do not discriminate on the grounds of sex, race or disability. It is an offence to serve alcohol to people aged under 18. Selling alcohol without a licence is illegal, as is the sale of raffle tickets without a licence where alcohol forms one or more of the prizes.

Under the **Theatres Act 1968** an organisation with a theatre licence can run a bar selling alcohol during performances without the need for an extra licence (see below). It must keep within permitted licensing hours and notify the clerk to the licensing justices in writing.

An organisation planning to sell alcohol on a regular basis will need a licence or a **registration certificate** under the **Licensing Act 1964**. A registered club would only need a registration certificate.

Before applying for a registration certificate, get financial advice on bookkeeping and accounts, and on liability for VAT and income or corporation tax. A charity should also seek advice on setting up a separate non-charity to run the bar. This non-charity will generally be required, under its constitution, to donate most or all of its profits to the charity under the Gift Aid scheme and so avoid income or corporation tax. For further details see *Trading*, in chapter 1.

Applications for a registration certificate are made to the local magistrates court, which will require a copy of the organisation's constitution and a plan of the premises. Copies of the application will be sent to the police service, fire authority and environmental health department, all of which may wish to inspect the premises. The application must also be advertised near the premises or in a local newspaper.

It is important to consider all the consequences of running a bar, particularly of opening a regular bar. These include:
* the security measures associated with handling large quantities of cash; these should include precautions against theft by servers
* the possibility of inconveniencing neighbours
* whether volunteers will put all their energy into running the bar at the expense of other activities
* whether alcohol consumption may deter some people from using the premises
* the need for additional insurance
* additional management time needed to manage the enterprise – especially if a separate organisation has to be set up to run the bar, which will need its own committee, meetings and minutes.

Entertainment licences
Public entertainment, theatre and cinema licences are issued separately by local authorities. The Home Office is encouraging local authorities to streamline the process for applications relating to premises catering for a maximum of 300 people. Its guidance *Community premises licensing: guidance to local authorities* proposes that:
* it should be possible to apply for two or more licences in a single application
* renewal notices should be issued for annual licences
* local authorities should provide a named contact for enquiries
* local authorities should impose only those conditions and restrictions strictly necessary for public safety and to avoid nuisance.

Music and dance
Organisations providing entertainment involving music or dance need a **public entertainment licence** (PEL) unless they are using premises already licensed for this purpose. **Occasional music licences** can be obtained from the licensing authority (the local authority). Applicants usually have to give 28 days' notice to the local authority, fire authority and the police. In Greater London, there is no fee for entertainment with an educational, charitable or similar purpose. The **Local Government (Miscellaneous Provisions) Act 1982**, which applies outside Greater London, allows the licensing authority to waive all or part of the licence fee where the entertainment has an educational, charitable or similar purpose. No fee is payable for church and village halls.

Theatre performances
A theatre licence is needed for plays and other stage performances. The application is similar to a PEL (see above), and restrictions may be imposed.

Films
Organisations planning to show films may need a licence under the **Cinemas Act 1985**.

There are exceptions. A licence is not required:
* to show films if they are for non-commercial exhibition and viewing is free or restricted to members
* if film showings are restricted to six days per year, provided that the local authority, police and fire authorities are informed.

Indoor sports
Organisations also need a licence to hold an event in which indoor sports is the principal activity. Occasional licences are available from the local authority, whose staff will inspect the premises. No licence is needed if sport is not the principal activity.

Forthcoming licensing laws

The **Licensing Act 2003** is expected to come into force early in 2005.

The key changes are:
- a new **single premises licence**, which can cover all the activities on the premises that require a licence under the Act, including:
- selling alcohol
- providing public entertainment – which includes live music, playing recorded music, dancing, showing films and performing plays
- providing an indoor sporting event
- providing refreshments between 11pm and 5am. The licence will include operating conditions (for example hours, noise, fire exits, capacity) tailored to the premises by the local licensing authority. The likely cost will be between £100 and £500, plus an annual charge of between £50 and £150.
- a new system of **personal licences** (issued for ten years), which will allow holders to serve or sell alcohol for consumption on or away from any premises covered by a premises licence. A personal licence will cost around £30
- both premises and personal licences will be issued by local authorities
- flexible opening hours with the potential to open 24 hours, seven days a week, subject to the views of local residents and other interested parties, the police and other responsible authorities
- a **club premises certificate** covering the sale of alcohol, public entertainment and late night refreshment may be granted if there are no representations from local residents, the police or health and safety officers The club committee will hold the certificate and the club will not need a personal licence (see above). The certificate would be valid for the life of the club.

Temporary event notices

Temporary event notices (TENs), which will cost around £20, will replace the current system of occasional permissions. The organisation will need to apply to the licensing authority no less than ten working days before the day on which the event period begins and send a copy of the application to the police. Each property will be able to have a maximum of ten TENs a calendar year, for a maximum total of 15 days. Each event can last a maximum of four days (96 hours), and attendance must be less than 500. The Act allows for these limits to be amended in the light of experience.

Exemptions for public entertainment events

Small-scale music events

To stage a music event an organisation will need a premises licence that authorises public entertainment. However, the Act will suspend conditions attached to a premises licence or club premises certificate imposed by a licensing authority if:
- the music is acoustic
- the premises hold no more than 200 people
- the music is performed between 8am and midnight.

The licence will remain under review.

Other exceptions

The following premises or types of entertainment do not require a licence under the Act:
- churches (unless alcohol is served or sold)
- Morris dancing or similar dancing
- incidental music
- garden fete or similar function (if not held for private gain).

Fee exemptions

The following will require a premises licence but will be exempt from the associated fees if only entertainment is provided (ie there is no alcohol or late night refreshment):
- church or chapel halls or other similar places of public religious worship, and village, parish or community halls and other similar buildings
- schools and sixth form colleges (where the entertainment is provided by the school).

For further information visit the Department for Culture, Media and Sport's website, *www.culture.gov.uk* or contact the Department on *alcohol.entertainment@culture.gov.uk* or 020 7211 6200.

Fundraising

Subscriptions

Charging a membership fee is a relatively easy way to raise a small amount of money. Provided it is permitted in the constitution, an organisation can charge certain people different fees, for example unwaged people could pay a reduced rate. Anyone willing to donate more than the standard amount could be given a title such as 'friend', 'patron' or 'life member'.

Before charging membership fees, consider the administration involved. The simplest method is to have a set membership period – the calendar year, financial year or the year starting from the annual general meeting – so that all reminders can be sent out at the same time. Depending on the subscription, members joining during the subscription year could pay a reduced rate. Keep a record of members' names, addresses and dates of payment. Companies and industrial and provident societies must keep a register of members (see chapter 2).

It is possible to alter a constitution that does not allow a charge for membership (see chapter 2). Alternatively membership could be free but the organisation could charge for services such as a newsletter.

It may be possible for members of charities to pay all or some of their membership subscription under the Gift Aid scheme (see below). This would enable the charity to recover tax on the subscription.

Gift Aid

The Gift Aid scheme enables UK taxpayers (both individuals and companies) to make tax effective donations to charities. Where donations are made by individuals, charities can reclaim from the Inland Revenue the basic rate of tax paid. With basic rate tax at 22%, the charity can reclaim £2.82 for each £10 donation. Donations can be regular or one-off and of any amount.

To enable the charity to reclaim the tax, an individual donor must give the charity a **Gift Aid declaration**. The declaration can be made in writing, by e-mail or orally. It can cover one or more donations, can be backdated to cover all donations since 6 April 2000, and can also cover future donations. Charities must send the donor a written record of an oral declaration. A model form is included in the Inland Revenue's Gift Aid toolkit *Gift aid it,* which can be downloaded from *www.inlandrevenue.gov.uk/charities/*

Charities that want to recover tax on donations made by individuals must write to IR Charities, with proof of their charitable status. They must keep sufficient records to show that their tax reclaims are accurate, otherwise they may have to pay back the tax reclaimed, with interest.

For companies wanting to make Gift Aid donations, the procedure is different. They donate an amount that includes the corporation tax they would have to pay on that amount. They then claim tax relief when calculating their profits for corporation tax.

For further details contact the Gift Aid helpline on 0845 3020203 or visit *www.inlandrevenue.gov.uk*

Legacies

An organisation could ask its supporters to remember it in their will. This is a sensitive subject, so requests for legacies must be handled carefully.

Inform existing donors of the possibility of making a bequest by including information and a legacy form in publicity material. It is also possible to advertise in journals such as the *Law Society Gazette* or *Charities Digest*. It may be worth contacting local solicitors as they sometimes advise people on charitable bequests.

Payroll giving

Under the payroll giving scheme employees can authorise their employer to deduct charitable donations from their pay before calculating PAYE tax. This means that employees will get tax relief on their donations at their highest rate of tax (but will still have to pay the usual rate of national insurance). There is no limit on the amount that can be given under the scheme.

The employer has to pay the donations to an agent approved by the Inland Revenue, who must pass on the donations to the nominated charities within 60 days of receipt.

As part of its campaign to promote payroll giving, the government will pay a 10% supplement on all donations until 5 April 2004.

For further details contact the IR enquiry helpline on 08453 020203 or visit *www.inlandrevenue.gov.uk*

Gifts of shares and securities

Individuals and companies can get tax relief for gifts of certain shares and securities to a charity when calculating their income or profits for tax purposes. The tax relief applies when an individual or company gives the shares or securities to the charity (with no conditions), or sells them to the charity for less than the market value on the day they are passed over.

For further information, including clarification of which shares and securities qualify for the scheme, contact IR Charities.

Collections

Collections are a relatively simple, low cost way of raising funds. To collect money on private premises such as pubs or supermarket forecourts the organisation simply needs the owner's permission. Under the **House to House Collections Act 1939** and the **Police, Factories, etc (Miscellaneous Provisions) Act 1916** there are strict rules governing house to house and street collections. These rules also apply to private premises where the public has right of access, such as railway stations and shopping arcades. An organisation wishing to raise money in this way must apply in writing to the licensing authority before the first day of the month preceding the month in which the collection takes place. In London this is the Metropolitan Police Service's Charities Office (020 7230 4015, *www.met.police.uk/charities*) or, for collections in the City, the Corporation of London (020 7332 3226). Elsewhere it is the local authority. The regulations apply to collecting goods as well as cash.

At the time of writing (December 2003) the law is not clear as to whether face to face fundraising (direct debit solicitation) requires a licence. Organisations should check with the local authority (or, in London, the police) for their rules.

Information requested will differ between authorities but they will usually need to know:
* the promoter's name
* the purpose of the collection
* where it is to be carried out
* how many collectors there will be and whether they will be paid
* the date(s) of the collection(s)
* whether the collection is for cash or goods
* the type of collection, ie street or house to house.

If a licence is refused or revoked, the charity can appeal to the Home Secretary within 14 days of receiving written notice.

Some national charities have been granted a **Home Office Exemption Certificate** enabling them to make house to

house collections anywhere in England and Wales at any time. However, as a matter of courtesy, a charity with such an exemption should inform the local authority (in London, the police) of its plans and try to avoid overlapping with other collections.

Further permission is needed to collect at tube or rail stations. For underground stations the request must be made on headed paper at least six weeks before the proposed date of the first collection. Individuals or fundraisers collecting on behalf of a charity must include a letter of authority from the charity. Most stations allow one collection a week, although some only allow one per month. For further details contact the London Underground Ltd Charity Coordinator on 020 7227 7892. Contact the station manager for collections at overground stations (ring Network Rail on 08700 00 20 20 for contact details).

The organiser of house to house collections is responsible for ensuring the following regulations are met:
* collectors must be aged 16 or over
* each collector must carry a certificate of authorisation and a prescribed badge (available from the Stationery Office) which must conform to Home Office regulations and be signed by the organiser
* collectors must produce their badges on request and give their names to the police if asked
* collectors must not annoy passers-by or householders
* any collecting boxes must be numbered and sealed
* any envelopes used must have a gummed flap
* if neither boxes nor envelopes are used, receipts must be given from a receipt book with consecutively numbered pages
* a record must be kept of each box, authorisation badge and permit issued.

After the collection, the boxes or envelopes must be opened in the presence of the organiser and a witness, unless the sealed box is taken to the bank. The contents should be recorded.

A statement of accounts must be sent to the licensing authority, showing the amount collected and the number of boxes distributed, and demonstrating that all have been returned and the expenses incurred.

The licensing authority can make rules covering street collections in its area. Contact the local licensing authority for details of local regulations. In most cases these rules are virtually the same as for house to house collections.

In the Metropolitan Police Service area it is possible to make a collection at an open air meeting without a police permit, unless the event is in a park or a similar open space, where bylaws may prohibit collecting. Check the position with the local authority.

Collection boxes can be purchased from Angal Collecting Boxes and Devices Limited (020 8390 9393).

Charities Bill

It is likely that a new, simplified scheme for licensing public collections will be included in the draft Charities Bill. At the time of writing (December 2003) consultation on the following proposals had just finished:

- Local authorities will be required to license all public charitable collections (including 'face to face fundraising' (direct debit solicitation) apart from very small and local ones, which will be exempt.
- Collections on the public highway or land commonly used by the public as a highway (such as supermarket forecourts and station concourses) will need to be licensed.
- National exemption orders will be replaced by a lead authority system.
- The right of appeal (currently restricted to house to house collections) will be extended to street collections, and appeals will be heard in the magistrates court.
- Responsibility for licensing street and house to house collections in London will be transferred from the police to local authorities.

The consultation also considered:

- the information organisers would need to submit when making a licence application
- basic safeguards necessary to secure collection proceeds
- how collection organisers might ensure that collectors are suitable
- record keeping and local authority monitoring.

For further information see *www.homeoffice.gov.uk*

Lotteries and raffles

The law relating to lotteries is contained in the **Lotteries and Amusements Act 1976**. The general rule is that lotteries cannot be run for private or commercial gain. Generally the law distinguishes between small lotteries and private lotteries, and 'society' (public) lotteries, which must be registered with the local authority or the Gaming Board for Great Britain.

Small lotteries

Small lotteries (or raffles) are those which are run for charitable, sporting or cultural purposes as part of an 'exempt entertainment'. This is defined in the Act as a 'bazaar, sale of work, fete, dinner, dance, sporting or athletic event or other entertainment of a similar character'. Section 3 of the Act gives full details of conditions to be observed. Some examples are:

- proceeds must not be used for private gain
- tickets can be sold only on the premises and during the course of the entertainment
- no more than £250 (in 2003/04) can be spent on buying prizes
- no money prizes can be awarded.

Private lotteries

A private lottery is one in which ticket sales are confined to either:

- members of one society, or
- people who work or live at the same premises.

Tickets must be printed with the price, together with the promoter's name and address and must state that tickets can only be issued to members. All tickets must be for the same price, so they cannot be sold at a discount (for example five for the price of four) or given away. The proceeds, less expenses, must go to the organisation or be used for prizes. The lottery can be advertised only on the organisation's or promoter's premises and tickets cannot be sent through the post. The promoter must be authorised to act by the organisation's management committee.

Society (public) lotteries

A society lottery is one promoted on behalf of an organisation wholly or mainly for one of the following reasons:

- charitable purposes
- participation in or support of athletic sports, games or cultural activities
- other purposes not for private gain or commercial undertaking.

All proceeds must go to a scheme approved by the organisation. There is no restriction on the number or frequency of lotteries.

Registration of the lottery

An organisation wishing to promote a society lottery must register with either the appropriate local registration authority (usually the local authority) or the Gaming Board.

Registration with the Gaming Board is essential if:
- the total value of tickets on sale in any one lottery will exceed £20,000, or
- the total value of tickets on sale in any one lottery, added to the value of those already sold or put on sale in all earlier lotteries in the same calendar year will exceed £250,000.

Lotteries not meeting these criteria are registered with the local authority.

Registration of the lottery manager
Under the Act anyone running a society lottery on behalf of an organisation has to obtain a **Lottery Manager's Certificate** from the Gaming Board. This does not apply if the lottery manager is an employee or member of the organisation for which the lottery is being run.

Tickets, prizes and expenses
Society lottery tickets must not cost more than £1 and all tickets must be the same price (so, for example five tickets cannot be sold for the price of four). Every ticket must specify:
- its price
- the name of the society promoting the lottery
- the promoter's name
- the date of the lottery
- the fact that the society is registered with the Gaming Board for Great Britain or, if registered with the local authority, the name of the local authority.

Society lottery tickets must not be sold to or by anyone aged under 16. They can be sold door to door but not on the street.

No prize may exceed £25,000 or 10% of the total value of the tickets sold, whichever is the greater. No more than 55% of the actual proceeds may be used to provide prizes. Prizes may be donated at a reduced cost or free of charge, but the value of any such single prize must not exceed the above limits.

Proceeds must not exceed £1 million for a single lottery or £5 million within one calendar year. Up to 35% of proceeds may be used to meet expenses without reference to the Gaming Board, and up to 80% of the proceeds can be used for prizes and expenses (when added together). The balance must be donated to the organisation.

Records
Within three months of each society lottery the promoter must submit a return to the Gaming Board or local authority, giving details of the proceeds, expenses and prizes, and showing how the balance of the amount raised was distributed. The promoter and a member of the society's management committee must sign the returns. Under the Lotteries and Amusements Act an organisation selling more than £100,000 worth of lottery tickets in any one year must submit audited accounts to the Gaming Board, together with a report prepared by a qualified auditor.

Other types of lottery
Other types of lottery covered by the Act include sweepstakes, tombolas and games where tickets with a tear open window or scratch panel are sold and cash prizes are given. These will all fall into one of the categories above.

For further details of all aspects of holding lotteries see *Lotteries and the law*, published by the Gaming Board, available from *www.gbgb.gov.uk*

Gaming machines
Gaming machines can be a good source of revenue for clubs but as some people object to them it is important to consult members before acquiring one. You will need to obtain a licence from the local magistrate. The machine can be used only by club members, can only pay out cash prizes and must not be played if non-members are on the premises. A club can have a maximum of three machines.

A notice from the firm renting out the machine must be displayed, showing how much money can be won, the minimum percentage payout and how much is retained. Only authorised people can remove money from the machine; these would usually be committee members or club employees.

A gaming machine can be used with a licence at a bazaar, fete or social as long as it is incidental to the event and none of the proceeds are going to private gain.

Check with the clerk at the magistrates court or the Gaming Board if in any doubt about the legal position, and with Customs and Excise about the VAT position of charging the machine owner for placing the machine in the club.

Amusement machines
Amusement machines also require permits from the local authority, and may have VAT implications. Coins or tokens can be won; the maximum pay out is £6 in tokens or £3 in coins.

Bingo

The **Gaming Act 1968** defines the following circumstances in which bingo can legally be played:

- if it is only one activity of a bona fide club with at least 25 members. In this case there is no need to register or obtain a licence. The admission fee can be no more than 60p, although people may stake as much as they want. All stakes must be distributed as prizes. The game cannot be advertised to the public or played on premises to which the public is admitted. There is no age limit on those who can play, but the club may set its own limit
- to charge more than 60p a day for admission, the club must register with the local licensing authority (in England and Wales the Licensing Justice). The club can charge a daily fee of up to £2 per person (on top of the stakes), but cannot advertise the game to the public. There is no limit on the stakes but all takings must be distributed as prizes. Bona fide guests (ie those not having to pay admission) may take part, but no person aged under 18 may be present in the room while bingo is being played
- if played to raise funds for a charitable or other non-profit making organisation, bingo or whist drives may be held without a licence or registration. The games can be advertised and the public admitted. The stakes and entrance fee must be no more than £4 and the total value of prizes cannot exceed £400. Proceeds, after deduction of reasonable expenses and prizes, must not be used for private gain
- if bingo is the main event, the club must have a licence and obtain a **certificate of consent** from the Gaming Board before applying for the licence from the local licensing authority.

For further information contact the Bingo Section of the Gaming Board for Great Britain (020 7306 6237/6238) or visit *www.gbgb.gov.uk*

Use of professional fundraisers

Charities' use of professional fundraisers is regulated by **Part II** of the **Charities Act 1992**. The regulations apply to fundraisers whose pay exceeds £5 per day, £500 per year or £500 for a particular fundraising venture. They do not apply to employees of the charity or to a charity's trading subsidiary, or to employees of a fundraising business.

Professional fundraisers appealing for money on behalf of a charity must have a written contract with that charity which satisfies legal regulations. Any request for funds has to be accompanied by a statement indicating who will benefit, the way in which the proceeds will be distributed and the method of calculating the fundraiser's remuneration.

Right to a refund

Anyone who gives £50 or more in response to a radio or television appeal made by a professional fundraiser using a debit or credit card will be entitled to a full refund, less reasonable administration expenses, if they decide to cancel their donation within seven days. The right to a refund must be made explicit in the appeal.

If a donor has bought goods where a percentage of the purchase price has been given to a charity, the refund is dependent on the return of the goods.

Breach of the above constitutes a criminal offence on the part of the professional fundraiser.

At the time of writing (December 2003) an independent commission was exploring models for a system of self-regulation for professional fundraisers. The draft Charities Bill is likely to include a power to introduce statutory regulation of fundraisers, should self-regulation fail.

Exempt fundraising events

Charities, and some other non-profit making bodies, are exempt from charging VAT on up to 15 fundraising events of any kind held in any one location, within a financial year. An exempt event is defined as one which is both organised and promoted primarily for the purpose of raising money, and includes those accessible through electronic communication.

There is no restriction on the number of small-scale events of any one kind, such as coffee mornings, as long as weekly gross takings for such events do not exceed £1000.

Any fundraising event that meets these criteria for VAT exemption automatically makes it exempt from tax on the profits (income tax if the organisation is a charitable trust, or corporation tax if it is an association or company). Events that do not meet these criteria may be subject to VAT and/or to tax on their profits.

For further information contact the Customs and Excise national advice service on 0845 010 9000 or visit *www.hmce.gov.uk*

Sponsored activities

Events such as sponsored walks or bicycle rides can be financially rewarding. However, finding sponsors and collecting sponsorship money can take a lot of organisation. Keep a record of the names and addresses of everyone who is being sponsored. Include the following information on sponsorship forms:

- a description of the event
- its purpose and date
- the name, address and age (if under 18) of the sponsored person
- each sponsor's name, address and amount pledged
- if the funds raised will be donated to a charity, a Gift Aid statement suitable for a sponsorship form and space for sponsors to tick if they want their donations to be treated as Gift Aid donations (for the correct wording, see the *Gift aid toolkit*, available from *www.inlandrevenue.gov.uk/charities*)
- the statement '*I certify that . . . has walked . . . miles/swum . . . lengths/danced for . . . hours*', followed by the signature of the organiser and the date.

The organiser should keep a record of the value of the sponsorship on each form and whether the money has been handed in.

It is very important to discuss with an insurance broker the insurance implications of any sponsored event, and where events involve children, to consider potential Children Act requirements. Where sponsored activities are held overseas or are intrinsically dangerous (such as parachuting) it is especially important to ensure that all insurances (see chapter 7) and consents are in order.

Charity shops and other trading

Charity shops are often run for short periods on a licence (see chapter 6) in shop premises which would otherwise be empty. The rent charged is usually low, but the organisation is responsible for rates, water charges, overheads and staffing.

Charities are not in general allowed to trade regularly. However, there are exceptions for:

- the sale of donated goods
- sales from activities which directly further the charity's primary purpose as set out in its constitutional objects (see chapter 1), for example a workshop for blind people selling products made by the beneficiaries
- sales which are incidental to the charity's primary purpose, for example, an arts charity can charge admission to its plays as primary purpose trading, and can sell ice cream and drinks to people attending the plays as incidental trading

- other sales provided the annual turnover is less than £5000, or is less than 25% of the charity's total income and less than £50,000. Note that these figures apply to turnover, not profit.

In other circumstances a charity may have to form a non-charitable subsidiary for trading purposes. For further information see the Inland Revenue booklet *Trading by charities*, IR 2001 or contact the Charities Advisory Trust (020 7794 9835).

Remember that goods or services sold by charities and other voluntary organisations may be subject to VAT. If the annual turnover of VATable goods and services sold by the organisation is more than the registration threshold (£56,000 in 2003/04) the organisation will have to register for VAT and then charge VAT to purchasers. For further information contact the Customs and Excise national advice line (0845 010 9000) Also see *Value Added Tax*, in chapter 8. It is an offence not to register for VAT and charge VAT if required to do so.

Car boot sales

Under the **Local Government (Miscellaneous Provision) Act 1982**, more than five cars or stalls constitute a market and therefore an application must be submitted to the local council at least a month before such an event. However, if all the proceeds of a car boot sale are for charitable purposes, or sales are carried out on private property with the owner's permission, the Act does not apply.

Regular events may require planning permission. If in doubt check with the local authority's planning department.

Minibuses and coaches

Organisations that own a minibus or coach may require a **Section 19 permit** or a **Public Service Vehicle (PSV) Operating Licence** if they use the vehicle for 'hire or reward'. This includes any arrangement where there is payment for the trip, even if the charge includes other items such as a meal, or the payment is treated as a donation. The rules apply to vehicles adapted to carry nine or more passengers. Application forms are available from the local Traffic Area Office, a designated body (a national voluntary organisation that can issue permits) or, in some cases, the local authority.

There is no need for a permit or licence if the organisation does not charge passengers in any way.

For further information contact the Traffic Area Network Division of the Department for Transport (*www.tan.gov.uk*) or the Community Transport Association (*www.cta.org.uk*).

Hiring to other organisations

It may be difficult for a permit holder to allow its minibus to be used by others who intend to charge passengers. Any organisation hiring the bus may need its own permit. This can be avoided if the permit holder also appoints the driver. Passengers must pay the permit holder and not the hiring organisation, although that organisation could collect the money.

Whatever arrangement is made, remember to inform your insurance company. A standard vehicle insurance policy excludes use for 'hire or reward' so the policy will need to be extended to cover this, which may greatly increase the premium. Also ensure the vehicle meets all safety requirements, and drivers are licensed to drive a vehicle of that type.

Looking after people
Health and safety

All organisations have a duty of care to employees, volunteers and others who carry out work for the organisation, service users and the general public If there is an injury (including physical injury, illness or death) or property damage caused by negligence, ie the failure to exercise reasonable care, the organisation could have to pay the user compensation. This would be covered by public liability insurance (see chapter 7) provided the organisation had informed its insurers about the activities undertaken.

However, public liability insurance only covers negligence arising from premises or non-professional activities. To ensure that the organisation is properly aware of risks and is taking all reasonable steps to minimise them, the management committee and senior staff should carry out risk assessments looking at all the risks to the organisation (not just health and safety). Consider, for example, the risks to the property of staff, users and the public; risks to money; risks arising from giving inaccurate or misleading information or advice; and risks to individuals' or the organisation's reputation. The organisation should consider, as part of its risk assessment, whether it needs public liability, professional indemnity, and/or product liability insurances, or any other insurances (see chapter 7). Any decision to take out or not to take out insurances should be made by the management committee and should be clearly minuted, along with the reasons for any decision not to take them out.

Under health and safety legislation an organisation must assess the risks to the health, safety and welfare of anyone affected by its activities, including users. If there is an accident as a result of any failure to comply with health and safety requirements, the organisation and its committee members and senior staff could be prosecuted by the Health and Safety Executive (see chapter 5).

If failure to observe health and safety requirements results in the death of a user (or anyone else), the members of the management committee could potentially be prosecuted for manslaughter. It is therefore essential for an organisation's health and safety policy to take into account the risks to users and include measures to avoid accidents.

Other public health laws apply if an organisation is running hostel accommodation or has a resident worker. For further details see *The quality of housing*, in chapter 6.

Physical restraint

Organisations that care for people who cannot always take responsibility for their own actions may in some circumstances be under a legal obligation to restrain them physically in order to protect them from injuring themselves or others.

To protect both users' and staff interests, organisations should have clear policies and procedures in place to safeguard the welfare of users and protect them from harm of all kinds. The policy should ensure that:
- staff are given guidance on:
- when physical restraint can be used, acceptable types of restraint, and the degree of force that can or should be used
- when physical restraint cannot be used and unacceptable methods. Make explicit the circumstances in which use of physical restraint will amount to gross misconduct and lead to disciplinary action
- the circumstances in which physical force should be used, the methods that can be used and how to explain reasons for restraint to the user
- staff are given regular training in defusing potentially violent situations and methods of restraint that do not involve physical contact
- any decisions to allow users to take risks as part of a care plan are carefully recorded to prevent staff being subsequently criticised if accidents occur
- all allegations of abuse are given urgent consideration and follow laid down procedures
- staff receive:
- guarantees on legal representation if they follow policies but an accident occurs
- training on safe techniques and ways of defusing tense situations

- first aid training
- care plans assess potential risks
- the organisation is insured to cover any legal expenses incurred through possible criminal prosecution or an inquest
- procedures are implemented to minimise the need for physical restraint and ensure that users are treated with respect and dignity
- safeguards are built into any procedures for using physical restraint including:
- recording use of and reasons for restraint
- interviews with users and staff to establish facts
- monitoring by senior managers of the use of restraint by individual staff and particular projects
- discussion of each incident at staff meetings
- disciplinary action in cases of obvious inappropriate use of restraint or excessive force
- a 'whistleblowing' policy enabling any user or staff member who believes that restraint is being misused to report it to senior management in confidence (see chapter 4).

National Minimum Standards

Under the **Care Standards Act 2000** organisations providing or managing a range of social care and independent health care services must register with the National Care Standards Commission* and ensure their services comply with minimum standards set by the Department of Health. Services covered by national minimum standards include:
- care homes
- domiciliary care
- children's homes
- adult placements
- voluntary adoption agencies
- independent fostering agencies
- residential family centres
- hospices.

For further information contact the National Care Standards Commission* (*www.carestandards.org.uk*).

* *The Commission for Social Care Inspection from April 2004.*

Organisations working with children may need to register with Ofsted and comply with its requirements. There are registration requirements and national standards for many other types of organisation, for example those which give advice on immigration matters or financial matters.

Abuse o

The **Sexual Offe**
young people fr
inappropriate sex

The Act makes unla
someone in a positi
(see below) and anyc
areas covered are:
- full-time education
- those detained unde
- those looked after by the local authority, whether in foster care, residential care or semi-independent accommodation
- those in a hospital (including private hospitals), a nursing home, children's home or other institution providing health and/or social care.

The two main defences are:
- if the person did not know, and could not reasonably be expected to know, that the younger party was under 18 or that they were in a relationship of trust with the young person
- if the parties were married to each other before the sexual relationship took place. As a matter of good practice, however, it would not be expected that those who were married would remain in a relationship of trust.

Human Rights Act

The **Human Rights Act 1998** incorporates the European Convention of Human Rights (ECHR) into domestic law. It includes the following key provisions:
- the right to life
- the right to respect for private and family life, home and correspondence
- the right not to be subjected to torture or inhuman treatment
- the right to a fair trial
- freedom of thought, conscience and religion
- freedom of expression
- freedom of assembly and of association
- the right to marry and found a family
- prohibition of discrimination in the enjoyment of Convention rights
- the right to peaceful enjoyment of possessions
- the right to education.

The Act makes it unlawful for public authorities, including private bodies that carry out public functions, to act in a way that is incompatible with the rights and freedoms guaranteed by the ECHR.

...with public functions

...anisations have a contract or service ...local or health authorities, and so may be ...to be carrying out public functions for the ...ses of the Human Rights Act.

Although the *functions* determine whether the organisation is a 'public authority', it is the relationship with the individual that will come under scrutiny when the Act is applied.

Implications

An organisation that breaches the Human Rights Act would be liable to remedies available in the courts. The level of damages awarded by UK courts must be commensurate with those awarded by the Court of Human Rights, which usually range between £5000 and £15,000.

Even if most voluntary organisations are relatively unlikely to be defined as carrying out public functions, they should build the principles of human rights into their policies and procedures to help develop and implement good practice and improve attitudes and behaviour towards people they work with and help.

For further information see *Charities and human rights* (OG 71 B3), available from *www.charitycommission.gov.uk*, and the Department for Constitutional Affairs' Human Rights Unit (*www.dca.gov.uk/hract*).

Chapter 10:
Closing down

Related chapters
Chapter 1 – Legal structures; charity trading
Chapter 3 – Self-employed workers
Chapter 4 – Reorganisation; redundancy
Chapter 6 – Premises; equipment leases
Chapter 9 – Contracts

There are many reasons why a voluntary organisation might close down. For example, it may have achieved its goals and decide to stop operating, or it may have no choice and be forced into closure through lack of funds. Whatever the legal status, facing closure becomes extremely serious if an organisation cannot meet itfs financial obligations.

There are certain procedures to follow when closing down. This is especially true if an organisation employs staff, rents or owns property, leases equipment and/or is a registered charity, a company or an industrial and provident society.

The Charity Commission publishes two useful documents: *Managing financial difficulties and insolvency in charities* (CC12) and *Small charities guidance – winding up* (SCU1) available from *www.charitycommission.gov.uk* or 01823 345427. Companies House has produced a booklet on winding up a company limited by guarantee, *Liquidation and insolvency* (GBW1), available on *www.companieshouse.gov.uk*. The government's Insolvency Service website *www.insolvency.gov.uk* includes information about insolvency matters and redundancy payments.

A note of caution: this chapter is not a substitute for expert legal and financial advice. When facing closure, professional expertise is essential.

Is closure necessary?

An organisation should consistently monitor its financial position to spot potential problems as early as possible. If the answer to any of the following questions is 'yes', then the organisation is running into financial difficulties, and should either start thinking of closure or implement a rescue plan.
- Is there an unanticipated overdraft?
- Is expenditure greater than income, with inadequate reserves available to cover the shortfall?
- Are there any large debts it has difficulty in paying?
- Is it regularly having to dip into reserves without being able to top them up?
- Is future income at considerable risk?

The next step is to work out the exact financial position to discover how long the organisation can remain solvent.

Liabilities: Forecast the likely expenses over the next few months. These could include:
- wages and employer's national insurance and pension contributions
- rent and rates for premises and rent on leased equipment
- the direct costs of providing the organisation's activities and services
- overheads, such as electricity, water, insurances, telephone and building repairs
- administrative costs, such as stationery, post and travel
- bank charges and auditor's fees
- VAT payments, if registered for VAT
- Inland Revenue payments.

Also consider the actual costs of closure. These include:
- legal and financial advice
- the legal fees for disposing of a lease
- any outstanding rent for the remaining period of leases on equipment and premises
- the legal and accountancy fees for winding up a limited company or an industrial and provident society (see *Winding up*, page 209)
- redundancy payments (see chapter 4)
- any outstanding holiday, maternity, paternity and adoption payments (see chapter 4).

Assets: Calculate the organisation's assets and likely income. These could include:
- money in the bank and cash in hand
- money owed to the organisation
- the realistic resale value of stock, for example unsold publications
- the realistic resale value of fixed assets such as land, buildings, furniture, equipment and vehicles.

Examine any restrictions attached to the assets. Many funders do not allow organisations to sell premises or equipment bought with their grants. Check whether the constitution includes restrictions on selling assets. Some sales of land and buildings by charities are regulated by the **Charities Act 1993** (see *Reducing costs of premises*, page 207).

Solvency and insolvency: The statement of assets and liabilities will show whether an organisation is insolvent, ie if its total assets are worth less than its total liabilities or it cannot pay its debts when they are due.

Sometimes the expression **technical insolvency** is used. An organisation can be described as being technically insolvent if either of the following apply.
- Its liabilities exceed its assets but it can still pay immediate debts. If there is a reasonable prospect of the assets becoming worth more than the liabilities, the organisation will not have to be wound up as being insolvent.
- Its assets are worth more than its liabilities but it has no ready cash to pay debts that are due immediately. If assets can be sold to pay the debts, or adequate funds can be borrowed, or creditors (the people to whom money is owed) are prepared to wait until cash is available, the organisation need not be wound up as being insolvent.

Committee members are personally responsible for the debts incurred by **unincorporated organisations** (unincorporated associations and trusts). Former committee members can also be liable if the debt was incurred while they were on the committee. An unincorporated organisation facing insolvency should take financial advice immediately. Individual committee members may consider taking their own, independent advice.

In an **incorporated organisation** (company or industrial and provident society), the committee members generally have limited liability (see *Liability of committee members*, in chapter 1) and are not liable for the organisation's debts. However, if the organisation has no reasonable prospect of being able to pay its debts when they are due or of being able to negotiate realistic repayment dates, the committee members must immediately seek advice from an insolvency practitioner (see *Incorporated organisations*, page 210). The practitioner will advise whether the organisation should stop trading immediately, start running down its activities, or implement a rescue plan.

Committee members may lose their normal protection against personal liability and be held personally responsible for the organisation's debts if they are involved in wrongful trading, that is:
- they continue activities against the advice of the insolvency practitioner, or
- they fail to call in an insolvency practitioner as soon as the committee members are, or should have been aware of the pending insolvency.

It is essential to identify any financial difficulties early as it may be possible to prevent insolvency and reduce committee members' risk of personal liability. Immediately seek advice from an accountant or solicitor if there are any concerns whatsoever about the organisation's financial position. Such advice should be in writing, and any remedial action suggested should be monitored, along with budgets and cashflows. The management committee should be prepared to meet more often, and must minute all decisions.

An organisation heading for insolvency has two choices. It can either implement a rescue plan to ensure that it remains solvent, or it has to wind up. The next section examines ways of rescuing an organisation in financial difficulties.

Planning for survival
This section looks at ways of reducing costs, increasing income and raising capital, and describes how to prioritise in order to make decisions.

Reducing staff costs
Reducing costs will involve difficult choices. As staff costs often form the largest proportion of expenditure, it is likely that the greatest savings can be made through redundancies or by changing terms and conditions. Although the committee is responsible for these decisions, it is essential to consult staff throughout the planning process, even if redundancy and redeployment are unnecessary, since restrictions on expenditure will affect working conditions and require staff cooperation. Consultation with staff or their representatives may be a legal requirement if redundancies are proposed (see *Notifying those involved*, in chapter 4).

Although redundancy is an obvious way of reducing costs, there may be other options. These include:
- restricting recruitment
- redeploying staff (but providing retraining if necessary)
- offering early retirement (making sure that there is no loss of pension rights)

- introducing short-time working (reducing hours), if this is allowed under the contract of employment or with the agreement of staff
- laying off staff temporarily, if this is allowed under the contract of employment, in the hope of obtaining new funding. People who are either laid off (ie receive no wages) for four weeks in a row or put on short time (ie receive less than half a week's pay) for six weeks in any thirteen, may claim redundancy payment. The claim must be in writing and employers may refuse payment if they believe they can offer at least 13 weeks' work within four weeks
- outsourcing a specific piece of work (for example writing a report or producing a newsletter) to a self-employed worker. This may be a cheaper option as the employer no longer pays costs such as employer's national insurance and pension contributions. There will also be savings on overheads such as training, holidays and sick pay. However, a self-employed worker's daily rate is invariably higher than those on an organisation's payroll, so consider the financial implications carefully. For further details see *Self-employed people*, in chapter 3. There may be particular problems in making an employee redundant and then outsourcing to that person the same work they were doing as an employee.

Chapter 4 looks at the legal rights of staff where reorganisation is necessary and results in redeployment, and describes the law and good practice governing redundancy procedures.

Reducing costs of premises

Premises can form another large element of expenditure. Moving to cheaper accommodation or sharing or subletting existing premises may reduce the costs, although there may be substantial upfront costs. Chapter 6 looks at the implications of these options in more detail. It also describes the process to be followed when disposing of property.

Reducing other costs

Equipment

It may be possible to sell equipment both to save on running costs and to raise capital. Before doing so establish who owns each item and any restrictions on selling, for example some funders attach conditions on grant aid which prevent organisations from selling off equipment purchased with a grant.

Once a company or industrial and provident society has become insolvent it can only sell equipment (or anything

else) if authorised to do so by the insolvency practitioner. As an insolvent organisation has a general responsibility to try to do its best for its creditors, the equipment must be sold for the highest possible price.

Another possibility is to give equipment to other organisations, thereby saving on running costs. A charity must give equipment to another charity with similar objects. Check the organisation's constitution and funders' restrictions to see whether this option is permitted.

Check the terms of the agreement of any equipment bought on credit or hire purchase. Under some credit agreements the purchaser merely rents the equipment until the payments are completed; with others it owns the purchases immediately. Also check warranties; they may be invalidated when the equipment is sold or transferred.

If equipment is rented, check the terms of the lease (see chapter 6). It may be for a fixed term, in which case the organisation could be liable for the rent of the whole period. As with premises it is possible – although unlikely – that the owner will be prepared to accept an early termination of the lease or allow it to be transferred.

Reducing administrative costs

Ways of cutting administrative costs include reducing telephone use, using second class post (or e-mail instead of post), reducing staff travel, limiting the use of external printing facilities and restricting the use of external consultants. It may be tempting to reduce costs associated with professionals such as auditors, accountants and solicitors, but remember that an organisation facing insolvency is likely to need more, rather than less, professional advice.

An organisation covering a wide geographical area could make savings by using the telephone, including conference calls, or through e-mail or faxes, rather than getting people together in one place for a meeting. The constitution must allow decisions to be made in this way, but if not, they could be made provisionally and ratified at the next proper meeting (see *Running the organisation*, in chapter 2).

Increasing income

As well as reducing running costs, there are ways of increasing income. The Directory of Social Change publishes a range of books on fundraising. Funding information services throughout the country can advise on funding sources and making applications. Contact your local council for voluntary service or rural community council for details. *FunderFinder*, the computerised database of grant making trusts and other funding sources, has information on funders, including their catchment areas and activities supported. A number of organisations – including the London Voluntary Service Council, other councils for voluntary service and the Directory of Social Change – have copies available for use, usually on an appointment basis.

The following possibilities may be appropriate, although most need to be implemented long before the organisation is facing possible insolvency and closure.

- **Trust funding**, particularly for specific work such as publications, conferences, research or an innovative project.
- **Business sponsorship**, particularly for pieces of work that will give the sponsor some publicity, for example publications or conferences. Take advice about the potential VAT and tax implications of this type of sponsorship.
- **Introducing or increasing charges** for membership or services. Although increased costs may discourage those most in need of services, it may be possible to introduce a tiered charging structure.
- **Improving marketing**. Some organisations may be able to raise substantial sums by marketing their services more effectively. As well as increasing income, an expanded market means an organisation is reaching many more people and improving its service delivery. But remember that any marketing will almost certainly incur extra costs. It is also important to be realistic about how much extra demand an organisation can cope with – especially at a time when it may have to wind down.
- **Putting funding on a more secure basis**. It may be possible to get a two or three-year commitment from funders, or to change from grant funding to contractual funding (which is legally more secure, provided the organisation complies with its side of the contract).
- **Setting up a profit-making subsidiary**. Some skills within an organisation could be provided on a commercial basis. A charity might have to set up a subsidiary company that transfers its profits to the charity (see *Trading*, in chapter 1).
- **Launching an emergency appeal**. Charity trustees must ensure that donors are aware that their funds may be used to pay off debts.

Merger

A further option is to amalgamate with, or be taken over by another organisation. The government intends to introduce legislation in the forthcoming draft Charities Bill to facilitate mergers between charities. The Charity Commission has endorsed a further recommendation that it should provide specific advice to enable mergers, and is examining ways of delivering advice, possibly through a dedicated mergers unit.

However, the Commission warns that merger should not be pursued primarily to keep a charity going, and that beneficiaries' best interests should be of central concern. It also advises that if a merger is initiated to rescue one or more of the parties, trustees of the stable or solvent organisation must ensure that this does not present an unjustifiable risk. The Commission says that trustees considering a merger should ensure that the proposed partners carry out an appropriate disclosure or due diligence exercise, proportionate to the size and nature of the merger.

For further details see the Charity Commission booklet *Collaborative working and mergers* (RS4).

It is essential to get legal advice if considering a merger, and in particular to be clear about whether the **Transfer of Undertakings (Protection of Employment) Regulations 1981** will apply (see chapter 4). It is also important to think carefully about the implications of bringing together two organisations that may have very different values, priorities, ways of working and organisational cultures.

The rescue plan

Prioritising objectives and services should be an integral aspect of managing an organisation but is particularly important when services may have to be reduced.

There is no single method of prioritising services to cut costs, but gathering the following information will help make decisions:

- services that must be provided under the terms of a contract where failure to do so could lead to breach of contract claims against the organisation
- the services, in order of priority, that must be provided to meet the organisation's objectives
- the best estimate of the cost of each service
- possible additional income from and/or for each service
- the additional cost of, and possible income from any new service
- any other methods of generating income, the amount that might be raised and the expenditure, including staff time, involved
- ways of reducing the costs of premises, equipment and administration, possible savings and the effect that any changes would have on services
- savings that could be made by freezing recruitment, redeployment, short-time working and redundancy.

Staff will almost certainly be affected by any decision to cut costs. It is therefore essential to consult them throughout the process of drawing up a rescue plan.

Winding up

Information and advice
The process of winding up an organisation will depend upon whether it unincorporated or incorporated, and whether it is solvent or insolvent. It is therefore imperative to get professional information and advice about the appropriate winding up procedures for your organisation.

Notification
Once a formal decision has been made to close an organisation down you should inform the following:
- the employees, employee representatives and unions (see *Redundancy*, in chapter 4)
- the organisation's accountant and auditor
- the organisation's solicitor
- the organisation's bank manager
- the Charity Commission, if appropriate
- the registration body, if appropriate (Companies House or the Financial Services Authority)
- the organisation's funder(s)
- past and current committee members
- anyone with a fixed charge or mortgage over the organisation's property
- all creditors
- service users.

In some cases notification will be the task of the appointed insolvency practitioner.

Solvent organisations
A solvent organisation may decide to close down, for example because it has achieved its goals, or because it wants to close before it becomes insolvent. If it can pay all its debts, including redundancy payments and the cost of disposing of premises and equipment, there are no restrictions on who can be paid during the closing down process. The management committee should select people to take responsibility for closing down the organisation and ensure that relevant agencies are informed.

The organisation should still take advice to ensure that all necessary procedures have been carried out thoroughly and correctly and that all legally required notifications have been made.

Unincorporated organisations
The procedure for winding up an unincorporated association will be set down in its constitution. The procedure would probably require a resolution agreeing to the dissolution to be passed at a general meeting. The constitution may also state how any balance or remaining assets should be distributed if the organisation is solvent.

A solvent organisation will need to consider how to transfer any assets remaining after it has paid its debts. The decision should be made at the meeting that formally winds it up. Most constitutions allow the committee or a general meeting to select another organisation to which the assets can be transferred. Any charity assets must be transferred to another charity with similar objects.

Before an organisation is wound up, it will need to prepare final accounts and submit them to the final meeting for approval. Once the organisation has been wound up, it should close the bank account and destroy headed notepaper. Trustees of registered charities must inform the Charity Commission if the organisation ceases to exist. Small, unincorporated charities whose income was not more than £10,000 and whose assets were valued at no more than £200,000 should send to the Charity Commission:
- a completed **declaration form – SCU2** (available from the Charity Commission), or
- a copy of the resolution or minutes of the meeting at which the decision to dissolve the charity was taken, certified by a trustee, the secretary or clerk.

The Charity Commission has published guidance for winding up a small unincorporated charity. See *Small charities guidance – winding up* (SCU1) available from *www.charitycommission.gov.uk*

Unincorporated charities with **income or expenditure above £10,000** should submit to the Charity Commission:
- a copy of the resolution to wind up the charity
- the final set of audited accounts
- a statement of the final distribution of assets if this is not shown in the accounts (this should be signed by the trustees and, preferably, also the external auditor).

After a charity has been wound up, the trustees have to make sure that its accounts and records are preserved for at least six years. If the property has been transferred to another charity, the Commission recommends asking the recipient charity to hold the records. Otherwise trustees may be able to arrange for records to be held by a former trustee, a solicitor or accountant, another local charity or an umbrella body.

Incorporated organisations

A solvent **company** can be wound up in a number of ways.

Voluntary striking off

If a company has been operating for less than three months it can apply to the Registrar of Companies to be struck off and dissolved. The advantages of this approach are that it is inexpensive (£10 in 2003) and the company may be restored in the future. Organisations should send **Form 652a**, signed by the majority of members, to the Registrar of Companies. Copies of the form should be sent to other directors (committee members), all company members, creditors and prospective creditors (including the Inland Revenue), employees, and managers and trustees of any employee pension fund. All VAT registered companies must notify the relevant VAT office. The Registrar advertises the proposed striking off, and if no one objects the company is struck off three months later.

Members' voluntary winding up

If the voluntary striking off procedure is not appropriate, the members must pass a special resolution for the company to be wound up voluntarily. In some cases the constitution may specify that a company is to be dissolved at a particular time. If so, members must pass an ordinary resolution. Notice of the special resolution for voluntary winding-up of the company must be published in the Gazette (published daily by HMSO) within 14 days of the general meeting. The company must also send a copy of the declaration and the special resolution to the Registrar of Companies within 15 days of the general meeting. As soon as the resolution is passed, the company ceases to operate apart from activities required to wind up.

The process of winding up is managed by a liquidator, using the following procedure:

- A majority of the company's directors must make a statutory **declaration of solvency** in the five weeks before a resolution to wind up the company is passed. This will state that the directors have made a full inquiry into the company's affairs and that they believe the company will be able to pay its debts in full within 12 months of the start of the winding-up. The declaration will include a statement of the company's assets and liabilities as at the latest practicable date before making the declaration.
- An insolvency practitioner is appointed at a general meeting, usually the meeting that passes the resolution.
- The insolvency practitioner and members decide on the disposal of assets. In practice, most constitutions will require these to be given to another organisation with similar objects.

- The insolvency practitioner presents a report and accounts to a general meeting, and submits these to the Registrar of Companies and the company's creditors.
- The company is dissolved three months later.

A solvent **industrial and provident society** (IPS) can be wound up in the following ways.

Instrument of dissolution

An instrument of dissolution must be signed by at least 75% of an IPS's members.

Amalgamation

Alternatively, many choose to amalgamate with another IPS or company. This creates a new organisation.

Transfer of engagements

A third option is a transfer of engagements to another IPS or company. The organisation being transferred to continues and the transferred IPS is generally wound up.

Insolvent organisations

If a rescue plan is not viable then closure is probably inevitable, particularly if the organisation is insolvent. If, by ceasing activities, an organisation can pay off all its debts, it could consider maintaining a legal existence. For example a company can remain an inactive shell, and an unincorporated association can retain a steering committee, ready to start again if new funding becomes available. The Charity Commission will want to be assured that any registered charity it is still fulfilling its objectives.

Once a decision has been taken to wind up an insolvent organisation, it must not interfere with its remaining assets, including money in the bank, cash in hand, stocks, equipment and possibly the premises. Also, an insolvent organisation must not pay any sums to its creditors unless authorised by the insolvency practitioner, as this could be **fraudulent preference**.

In practice, this means an organisation cannot pay any money into an overdrawn account, allow any equipment to be moved from the premises, or even pay staff wages. The organisation should, however, continue to collect any money it is owed, but may only put it into an account that is in credit.

Each day the organisation remains in its premises or employs staff it is incurring debts that it may be unable to pay. The creditors would include the utility companies, phone companies and the landlord.

The organisation must keep records of decisions and actions, to protect its committee members against charges of wrongful trading or fraudulent preference.

Unincorporated organisations

Legal advice is essential if an unincorporated organisation becomes insolvent. Any liabilities incurred can be treated as personal liabilities for its management committee members (see *Who is liable for debts*, page 212). There is no legal procedure for winding up unincorporated associations, but they are generally advised to pay debts in the same order of preference as companies (as set out in the Insolvency Acts).

The management committee should select people to take responsibility for closing down the organisation, for example the chair, finance officer and treasurer.

If the organisation is in debt, it may be best to call a creditors' meeting to see whether they will accept a share of what remains. This should be done only with specialist legal advice from accountants and lawyers who understand the voluntary sector.

Incorporated organisations

It is important to realise that a company or industrial and provident society (IPS) does not become insolvent when it has no more money. It becomes insolvent at the point when the directors know, or should have realised, that the organisation has no reasonable prospect of meeting its financial obligations when they are due.

Under the **Insolvency Act 1986** an insolvent company or IPS must appoint an **insolvency practitioner** (an individual – usually an accountant or solicitor – licensed under the Act to carry out liquidations). The practitioner will decide whether the organisation should cease operating and will notify the appropriate people and organisations (see *Notification*, below). Once the liquidator is appointed, the committee members lose their powers completely; the liquidator makes all crucial decisions. The organisation must cease carrying out its business from the date of the resolution to wind up except where carrying on the business is beneficial to the winding up. The liquidator will decide this.

An insolvent incorporated organisation can be wound up by:
- company voluntary arrangement
- administrative orders
- creditors' voluntary liquidation
- using the courts to appoint the Official Receiver (compulsory liquidation).

Company voluntary arrangements

A company voluntary arrangement (CVA) is a procedure whereby a company owing money comes to an arrangement with its creditors about how it will repay its debts.

The CVA may be proposed by:
- the administrator, if there is an administration order (see below)
- the liquidator, if the company is being wound up
- the company directors, in other circumstances.

When the directors have proposed the arrangement, they appoint an insolvency practitioner as nominee to supervise the arrangement. The insolvency practitioner will report to the court within 28 days on whether, in their opinion, it is necessary to call meetings of the company and of its creditors.

If a creditors' meeting is held, the arrangement must be supported by at least 75% by value of all creditors voting in person or by proxy. Once approved, it binds all creditors who had notice of the meeting, whether or not they voted for it.

Once agreement is reached, the nominee becomes the supervisor with responsibility for implementing the arrangement.

Administration orders

An administration order is a court order made to appoint an administrator to manage the company's affairs. Its aim is to save a failing company, approve a voluntary arrangement, agree a compromise arrangement or get a better price for the company's assets when it is liquidated.

The company itself, its directors or one or more of its current or prospective creditors can make a petition for an administration order. The court appoints an administrator, who becomes responsible for managing the company's property and affairs with the approval of the company's creditors.

Creditors' voluntary liquidation

In this case the company's members pass an extraordinary resolution at a general meeting saying they cannot continue operating because of liabilities and that it is advisable to wind up. Within 14 days of this meeting, the company calls a meeting of all its creditors and presents them with a statement of affairs. Notice of the meeting must be sent to the creditors at least seven days beforehand. Also, the directors must prepare a statement of affairs for the meeting, and appoint one of themselves to preside over it.

The creditors now in effect own the organisation's assets, and must decide how they are to be distributed. To do this they appoint a liquidator and agree a fee. As with a members' voluntary liquidation, the liquidator must be a qualified insolvency practitioner. Alternatively, the creditors may petition the court to appoint the Official Receiver as the liquidator. Once the assets have been distributed, the liquidator will call a general meeting of the creditors and members to report on the liquidation.

Compulsory liquidation
Compulsory liquidation of a company is when a court orders the company to be wound up.

The following can also petition the court to appoint the Official Receiver, who will decide whether the company should be wound up:
- the company itself
- the company's directors or one or more members
- the Secretary of State for Trade and Industry
- the Financial Services Authority
- the Official Receiver.

An accountant should prepare a statement of affairs, which analyses the organisation's history and details its assets, liabilities and debts, within 14 days of the appointment of the Official Receiver. A liquidator is then appointed. This could be the Official Receiver or another person chosen by the creditors.

Liability for debts
The final responsibility for debts depends on the organisation's legal structure (see chapter 1).

Incorporated organisations
If the organisation is registered as a company limited by guarantee or an industrial and provident society (IPS), then the organisation, rather than the members of the management committee, is responsible for the debts. In companies limited by guarantee, members are liable only up to the value of the guarantee set out in the memorandum of association (usually £1 or £5). In IPSs they will have to pay only the amount due on any shares (usually £1).

However, committee members who carry on running a company or IPS when they know it is insolvent could be found guilty of **wrongful trading** under the **Insolvency Act 1986**. The Act says that if a company or IPS is wound up because it is insolvent, committee members can be personally liable for any outstanding organisational debts if they carry on its activities after they knew, or ought to have known that there was no reasonable prospect of avoiding insolvency. Committee members could also be found guilty of **fraudulent preference** if they allow an insolvent company or IPS to pay debts without following the very strict order of preference set out in the Insolvency Acts.

Individuals who back a loan with a personal guarantee remain responsible for its repayment, even if the organisation is incorporated. Likewise, individuals who have guaranteed payment of rent or equipment under a lease will remain personally responsible for payments.

Unincorporated organisations
An unincorporated organisation does not have a separate legal existence independent of its members. This means it cannot enter into any financial or legal commitments in its own right, instead the members themselves – or more commonly the committee members – have to act on behalf of the organisation. So if the organisation cannot pay its debts, a creditor is entitled to bring a court case against those responsible for authorising transactions to recover the money owed – usually the current and/or past members of the committee.

A committee member cannot avoid liability by resigning before the organisation runs into debt.

In practice committee members are not often held personally liable for an organisation's debts – either because they have not allowed the organisation to get into debt, or because they are able to negotiate with creditors to waive the debts or can raise funds to cover the debts. But committee members should not depend on debts being waived or adequate funds being raised. They should ensure the organisation does not make long-term financial commitments unless it has long-term financial security, and should closely monitor financial reports and be sure they understand the organisation's current and long-term financial position.

Contacts

Sandy Adirondack
39 Gabriel House
Odessa Street
London SE16 7HQ
www.sandy-a.dircon.co.uk/legal.htm

ACAS
08457 47 47 47 (helpline)
08456 06 1600 (textphone)
08702 42 90 90 (publications orders)
www.acas.org.uk

Advice^UK
12th floor
New London Bridge House
25 London Bridge Street
London SE1 9ST
020 7407 4070
general@adviceuk.org.uk
www.adviceuk.org.uk

Age Positive Team
Department for Work and Pensions
Room W8d
Moorfoot
Sheffield S1 4PQ
agepositive@dwp.gsi.gov.uk
www.agepositive.gov.uk

Amicus
33-37 Moreland Street
London EC1V 8JA
020 7505 3000
www.amicustheunion.org

Angal Collecting Boxes and Devices
Building A, 91 Ewell Road
Surbiton
Surrey KT6 6AH
020 8390 9393
sales@angal.co.uk
www.angal.co.uk

ASH (Action on Smoking and Health)
102-108 Clifton Street
London EC2A 4HW
020 7739 5902
www.ash.org.uk

British Insurance Brokers' Association
14 Bevis Marks
London EC3A 7NT
020 7623 9043
enquiries@biba.org.uk
www.biba.org.uk

British Standards Institute
bsonline@techindex.co.uk
http://bsonline.techindex.co.uk

Centre for Accessible Environments
Nutmeg House
60 Gainsford Street
London SE1 2NY
020 7357 8182
info@cae.org.uk
www.cae.org.uk

Charities Advisory Trust
Radius Works, Back Lane
London NW3 1HL
020 7794 9835
people@charitiesadvisorytrust.co.uk
www.charitiesadvisorytrust.co.uk

Charities Digest
www.charitycoice.co.uk/orderbook.htm

Charity Commission
Harmsworth House
13-15 Bouverie Street
London EC4Y 8DP
0870 333 0123
0870 333 0125 (textphone)
01823 345427 (publications)
enquiries@charitycommission.gsi.gov.uk
www.charity-commission.gov.uk

Registration enquiries — under £10,000
20 Kings Parade
Queens Dock
Liverpool LS3 4DQ

Registration enquiries — £10,000 plus
Woodfield House
Taunton
Somerset TA1 4BL

Charity Law Association
charitylaw@aol.com
www.charitylawassociation.org.uk

Commission for Racial Equality
St Dunstan's House
201-211 Borough High Street
London SE1 1GZ
0870 240 3697
info@cre.gov.uk
www.cre.gov.uk

Community Development Foundation
60 Highbury Grove
London N5 2AG
020 7226 5375
admin@cdf.org.uk
www.cdf.org.uk

Community Fund
Camelford House
89 Albert Embankment
London SE1 7UF
020 7587 6609
020 7587 6620 (minicom)
www.community-fund.org.uk

Community Matters
12-20 Baron Street
London N1 9LL
020 7837 7887
communitymatters@
communitymatters.org.uk
www.communitymatters.org.uk

Community Recycling Network
Trelawny House
Surrey Street
Bristol BS2 8PN
0117 942 0142
info@crn.org.uk
www.crn.org.uk

Community Transport Association
Highbank
Halton Street, Hyde
Cheshire SK14 2NY
0870 774 3586
CTAUK@CommunityTransport.com
www.communitytransport.com

Companies House
Crown Way
Maindy
Cardiff CF4 3UZ
0870 33 33 636
enquiries@companies-house.gov.uk
www.companies-house.gov.uk

Criminal Records Bureau
PO Box 110
Liverpool L3 6ZZ
0870 90 90 811
0870 90 90 344 (textphone)
www.crb.gov.uk

Contacts

Department for Constitutional Affairs
Selborne House
54-60 Victoria Street
London SW1E 6QW
020 7210 8614
general.queries@dca.gsi.gov.uk
www.dca.gov.uk/

Department for Work and Pensions
Correspondence Unit
Room 540
The Adelphi
1-11 John Adam Street
London WC2N 6HT
020 7712 2171
www.dwp.gov.uk

Department of Health
Richmond House
79 Whitehall
London SW1A 2NL
020 7210 4850
020 7210 5025 (textphone)
dhmail@doh.gsi.gov.uk
www.doh.gov.uk

Department of Trade and Industry
DTI Enquiry Unit
1 Victoria Street
London SW1H 0ET
020 7215 5000
020 7215 6740 (textphone)
dti.enquiries@dti.gsi.gov.uk
www.dti.gov.uk

Directory of Social Change
24 Stephenson Way
London NW1 2DP
020 7391 4800
020 7209 5151 (publications)
info@dsc.org.uk
books@dsc.org.uk
www.dsc.org.uk

Disability Rights Commission Helpline
Freepost MID 02164
Stratford upon Avon
CV37 9BR
08457 622 633
08457 622 644(textphone)

Disabled Living Foundation
380-384 Harrow Road
London W9 2HU
0845 130 9177 (helpline)
020 7432 8009 (textphone)
www.dlf.org.uk

Energy Saving Trust
21 Dartmouth Street
London SW1H 9BP
020 7222 0101
info@est.co.uk
www.est.org.uk

Environment and Energy Helpline
0800 585 794

Equal Opportunities Commission
Arndale House
Arndale Centre
Manchester M4 3EQ
0845 601 5901
info@eoc.org.uk
www.eoc.org.uk

Financial Services Authority
25 The North Colonnade
Canary Wharf
London E14 5HS
0845 606 1234
consumerhelp@fsa.gov.uk
www.fsa.gov.uk

Funder Finder
65 Raglan Road
Leeds LS2 9DZ
0113 2433008
www.funderfinder.org.uk

Gaming Board for Great Britain
Berkshire House
168-173 High Holborn
London WC1V 7AA
020 7306 6200
www.gbgb.org.uk

Gift Aid helpline
0845 3020203

HMSO
www.hmso.gov.uk

Home Office
50 Queen Anne's Gate
London SW1H 9AT
0870 000 1585 (public enquiry team)
020 7273 3476 (textphone)
public.enquiries@homeoffice.gsi.gov.uk
www.homeoffice.gov.uk

HSE Books
01787 881165

HSE Infoline
Caerphilly Business Park
Caerphilly CF83 3GG
08701 545500
02920 808537 (textphone)
hseinformationservices@natbrit.com
www.hse.gov.uk

Information Commissioner
Wycliffe House
Water Lane
Wilmslow
Cheshire SK9 5AF
01625 545740
mail@ico.gsi.gov.uk
www.informationcommissioner.gov.uk

Inland Revenue Charities Helpline
www.inlandrevenue.gov.uk/charities
0845 3020203

Inland Revenue Employers' Helpline
0845 7 143 143
0845 602 1380 (textphone)

Inland Revenue National Insurance Contributions Office
www.inlandrevenue.gov.uk/nic

Inland Revenue OrderLine
0845 7 646 646

Joint Council for the Welfare of Immigrants
115 Old Street
London EC1V 9JR
020 7251 8708
info@jcwi.org.uk
www.jcwi.org.uk

LASA
Universal House
88-94 Wentworth Street
London E1 7SA
020 7377 1226
info@lasa.org.uk
www.lasa.org.uk

London Voluntary Service Council
356 Holloway Road
London N7 6PA
020 7700 8107
lvsc@lvsc.org.uk
publications@lvsc.org.uk
www.actionlink.org.uk/lvsc

National Association of Councils for Voluntary Service
177 Arundel Street
Sheffield S1 2NU
0114 278 6636
0114 278 7025 (textphone)
nacvs@nacvs.org.uk
www.nacvs.org.uk

The National Centre for Volunteering
Regent's Wharf
8 All Saints Street
London N1 9RL
020 7520 8900
Volunteering@thecentre.org.uk
www.volunteering.org.uk

National Council for Voluntary Organisations (NCVO)
Regent's Wharf
8 All Saints Street
London N1 9RL
020 7713 6161
0800 2 798 798 (helpline)
0800 01 88 111 (textphone)
www.ncvo-vol.org.uk

Publications
NCVO, PO Box 5001
Manchester M60 3SW

Occupational Pensions Regulatory Authority
Invicta House, Trafalgar Place
Brighton BN1 4DW
helpdesk@opra.gov.uk
www.opra.gov.uk

Office of the Deputy Prime Minister
26 Whitehall
London SW1A 2WH
020 7944 4400
www.odpm.gov.uk

ODPM free literature
PO Box 236
Wetherby
West Yorkshire LS23 7NB
0870 1226 236
0870 1207 405 (textphone)
odpm@twotenpress.net

Office of the Pensions Advisory Service
11 Belgrave Road
London SW1V 1RB
0845 6012923
enquiries@opas.org.uk
www.opas.org.uk

The Pensions Trust
6 Canal Street
Leeds LS11 5BQ
0113 234 5500
www.thepensionstrust.org.uk

Planning Aid
Unit 319, The Custard Factory
Gibb Street
Birmingham B9 4AA
0121 765 5282
planaidcoord@rtpi.org.uk
www.rtpi.org.uk/planning-advice

Quit
Ground floor, 211 Old Street
London EC1V 9NR
020 7251 1551
0800 00 22 00 (helpline)
stopsmoking@quit.org.uk
www.quit.org.uk

Refugee Council
Bondway House
3-9 Bondway
London SW8 1SJ
020 7346 6777 (advice line)
020 7820 3087 (infoline)
info@refugeecouncil.org.uk
www.refugeecouncil.org.uk

Registrar of Companies
see Companies House

RoSPA
Edgbaston Park
353 Bristol Road
Birmingham B5 7ST
0121 248 2000
help@rospa.co.uk
www.rospa.co.uk

Scottish Council of Voluntary Organisations
The Mansfield
Traquair Centre
15 Mansfield Plane
Edinburgh EH3 6BB
0131 556 3882
0131 557 6483 (textphone)
www.scvo.org.uk

Shap Working Party
PO Box 38580
London SW1P 3XF
020 7898 1494
www.shap.org

The Stationery Office
0870 600 5522
www.tso.co.uk

Transport and General Workers' Union
Transport House, 128 Theobald's Road
London WC1X 8TN
020 7611 2500
www.tgwu.org.uk

TUC
Congress House, Great Russell Street
London WC1B 3LS
020 7636 4030
www.tuc.org.uk

Unison
1 Mabledon Place
London WC1H 9AJ
0845 355 0835
www.unison.org.uk

Voluntary Voice
see London Voluntary Service Council

Wales Council for Voluntary Action
Baltic House, Mount Stuart Square
Cardiff CF10 5FH
0870 607 1666
029 2043 1702 (textphone)
help@wcva.org.uk
www.wcva.org.uk

Waste Watch
96 Tooley Street
London SE1 2TH
020 7089 2100
info@wastewatch.org.uk
www.wastewatch.org.uk

Waste Watch Wasteline
0870 243 0136
www.wasteonline.org.uk

Work Permits (UK)
Level 5
Moorfoot
Sheffield S1 4PQ
0114 259 4074
customrel.workpermits@wpuk.gov.uk
www.workingintheuk.gov.uk/

Working Families
103 Berry Street
London EC1V 0AA
020 7253 7243
office@workingfamilies.org.uk
www.workingfamilies.org.uk

Index

Index

Index